Rumi: A Philosophical Study

by

Gholamreza Aavani

ABC International Group, Inc.

ISBN 10: 1567444318
ISBN 13: 978-1567444315

Library of Congress Cataloging-in-Publication Data

Gholamreza, Aavani
1. Rumi. 2 Sufism. I. Title

All translations from *Mathnawi* are taken from Nicholson with modifications.
All translations from *The Discourses of Rumi* (*Fihi Ma Fihi*) are from Arberry.
All translations from the *Maqalat-i Shams* are from Chittick's *Me and Rumi*.

Cover design by Samira Ardalan
Painting by Mahmoud Farshchian

Published by ABC International Group, Inc.
Distributed by Kazi Publications, Inc.
3023 West Belmont Avenue
Chicago, IL 60618
Tel: 773-267-7001; Fax: 773-267-7002
email: info@kazi.org/www.kazi.org

This book is dedicated to

Professor Tu Wei-ming

with gratitude

O Giver of intelligence, come to my help.
None wills unless Thou will it.
Both the desire for good and the good action itself
proceed from Thee.
Who are we?
Thou art the First, Thou art the Last.
Do Thou speak and do Thou hear and do Thou be!
We are wholly naught
notwithstanding all this exertion.

Mathnawi, 6:1438–40m.

O God who art without peer,
show favor!
since Thou hast bestowed on our ear
this discourse as an earring.
Take hold of our ear and draw us to that assembly
where the joyous revelers drink of Thy wine.
For as much as Thou hast caused a waft of its perfume to
     reach us,
do not stopple the mouth of that wineskin,
O Lord of the Judgement!
Whether they are male or female
they, all Thy creatures, drink from Thee.
O Thou whose help is besought,
Thou are generous in giving.

Mathnawi, 5:305–8m

Contents

Preface
by Seyyed Hossein Nasr

Those familiar with Islamic intellectual history and the development of Sufism might be surprised at the title of this book. They might ask: "Was not Rumi against the philosophers (*falasifah*), and did he not write *pay-i istidlaliyan chubin buwad* ("The leg of the rationalizers is a wooden-leg")? To answer this question, we must turn briefly to the understanding of the term "philosophy" (*falsafah*) in the Islamic tradition on the one hand, and the most universal meaning of "philosophy" in the English language, which is the language of this book, on the other. In Islamic civilization, *falsafah* is clearly defined as one of the recognized intellectual schools along with *kalam*, or theology, *ma'rifah/'irfan*, *usul*, etc. In English, philosophy on the highest level, going back to Pythagoras, Plato, Aristotle, and Plotinus, is the supreme science of Being, of the ultimate nature of things, and of the principles and epistemology of all the sciences. Of course modern Western philosophy from the Renaissance onward has moved in the direction of even greater distance away from "the love of wisdom" to the forgetting of *sophia* and even its denial, resulting in agnostic and atheistic philosophies that should be called "misosophy" rather than "philosophy." But the universal meaning of the term "philosophy" has not disappeared in the English language.

[Rumi was not a philosopher in the sense that Boyle, Marx, the deconstructionist philosophers, or logical positivists are called philosophers. But if St. Bonaventure, Nicholas of Cusa, and Franz von Baader are called philosophers, the Rumi can also be called a philosopher in English, and we can speak legitimately of the philosophy of Rumi.] Within the Islamic tradition, however, while Rumi knew much about the ideas of philosophers such as al-Farabi and Avicenna, he is not called a *faylasuf* but an *'arif*, or gnostic, who also possessed knowledge of *fal-*

safah along with other major Islamic intellectual disciplines. In the most universal sense of philosophy, he was one of the greatest philosophers any civilization has produced, while being at the same time a critic of the *falasifah*, and while being also one of the greatest mystical poets and troubadours of Divine Love.

What are the basic elements of Rumi's "philosophy"? The most basic and fundamental element, which is the basis and foundation of everything else, is metaphysics in the universal sense of the term. It is the supreme science of the Real, the Absolute, and the Infinite, and the science of the apparent and the relative in light of the Real and the Absolute. In his inimitable way Rumi summarizes the content of this supreme science in a single verse,

> *ma 'adamha'im hastiha nama*
> *Tu wujud-i mutlaqu hasti-yi ma*

We are non-beings parading in the guise of being,
Thou art Absolute Being and our being besides.

The *Mathnawi* is one of the most important works on metaphysics and gnosis, and teachings concerning the supreme science of the Real are to be found in all of its six books.

The *Mathnawi* is also the richest source in the Persian language of anthropology, or the science of man, understood traditionally. Rumi discusses in both a didactic manner in philosophical terms as well as through stories and symbols the human state and the complexities of the human soul. He reveals himself as an incomparable healer of souls and master of traditional psychology. In the traditional world, where the complementarity and correspondence between the macrocosm and microcosm are central, cosmology and sacred psychology go hand in hand. And so the *Mathnawi* is full of cosmological teachings that demonstrate the mastery that Rumi had of the various cosmologies that had been developed in the Islamic world from the purely Quranic to the Peripatetic and Hermetic.

When someone asks me what the most important source is for the understanding of Islamic aesthetics and philosophy of art, I always answer the *Mathnawi*. There is no richer and more profound source in Islam for the understanding of the meaning of beauty, the relation of form to essence, and the spiritual significance of art than the works of Rumi, and in this domain the *Diwan-i Kabir*, which combines poetry and music in an incomparable way, is as important as the *Mathnawi*. Rumi was both a supreme artist and himself a supreme work of art created by the Supreme Artisan. Who else could have addressed God in such a way as we find in this verse of Rumi?

Ma chu changimu tu nakhun mizani

We are like the lyre that Thou pluckest.

Rumi's works, especially the *Mathnawi*, also contain the most profound exposition of what is now called the philosophy of religion, and in fact religion in its universal sense is like the marrow of the bone of his whole opus. Also, along with Ibn 'Arabi, he is the foremost defender and expositor of what has now come to be known as "the transcendent unity of religions," following the title of Frithjof Schuon's famous work. Schuon in fact considered Rumi as the most universal saint of Islam.

No single book could deal with all of the above-mentioned aspects of Rumi's "philosophy," not to speak of issues not mentioned above. Dr. Aavani's book does deal, however, with many of the central aspects of his "philosophy." He begins with a scholarly account of the life and works of Rumi as well as Shams al-Din Tabrizi, but the main part of the book is devoted to the nature of man and his spiritual development, including such philosophical issues as form (*surat*) and inner meaning (*ma'na*) and the theory of knowledge and epistemology. Dr. Aavani also deals with certain theological issues, the symbolic language of Rumi, and the "stations" of the spiritual path with which so many classical Sufi works have been concerned.

xiii

Before concluding, a word must be said about the author of this book. I first met Dr. Aavani in 1964 in Beirut, where I spent a year inaugurating the Aga Khan Chair of Islamic Studies at the American University, where he was studying as an undergraduate, planning to go to Europe or America for his doctorate. After that year, however, he decided to come back to Tehran to do his Ph.D. with me at Tehran University, where I was teaching. I have therefore known him for over fifty years and been witness to his growing into a major Iranian scholar and thinker. Today he is considered as one of Iran's foremost Islamic philosophers and teachers of philosophy and Sufism. He has remained for over half a century a close friend and colleague. We have participated in many projects together, and he succeeded me as president of the Iranian Academy of Philosophy, which I founded in 1973. He did much to revive and enhance the activities of the Academy after the Iranian Revolution and to spread the cause of Islamic philosophy. I congratulate him for the writing of this important work on Rumi and pray that he has a long and continuously fruitful life.

wa'Llahu a'lamu bi'l-sawab

Seyyed Hossein Nasr
Washington, D.C.
August, 2016

Introduction

Jalal al-Din Muhammad ibn Muhammad ibn Husayn Balkhi, known as Rumi, is one of the greatest, if not the greatest, of the Sufi poets of Islam. He is perhaps unparalleled in the annals of world literature in expounding the inmost secrets and mysteries relating to man, the cosmos, and the Divinity, about the ultimate nature and becoming of the human, the universal wisdom, underlying all the holy scriptures and the teachings of prophets and sages and their ranks in the ladder of Divine proximity. Few books can match his *Diwan* in disclosing the mysteries of Divine Love, and still fewer books can equal and rival his *Mathnawi* in explicating the deeper layers of wisdom attainable by man.

Rumi has been studied, especially through his *Mathnawi*, as a great Sufi and gnostic (*'arif*). But seldom has he been viewed as a sage-philosopher. In the present book he has been studied from both vantage points, bringing to light the complementarity of the gnostic and philosophical aspects of Rumi's thought.

It might be irksome to some to speak of Rumi as a philosopher. This is to some extent understandable, given that Rumi does not compose his thought according to the conventions of the Islamic *falsafah* tradition; but we should bear in mind that many problems that are philosophical in nature are discussed in his *Mathnawi*, and they are most often debated or refuted, and alternative answers from another viewpoint are provided. The number of such problems and issues is by no means small, and so they deserve a studied and careful consideration.

In reality, almost all problems are held common between discursive philosophy, gnosis, speculative Sufism, and dogmatic theology, but the difference among these fields rests mostly in their respective methodologies. The method employed by one, for example, might be eristic, disputation, and debate. For another it might be proof and demonstration, and for still another unveiling

1

(*kashf*), or the science of realization achieved through purification and spiritual wayfaring. If, for instance, Rumi criticizes both discursive philosophers and dogmatic theologians, it is because they have missed the target, or have misplaced the mirror of their understanding, or have directed it in a crooked way.

In addition, although Rumi's teachings are trans-historical and perennial in nature like those of many other great Sufi masters, we should not forget that as a person he flourished and lived in particular historical circumstances. He came from a specific traditional background, spoke a specific language, and lived in a specific cultural milieu, which was rife with speculative issues in their philosophical, theological, and Sufi-mystical aspects. Indeed, some of the greatest representatives of all three trends of Islamic thought, and as a matter of fact of all other branches of the Islamic sciences, were contemporaries of Rumi, some of whom Rumi might have met either in his childhood in Khwarazm, or in the company of his father while migrating to Anatolia, or during his stay in Konya.

Rumi was the contemporary of distinguished philosophers such as Nasir al-Din Tusi, Athir al-Din Abhari, and Siraj al-Din Urmawi, all three being great exponents of Peripatetic Philosophy, and the last-named being the chief Judge in Konya, who is said by some to have performed Rumi's funeral prayers. He might have met great luminaries of Sufism, such as Ibn 'Arabi, Sa'd al-Din Hamawayh, and Awhad al-Din Kirmani. He was, moreover, a close friend of Sadr al-Din Qunawi, the stepson and the successor of Ibn 'Arabi, who can be said to have systematized Ibn 'Arabi's Sufi doctrine in his various works. Fakhr al-Din Iraqi, the author of the *Lama'at* (or *Flashes of Divine Light*) on Divine Love, was an intimate spiritual companion of Rumi. Najm al-Din Razi, the author of the famous *Mirsad al-'Ibad*, one of the great masterpieces of Sufi literature, and one of the disciples of the great Sufi master Najm-al-Din Kubra, the founder of the Kubrawiyyah order, is said to have been in Konya and to have met both Rumi and Sadr al-Din Qunawi. There is no doubt that all these Sufi masters belonged to different initiatic

2

orders and either founded or followed different trends in Sufism.

In addition, the Mongol invasion had caused tremendous devastation in all the conquered regions, destroying all the great centers of learning and leading to the death of some of the greatest scholars. It was natural for scholars, sages, and Sufi masters to seek refuge in safe cultural and spiritual havens, immune from the Mongol invasions. One of the safe asylums for these refugees was Asia Minor, where the Seljuqs reigned. Another safe refuge was Syria, especially the two great cities of Damascus and Aleppo. These two great cities, along with Konya, became centers for the assembly of great scholars in almost all branches of learning, including theology, jurisprudence, philosophy, and Sufism. These few cultural centers became the rallying places for scholars of the Eastern lands of Islam seeking refuge from the ferocious Mongol assaults. It is natural that these towns and cities became the meeting places of scholars belonging to different schools with multifarious viewpoints.

But Mawlana Rumi was most of all impressed and influenced by Shams-i Tabrizi, who was a living witness to all these spiritual and intellectual trends, and from whose all-embracing and penetrating insight nothing could escape. Being an intellectual itinerant, like Socrates, he would go not only to craftsmen, artisans, and poets, but to Sufis, jurisprudents, and philosophers as well. His agora would not be confined to Athens, but included the whole region from Eastern Iran to Konya, Anatolia, down to Damascus and Aleppo. The temporal span he contemplated, moreover, included the wide expanse of history, from Plato to Avicenna and Suhrawardi; from Adam, Noah, and Abraham to the Holy Prophet; from the early Sufi masters such as Junayd and Bayazid to Ibn 'Arabi. In his *Maqalat*, which are his private and intimate talks with Rumi jotted down by scribes, we see him not only as a great Sufi master, but also as a critical witness to all the currents of thought and spirituality in his age. No one, even the great saints in Sufism, such as Bayazid and Hallaj, was immune to his harsh and relentless criticism, most of which can be seen reflected in one way or another in Rumi's *Mathnawi*.

This book attempts to provide an outline of some of the main and essential features of Rumi's thought as enunciated in his masterpiece, the *Mathnawi*. It began as the notes for a course on Rumi that I offered at Peking University in the Institute for Advanced Humanistic Studies (IAHS) in the Fall term of 2014. I am especially grateful to Professor Tu Wei-ming, the Director of the Institute, for inviting me to teach as the distinguished Kenan Rifai Professor of Islamic Studies in the Institute.

My thanks are also due to Halideh Cemalnur Sargut, the President of the Turkish Women's Cultural Association, TURKKAD, and founder of Kerim Education, Culture and Health Foundation for supporting the chair. I also have an obligation of thanks due to professor Wang Yidan, Professor of the Department of West Asian Languages and Cultures, School of Foreign Languages, and the Director of the Institute of Iranian Culture at Peking University, for her constant encouragement with regard to the course. I would also like to express my gratitude to professor Yang Guiping, Professor and Director of the School of Philosophy and Religious Studies at Minzu University of China for providing the opportunity to teach several courses in Islamic philosophy and Sufism at Minzu University. My special thanks are also due to the following: Dr. Wang Xi of the Institute for World Religions, Chinese Academy of Social Sciences; Yang Yan, doctoral candidate, Department of English Language and Literature, School of Foreign Languages, Peking University, and Assistant at the Institute for Advanced Humanistic Studies, Peking University; and Ma Ruizhi, an undergraduate student, School of International Studies, Peking University, and Coordinator, Institute for Advanced Humanistic Studies, Peking University, for typing my manuscripts and coordinating the course; and Ma Zhengfeng, master's student at the School of Philosophy and Religious Studies, Minzu University, Peking, for typing and translating my lectures into Chinese.

Also my special thanks go to Nicholas Boylston for reading and editing the text, and to Dr. Laleh Bakhtiar of Kazi Publications for including this book among their publications.

I should also express my special debt of gratitude to my wife, Tahereh Kianifar, whose exemplary patience, forbearance, and support made the writing and publication of the book possible.

I have used Nicholson's translation of the *Mathnawi*, but have found it necessary to make some modifications in the translation. Where there is any modification greater than simply omitting words in parentheses, an "m" has been added in the footnotes. The quotations from the *Maqalat* of Shams Tabrizi are all from *Me and Rumi*, translated, introduced, and annotated by William Chittick (Fons Vitae, 2004). All other translations in the book, unless specified, are my own.

The chapter "Humankind in the Thought of Rumi" was originally a paper presented at the International Symposium on Rumi held in the UNESCO Headquarters in Paris on the occasion of the 800th anniversary of his birth.

A Note on Transliteration

Given the importance of the shared heritage of technical terms in Islamic languages, all terms have been transliterated according to standard Arabic-Persian transliteration, without diacritical markings. The one exception to this rule is the Persian silent *h*, which has been transliterated as *-eh*.

The Life of Rumi

Jalal al-Din Rumi (604 AH/1207 AD–672/1273) is no doubt one of the greatest Sufi poets of the world. Scarcely do we know of any person who can be compared to him in expounding the mysteries of human existence, the cosmos, and the Divine Being in such sublime and beautiful verse. His *Mathnawi* is perhaps the finest example of Sufi didactic poetry, just as his *Diwan* represents the pinnacle of mystical achievement in Divine love.

Despite the difficulties of briefly summarizing Rumi's life, we can take a clue from a verse famously attributed to Rumi, distinguishing three different stages in his life:

> The upshot of my life was no more than three words:
> I was raw, I was cooked, and then I burned.[1]

Accordingly, we can divide Rumi's life into three stages. The first period of his life extends roughly from his birth in 604/1207 to the death of his father in 628/1231, when Rumi was about twenty-four years old. The second phase in his life is the period from the death of his father to his miraculous meeting with Shams-i Tabrizi in 649/1251; the most important event in this second stage is Rumi's spiritual initiation by Burhan al-Din Muhaqqiq Tirmidhi, the successor of his father in the chain of spiritual initiation. But the most spectacular and spiritually rewarding phase of his life is the third stage, in which he underwent a profound spiritual transformation through his encounter with Shams, betokening the extent to which a spiritual master is needed in the realization of the spiritual life.

This division of Rumi's life into three stages, more than being merely historical and chronological in nature, is based on a sort of ascension of the ladder of spiritual realization or the degrees of certainty. These stages correspond to the three degrees of certainty mentioned in the Quran. The first degree of certainty, called "the knowledge of certainty" (*'ilm al-yaqin*),[2] is also spoken of by Rumi as "knowledge by imitation" (*'ilm-i taqlidi*), and

7

can be compared to arguing that there is fire because there is smoke, without having seen the fire for oneself. The second stage of certainty is called "the vision of certainty" (*'ayn al-yaqin*),[3] which would mean seeing the fire burn. The highest stage is called *haqq al-yaqin*[4] or "the realization of certainty," and would mean putting one's hand directly in the fire and feeling it burn.

> If your knowledge of fire
> has been turned to certainty
> by words alone,
> seek to be burned by the fire itself
> and do not abide in the knowledge of certainty.
> There is no actual certainty until you burn.
> If you desire this certainty sit down in the fire.[5]

Rumi also names the third stage "the knowledge of realization" (*'ilm-i tahqiqi*), and he who possesses this knowledge is called "the realizer" (*muhaqqiq*).

> Between the true knower [the realizer] and the blind imitator
> there are great differences;
> For the former is like David, while the other is but an echo...
> Beware! Be not duped by those sorrowful words:
> the ox bears the load but it is the cart that creaks.[6]

> Imitative knowledge is for purchase and sale;
> when it finds a customer, it glows with delight.
> The purchaser of realized knowledge is no one but God;
> its market is always thriving indeed.[7]

Now let us trace in brief outline some of the main features of the three stages in the life of Rumi.

The First Stage

Jalal al-Din Muhammad, better known by his honorific titles, *Mawlana* ("our Master") and *Mawlavi*, and "Rumi,"[8] was born in Balkh in present-day Afghanistan on the sixth of Rabi' al-Awwal of the Muslim lunar calendar in

604 AH, which is to say September 30, 1207 AD.[9] His father, Shaykh Baha' al-Din Walad, known as "Sultan al-'Ulama," "the King of Scholars," is said to have received this honorific title from the Prophet Muhammad in a dream.[10] His grandfather, Husayn Ibn Ahmad, known as Khatibi, was also a distinguished religious scholar of the time with whom certain eminent scholars of the age had studied.[11] Late in life, Baha' Walad was compelled to leave Balkh, never to return. The reasons for his migration are not known for certain, but biographers have mentioned several possible causes for his departure:

It is said by some that Baha' Walad had stood against the philosophers and theologians, publicly criticizing them on the pulpit. He was especially averse to Fakhr al-Din Razi, the most eminent religious scholar and Ash'arite theologian of the time, who was the teacher and favorite scholar of Muhammad Takash, the Khwarazm-Shah. Some biographers have mentioned that Baha' Walad had to leave because of the instigation of Razi, but this cannot be corroborated historically, especially because of the fact that Razi had died about ten years before Baha' Walad's departure. But in any case, Baha' Walad's outspokenness regarding philosophers and theologians, and particularly his animosity towards Razi, might have provoked the rage and fury of the Khwarazm-Shah.[12]

Biographers have also mentioned that Baha' Walad was a disciple of Najm al-Din Kubra, the founder of the Kubrawi Order, known in Persia as the saint-carving spiritual master (*shaykh-i wali-tarash*) because of the fact that nearly all his disciples are considered to be very distinguished saints and gnostics in the annals of Sufism. The Khwarazm-Shah had distaste for Najm al-Din, so much so that he had ordered that Majd al-Din Baghdadi, the successor of Najm al-Din, be drowned in the Oxus river in 616/1219. For this reason, the Khwarazm-Shah's oppression of the disciples of Najm al-Din Kubra has also been mentioned as one of the possible causes of Baha' Walad's migration.[13]

Sufi masters, unlike the authoritarian despots who were abhorred by the people, were much liked and praised by the common run of men because of their piety, their exquisite moral traits, their saintly characters, and their lack of attachment to all things worldly. Baha' Walad, in addition to sharing copiously in the aforementioned excellences, had a rare gift for oratory, as evidenced by his extant exhortations and sermons, which are rare masterpieces of Persian prose-writing.[14] It is evident that these would have made deep impressions on his audience, and there surely would have gathered around him a large number of disciples and followers. Rulers were generally either apprehensive or envious of Sufi masters' influence, and this might have been another factor that led to the emigration of this great shaykh.

Another probable cause of his migration might be the prognostication of the impending Mongol invasion, which was threatening the Khwarazm-Shah's empire and came to pass only few years after Baha' Walad's departure. It is probable that more than one of these causes or all of them together might have induced Baha' Walad to bid farewell to his hometown forever.[15]

Baha' Walad most probably left Balkh with his son Jalal al-Din Muhammad and some of his fervent disciples in 616/1219 for a pilgrimage to Mecca. En route, in the city of Nishapur they are said to have met the famous Sufi poet 'Attar, whom he had known as the fellow-disciple of Najm al-Din Kubra.[16] 'Attar is said to have given a copy of his *Asrar-Namah* (*The Book of Divine Mysteries*) to Jalal al-Din Muhammad, who was then about thirteen years old, divining to his father that "very soon your son shall kindle fire in the burning lovers of the world."[17]

In the classical biographies of Rumi—such as the *Walad Nameh*[18] by Rumi's son, Sultan Walad, which is considered to be the most authoritative; the treatise by Sipahsalar,[19] who was Rumi's disciple and companion for forty years; the *Manaqib al-'Arifin* by Aflaki,[20] written about eighty years after Rumi; and in later sources, such as Jami's *Nafahat al-Uns*,[21]—there are different reports about the nature of Baha' Walad's return from Mecca. According to some sources, Baha' Walad stayed in Arzanjan that winter and possibly for a few years later at the invitation of Fakhr al-Din Bahram-Shah or his son 'Ala' al-Din, the governor of the province.[22]

After that, Baha' Walad moved to Larandeh,[23] a town in the southeast of Konya, where Jalal al-Din Muhammad married Gawhar Khatun, the daughter of Khwajeh Lala Samarqandi,[24] who bore him two sons, Baha' al-Din (Sultan Walad) and 'Ala' al-Din. Rumi's mother, known as "Madar-i Sultan," is buried in this town, and a certain Amir Musa is said to have built a school-mosque (*madrasah*) there for the Shaykh.[25] These facts all attest to Baha' Walad's long stay in Larandeh.[26]

According to the *Walad Nameh*, Baha' Walad spent the last two years of his life in Konya, the capital of the Seljuq Kingdom in Anatolia, at the invitation of Sultan 'Ala' al-Din Kayqubad, the Seljuq Sultan who commanded his chamberlain, Gawhar Tash, to construct a *madrasah* for the Shaykh.[27] This *madrasah* would later become Rumi's teaching center, which Aflaki calls the "the school-mosque of our lord" (*madrasah-yi hazrat-i khudawandigar*)."[28] Baha' Walad passed away in Konya on Friday the eighteenth of Rabi' al-Akhar of the year 628 AH, February 23, 1231 AD.[29]

The Second Stage

Rumi was about twenty-four years old when Baha' Walad died. Either by the last will and testament of his father or at the request of Sultan 'Ala' al-Din Kayqubad, or perhaps at the behest of his father's disciples, he accepted his father's seat in teaching, preaching, and other religious duties, including issuing verdicts on religious and legal matters.[30] This continued until the decisive moment in the second phase of Rumi's life occurred, as Burhan al-Din Muhaqqiq Tirmidhi visited Konya.

Burhan al-Din was a close associate and an eminent disciple of Baha' Walad in Balkh. Some sources even claim that he was entrusted with the education of Rumi as a child.[31] At the time of Baha' Walad's migration, Burhan al-Din had been taking a retreat in his native town of Tirmidh. When he heard later of his master's migration to Western Anatolia, he immediately set out in search of his master. Reaching Konya in 629/1232, he earnestly searched for his spiritual master, but found out that he had passed away the year before.[32]

According to Aflaki in his *Manaqib*, after testing Rumi in all disciplines, Burhan al-Din praised him greatly and told him:

> You have surpassed your father a hundred times in all particular branches of religious science. But your father was perfect both in discursive, formal sciences and in the science of spiritual states. So I want you to tread on the path of spiritual states and to obtain from me those mysteries and truths that I received from my revered spiritual master.[33]

Upon hearing this, Rumi declared his consent and paid initiatic allegiance to Burhan al-Din, accepting him as his *pir*, or spiritual master. Even though Baha' Walad had been much engaged and concerned with the formal training and education of his son in the multifarious branches of religious sciences, all our sources are silent about any spiritual initiation of Rumi in the Sufi path by his father. It therefore seems that he was first initiated into the Sufi path by Burhan al-Din. According to Sultan Walad,

> (Rumi) wholeheartedly became his disciple and laid his
>   head before him,
> falling down in obedience like a dead body.
> When he died before him, the master gave him new life:
> removing his sprinkling tears, he made him a mine of
>   laughter.[34]

Our sources also speak of several spiritual retreats undertaken by Rumi at the behest of his spiritual master at this time.[35]

If one takes even a cursory glance at the *Mathnawi* of Rumi, one will immediately recognize the profundity and depth of his knowledge in nearly all branches of Islamic sciences, be they the so-called intellectual (*'aqli*) or transmitted (*naqli*) sciences, including fields such as literature (*adab*), jurisprudence (*fiqh*), the principles of jurisprudence (*usul al-fiqh*), the science of prophetic traditions (*'ilm al-hadith*), Quranic exegesis (*tafsir*), the history of Islam (*tarikh*), the science of religious creeds and heresiography (*al-milal wa'l-nihal*), the science of dogmatic theology (*kalam*), and philosophy (*falsafah*). Nonetheless, his spiritual master wanted him to delve more deeply into the formal religious sciences, and after almost a year of spiritual training advised him to go to Syria in order to deepen his knowledge in these fields. Following the advice of his spiritual mentor, he left for Aleppo and studied there in the famous Halawiyyah *madrasah* for two years with such distinguished masters as Kamal al-Din Abu'l-Qasim Ibn al-'Adim, who was well-versed in diverse disciplines such as literature, jurisprudence, the science of prophetic traditions, and the science of the chain of transmitters (*'ilm al-rijal*), and who was one of the most well-known calligraphers of his age.[36]

It should be mentioned that because of the Mongol invasion, which had decimated the populations of the towns and cities that stood in its way, most of the eminent scholars had taken refuge in Syria, especially in Damascus, which became a safe-haven for gnostics, philosophers, theologians, jurisprudents, and every caliber of erudite savants. It was therefore natural that after two years of study in Aleppo, Rumi set out for Damascus to continue his studies there. He is estimated to have studied there for four years, perhaps with such distinguished Sufi adepts and scholars as Ibn 'Arabi, who for more than a decade had chosen Damascus as his final abode of residence. After six or seven years of study in Syria, Rumi came back to Konya where he was "well received by men of learning, dignitaries, and gnostics."[37]

According to some historical reports, in Konya Rumi took three more spiritual retreats, following the advice of his spiritual master, after which he said to Rumi:

O my son, you were without peer in intellectual and transmitted sciences and in the science of unveiling. Now you have become the beloved example of all prophets and saints in the knowledge of hidden spiritual secrets, the mysteries of the folk of truth, the unveilings of the Divine men, and in the vision of the invisible realities.[38]

He then permitted Rumi to give initiation to aspirants in the spiritual path.

The spiritual companionship of Rumi and Burhan al-Din lasted for nine years,[39] and since the arrival of the latter in Konya was in 629/1232, his death must have occurred in 638/1240.[40]

The Third Stage

After the demise of Burhan al-Din in Ceasara, Rumi went to that city and on the instructions of Burhan al-Din's will, took his library and some other belongings to Konya.[41] After him, Rumi took over his functions of teaching and spiritual guidance, and like his father taught religious law, jurisprudence, and other religions sciences, while also attracting large audiences at the pulpit. "Like religious scholars he used to wind his turban and place it (under his chin). He also used to wear wide-sleeved garments as was the custom of the other orthodox scholars."[42]

According to the *Walad Nameh*, Rumi then had more than ten thousand disciples and students, and was moreover highly esteemed by the great *muftis* (Sunni religious scholars) of the province.[43]

But as dictated by the vicissitudes of fortune and by Divine Decree, there occurred the most crucial event in the life of Rumi—that is, his sudden and unexpected encounter with Shams-i Tabrizi—which transformed Rumi's life to such an extent that it turned him from an erudite scholar into an ecstatic troubadour of Divine Love.

> I was the ascetic of the nation.
> I was the possessor of the pulpit.
> But then Divine Destiny made my heart
> your hand-clapping lover.[44]

Out of your love I became the clapping composer of love
    poems.
Your love consumed whatever I had of conventions and
    modesty.
I was chaste, ascetic and staunch as a mountain.
What a mountain! Your wind robbed it like straw.[45]

You had become a scholar of high rank,
you showed erudition and demonstrated proofs.
Now, there came the touchstone of love;
where are your questions, where are your answers?[46]

Our Shaykh who was a Mufti became a poet from love;
even if an ascetic, he became a wine-drinker.
But not from a wine that was made of grapes;
his luminous soul drank not save the wine of illumina-
    tion.[47]

Who was Shams, who caused such a transformation
in the spiritual life of Rumi? As his name indicates, he
was from Tabriz, a city in the northwest of Iran, famous
for its Sufi saints at that time. His name was Muhammad
ibn 'Ali ibn Malikdad. Sepahsalar describes him in this
way:

Both perfect and making others perfect, possessing both
discursive knowledge and spiritual states and the science
of unveiling (kashf), the pole of the beloveds of the Unique,
and the most intimate in the threshold of the Self-Sufficient
God; he was among those concealed in the Divine Sanctu-
ary and accepted in the chambers of intimacy. The folk of
realization referred to him when it came to Divine sciences
and realities, and he showed the path of the attainment of
sanctity to the wayfarers. In his speech and his way of
proximity (to God) he had the manner of Moses, and in spirituality and seclusion he had the character of Jesus. He
always treaded the path of contemplation and passed his
time in spiritual self-exertion. Until the meeting of his ex-
cellency our lord (Rumi), no creature was aware of his spiritual state, and even now no one is cognizant of the reality
of his mysteries. He always used to conceal his miraculous
feats and hide himself from the rabble, lest he become

15

known. He always showed the manner and wore the garment of merchants, and at every town to which he traveled he used to stay in the caravanserai and would fasten fast a large padlock (in the manner of merchants).[48]

According to Aflaki, Shams was first the disciple of Abu Bakr Sallehbaf (the basket-weaver) Tabrizi, who was unique in his age for his Divine proximity (*walayah*) and the unveilings of the heart.[49] But Shams searched wherever possible for a more perfect spiritual guide, and that is why he was called "the flying Shams" (*Shams-i parandeh*).[50]

According to others, among them Jami in the *Nafahat al-Uns*, he was a disciple of Baba Kamal Jandi, himself a disciple of Najm al-Din Kubra.[51] Still others surmise that he received his spiritual initiation at the hands of Rukn al-Din Sijasi of the Abhariyyah order.[52] Others yet hold him to be an *uwaysi*, which in Sufi terminology means having no human spiritual guide, but being invisibly guided by God through the immortal Green prophet, Khidr.[53]

According to Aflaki, one day Rumi was riding a mule, passing through the cotton-sellers' market, surrounded by scholars and students. All of a sudden, he met Shams, who asked Rumi this question: "Who is greater, Bayazid Bastami or the Prophet Muhammad?"

Mawlana (Rumi) said: "What kind of question is this? Muhammad is the seal of the prophets! How can you compare Bayazid with him?" Whereupon Shams retorted: "So why did Muhammad say: 'We have not known You (God) as we should have'? And why did Bayazid say: 'Glory be to me! How great is my majesty!'?"

On hearing this, Mawlana fainted, and when he came to, he reverently took Shams's hand and took him to his *madrasah* on foot. They secluded themselves in his chamber, and for forty days no one was allowed to enter.[54]

Jami repeats the same story, explaining that Muhammad's statement issued from his great thirst and the in-

16

finite expansion of his breast, while Bayazid's ecstatic utterance was the outcome of the paucity of his thirst and
the narrowness of his forbearance.[55]

In the *Walad Nameh*, Rumi's son, Sultan Walad, likens the relationship of his father and Shams to that of
Moses and the Green Prophet, Khidr, whose story is mentioned in the Quran:

> Shams-i Tabrizi was his Khidr,
> he with whom if you were to associate
> you would never purchase anyone else for a grain;
> you would rend asunder the veils of darkness.
> He who was concealed even from those hidden (the Friends
>   of God),
> he was the great king of all those who had attained.
> If the Friends of God are concealed from creatures
> (it is because) creatures are the body and they are the
>   soul.[56]

In the wake of this meeting, Rumi disappeared for a
long time from the public scene. He abandoned teaching,
preaching, and exhorting the public from the pulpit. He
even left the spiritual sessions that he had held with his
disciples. According to the *Walad Nameh*:

> The Shaykh, the master, became a novice;
> he would take a lesson in his presence each day.
> He was an accomplished master, he turned a beginner;
> he had been the leader, he became a follower.
> Although he was perfect in (spiritual) poverty,
> it was a new knowledge that was shown to him.[57]

Rumi also distributed whatever he possessed in the
way of God for Shams's sake. This no doubt brought
about the hatred and enmity of Rumi's followers towards
Shams. They blamed Rumi for neglecting his followers.
The fire of envy and jealousy blazed in their hearts.
"Unanimously they agreed to murder Shams; there occurred a great confusion among the companions."[58]

Shams was no doubt irritated by such behavior, and
he decided to leave Konya after a sojourn there of about
sixteen months.[59] The more Rumi implored him to stay,

17

the more resolved he became to leave Konya, because he saw that his own life was in danger. He left Konya on the 21st of Shawwal in the year 636, May 27, 1238. His disappearance caused great joy for the disciples but great sorrow and grief for Rumi.

Rumi ordered his son, Sultan Walad, and some of his intimate disciples to search for Shams. For nearly a month they looked for him, but they found no trace. Finally, there came news of the rising of the sun in Damascus (as *shams* in Arabic means "sun"). Rumi immediately sent letters and envoys one after another, sending four poems in praise of Shams to Damascus with many gifts.[60]

In the meantime, Rumi had become furious with his disciples, who had caused this separation between him and his beloved master. He would speak to them no more. He even threatened that he would leave Konya forever. The disciples became remorseful and showed much regret for their bad conduct, asking for their master's forgiveness.

> They came to their Shaykh with supplication:
> "Forgive us, do not depart.
> We repent. Have mercy on us.
> Curse us if we do this once more.
> Accept our repentance out of your grace,
> even if we have committed offenses from impertinence."[61]

Mawlana accepted their apology and sent his son, Sultan Walad, together with twenty of his disciples, to Damascus.

Among the poems that Rumi sent to Shams after he had learned about his whereabouts was the following:

> By God, who has been from eternity
> Living, Knowing, Omnipotent and Everlasting.
> By Him whose light kindled candles of love,
> such that a hundred thousand mysteries were known.
> And by His one decree the universe was filled
> with lovers and love, the commander and the commanded.
> And in the talismans and spells of Shams of Tabriz,
> the treasure of His wonders became hidden.

18

I swear that from the moment you departed
I was separated from sweetness like wax.
Like a candle, I burn every night,
a mate of fire, ever deprived of honey,
Separated from your beauty my body is
as desolate as wilderness, my soul in it like an owl.
Now twist your bridle this way
and thicken the trunk of the elephant of love.
In your absence the spiritual dance is not lawful
and merry-making is damned like Satan.
Without you no poem was ever composed
until your most noble letter was received.
Then after the delight of tasting the audition
of your letter, five or six ghazals were composed.
May my night (*sham*) become luminous by you like the
    dawn,
by you, O the glory of Syria (*Sham*), Armenia, and Byzan-
    tium.[62]

In another famous poem Rumi recommends that his
son and the delegation bring Shams to Konya at any cost
and not be deceived by his promises and procrastination:

Go, my comrades, and fetch me my beloved companion.
Bring to me at last my runaway idol.
With sweet pretexts, with melodious songs,
attract homewards that beauteous, graceful moon.
If he promises you that he will come the next moment
all his promises are cunning, and he will deceive you.
He has such fiery breath, that with magic and incantation
he will tie a knot on water and put a seal on the air.
When in blessedness and joy my sweetheart comes in,
sit down and behold the wonders of the Creator.
When his beauty glitters, what is the beauty of the fair?
Since his sun-like face extinguishes all lamps.
O my swift-footed heart, go to Yemen to my sweet darling.
Convey my greetings and goodwill to that priceless
    agate.[63]

Splash water on the way, the sweetheart is coming.
Give glad tidings to the garden, the perfume of spring is
    coming.
Open the way for the beloved, that four and ten nights'
    moon,

from his light-giving visage, strewn light is coming,
The heaven has become cleft, there is tumult in the world,
ambergris and musk waft in, the beloved's banner is com-
    ing.
There is coming the splendor of the garden, there is com-
    ing the light of my eye.
My sorrow shall be set aside, to my bosom my moon is
    coming.
The arrow is set going, running to the target,
Why are we sitting here, for the king from the hunt is
    coming?
The garden gives its greetings, the cypress is standing up-
    right,
the greenery goes barefoot, and the buds, mounted, are
    coming.
Of what wine do the solitaries of heaven drink that the
    spirit
is ruined and inebriated, and reason, intoxicated, is com-
    ing?
When you reach our quarter, silence is our habit,
because from our discourse the dust of vexation is com-
    ing.[64]

Shams's residence in Damascus is said to have lasted
about fifteen months.[65] After a long search they finally
found him and offered him some of these heart-burning
poems betokening Rumi's agony of separation.

The poems of Mawlana, coming from his enflamed
heart, had their effect on Shams, and he decided to go to
Konya once more. Shams journeyed on horseback while
Sultan Walad was holding the stirrups, traveling the
whole way from Damascus to Konya on foot.[66] Rumi, with
great joy and exhilaration, came to welcome them. He
was greatly relieved from his long grief and agony. Rumi's
companions prepared great feasts for the occasion and
arranged sessions of spiritual dance for them, having repented of their previous behavior.[67] But the whole affair
did not last long:

But once more the insolent fellows ceased to be courteous
and planted the seeds of ingratitude and jealousy.[68]

20

Rumi's companions and disciples once more became furious and started to slander them, mostly because Rumi had abandoned teaching his courses and had started instead sessions of spiritual dance (sama'). What irritated them most of all was that he had abandoned all his close companions, associating with Shams all the time and engaging with him in spiritual discourse. Thanks to the presence of some scribes in their private assembly, we fortunately have some of their discourses transcribed, which are known and published as Maqalat-i Shams (The Discourses of Shams).[69] They tell us a great deal about the Divine personality of Shams and how he was able to exert such a profound spiritual influence on Rumi.

Rumi, moreover, had many rivals and enemies, envious of his reputation. They started to slander him and besmear his reputation in the town: "Alas it is a pity that such an excellent and dear scholar and prince was suddenly turned mad, confounded, and deprived of intelligence."[70]

The common people considered Shams to be a magician and a disbeliever, but Rumi considered him to have the kernel of religion and possess the sublime mysteries of God, a fact that brought about his anathematization by some religious scholars.[71] To make matters worse, some of the close relatives of Rumi were engaged in this tragedy, foremost among them being Rumi's second son, 'Ala' al-Din Muhammad, who was the archenemy of Shams.[72]

According to Franklin Lewis, 'Ala' al-Din's enmity might have had several causes: that Shams had suggested that 'Ala' al-Din might have something to learn from him, or that Sultan Walad received more praise and attention, or that 'Ala' al-Din eventually hoped to take his father's place, but that with Shams around, this proved impossible.[73]

Golpinarli, one of the most distinguished Turkish scholars of Rumi, basing himself on the Maqalat, argues that Shams had threatened 'Ala' al-Din because the latter never accepted his authority.[74] In any case, according to the *Walad Nameh*, being disturbed by these chaotic circumstances, Shams once more disappeared from the scene, never to appear again.

> Again, when the sun of religion came to know
> that that assembly was full of hatred and rancor,
> that love had departed from their hearts,
> and their hearts were rendered captive to their clay (bodies),
> once more the malicious souls were agitated
> and tried again to exterminate the king.
> The king then said to (Sultan) Walad,
> "Do you see how once more they have become friends in wretchedness,
> trying to cast me away from Mawlana's presence
> like whom there is no guide as learned and wise,
> trying to separate and distance me from him
> and after that rejoice all together?
> This time I shall go away suchwise
> that nobody can ever know where I am.
> All will become hopeless of finding me,
> none would ever be able to give a sign of me.
> Many years will elapse
> and no one will find a trace of my dust.
> When I draw out this time, they will say
> 'Someone for sure has killed him from enmity.'"
> He repeated these words many times,
> confirming them for the sake of emphasis.
> All of a sudden he was lost in the midst of all
> and sorrow departed from all their hearts.[75]

As we can see from the above quotations, Shams, seeing the adversity of fortune, decided to leave Konya forever, never to return there again. But there is another report by Aflaki, quoted also by Jami, to the effect that Shams was murdered by some of the disciples:

Shams was sitting in the presence of Mawlana in a private apartment. Somebody silently motioned to him to come out. He immediately got up and said to Mawlana: "They want to kill me."

After much hesitation, my father said: "To Him belong both the (worlds of) creation and command" (Quran 7:54). Blessed be God! Therein lies some (Divine) expediency."

They say that seven wayward and jealous rogues, who were as unanimous as a single hand, lay in ambush, and taking the opportunity, stabbed him. Shams al-Din uttered such a powerful cry that the whole group fell unconscious. When Mawlana heard the news, he said: "God does what He decrees and judges as He wills."[76]

Jami, repeating the words of Aflaki, has added: "When they came to, they did not see more than a few drops of blood, and from that day on no sign has appeared from that spiritual king."[77]

Furuzanfar, the Persian scholar and perhaps the foremost authority on Rumi of the twentieth century, has categorically denied the murder of Shams at the hands of his adversaries, basing his argument mainly on the fact that Rumi went twice to Damascus in search of him, in addition to the explicit statement of both Shams and Sultan Walad in the above quotation.[78]

Golpinarli, on the other hand, on the basis of some contradictory and uncritical reports from Aflaki's *Manaqib*, has persistently advocated the theory of the murder of Shams by his enemies.[79] However, by carefully analyzing the data about the murder, Lewis has undermined their authenticity.[80]

After the disappearance of Shams, rumors spread in the city that Shams had been murdered, and Rumi no doubt heard and denied them.

Who said that the eternally living has died?
Who said that the sunshine of hope has died?
That enemy of the sun (Shams) went up to the roof;
closing his two eyes he said, the sun has died.[81]

Somebody said that Khwajeh Sana'i[82] has died;
the death of such a venerable master is not a petty affair.
He was not a wisp of straw to fly with a wind.
He was not water to be frozen by the cold.
He was not a comb to be broken by a hair.

He was not a seed to be pressed by the earth.
He was a treasure of gold in this earthly dungeon.
He did not reckon the two worlds as much as a barley
    grain...
Do not say that Shams, the glory of Tabriz, (has died);
whoever died of these two worlds, he died not.[83]

Furuzanfar explains:

> Whenever somebody brought the news that he had seen
> Shams in such-and-such a place, even when telling a lie,
> Mawlana would immediately give him his turban and his
> garment and would give him many gifts with gratitude, and
> would be very much delighted. One day somebody reported
> that he had seen Shams in Damascus. He was overjoyed
> as cannot be described, and he gave him what he had, his
> turban, garment, and shoes. A dear one told him that the
> man was telling a lie! He had not seen him. Mawlana said:
> "I gave him my turban and my garment for his lie. Had his
> report been true I would have given him my soul."[84]

According to Sultan Walad, Mawlana spent most of
the time engaged in the spiritual dance, revolving round
himself like the revolution of the celestial spheres. Again
there was a rumor in the town that this great pole and
mufti of Islam was creating agitation and causing commotion like the insane, that all people had turned away
from religion and had become pledged to love, such that
they knew no religion and creed except love. So his denigrators, with utmost strength of denial, said that such
things were against religion and the Divine Law.[85]

Rumi, on the other hand, inattentive and indifferent
to such repeated calumniations, tried once more to look
for Shams in Damascus, since Shams had met him first
in this city,[86] and also because after his first departure
from Konya, Sultan Walad had found him there. The
wrongdoing and bad conduct of some of his companions,
which had caused him much grief and despondency, im-
pelled him to leave Konya for a while. In Damascus he
would search for Shams in every nook and corner, but in
vain.[87]

How much do I seek you, from house to house,
from door to door?
How much do you flee from me, from corner to corner,
from quarter to quarter?[88]

During this trip, Rumi held many spiritual sessions in Damascus to which many people were attracted and "they scattered much wealth and money at his feet."[89]

He set out for Sham (Syria) and journeyed there,
and after him set off many people, both raw and ripe.
When he reached Damascus on that journey,
he burned many in the fire of love.
He made all famished and fascinated.
All of them were ravished beyond themselves,
sacrificing for him all their belongings.
Obeying his commands whole-heartedly,
all in sincerity became his disciples and servants
cast in his wake like fading shadows.
All sought him out: infants, the aged, and the youth.
All chose him, with heart and soul.[90]

But they were all amazed at his longing search for Shams.

All of them said, it is cause of amazement
that such an eye, which is God-viewing,
like which we have not heard of from time immemorial...
Nor have we seen one like him in this age.
Who in the world is better than he
in greatness, majesty, and grandeur?
Whom is he seeking so zealously,
wandering after him so obstinately?
Who is he, the so-called Shams of Tabriz,
after whom the unique one of our time is chasing?
We wonder what the Shaykh is looking for
that he wanders after him in every direction.[91]

Rumi's search for Shams came to nothing, and so he went back to Konya, staying there a while and taking care of the spiritual needs of his disciples. But the ardent desire to see Shams once again overpowered him and made him return once more to Damascus.[92] The duration of his stay in this city is not specified by the sources and is vaguely referred to as "some years and some months," but Furuzanfar surmises that this must have taken place between the years 645/1248 and 647/1250.[93]

During Rumi's last stay in Damascus, the people of Konya were much depressed and agonized by his absence. Fearing that he might not come back to that city, they presented the situation to the Seljuq Sultan and sent an authenticated document, attested to and stamped by all scholars, shaykhs, judges, magistrates, and dignitaries of the Anatolian cities, inviting him back to his accustomed homeland and the mausoleum of his dear father.[94]

But strangely enough, though Rumi could not find Shams outside, he found him finally within himself.

> He did not see the Sun of Tabriz in Damascus,
> but he saw him apparent within himself like the full
>   moon.
> He said: "Even if we are distant from him in body,
> without body and soul, we are from the same light.
> Whether you behold him or you behold me,
> I am he and he is I, O you the seeker…"
> He said: "Since I am he, what am I seeking?
> I am the same as he, now I shall speak of myself.
> The more I increased the description of his beauty,
> I was the same as that beauty and grace myself."[95]

This may indicate that the spiritual seeker who is earnest and zealous in his search is finally identified with the master, or becomes the mirror of his perfections and is able to envision his reality in himself.

The Personality of Shams in Rumi's Poetry

The extent of Rumi's adoration and emulation of Shams might seem to some as somewhat exaggerated. But this love for Shams would seem quite natural to us if only we could know the role of the spiritual master and his relationship to the disciple in the spiritual path.

A spiritual master, by definition, is one who has lost his self in its origin, that is, the Divine Self, such that there is not one iota of selfish egoism or trace of carnal passions in his being. In other words, for the disciple he is the total manifestation of the Divinity and the Divine Attributes. By his treading of the stations of the spiritual path, his utterly human attributes have taken on the hue of the Divine Attributes of which they are the manifestation, or according to a simile in the *Mathnawi*: "The dark charcoal of his being, having been burned up in the blazing fire of Divine Love, has turned into fire and tells you: 'I am fire, I am fire!'"[96]

A spiritual master, moreover, is one who has attained proximity to God. This means that he has attained Divine intimacy, and that is why he is called the Friend of God (*wali Allah*). He is, in other words, the perfect mirror, which reflects in itself the Most Beautiful Names and Attributes of the Divinity.

> Whoever wishes to sit with God,
> let him sit in the presence of His friends.
> If you are separated from the presence of His friends,
> you are in perdition because you are a part without the
>   whole.
> Whomsoever Satan cuts off from the noble (friends of
>   God),
> he finds him without anyone to help him and he devours
>   his head.
> To go for one moment a single span apart from the com-
>   munity of friends,
> is Satan's guile, listen and know this well.[97]

It is for this reason that Rumi considered Shams to be the radiation of the Divine Light, which like a spiritual sunlight illuminated his innermost being.

> The Shams of Tabriz who is absolute light
> is the sunshine and an irradiation of the Divine light.[98]

> My master, my Lord, you, the Sun of the Real from Tabriz,
> you are both the light of the earth and the Sun of
>   Heaven.[99]

Spiritual masters, moreover, are like lions who chase after spiritual game.

> The spiritual pole is a lion and it is his business to hunt;
> the rest of creatures eat his leavings.[100]

That is why Rumi considered Shams to be a lion before whom the rest of the creatures, including himself, were as a flock of deer.

> I see a lion before whom the world is like a flock of deer;
> I do not know this lion, I do not know this deer.[101]

In the *Mathnawi*, composed many years after the disappearance of Shams, whenever the sun (*shams*) is mentioned, Rumi is immediately reminded of his spiritual master and is overtaken by a sort of ecstatic enthusiasm for his beloved mentor, who is a total manifestation of the Divine Sun.

> Hundreds of thousands of times have I abandoned hope—
>   of whom?
> Of the Sun (*Shams*)? Do you believe this?
> Do not believe of me that I can endure
> to be without the Sun, or the fish without water.
> And if I become despairing, that is the objective manifes-
>   tation
> of the Sun's work, O goodly friend![102]

> There is nothing in the world so wondrously strange as
>   the sun (*Shams*);
> but the Sun of the spirit is everlasting: it has no yester-
>   day.
> Although the external sun is unique,
> it is possible to imagine one resembling it.
> The spiritual Sun, which is beyond the aether
> has no peer in the mind or outside.
> Where is there room in the imagination for his essence,
> that the like of him should come into imagination?
> When news arrived of the face of Shams al-din (the Sun of
>   Religion)
> the sun of the fourth heaven drew in its head from shame.
> Since his name came to my lips,

28

it behooves me
to set forth some hint of his bounty.[103]

Rumi, moreover, has dedicated his great *Diwan* to his spiritual master by calling it *Diwan-i Shams-i Tabrizi* and also by choosing the pen-name "Shams" or "Shams al-Haqq" (the Sun of the Real), which with only a few exceptions is reiterated in the final lines of all the poems in this book.

Rumi After Shams

Rumi, desperate and hopeless of finding Shams, returned to Konya. Having abandoned teaching and academic discourse, he spent his time in worship, spiritual sessions, *sama'* (spiritual dance), and training the disciples. From the departure of Shams (647/1250) to the end of his life (671/1273), he spoke in the language of love and Divine gnosis in verse—in long and short poems, sonnets, and rhymed couplets—and in prose.

Rumi, moreover, was so much immersed in the contemplation of the splendor of Divine Beauty and Majesty that he delegated the function of spiritual guidance of his disciples, including his own children, to Shaykh Salah al-Din Zarkub of Konya, who in the absence of Shams also played the same role in the life of Rumi and filled, so to speak, his spiritual vacuum.[104]

Shaykh Salah al-Din Zarkub

Salah al-Din Zarkub of Konya was the disciple of Burhan al-Din Muhaqqiq of Tirmidh, and Rumi no doubt was his friend as a co-disciple. But during Rumi's turbulent days in Konya and his journeys to Damascus, Salah al-Din was residing in his native village near Konya, having got married there, uninformed about what was going on in the city:

> ...until one day he came to Konya and attended the congregational Friday prayer in the Bu'l-Fadl Mosque. That day, Mawlana Rumi was preaching from the pulpit. He was

causing great commotion in the audience. He quoted many delicate points from Sayyid Burhan al-Din. All of a sudden the spiritual states of the Sayyid manifested themselves in Salah al-Din through Mawlana's person. He uttered a clamorous outcry, rose up, and came to Mawlana's feet. He unturbaned his head and laid many kisses on the feet of Mawlana.[105]

Having despaired of finding Shams, Rumi turned his whole attention to Salah al-Din and appointed him as his successor, commanding all his companions and his family to obey him. Let us listen to Sultan Walad's eye-witness account in the *Walad Nameh*:

> The story has no end, O wise man.
> Reiterate here what Mawlana said,
> out of sheer love, he said to the companions:
> I have no care for anybody in this world.
> I have no patience for you, so depart from me
> and pay allegiance to Salah al-Din.
> Since I have no whim in my head to be a spiritual master (*shaykh*)
> no bird is able to flutter its wings with me.
> I am happy by myself.
> I do not want to be with anybody.
> Everybody is a nuisance to me as a fly.
> Henceforth, run about in search of him, you all.
> May you all seek his union with heart and soul.[106]

Sultan Walad then explains that after appointing Salah al-Din as his successor, Rumi's inner agitation was alleviated. Salah al-Din's spiritual guidance was different from that of Shams, that is, it was more peaceful, which had much effect in pacifying the agonized spirit of the master. They associated with each other "as sugar and milk," and intermingled as two pieces of gold. But he was so much the focus of the attention of Rumi that once more it caused the envy, jealousy, and rancor among his disciples.

> Then there was a clamor among the denigrators.
> Once again the men of iniquity were embroiled.

They said to one another: We were delivered from that one
    (Shams),
but when we consider well, we are in (a new) snare.
This newcomer is much worse than the first one.
That one was light, this one a mere spark.
That one was both eloquent and discoursed well.
He was a man of erudition, knowledge, exposition, and
    style...
It is a great pity and cause of loss
that our master exchanges the better for the worse.
Would that the first one were the companion
and comrade of our Shaykh once again![107]

Salah al-Din Zarkub, moreover, as his name signifies
in Persian, was a goldsmith, a plain and simple man
without any academic training. He would stutter when
pronouncing certain words, and hence he could not articulate these words when saying his ritual prayers. Because he was born and raised in Konya, the inhabitants
of that city knew him from childhood and were surprised
that a common, and in their view vulgar, man should be
promoted to such an exalted and lofty spiritual rank and
function as Rumi's representative. This spiritual kinship
was besides strengthened by a matrimonial kinship.
Mawlana accepted Salah al-Din's daughter, Fatimah
Khatun, in marriage to his beloved son, Sultan Walad.
He composed some very beautiful poems at their wedding
party. He himself taught Fatimah Khatun the art of writing and the recitation of the Quran, and always recommended to his son that he treat her in the best manner
possible, as we can infer from some of his letters to him.
This might have been a further cause for the provocation
of the jealousy of denigrators.

We all know this man and his lineage.
We are all fellow-townsmen living in the same quarter.
We have seen him grow up among us as a child.
He is the same, even if he has grown sturdy.
He has neither handwriting, knowledge, nor speech,
having had no value and worth among us.
Purely illiterate, simple-hearted and ignorant,
good and bad are of equal worth to him.

31

Always in his shop beating the gold,
and all his neighbors disturbed by his strokes.
He cannot even read correctly the opening chapter (of the
    Quran).
If somebody asks him a question, he is helpless.
It is a wonder for what reason our master,
who has had no peer among wise men,
prostrates before him day and night
and esteems him more highly than he esteems the doctors
    of religion.
He gives him whatever he has of gold, silver, and fair gar-
    ments.
Before, he used to sit in the last row near the shoerack,
now he boasts among men of being our companion.
How is it that we are now calling him "Shaykh"
or even greater than that?[108]

They even plotted to kill him, and all of them took an
oath that it would be a sign of irreligion to let him survive.
But a disciple informed Salah al-Din of their evil plot, and
upon hearing it:

He made a sweet smile and said: "Those blind ones,
who, losing the way have become infidels, without faith,
are not so much aware of the Real as to know
that without His decree no blade of grass moves.
They are offended to see that our master
has favored me among all in particular.
Have they not known that I am but a mirror?
I have in myself no visible image.
He sees in my mirror his own visage,
so why should he not choose and prefer himself?
He is in love with his own beauty,
do not think he is wicked and evil-minded to others.[109]

This self-description of Salah al-Din might seem to us
a condescension or self-aggrandizement, but we should
not forget that it is uttered in a critical situation where
his life was endangered by his enemies.

In addition to the accounts of Mawlana's love for Salah al-Din reported by Sultan Walad, Mawlana himself

has praised him highly and adulated his spiritual qualities in seventy-one poems of the *Diwan* and in several
places in the *Mathnawi*.[110]

> When you have escaped from self
> you have become wholly the proof of God.
> When the slave in you has become naught
> you have become the King.
> And if you wish to behold this mystery plainly,
> Salah al-Din has shown it forth:
> he has made the eyes to see and has opened them.
> From his eyes and mien, every eye
> that has the light of God has discerned mystical poverty.
> Shaykh Salah al-Din is one who, like God, acts without
>   instrument,
> giving lessons to his disciples without anything said.
> In his hand, the heart is submissive like soft wax:
> his seal makes the impression, now of shame, now of
>   fame.[111]

Sufism, moreover, is based on the purification of the
soul or on the annihilation of the egoistic self in the Divine Self. After returning from that station to what is
called the station of self-subsistence in God (*baqa*), the
servant becomes the mirror of God, in the sense that God
witnesses the total manifestation of his Names and Attributes in the mirror of his servant; and God becomes
the mirror of His servant, meaning that the servant witnesses everything in God and by God.

> The Sufi's book is not composed of ink and letters;
> it is naught but the heart white as snow.
> The scholar's provision consists of pen-marks.
> What is the Sufi's provision?
> Footmarks (of the spiritual journey).[112]

The companionship of Rumi with Salah al-Din(*baqa*)
after the demise of Shams, lasted for ten years (647–
57 / 1249–59).[113]

> The Master and he were like one soul in two bodies.
> They were tranquil, gladsome, and joyous together,

33

intoxicated with each other for ten years,
without the hang-over of separation, they had union.[114]

At his funeral ceremony Rumi composed a thrilling
elegy, with this as its opening verse:

O you from whose separation heaven and earth are weeping,
the heart seated in blood, the intellect and the spirit are
weeping.[115]

Husam al-Din Chelebi

After the demise of Salah al-Din, the master appointed
Husam al-Din (literally, "the Sharp Sword of Religion") as
his spiritual successor and ordered his disciples to follow
and obey him. We read in the *Walad Nameh*:

When Salah al-Din passed away from this world,
the master said: "O you, the truth-seeking Husam al-Din,
henceforth you are my vicegerent, my deputy,
because there is no duality in our midst."
The master replaced this one with that one
and strewed shafts of light over his head.[116]

Husam al-Din Hasan ibn Muhammad, whom Rumi in
the preface to his *Mathnawi* calls "the exemplar for them
that know God and the leader of them that possess right
guidance and certainty...the charge deposited by God
among his creatures...the key of the treasuries of the empyrean, the trustee of the riches of that stored in the
earth, the father of virtues,"[117] was originally from Urmia
in north-western Iran; his ancestors were apparently of
Kurdish origin and had migrated to Urmia and settled
there.[118]

Husam's grandfather moved to Konya, where Husam
was born in 622/1225. Rumi and some biographers also
call him Chelebi (meaning "my lord," a general Turkish
term that was specifically applied first to Husam). He was
also known as Ibn Akhi Turk, because of the fact that his
ancestors belonged to the orders of chivalry whose head
in Turkish was called "Akhi."

Husam's father passed away when he was in his teen-age years. The dignitaries of the time and the members of the order of chivalry all invited him to join them, because all the spiritual chevaliers of the age were novices trained by their fathers and forefathers. He accepted their companionship with penetrating circumspection. Together with all his chevaliers and servants, he came to Mawlana and laid his head before him, as they all willingly chose to serve the master. Husam, and moreover commanded his chevaliers and servants to engage themselves in their own professions and to use their earnings to provide the means of livelihood and other necessities of life for the master.[119]

On many occasions Husam presented to the master whatever he possessed, such that he had nothing more left to offer. The servants started to taunt him, saying that he had no means and possessions left for himself. So he replied: "In that case, sell all the utensils in my house!"

After some days they said: "We have sold everything, and there remains nothing but ourselves."

He said: "Thanks be to God, the Lord of the universe, Who made the emulation of the practice of the Holy Prophet feasible for me. I manumit you all for the sake of God, seeking His pleasure, and for the love of our master."[120]

Mawlana loved Husam al-Din to such an extent that he would not hold a spiritual session of the invocation of God, the spiritual dance, or an exhortation without the latter's presence. He had, moreover, made him the superintendent of all his properties, such that his son, Sultan Walad, complained to his father that the family depended for their daily bread on Husam al-Din. Mawlana rejoined: "O Baha' al-Din (i.e. Sultan Walad), by God, if a hundred thousand ascetic and perfect men were starving and about to die, and I had only one loaf of bread, I would send it to Chelebi (Husam)."[121]

The Composition of the *Mathnawi*

We are all indebted to Husam al-Din for the production of Rumi's *Mathnawi*, because it is he who instigated Rumi to compose this great masterpiece, which is no doubt one of the greatest works of mystical poetry in world literature. Husam al-Din saw that most of Rumi's disciples and companions were engaged in reading and reciting the Sufi poetry of other poets, especially Sana'i and 'Attar. Rumi had composed many long and short odes and sonnets, but scarcely anything like the great works of didactic Sufi poetry of these older poets, which ingeniously exhibit the subtle mysteries of the Sufi Path.

So one night in private company with Rumi, Husam complained of this fact and asked him to compose a book in the style of *The Garden of Truth* (*Hadiqat al-Haqiqah*) of Sana'i and the *Conference of the Birds* (*Mantiq al-Tayr*) of 'Attar.[122]

Upon hearing this request, Mawlana immediately composed the first eighteen lines of the *Mathnawi*, and so the great masterpiece had its beginning. Hence until almost the end of his life, Mawlana was engaged in composing the *Mathnawi*. Husam would sit in his presence through the night, sometimes until dawn, and Mawlana would compose impromptu the rhymed couplets. Husam would write them down, and at the end of the session he would read them out and sing them for him in a fashion that has come to be known as *Mathnawi-khwani* ("the recitation of the *Mathnawi*").

Around the same time that the first book of the *Mathnawi* was finished, Husam's wife passed away, and Husam was so grieved and disquieted that the composition of the *Mathnawi* was delayed for two years. When Husam regained his peace of mind, the formidable task was resumed once more.[123]

In the beginning of the second book of the *Mathnawi*, Rumi hints at this incident and mentions the starting date of the second book of the *Mathnawi*.

This *Mathnawi* has been delayed for a while;
an interval was needed in order that the blood might turn
    to milk.
Blood does not become sweet milk until thy fortune
gives birth to a new babe. Listen well.
When the light of God, Husam al-Din, drew back
the reins (of the spirit) from the zenith of Heaven;
for after he had gone in the ascension to realities,
without his life-giving spring, the buds (of knowledge)
    were unburst (in my heart).
When he returned from the sea towards the shore,
the lyre of the poesy of the *Mathnawi* became attuned
    again.
The *Mathnawi* was the polish of spirits;
Husam's return was the day of my seeking
an auspicious commencement again.
The date of beginning this gainful trade
was in the year six hundred and sixty-two.[124]

Since Husam al-Din encouraged Rumi to compose the *Mathnawi*, the latter mentions him on many occasions, by name or by allusion. In the beginning of most of the six books of the *Mathnawi*, he dedicates the book to him or reminds us that the book has seen the light of day because of his inspiration. Most often he calls Husam al-Din "Dia' al-Haqq"[125] ("the Radiance or Splendor of God"). For example, in the beginning of the fourth book we read:

O Dia' al-Haqq, Husam al-Din, thou art he
through whose light the *Mathnawi*
has surpassed the moon.
O thou in whom hopes are placed, thy lofty aspiration
is drawing this poem God knows whither.
Thou hast bound the neck of this *Mathnawi*;
thou art drawing it in the direction known to thee.
The *Mathnawi* is running on, the drawer is unseen,
unseen by the ignorant one who hath no insight.
Inasmuch as thou hast been the origin of the *Mathnawi*,
if it become increased, it is thou who hast caused it to in-
    crease.
Since thou wishest it so, God wishes it so:
God grants the desire of the devout.[126]

37

Furthermore, in the beginning of the sixth book, Mawlana calls the *Mathnawi* "*Husami Nameh*" ("The Book Dedicated to Husam al-Din"):

> O life of the heart, Husam al-Din,
> desire for a Sixth Part has long been boiling within me.
> Through the attraction of a sage like thee,
> a Book of Husam has come into circulation in the world.
> Now, O spiritual one, I bring to thee an offering,
> the Sixth Part to complete the *Mathnawi*.[127]

Now, from the last line it is evident that Rumi intended to complete the *Mathnawi* in six books, and thus it seems likely that the hypothesis of some scholars who claim that Rumi wanted to add a seventh book at the end of his life has no foundation.

The Death of Rumi

The *Mathnawi* had come to an end. Rumi seems to have been exhausted, spending so much time and sitting up late at night to accomplish this formidable task. But in addition, he had undergone unbearable suffering during his lifetime: his migration from his hometown in early life; his long journeys in search of knowledge, or in his search for Shams; his tragic experience of separation from the latter; the impropriety of the inhabitants of Konya towards Shams and Salah al-Din; the disobedience of his son 'Ala' al-Din and his bad conduct towards Shams; and the turmoil and vicissitudes of the time in which the reigning Seljuqs in Anatolia were constantly clashing with the Mongols. All these were heavy blows from which Rumi had suffered much.

Moreover, being a great gnostic and sage, Rumi never bowed to any temporal authority. He came into this world as a stranger, lived in it, and left it as a stranger. Because he was a veritable lover, his visage was growing paler and paler, and his vital powers were in decline. He lived, moreover, by the power of the spirit and not by victuals:

The power of Gabriel was not from the kitchen;
it was from beholding the Creator of existence.[128]

Late in life he was ill and bed-ridden, and probably suffered from a severe hectic fever.[129] When the inhabitants of Konya came to know about his illness, they came to call on him. On the last occasion:

Shaykh Sadr al-Din (Qunawi)—may God bless him—came to visit him. He said: "May God give you immediate health! It is a cause of lifting the (spiritual) ranks; there is hope for recovery. The gracious Mawlana is the Spirit of the world!" Whereupon Mawlana said: "May God grant all health to you. Between the lover and the beloved there remains no more than a thin hair shirt. Don't you want that light be joined to light?"[130]

> Now I am denuded of my body and He of the veil of fantasy.
> I am sauntering towards the consummation of union.[131]

Shaykh Sadr al-Din wept bitterly, and Mawlana is said to have extemporized the poem beginning with the verses:

> How do you know what a King within me I have as my companion?
> Do not look at my golden face, for I have an iron pace.
> I have turned my face wholly to the King who brought me here,
> and thousands of benedictions do I have from Him who created me.
> Sometimes I am like the sun, sometimes a sea of pearls,
> I have the spheres within my heart, and the earth revolving around it.
> Within the hive of this world I hum around as a bee;
> do not see my lamentations alone, for I have a mansion of honey.[132]

In the last poem Mawlana is said to have composed, he refers to his imminent death. Its last line might be a reference to what Jami has reported as Rumi's last

39

words: "Our companions draw me from this side, and my beloved master Shams al-Din calls me from that side."

> In my dream last night I saw an angelic man in the quar-
> ter of love,
> with his hand motioning towards me he said:
> turn your reins towards us with resolution.[133]

Mawlana passed away towards sunset on Sunday the 5th of Jumadi al-Akhirah in 672, December 17, 1273.[134] At his funeral ceremony, all the townsmen of Konya were present. Men from all walks of life, from all religions and creeds, Muslims, Jews, and Christians participated. In accordance with Mawlana's will, Qunawi performed the funeral prayer. Some sources relate that he fainted while saying the funeral prayer, and it was resumed by the Chief Justice of Konya, Saraj al-Din of Urmia.[135] The people of Konya held mourning rituals for forty days, described as follows by Sultan Walad:

> The people of the town, minor and major,
> were all heaving sighs in lamentation.
> The villagers too, both Byzantines and Turks,
> pain-stricken had all rent their collars.
> They all attended his funeral
> out of kindness and love, and not for gain.
> The adherents of all creeds attested to his veracity,
> the folk of every community expressed their love.
> Followers of the Messiah made him the object of adora-
> tion,
> Jews had seen him as good in character as Hud.
> The Christians said: "He is our Jesus."
> The followers of Moses said: "He is our Moses."
> The believers called him the secret and light of the Mes-
> senger;
> they said he was a great and unfathomable ocean.[136]

> The mourning rituals lasted for forty days,
> where moaning and wails did not cease for a moment.
> After forty days they went to their homes;
> they were all engaged in the same story.
> Day and night this was their tale,
> that that treasure had been interred in the earth.

Everywhere there was mention of his states and life,
mention of his words, which he strewed like pearls,
mention of his angelic figure having no peer,
mention of his noble demeanor without parallel,
mention of his love of God and his non-attachment,
mention of his Divine intoxication, and the veracity of his
    unification,
mention of his utter abandonment of this world
and his heart-felt longing for the hereafter,
mention of his gracefulness, humility and munificence,
mention of his spiritual state and dance, like the
    spheres. [137]

Mawlana was buried near the tomb of his father. Mu'in al-Din Parwaneh, the Seljuq grand vizier, built a mausoleum for him,[138] which is known as Qubbat al-Khadra ("the green dome"), perhaps in imitation of the green dome of the Holy Prophet.

On the seventh day after the demise of Rumi, Husam al-Din together with his companions and disciples went to visit Sultan Walad, asking him to become the successor of his father in the spiritual path. But Sultan Walad refused the offer, saying: "As you were the successor of my father during his life, so too to you belong his vicegerency and his throne."[139]

So Husam replaced Rumi as the spiritual master of the *tariqah*, to become known later as the Mevlevi Order. He functioned in this capacity for eleven years until his death in 683/1284.[140] After Husam, Sultan Walad was unanimously chosen as the Khalifah, and during the thirty years of his vicegerency, he consolidated the fundamental rules of the *tariqah*, which persist to the present.

Rumi's Works

Rumi was a prolific poet and writer. At least some, if not most, of his works were not written by his own hand. His poems were generally extemporized and written down by his disciples or by his son, Sultan Walad. Since his teachings were oral, it is probable that at least some of these oral teachings in public or private sessions were never copied down by scribes. His works can be divided into two categories: verse and prose.

His works in verse comprise the following:

The *Mathnawi*: In Persian prosody the term *Mathnawi* is generally applied to poetry in which the hemistiches in each line have the same rhyme. Poems in *Mathnawi* style were current in Persian from the early period, but this term is specifically applied to Rumi's masterpiece as a proper name, so much so that the name of the style and this work have become almost synonymous. As mentioned earlier, the *Mathnawi* was composed at the request of Husam al-Din, who asked Rumi to compose a book for the disciples in the style of the *Garden of Truth* of Sana'i and the *Conference of the Birds* of 'Attar. Rumi composed the first book between the years 657/1259 and 660/1262. The second book was started in 662/1264, i.e. after a delay of two years. The whole work comprising six books is estimated by Furuzanfar to have been finished by 666/1268[141] and by some others to have continued to the end of his life.[142] The best edition is that by Reynold A. Nicholson, which is accompanied by an English translation and notes.

The *Diwan-i Shams-i Tabrizi*: Also known as *Kulliyat-i Shams* (*The Collected Works of Shams*) and *Diwan-i Shams*, the *Diwan* mainly consists of poems that Rumi composed and dedicated to Shams, with the addition of a few dedicated to Salah al-Din. The *Diwan* comprises about 35,000 couplets. From the point of view of prosody, it contains perhaps the most diverse range of meters and rhymes in Persian poetry. His poetic style is categorized as Khurasani, that is, the style current among the poets of Khurasan and developed in the early period of Persian literature, despite the fact that Rumi was the contemporary of poets like Sa'di, who followed the Iraqi style.[143] The *Diwan* was edited by B. Furuzanfar and published by the Tehran University Press.[144]

Ruba'iyyat (*Quatrains*): A *ruba'i*, or quatrain, is any poem consisting of two lines in which the first, second, and fourth hemistiches rhyme with one another. More than 1600 quatrains have been attributed to Rumi, some of which appear to be spurious. Since composing quatrains was fashionable among Persian poets, and even some philosophers and many Sufis who are not known as poets composed quatrains of various sorts, it is natural that they were falsely attributed to other authors. The *Ruba'iyyat* are published in Volume 8 of Furuzanfar's edition of the *Kulliyat-i Shams*.

His prose works are the following:

Fihi Ma Fihi (*In It Is What Is In It*, also known as *The Discourses of Rumi*): In Sufi orders it was common practice for disciples to note down the utterances of their masters and later compile them in book form. Rumi's discourses in his spiritual sessions (*majalis*) were compiled as *Fihi Ma Fihi*, and include records of Rumi's answers to particular questions posed to him and discourses on issues regarding the path of initiation and the stations leading to ultimate Union. Many verses of the Quran, Prophetic traditions, and sayings of Sufi masters are mentioned and allegorically interpreted. Some of the stories mentioned in the discourses are also found in the *Mathnawi*, and so help one to understand the poetic expressions of the latter in a more direct and simple way.

Furuzanfar, after elucidating that the title *Fihi Ma Fihi* was a later insertion not to be found in the older manuscripts, surmises that the title may have been taken from verses of Ibn 'Arabi in which the same term is employed.[145]

Al-Majalis al-Sab'ah (*The Seven Sessions*): These are transcriptions of seven sermons that Rumi preached from the pulpit. They are works of very high literary and spiritual quality. Most probably, these sermons were delivered by Rumi during Friday congregational prayers before his encounter with Shams, at which time he abandoned teaching and public discourse. The sermons, written in rather simple Persian style, usually begin with an introduction in Arabic followed by a prayer in Persian, and are based on commentary upon a verse or verses from the Quran or a tradition from the Prophet. Among the different editions of the text one can mention that of Fereydoun Nafiz[146] published in Istanbul and the critical edition by Tofiq Subhani.[147]

Maktubat (*The Letters*): These are the collected letters of Rumi, written to different persons on various occasions. Sometimes they are in the form of recommendations written to various viziers or potentates, or to solve the specific problems of his disciples. Among his letters we can find one addressed to his daughter-in-law, Fatimah Khatun, apparently to apologize for possible maltreatment by his son Sultan Walad:

> ...I expect from my dear son Baha' al-Din (Sultan Walad) that if he does something to offend you, really and truly I will renounce him; I will not answer his greetings, I will not even allow him to attend my funeral services. I want you not to be grieved and not to feel sad. God the Almighty will help you, and all the servants of God are at your aid. As for anyone who tries to diminish and damage you, know that the sea is not polluted by a dog's mouth, nor a bowl of sugar by the molestation of a fly.[148]

Rumi wrote a similar letter to his son:

> I recommend to you concerning our princess (Fatimah Khatun), the light of our heart and our eyes and of all the worlds. She is now under your bond (of marriage) and your custodianship. She is entrusted to you as a great trial (from God). It is expected of you to set fire to the foundation of all your pretexts and not to make a motion whether willingly or unwillingly for a single moment, and not to shun the obligations of attending to her, lest she should feel an iota of agitation, disloyalty, or vexation. She herself, out of the purity of her essence and her noble royal character, does not complain of anything...By God (repeated seven times) and for the sake of your and your father's everlasting honor, I recommend that you hold her and all her family dear and consider all your days and all your nights as your first day in the nuptial chamber in continuously hunting her heart and spirit, and you should not think that she has been hunted and you no longer need hunt her. That is the way of those who see only the appearance of things...[149]

Shams-i Tabrizi

As we have explained, the meeting with Shams of Tabriz totally transformed Rumi's spiritual life. It changed him from a traditional scholar with some formal Sufi training into a troubadour of Divine Love. The alchemy of Shams's vision had transmuted him into gold. He saw in the personality of his master "the actual living embodiment of the true Beloved, who is God Himself."[150]

It is interesting to note that nearly all the works of Mawlana were written after his encounter with Shams. We can therefore see the personality of Shams present in almost all the works of Rumi. Mawlana has devoted his whole *Diwan* to him, naming it the *Diwan-i Shams-i Tabrizi* (*The Collected Poems of Shams of Tabriz*). This appellation might suggest that the collection of poems belongs to Shams, but they do indeed belong to Mawlana, who in his enthusiastic adoration for his beloved master has chosen his master's name as his own pen-name.

But if we are to trace some of the reasons for this unaffected and sincere devotion, it is best to look into the private and intimate discussions of the master and the disciple jotted down by some scribes, later entitled *Maqalat-i Shams-i Tabrizi* (*The Discourses of Shams*). We can in fact find the root and origin of most of Mawlana's ideas as elaborated in the *Mathnawi* and elsewhere in these intimate discussions. Shams, through his spiritual magic and also through his undaunted critiques, changed Mawlana's views concerning many problems, and especially about many great Sufi luminaries, scholars, theologians, and philosophers, with critiques that were in a sense directed at Mawlana himself. As we can see, most of the key ideas of Mawlana as enunciated in his *Mathnawi* and his other works are prefigured in the enigmatic utterances of Shams in his discourses.

The Personality of Shams in the *Maqalat*

We can come to understand the personality of Shams better through his own words, as we have them recounted in the *Maqalat*.

In his childhood strange apparitions came to him. No one was aware of his state, and even his father did not know what was wrong with him. Addressing his father, he said that the latter was like a hen who had duck eggs under him. After they hatched, the hen nurtured the baby ducks, but when the ducks became a bit larger and went with their mother to the edge of a stream, they entered the water and began to swim. Their mother, the hen, was not able to swim, so she stayed at the edge. "Now father! See that the ocean has become my mount and this is my homeland and state."[151]

Shams was an itinerant Sufi who had to provide for his own food and lodging. Unlike other scholars and Sufis, he would not stay in the *madrasah* or the *khanaqah*, and would rather take his residence in the caravanserais. He would make himself appear to be a merchant, wearing a merchant's robes and putting a big padlock on his door, though inside there was nothing more than a pillow and a reed mat. In his journeys if he stayed longer in one place, he would earn his livelihood by weaving trouser strings, would work as a laborer, or would engage in teaching children. He had a special way of teaching that would accelerate the learning process. "I taught that child the Quran in three months, as I had said I would." The child's parents, instead of the promised two hundred, paid him five hundred dirhams.[152]

In spite of his apparently harsh and crude behavior, he was inwardly very lenient and extremely tolerant. "It is my disposition to supplicate for Jews: 'O God guide them!' When someone curses me I say in supplication: 'O God, give him something better and more pleasant to do than to curse people.'"[153] But in no event would he compromise the truth. If something had to be said, he would say it, even if the whole world grabbed him by the beard and commanded him not to do so, because even after a thousand years those words would reach those for whom

46

they were intended.[154] Ever since he was a child, God had inspired him to use words to train people, "so that they might be delivered from themselves and go forward."[155]

Like many great Sufi masters, Shams's spiritual instructions were oral. He was not accustomed to writing: "Since I never write anything down, the words stay with me. At every instant they show me another face. Words are a pretext. The Real has thrown off His mask and is showing His Beauty."[156] He would answer the difficulties of everyone in the inhabited quarter, no matter what they might come up with.[157] Like all the great messengers, sages, and saints, he felt it to be his duty to awaken people from the deep slumber of ignorance, negligence, and forgetfulness. He believed that great scholars, instead of awakening the people, immersed them ever more in their cozy dreams: "The great scholars are far away. Completely dead, totally asleep, they talk in their dreams."[158]

Shams and Mawlana

The encounter between Mawlana and Shams was not coincidental. How could that great event happen by chance? As Shams himself recounts, he had been pleading with God to make him a companion of one of His Friends. In a dream he was given the glad news that He would make him the companion of a great Friend. Shams was wondering the next day, who was that Friend? The next night he was told in another dream that that Friend was to be found in Anatolia: "When I finally saw him after a long time, it was said to me: 'It is not time yet.' All affairs depend on their due times."[159]

From the above statement it appears that Shams had already met Mawlana before their final encounter in Konya. Commentators maintain that their first encounter occurred in Damascus, while the young Mawlana was studying there with the great masters. But the question arises as to the exact date when this happy incident took place. There are clear hints in the *Maqalat* that shed some light on this question.[160]

47

There are four allusions in the *Maqalat* that indicate that Shams and Mawlana had met each other fifteen years before their second encounter in Konya. In one context Shams mentions his fifteen years' patience for Mawlana, which proves that the first meeting had been more than a casual incident. "When you compare others' patience to his, it seems to be too much. Compare his patience to God's patience! There fifteen years would be too little! [It makes no difference] whether fifteen years or a thousand years."[161]

In the second passage, Shams makes an allusion to the fact that the more a seeker sits in expectation in the way of the beloved, the more mature and perfect he is in the Path of Love. In this regard he compares Jesus, who spoke as an infant child in the cradle, with the Prophet Muhammad, who was chosen as a prophet at the age of forty. It is evident that here the seeker is Mawlana, and by "the sought" is intended Shams: "When the friend is at hand, does anyone still say 'seeker'? The seeker is boiling and speaks quickly like Jesus. After forty years the sought! The one sought for sixteen years gazes upon the face of the friend, after fifteen years the seeker has found him qualified to speak."[162] One can infer from this quotation that Shams had known Mawlana for sixteen years, but after fifteen years he had become the focus of Mawlana's attention. In other words, this conversation took place one year after their second meeting.

In a third passage, Shams reminds Mawlana of their previous meeting: "I hardly mix with anyone. Even with a chieftain like him if you sift the whole world, you won't find another. It was sixteen years before I began with 'Peace be upon you.'"[163]

In yet another passage, Shams mentions that in his first meeting with Mawlana, sixteen years before, he was mentioning that forms are diverse but the meaning is one: "He was saying that creatures are like numerous grapes. They have number in respect of form. If you squeeze them in a pot, will any number be left? If anyone can put these words into practice, his work will be complete."[164]

But at the same time Shams acknowledges that though he was strongly inclined towards Mawlana, he could see from his talk at that time that he was not mature enough and receptive to the symbols. Nothing could have been done during that time. If he had spoken, his words would have been wasted. "At that moment you didn't have this state."[165]

Shams considered his meeting with Mawlana to be a boon and a blessing. Not being able to find a befitting spiritual companion was like "water bubbling in itself, twisting in itself and beginning to stink. Then Mawlana's existence struck against me and the water began to flow. Now it goes forth happily, fresh and splendid."[166]

Mawlana, on his part, in Shams's view was surrounded by a host of miscreant rascals, from whom he was under a Divine obligation to rescue Mawlana. "I was sent because this servant of ours was caught in the midst of unfit people. It would be a pity if they were to take him to harm."[167]

Again, comparing himself to Mawlana, Shams declares that Mawlana is so immersed in the love of God that he has forgotten both this world and the afterworld. "The reason is that Mawlana is drunk in love, but has no sobriety in love. As for me I am drunk in love, but I am sober in love. In my drunkenness I don't forget like that. How could this world have the gall to veil me or to be veiled from me?"[168]

Mawlana, according to Shams, had no equal in all fields of knowledge, whether in theology, jurisprudence, or grammar. If he wanted to do it and boredom did not prevent him, he could practice logic better than its masters, "with more flavor and more beautifully than they."[169]

Shams Criticizes Some Sufi Saints

In several places in his *Maqalat*, Shams criticizes certain distinguished Sufi masters, including Hallaj, Bayazid Bastami, and Ibn 'Arabi, while praising them highly in other contexts. In order to better understand his stance *vis-à-vis* these great spiritual luminaries, it is well to bear in mind the fact that Shams should be reckoned among those saints who are the spiritual heirs (*warith*) of the Prophet Muhammad, following in his footsteps. For this reason, he harshly reprimands those who, though belonging to the Prophet's community, digress from his spiritual path.

Aside from these criticisms, Shams does in fact praise these figures very highly. One example of these attitudes is found in the story of a disciple who was claiming that he could see God face-to-face seventy times a day. His master rebuked him and said that if he were to see Bayazid once, that would be better than seeing God seventy times. But nonetheless, he openly declares that a hundred thousand Abu Yazids could not reach the dust of Moses's sandals.[170] Yet, Shams also time and again reiterates the Holy Prophet's famous statement that if Moses were living in his era, he would have no choice but to follow him. He openly declares: "I have raised objections to the words of great ones, but I have never objected to the words of Muhammad."[171]

Elsewhere, Shams says that Bayazid did not eat the Persian melon because he did not know how the Prophet used to eat it. But this is merely the outward form of following the Prophet, and not its reality. Instead Bayazid ruined the reality of following by saying: "Glory be to me! How magnificent is my status," whereas the Holy Prophet said: "Glory be to you! We have not worshiped you as you should be worshiped." Indeed, "If anyone supposes that his state was stronger than that of Muhammad, he is very stupid and ignorant."[172]

Again criticizing Abu Yazid for the ecstatic utterance mentioned above, he asks whether the speaker was the Real Who was wondering at His kingdom, or whether it was Bayazid. Shams notes that the speaker no doubt was Bayazid himself, but he is quick to add that he should not be taken to task for this utterance, because it was uttered in a state of selflessness, or in other words of spiritual intoxication.[173] But if someone is in the state of intoxication, he cannot follow Mawlana, who is on the other side of drunkenness.[174] To live a life of seclusion, moreover, like Bayazid, would be an innovation in Muhammad's religion.[175]

But Shams is more critical of Hallaj, especially with regard to his ecstatic utterance "I am the Real" (*ana al-Haqq*). By enunciating such an expression, one is no longer the true follower of the Prophet: "The fault was with the great ones, for they spoke words out of infirmity—'I am the Real.' They left the following. Then words like this fell out of their mouths."[176] Elsewhere, Shams says: "The beauty of the spirit had not completely shown itself to Hallaj. Otherwise, how could he have said 'I am the Real'? If he had annihilated his 'self' in the Divine 'Self' and immersed himself in the world of Spirit, then how could words like 'I' and 'am' be congruent with that claim?"[177]

Referring to the Prophetic tradition that one should hold to the religion of old women, Shams comments that for old women God is everything. Addressing God, they say: "O You! Oh, all is You!" This is better than saying: "I am the Real." "Although he arrived at God, he did not arrive at the reality of God. If he had been aware of God's reality, he would not have said 'I am the Real.'"[178] It was due to these wild utterances that he lost his life, as summed up in the poem:

That fellow who kept on bragging I am the Real
Enough that he hung himself on the rope.[179]

But most interesting are Shams's amiable and reverential criticisms of Ibn 'Arabi, whom he often refers to as Shaykh Muhammad. In one place Shams mentions that Shaykh Muhammad used to say that so-and-so was mistaken. But sometimes Shams would point out to him that he was mistaken. "He would throw down his head. He would say: 'Child, you strike a hard whip.'...At first he would say: 'Child,' and in the end he would say: 'Child.' Then he would laugh, meaning: 'What place is this for a "Child"?'"[180]

Comparing him to the scholars of his time, he remarks: "He was a mountain, a mountain! I have no purpose here but every time he spun the wheel, a hundred thousand like these [scholars] would fall flat and be shucked off."[181]

On another occasion, Shams recounts their debate about the spaciousness of the plain of speech and the plain of meaning. Ibn 'Arabi (Shaykh Muhammad) maintains that the plain of speech is spacious because everyone says whatever he desires. But Shams rejoins that the plain of speech is very narrow, but the plain of meaning is very spacious: "Come forth from speech so that you may behold spaciousness and the plain."[182]

Still elsewhere he relates that Ibn 'Arabi used to say that if he were to say that something should have been like this, or it should have been like that, that would be utter disbelief. Shams tells us that he was patient until one day he (Ibn 'Arabi) was giving advice to someone. "I said to him: 'So with this advice you are saying you should be like this but for you that is unbelief.'"[183]

As we can see in his *Fusus*, Ibn 'Arabi very much liked the metaphysical expression "Necessary Being," and he used it along with the theological expression *Qadim* (Eternal) and the Quranic expression *Ghani* (Self-Sufficient) for God. According to Avicenna, God is the "Necessary Being by His Essence." According to Shams, Ibn 'Arabi would rejoice when hearing this expression: "As for our Shaykh Muhammad, he was a great man. 'Necessary in existence by His Essence'—He sat back and said 'Allah.' He laughed: 'What kind of name have they given Him.'"[184]

But nonetheless, Shams preferred Mawlana to Ibn 'Arabi. According to Shams, Ibn 'Arabi would oftentimes make ritual genuflections and prostrations and would say: "'I am the servant of the Folk of the [Divine] Law.' But he did not have a following. I took much benefit from him, but not as much as from you. What is from you is not like what is from him. *'How different a pearl from a pebble.'*"[185]

Some chroniclers have ascribed the spiritual lineage of Shams and even of Rumi's father to Ahmad Ghazali, who, unlike his elder brother, Muhammad Ghazali, was a supreme spiritual master in certain Sufi chains of initiation. Shams had a very high admiration of him. "He

52

was a man who, when he would gaze on heaven in the direction of the spheres would make it crumble to dust."[186]

Ahmad, being the author of the *Sawanih*, one of the best treatises ever written on Divine Love, is said to have been enchanted and infatuated by earthly beauty, especially as manifested in human forms. Shams goes on to add how he was misunderstood by the common run of men who saw in this a kind of concupiscent love.

> He did not incline to these beautiful forms out of appetite. He saw something that no one else saw. If they had taken him apart piece by piece, they wouldn't have found an iota of appetite. However, because of this behavior, some people acknowledged him, and some people denied him.[187]

Shams is also critical of the lukewarm dervishes of his time who were strangers to the lifestyle of true dervishes. He tells us that at first he kept aloof from the jurisprudents and used to associate with the dervishes. "Then I came to know what it is to be a dervish and where they are, and now I would rather sit with jurists than with these dervishes." This is because the jurists have indeed taken much trouble in gaining the knowledge of jurisprudence. But those idlers only brag about being dervishes.[188]

Shams, a Critic of Philosophers

Shams is not hesitant in criticizing philosophers, especially when they deny the mysteries attained by gnostics through unveiling and by Divine instruction. They deny, for example, the speech of inanimate things, which is visible to the inmost being of the prophets and the Friends of God. They blatantly deny the Hadith of the Moaning Pillar.[189]

Philosophers, moreover reprimand the prophets because they think that prophets have engaged themselves with the common people, and they have thus held themselves back from disengagement and seclusion. "They also say that the fact that prophets wanted wives was a defect and a taint."[190]

He also blames the "silly philosophers" for holding that "the intellects are ten" and that they encompass all possible things.[191] They also deny the miracles of prophets, and say that they accept the truths of the intellect alone and not that which contradicts them. Shams counters their argument by saying: "Intellect is God's Proof, but when you do not employ it correctly, it comes up with contradictions."[192]

Comparing Avicenna to Plato, Shams maintains that Avicenna was "half a philosopher," but Plato was a "full philosopher" because he laid claim to love;[193] but nonetheless a single servant of God could empty Plato in one moment of all those sciences.[194]

Pretenders to philosophy make many interpretations about the life after death and make expositions through rational demonstrations. But they are much inclined to worldly possessions, women, honor, and wealth on this side. But if someone were to mention the name of death to them, they would suffer a thousand deaths.[195]

Criticizing those who desire to attain the Divine science merely by discursive reasoning, Shams remarks that this science cannot be obtained by scholastic studies in the *madrasah*. If one studies six thousand years, that is, six times the life-span of Noah, that science cannot be obtained. One should enter under the shadow of God and realize in oneself all the Divine Attributes, and one will become aware of the Living, the Ever-Standing.[196]

Referring to the prophetic tradition that most of the inhabitants of Paradise are the simple-minded (*al-bulh*), Shams remarks: "The majority of the denizens of Hell are from among these clever people, these philosophers, these knowledgeable people, the ones for whom cleverness has become a veil."[197]

According to philosophers, the world is the macrocosm and the human make-up is the microcosm. But according to the prophets, the macrocosm is man and the microcosm is the world. "Thus this world is a sample of the human world."[198] You are a world without end.[199]

"The whole universe is in one person. When he knows himself, he knows all."[200]

Philosophers claim that God knows the universals without particulars. But how can one know the universals without knowing the particulars? "If He does not know the particulars He does not know the universals."[201]

Only two or three decades had elapsed since the martyrdom of the Master of Illumination, Shaykh Shihab al-Din Suhrawardi. According to Shams, Suhrawardi was much admired and respected by the king of Aleppo (Malik Zahir), and so he became the object of the envy of exoteric scholars. Shams only alludes to the letter that the jurisprudents wrote to Saladin (Salah al-Din Ayyubi), Malik Zahir's father, asking him to do away with the philosopher. But he says: "When he (Malik Zahir) read the letter, he took away his turban and had his head cut off." But he at once regretted what he had done, and the deception of the enemies became manifest to him "and he killed two or three of them." Shams reiterates what is reported by some other sources that Shihab al-Din's knowledge dominated over his intellect, but the intellect must dominate over knowledge. Comparing the two, Shihab al-Din of Suhraward, a philosopher-sage, on the one hand, with a Sufi master, he prefers the philosopher-sage.[202] He harshly rebukes those who called Suhrawardi an unbeliever: "Those dogs used to call Shihab an unbeliever openly. I said, Beware! How could Shihab be an unbeliever? He is luminous!"[203]

Shams is also a staunch adherent to belief in free choice as opposed to predestination. He regrets that some great men have fallen into the snare of the latter doctrine. God has said that we are in possession of free choice, so why do we call ourselves predestined? And besides, "commandments and prohibitions, promises and threats, and sending messages all demand free choice."[204]

Shams and the Dogmatic Theologians

Shams was in close contact with some of the Muta-kallimun or dogmatic theologians, and even had great sympathy and affection for Shihab Hariwa (hailing from Herat), the most distinguished student of the famous theologian Fakhr-i Razi. Every now and then he quotes and criticizes Shihab, who, for example, believed that since God is necessary by Essence, He is determined, and He cannot choose freely. Shams declares that he would not accept that doctrine even if all the prophets had said that He is so. "I don't want that God. I want a God who acts by free choice...Every moment He destroys a thousand worlds...If the whole world were to accept that from Shihab, I wouldn't accept it."[205]

Elsewhere Shams intimates that if Shihab Hariwa were to hear what he was saying about the weeping and the laughter of inanimate things, he would have said in the dialect of Nishapur: "What is this? Philosophical reason does not accept it."[206]

Quoting a verse from an ode by Fakhr-i Razi himself:

Our spirits are in dread of our bodies.
The upshot of this world is
naught but calamity and disaster.[207]

Shams remarks that this is the essence of the knowledge attained by those who have vainly immersed themselves in discursivity.

Again, he says that if truth were to be attained by mere study and by debate, then great Sufi masters such as Bayazid and Junayd would have to die out of regret before Fakhr-i Razi, and they would have to become his students for a hundred years. But even if Fakhr-i Razi has written a commentary of the Quran in a thousand folios, nonetheless a hundred thousand Fakhr-i Razis could not even touch the dust of Bayazid.[208] How impudent and brazen was Fakhr-i Razi when he put himself on a par with the Prophet Muhammad and said: "Muhammad Tazi [the Arab] says this, and Muhammad Razi [meaning himself] says that. Isn't he the apostate of the time! Isn't he an unqualified unbeliever? Unless he repents."[209]

Being too much engaged in polemics and the art of disputation becomes a spiritual veil for the Friends of God and is a great hindrance in the path of Divine proximity. That is why the Holy Prophet is said to have prohibited wrangling and disputation in religion. He is again said to have recommended the religion of old women ('alaykum bi-din al-'aja'iz). Their neediness is better than all. "Fakhr-i Razi and a hundred like him should be proud to lift the corner of the face-covering of that needy, truthful woman so as to take blessing. And still—what a pity for that face-covering."[210]

Shams, like Rumi, prefers the school of the Sunnis to the school of the Mu'tazilites. "The school of the Sunnis is closer to the work than the school of the Mu'tazilites. The latter is near to philosophy."[211] Perhaps by the school of the Sunnis he means the Ash'arites.

According to Shams, Ghazali used to study the *Isharat* of Avicenna with 'Umar Khayyam without letting anyone know about it. That is why some criticize Ghazali's *Ihya' 'Ulum al-Din* (*The Revivification of the Religions Sciences*), because of his deductions from that book. Ghazali read the *Isharat* once, but he did not understand it. He read it for a second time, and he still did not understand it. Again, he read it with Khayyam a third time. But though he studied philosophy with Khayyam, he did not want to make it known to the public. But in order to divulge the secret, Khayyam ordered some minstrels, musicians, and drummers to play when Ghazali was leaving the house, so that everybody would come to know that Ghazali had studied philosophy with him and had benefited from him.[212]

Prophets

The Holy Prophet said that a believer is a mirror unto the believer. So a believer is a true mirror, which represents things as they are. Prophets are like so many straight and clear mirrors who show one and the same thing, each one confirming the other. Like different lights, they are all friends of each other. But one who is lazy and does not use his intellect properly is like one who holds his mirror crookedly.

If, for example, many people with clear eyes are standing in the sunshine, and a person is approaching them from afar playing a drum and dancing, they will not disagree. If in the darkness of the night they hear the sound of a drum, there will be a hundred disagreements among them. One will say that it is an army and another that it is a circumcision party. If there were a lamp in their hands, there would be no disagreement.[213]

He says:

> Prophets all make each other known. Jesus says: "O Jew, you did not know Moses well. Come and see me so that you may know Moses." Muhammad says: "O Christian, O Jew, you did not know Moses and Jesus well. Come and see me so that you may know them." The Prophets all make each other known. The words of the prophets explain and clarify each other.[214]

The path to God is one of two: one is the way of opening up the inwardness, and that is the way of the prophets and saints, and the other is by way of acquiring knowledge through self-exertion and purification.[215]

Elsewhere, Shams advises us to estrange ourselves from people and not to attach to them. What can one gain from them? How can they cause our liberation and from what can they liberate us? To what can they bring us near? But on the other hand one should adopt the conduct of the prophets and should follow their example. They seldom mixed with people. "They were attached to God, even if outwardly people gathered around them."[216]

Nabi, "prophet," etymologically speaking, means one who brings news from God or from the spiritual world. But according to Shams, to bring news means to awaken. *Nabi* means an awakener. He is awakened to the Real, and he awakens others to the reality of the Real.[217]

Prophets have two kinds of revelation: a revelation from Gabriel and a revelation in the heart. Friends of God have only the latter.[218]

You can see the reality of everything, including all prophets, in yourself. You can see Moses, Jesus, Abraham, Noah, Adam, Eve, Asiya (Pharaoh's wife), the Antichrist, Khidr, and Elias within yourself. You are a world without end. How can the heavens and earth embrace you? As the *hadith qudsi* states: "My heavens and my earth do not embrace Me, but the heart of My believing servant does embrace Me." "You shall not find Me in the heavens. You shall not find Me on the Throne."[219]

Shams had a tremendous love and adoration for the Prophet Muhammad. He is the seal and perfection of all prophets. Nobody would be compared to the Holy Prophet and his Household even if they happened to be such eminent figures as Socrates, Hippocrates, or the Ikhwan al-Safa (the Brethren of Purity).[220]

He even declares that he does not revere the Quran because it is the word of God, but because it came out of Muhammad's mouth.[221]

Again, he asserts that he would not exchange the least report from Muhammad with a hundred thousand treatises by Qushayri, Qurayshi (a pun on words), and others, because they are insipid and have no flavor.[222] It is only God Who is God. That which is created is not God, whether it is Muhammad or other than Muhammad.[223]

In various places in the *Maqalat*, Shams places stress on the complete following of the Prophet Muhammad. But a perfect following is this, that if he went on the nocturnal journey, you should also follow suit and go in his tracks. You should also endeavor to gain a settling place in your heart.[224]

We saw earlier that Shams launches his pungent criticism not only against philosophers and dogmatic theologians, but also against some Sufi masters such as Bayazid and Hallaj. But he never raises any objections against the Prophet Muhammad: "I have often raised objections to the words of the great ones, but I have never objected to the words of Muhammad."[225]

When God says in the Quran: "The All-merciful sat upon the Throne" (20:5), that Throne is the heart of Muhammad. If there had been no sitting before him, how was it during his time? He is telling him his own story when he says: "*Taha!* Don't suffer, don't suffer. Don't see any suffering. I did not bring this story so that you should suffer."[226]

What other prophets gained in a thousand years, Muhammad passed through in a brief period. If Jesus spoke that one word in the beginning of his infancy, it was not out of his free choice

> Although Muhammad spoke late and after forty, his words were more perfect. I mean the words of both of them hit the mark.[227]

> If they ask me, "Was the Messenger a lover?" I will say, "He was not a lover. He was the adored and the beloved." However, intellect becomes perplexed by the explication of the beloved. So I'll call him a lover in the sense of a beloved."[228]

If it is said to someone who sees the Dominating One, and sees the Giver of Being giving being to all things, and opens his eyes and sees the Creator without imitation and veil...Now if it is said to him to go and see the light of Muhammad, he would see that

> ...infirmities sit on this sun and moon, but no infirmity sits upon that. It has no infirmity. The face of this sun becomes black, but the face of that sun does not become black. That sun has taken on the light of His majesty, but this sun stands in the station of *When the sun in darkened* (Quran 81:1).[229]

Friends of God

Awliya' (the plural of *wali*), rendered in the Christian context as "saints" and meaning literally "Friends of God," are the intimates of God or those who are the most proximate to God. Friends of God are the criterion, the test, measure, and proof of their religions. Recognizing these folk is more difficult than recognizing the Real, because you can come to know Him by demonstration and inference. But these folk are like other people in outward appearance, although they have a meaning far from our conceptions and thoughts.[230]

The Friend of God is the real Book of God. The Book of God is not merely this bound volume in your hand. It also means the Friend of God, who is the realization of the Book and the true spiritual leader. He is the verse and the chapter of that Book. And how many verses there are in that verse! And what in the final analysis will save us is that servant of God and not merely that written book.

The Friend of God, moreover, is hidden among the pretenders, as "the Night of Power" (*Laylat al-Qadr*) is hidden among other nights. He is hidden not out of his contemptibleness, but because of his extreme manifestness. People usually deny the Friends of God because their love for this world is very strong. But in the Hereafter, when they behold their glory and majesty, they will regret this denial and shout: "Alas for me for what I neglected in the side of God. Indeed, I was among the scoffers" (Quran 39:57).[231]

People are usually mistaken about the nature of Divine friendship. They are mistaken about the nature of the Divinity, that is, about that God Who has created the heavens and the earth and has caused this universe to appear. Can His friendship be gained so easily, as with the one who enters a soup kitchen, buys some soup, drinks it down, and then leaves?[232]

They are those who have Divine discernment. They see with the Light of God. They see with a view that subsists after the annihilation of all views. They see that what most people see as excellence and subtle vision is nothing but stupidity and veiling.[233]

Friends of God are of two kinds. They are either manifest and known (*mashhur*), or they are hidden and unknown (*mastur*). The first ones are the lovers, and the latter are the beloveds. The manifest Friends are the seekers, and the hidden ones are the sought. The lovers

61

are known for their love, but the beloved ones are hidden from the view of all but a few. As Sultan Walad notes:

> Some Friends of God are well known and some of them are concealed among humankind. The spiritual rank of the concealed ones is higher than that of those who are well known. That is why all the great and eminent spiritual masters have always desired to find one of those hidden Friends.[234]

The manifest Friends play an intermediary role between the hidden Friends and creatures. The hidden Friend is like the sun, and the manifest one is like the moon.

> God has servants whom He brings into the veil and to whom He talks of the secrets.[235] Beyond these outward Shaykhs who are famous among the people and mentioned from the pulpits and in the assemblies, there are hidden servants, more complete than the famous ones. And there is a sought one who is found by some of them. Mawlana thinks that I am he. But that's not my belief.

> If I'm not the sought one, I am the seeker. In the end the seeker will bring up his head in the midst of the sought. Right now, God is seeking me.

> However, the story of the sought one is not found in any book, nor in the explanations of the paths, nor in the treatises—all those are explanations of the road. About that one person we have heard this, nothing else.[236]

In the above quotation, though Shams seems to deny being a hidden Friend of God, he implies that he is one of them because he is sought by God. But elsewhere he compares himself to the sun and Mawlana to the moon:

> ...should I make hypocrisy or should I say it without hypocrisy? This Mawlana is like the moon. No eye can reach the sun of my existence, but it can reach the moon. The eye cannot afford to see the sun because of its luminous rays and brightness. Even that moon cannot reach the sun,

but the sun can reach the moon. *"The sight comprehends him not but He comprehends the sight"* (Quran 6:103).[237]

Mawlana in his *Discourses* considers Shams to be one of the hidden Friends of God (*awliya' mastur*).

> They say we have seen Shams al-Din Tabrizi. O Venerable man, we have seen him! O bastard, where did you see him? In the world there are many Friends of God who are insightful and have attained Union. There are other Friends beyond them who are called the hidden ones of the Real. Those Friends make many supplications as: "God! Show us one of those your hidden Friends!" Even though they have insight, they cannot see them unless they wish it and unless it behooves them...

> The face of the sun is toward Mawlana because Mawlana's face is toward the sun.[238]

> If someone falls into the ocean and strikes the ocean with his hands and feet, the ocean will break him. It is the ocean's habit to swallow someone, until he is drowned. When he is immersed and drowned, then the ocean will become his bearer. That is why the Holy Prophet said that if someone wants to see a dead body walking on the earth, let him look at Abu Bakr; he was liberated from the dustbin of this earth. He settled in the companionship of the pure and life-giving water. That ocean is a servant among the servants of God.[239]

Discursive Knowledge

For Shams, true knowledge comes through unveiling and by the vision of things in God, and not through mere study. Most often studying is a great veil. People are immersed in it as if they have fallen into a well or a moat. In the end they will come to regret it because they have busied themselves with licking the bowl, and they have held themselves back from that enduring and eternal food. Letters and sounds are like the bowl.[240]

If discursive knowledge were sufficient for the attainment of truth and reaching the goal of Union, the great

63

discursive philosopher Avicenna would not have said at the end of his life:

My knowledge reached that far
That I came to know that I know nothing

"You can catch the scent of something from this one word. They showed him something, 'I came to know that what I said from the beginning to the end was nothing.'"[241]

True knowledge is the work of the heart, not of the brain and the forehead. He who is more learned is further from the goal. The more abstruse his thinking, the further he is from the goal.[242]

The reason why most people study in the *madrasahs* is that they think they will become tutors and assistant professors and that they will run schools...They talk of beautiful things in the assemblies so that they can get positions. But why should one barter knowledge for worldly things? The rope of knowledge is for people to come out of the well, not for them to go from this well into that well.

"You must bind yourself to knowing this: 'Who am I? What substance am I? Why have I come? Where am I going? Whence is my root? At this time what am I doing? Toward what have I turned my face?'"[243]

The Microcosm and the Macrocosm

Who can understand the words of God but the servant of God? If you become the servant of God, you can know the tongue and the words of God. One can understand the word of God because the reality of all plants, animals, and minerals, and of the ethereal subtlety of the spheres can all be found in man, but what is in man cannot be found in them. He is in reality the macrocosm. After all, God says: "My heaven and my earth do not embrace Me but the heart of my believing servant does embrace me."[244]

In the view of philosophers, the human being is the microcosm, and the world is the macrocosm. But in the view of prophets, the world is the microcosm, and the human being is the macrocosm. The world is made in the image of man.[245]

Someone said to a Sufi: "Lift up your head and gaze upon the traces of God's mercy."[246] He said: "Those are traces of traces. The roses and tulips are inside."[247]

According to Shams, Moses was the beloved of God and he to whom God spoke. He is mentioned more often in the Quran than any other prophet, and when someone loves something, he mentions it often. As stated in the Quran:

> When Moses came to the appointed meeting and his Lord spoke to him, he said: "My Lord, show me that I might look upon thee." He said: "Thou shalt not see Me; but look upon the mountain; if it remains firm in its place then thou wilt see me." And when his Lord manifested himself to the mountain, He made it crumble to dust and Moses fell down in a swoon. (Quran 7:143)[248]

When the reality of vision turned its face to Moses and he was immersed in vision, he said: "Show me." He replied: "You will never see Me." Since he was immersed and drowned in seeing, how could he say: "Show me so that I may see"?

That mountain is a reference to Moses's own essence. He called it a "mountain" because of its grandeur, immovability, and stability. In other words, God meant: "Look into yourself and you will see me." According to Shams, this is equivalent to the saying of the Prophet: "He who knows his own self, knows his Lord."

When God manifested Himself, then Moses's self, which was like a mountain, crumbled to dust...then Moses said: "I have repented to Thee," that is, I have repented from the sin of being immersed in vision and then asking for vision.[249]

Our hearts are God's storehouse. So why should we put down the goods of a camel-driver there? I will throw them all out. My heart cannot bear but to be the King's storehouse.[250]

65

The Holy Quran

There is nothing above the Quran. However, that Quran that is addressed to the common people concerning commandments, prohibitions, and showing the way has one taste, and that addressed to the elect has another taste.[251]

The reciters of the Quran have different levels. There are many reciters of the Quran who, as the Prophet has said, recite the Quran, but the Quran curses them. There are some other reciters whom the Prophet has named the folk of God and His elect. They are aware of the seven layers of meaning, because the Prophet said: "The Quran has an outward sense and an inward sense, and its inward sense has another inward sense up to seven inward senses." These seven layers of meaning are not what is customary and known among the people.

Beyond these two main senses, there is still another level for those who are the most elect. They are neither of this sort nor of that sort. They are not mentioned in the Quran except by allusion.[252]

Some commentators of the Quran make only a literal interpretation. How do they interpret this verse: "We shall show them our signs in the horizons and in themselves until it becomes manifest to them that He is the Real"? What do they say about 'horizons"? "Winter and summer"? About "in themselves"? "Illness and health"? "Well done, O exegetes"?

"Another exegesis! 'horizons' means 'splitting the moon and the miracles.' 'In themselves' means 'expanding the breast.' That 'He is the Real' means that God is the Truth and Muhammad is the true. 'A fine exegesis.'"

But the true interpretation is consigned to spiritual travelers and wayfarers. For them each verse is a message and a love-letter from the Beloved. They truly know the Quran. The beauty of the Quran presents and manifests itself to them.

"The All-merciful taught the Quran" (Quran 55:1–2) indicates that one should listen to the Quran's exegesis from God. If you listen to any exegesis other than God's, that is the exegesis of the speaker and shows the speaker's state. It is not the real exegesis of the Quran. As to the literal translation of the Quran, that is what five-year-old children can do.[253]

There are some who believe that the Quran is the Word of God but the Hadith is the speech of Muhammad. "What hope is there for him? If this is his beginning, where will he reach in the end? All these things should be known by him in childhood, but he's remained in narrowness."[254] Sometimes there are more secrets in the Hadith than in the Quran. Look at the verse "The heart lied not in what it saw" (Quran 53:11), and the hadith "I have prepared for my righteous servants what no eye has seen and what no ear has heard, nor has it occurred upon the heart of any human being…"[255]

In the Quran it is said: "Had we sent this Quran down on a mountain thou wouldst have seen it humbled, rent asunder in fear of God" (59:21). That which He places on a mountain and that mountain cannot bear it, that light strikes him.[256]

The Glorification of Beings

In one of the most significant verses of the Quran, God declares that all beings glorify Him. "The seven heavens and the earth and all beings therein glorify Him, and there is nothing that does not proclaim His praise; but you do not understand how they declare His glory" (Quran 17:44).

Some of the theologians, the Mu'tazilites for example, short of understanding the real purport of this verse, have taken it to mean that all beings, as signs of God, signify the existence of God.[257] This, however, is contrary to the tenor of the verse. For some Sufi masters and certain sapiential philosophers, such as Mulla Sadra, the meaning of the verse is too evident to be interpreted in such a way as to negate its literal import. Several of them have dealt extensively with the problem, and have even written treatises on this subject. For Rumi, the glorification of all beings is so evident that it is as if he witnesses their glorification by a sort of spiritual vision. One only has to understand the language of beings and to penetrate into their inmost essence in order to be able to listen to their inward praise and glorification. God has made every thing declare His Glory, whether that thing possesses discernment or not. Each one glorifies Him in a different fashion, but the problem is not only that we do not understand their glorification, but that scarcely any being understands the glorification of another.

> Each glorifies Thee in a different fashion,
> and that one is unaware of the state of this one.
> Man disbelieves in the glorification uttered by inanimate
>   things,
> but those inanimate things are masters in performing
>   worship.
> Nay, the two-and-seventy sects, every one,
> are unaware of each other and in great doubt.
> Since two speakers have no knowledge of each other's
>   state,
> how will it be with wall and door?

Since I am heedless of the glorification uttered by one who
    speaks,
how should my heart know the glorification of that which
    is mute?[258]

Rumi goes to some length to elaborate the differences
between various schools, their animosity and adverse-
ness to, and indeed their total lack of understanding of,
one another—which is to say, their lack of awareness of
each other's modes of glorification. If people, as rational
and speaking beings, are unable to understand each
other and have become divided into seventy-two sects,
how can we expect them to understand the glorification
of mute things? After elaborating the point by citing some
examples, Rumi concludes by saying:

No one knows except the deified man
in whose heart is a spiritual touchstone.
The rest hold only an opinion;
they fly to their nest with a single wing.[259]

The difference between those who know and those
who do not know is the difference between knowledge
and opinion. Knowledge is a bird with two wings, whereas
opinion is a bird with one wing alone, the flight of which
as a consequence is defective and impaired.

The one-winged bird falls headlong and then flies up
a little and might never reach the nest, whereas the two-
winged bird, endowed with knowledge and delivered from
mere opinion, spreads its wings and flies straight to its
nest, not listening to the praise or the blame of the entire
world. Rumi's simile of one-winged and two-winged birds
could be compared with Plato's parallel simile of the
winged horses in the *Phaedrus*.[260]

Given that human language is speech or a vocal sort
of expression, when we say that all beings praise or glorify their Lord, we might mean that they have a language
like ours that is vocal in nature. But this is far from being
the case. According to the ancients there are other kinds
of expression. Consider, for example, a child who laugh-
ingly gazes at her mother, without uttering a word: this

is an inner expression that betokens a sort of affection or love for her mother that is stronger than uttering mere words about love for her.

Animals too, though many have their own particular kind of vocal expression, communicate their wants and desires non-vocally. Consider a cat, for example, who comes and politely sits by your table, opening and shutting its eyes, and every now and then looking covetously at the food. Without uttering a sound, she is more than able to communicate her desire.

In some verses, Rumi calls vocal expression the "language of discourse" (*zaban-i qal*) and non-vocal expression the "language of one's (inner) state" (*zaban-i hal*). For Rumi, the latter is of course the more real language. In one famous verse, which has become an almost proverbial expression in the Persian language, Rumi represents God as saying to Moses: "I look not at the tongue and the speech; I look at the inward spirit and the inner state."[261]

But there is a third and much more exalted language, beloved to the ancient sages and scarcely understood and even denied today, and that is the language of being. If language is expressivity, what language is more authentic than being itself, by which things show themselves to us as they are? Furthermore, being is the root and the principle behind the other two types of language and behind every other possible kind of expression.

I said that ancient sages were very fond of understanding the language of being. To give but one example from China, take the case of Lao Tzu in his *Tao Te Ching*. This precious diamond expresses the language of being in the best way. It tells us how the Tao, without a name, by becoming named has expressed and manifested itself in the world of multiplicity or in the Ten Thousand Things. Lao Tzu, having identified himself with the Tao, or by realizing the Tao in himself, has witnessed the *modus operandi* of the Tao, and having fully understood the ontological language of this universal and cosmic principle, has given us a human expression in vocal or written language.

To give another example from Presocratic philosophy, the philosophy of Heraclitus explains to us in brief terms how the *arche*, or the First Principle, which he considers to be the Logos, has manifested itself in multifarious and indefinite things, each of which is an aspect of the Universal Logos. Philosophy, according to Heraclitus, is *homo-legein*, that is, "to speak as the Logos speaks," or in other words it is to understand the language of being. Common people, according to Heraclitus, are like dreamers, each of whom has his or her own private dream. It is only the sage who has awakened from his slumber and comprehends the universal functioning of the Logos.[262] A similar perspective is voiced by Muslim sages such as Avicenna, Suhrawardi, Ibn 'Arabi, and Mulla Sadra, each of whom deciphers for us the mysterious script of being from converging but different points of view.

Rumi, too, talks often about the language of being, and his *Mathnawi* can in a way be regarded as an expression of that language. But Rumi avows that to understand the language of being is extremely difficult. He wishes that being had a tongue like human beings do so that it could divulge its secrets and could remove the veils from existent things. Whatever words and statements we utter about being, it is as if we have added other veils by our mere utterance:

> Would that Being had a tongue
> that it might remove the veils from existent beings!
> O breath of existence, whatsoever words thou mayest utter,
> know that thereby thou hast bound another veil upon it.
> That utterance and that state of existence
> are the bane of perception:
> to wash away blood with blood is absurd, absurd.[263]

For those who understand the language of being, according to Rumi, all particles speak, saying in their inwardness that they hear and see and are full of joy. But for those who are not intimate with their language, they seem to be deaf and mute.

What is the reason for such incomprehension? It is due to the fact that the human, by nature a spiritual being but forgetting himself, tends towards material things and hence becomes unable to penetrate into their mysteries. One should, on the contrary, ascend from the mineral to the spiritual stage, and from that vantage point behold the inner tumult of all particles.

> All particles of the world in their inwardness,
> addressing you, say all day and night:
> "We have hearing and sight and are happy;
> but with you, the uninitiated, we are mute."
> For as much as ye are going toward inanimateness,
> how shall ye become familiar
> with the spiritual life of inanimate beings?
> Go forth from inanimateness into the world of spirit,
> hearken to the commotion of the particles of the world.
> The glorification of God by inanimate beings
> will become evident to thee.
> The doubts suggested by false interpretations
> will not carry thee away from the truth.
> Since thy soul hath not the lamps for seeing,
> thou hast made interpretations.[264]

Rumi, too, like all other beings, takes part in this universal hymning of the Divine Glory, and it is as if his spiritual dance (*sama'*) is his participation in such a celebration. One could even say that the glorification of the perfect man is the pinnacle or the sum total of the glorification of all beings.

If everything in the universe glorifies God, if every particle, nay every atom, praises him, if all beings in the universe, in Heaven and on earth, the angels and cherubim, the heavenly spheres, galaxies, and stars, the sun and the moon, the elements, and the three kingdoms of minerals, plants, and animals glorify His praise, so too human beings, who, according to Rumi are the consummation of the chain of being and the highest rung in the ladder of existence, should also attune themselves with this universal harmony and take part in this sweet psalmody of the Divine praise.

The human being, as we shall see later in our discussion about humankind in Rumi, is in some respects different from other beings. For example, among all creatures he has been endowed with the Divine gift of free choice. So he is free to either glorify and praise the Lord of the universe or not. But if he makes this choice, especially if it be as a result of a profound knowledge that he has obtained about himself, the cosmos, and the Divinity, his glorification, being voluntary and founded on the supreme knowledge of reality, is of an insuperably superior order.

The human being, moreover, rather than the cosmos, is made in the image of God. He is the theophany of all the Divine Names and Attributes. He embodies in himself the reality of the world, and the world is his reflection or his image. He is the substance and the world is his accident.

The perfect saint or sage, according to Rumi, is the intermediary between Heaven and Earth, between God and creation, and, as such, is the guardian of the Divine treasury and the consummation of creaturely existence. Being the realization of all Divine Names and Attributes, he glorifies God with all His Names. Since the cosmos is also a manifestation and reflection of the Divine Names and Attributes, this signifies that the glorification of the Perfect Human is equivalent to the glorification of all beings. In the terminology of the Quran, each being glorifies God with its own special and peculiar praise (*bi-hamdihi*); it is only the Perfect Man who glorifies Him with an all-encompassing and universal praise (*al-hamd*).

We said earlier that the human being among all other beings is endowed with free choice by which he can opt for the glorification of God. But according to Rumi, human choice is not consequential if it is not bolstered by Divine Grace or Divine Favor. In the final analysis, our choice is not totally autonomous or independent of Divine Providence. This is why Rumi always calls for Divine Succor. Ultimately, even though the human being has been given free choice, his perfection and salvation rest in seeking the infinite Mercy of God.

> O God,
> put into our heart subtle words
> which may move Thee to mercy, O Gracious One!
> From Thee come both the prayer and the answer,

from Thee security, from Thee also dread.
If we have spoken faultily, do Thou correct it.
Thou art the Corrector, O Thou who art the Sultan of
    speech.
Thou hast the alchemy whereby Thou mayst transmute it,
and though it be a river of blood, mayst make it a Nile.
Such alchemical operations are Thy work,
such elixirs are Thy secrets.[265]

God has wrought many miracles in His creation. From a single soil He has brought forth multifarious plants and flowers with different shapes, colors, flavors, scents, and beauties. He has transmuted the same soil into different minerals. He has transformed one kind of earth into gold and another into human beings. He can do the same alchemical operation in our consciousness and change our spiritual darkness into enlightenment. He can transform our ignorance into knowledge, our negligence and forgetfulness into vigilance and remembrance, and our anger and irascibility into patience and forbearance.

O Thou who hast transmuted one clod of earth into gold
and another clod into the father of humanity,
Thy work is the transmutation of essences and munifi-
    cence.
My work is oversight, forgetfulness, and error.
O Thou who makest brackish earth to be bread,
and O Thou who makest dead bread to be life!
Transmute oversight and forgetfulness into knowledge.
I am all wrath. Make me patience and forbearance.[266]

Since both prayers or invocation and their response come from Him, the servant should only resort to Him and Him alone. It is He who gives us the yearning to call Him, to glorify and praise Him, and He it is who listens and responds to our prayers and supplications. In the true prayer or invocation, the servant is totally lost in Him, and He alone remains as the invoker and the invoked.

75

To whom but Thee should Thy servant lift his hand?
Both the prayer and the answer are from Thee.
Thou at first givest the desire for prayer
and Thou at last givest likewise the recompense.
Thou art the First and the Last and we between are nothing,
a nothing that does not come into expression. [267]

The best kind of prayer and supplication is that of
those who have annihilated their selves in the Divine Self.
In such a station He is both the invoker and the invoked;
both the prayer and its answer proceed from Him.

The invocation of the selfless is in truth different.
That invocation is not from them;
it is spoken by the Divine Judge.
God is making that invocation
since the speaker is naughted.
The invocation and the answer are both from God. [268]

Finally, Rumi advises us not to dismiss and neglect
prayer and glorification of God. The act of praying and
invocation is in itself praiseworthy, irrespective of the
benefit or the result that might accrue therefrom.

My brother, do not refrain from invoking God.
What business have you with His acceptance or rejection? [269]

Returning to the universal glorification of God by all
of creation, Rumi explicitly says that all beings have their
own peculiar speech, but it is not comprehended by any
and every one. One should attain to a special spiritual
rank in order to be able to apprehend the whisper of beings.

The speech of water, the speech of earth and the speech
of mud
are apprehended by the senses of them that have
hearts. [270]

Some philosophers may deny the inner speech of things, just as they may cast into doubt the complaint of the moaning pillar (*hannanah*) on which the Prophet leaned when it served as his pulpit. Mawlana responds by saying that the saints and Friends of God have a special kind of perception of which ordinary people are deprived, even if they possess it virtually.

> The philosopher who disbelieves in the moaning pillar
> is a stranger to the senses of the saints.[271]

The question might be asked, how do the saints or the Friends of God perceive something that is not accessible to others? To answer this question in a summary fashion, one should be reminded that according to Rumi and nearly all Sufi saints, human beings have seven vertical (or spiritual) levels within themselves, one above the other, corresponding to the seven heavens mentioned in the Quran and the seven Sufi stations (ultimately leading to Union), and probably also corresponding to the seven layers of interpretation of the Divine Word.

These seven stages are called 1. the body (*jism*); 2. the breast (*sadr*, corresponding to the soul); 3. the heart (*qalb*); 4. the spirit (*ruh*); 5. the secret (*sirr*); 6. the hidden (*khafi*); and 7. the most hidden (*akhfa*). All of these expressions are to be found in the Holy Quran.

It is interesting to note that according to the Sufis, each of these seven stages has its own peculiar kind of perception, or its special kind of sensation. Just as, for example, the bodily eyes see physical objects, so too each level has its own specific kind of vision, hearing, and other senses. Just as the child in the womb has all the five senses potentially, which only become actually operative when the child is born into this world, so too all humans have the mentioned spiritual faculties potentially, but they must be actualized through spiritual rebirth. That is why Rumi often speaks about "the eye of the heart" or "the eye of the spirit," or about spiritual audition and olfaction.

Besides the understanding and the soul which is in the ox
   and ass,
man has another intelligence and soul.
Again, in the saint, who has that Divine Breath,
there is a soul other than the human soul and intelligence.[272]

Ordinary people are so engaged in sensory perception
and sensual pleasures that they are as if debarred from
transaction with the higher stages of their own being.
These stages are already there, and one has only to remove the obstacles hampering spiritual perception. One
should cast these obstacles away to get ready for a new
spiritual audition.

If thou wouldst not have the mind of thy spirit in perplex-
   ity
do not stuff this cotton-wool into thy spiritual ,
so that thou mayst understand those riddles of His,
so that thou mayst apprehend the secret sign and the
   open.
Then, the spiritual ear becomes the place
where inspiration (*wahy*) descends.
What is *wahy*? A speech hidden from sense-perception.
The spiritual ear and spiritual eye are other than this
   sense-perception,
the ear of reason and the ear of opinion are destitute of
   this (inspiration). [273]

If one wants to taste the water of Divine Mercy, one
must become lowly and humble like water. If one wants
to hear the voice of celestial music, one must remove
from one's ear the cotton of doubt and evil temptations.
If one desires to behold the beauties of the unseen world,
one must cure oneself of chronic spiritual myopia. If one
longs to taste the sugar of Union, one must remove from
oneself the traces of fever and bile.

Bring the sky under thy feet, O brave one.
Hear from above the firmament the noise of celestial music.
Take out of thine ear the cotton of evil suggestion,
that the cries from heaven may come into thine ear.

78

Purge thy two eyes from the hair of defect
that thou mayst behold the cypress garden of the world
   unseen.
Eject the phlegm from thy brain and nose,
that the wind of God may reach thy sense of smell.
Do not leave in thyself any trace of fever and bile,
that thou mayst get from the world the taste of sugar...
Tear the fetter, which is the body, from the foot of the soul
so that it may race round the arena of the Divine Assembly.
Take off the shackle of avarice from thy hands and neck;
seize and enjoy a new fortune in the old heaven.[274]

We are probably all familiar with Plato's allegory of the
cave in *The Republic*. In this allegory, we human beings
are like prisoners in the cave, with our necks and feet
turned towards the wall and bound by fetters and shackles, unable to move, only able to look at the screen on the
wall on which appear the images of things, shown by the
invisible men on the parapet behind the prisoners. If by
Divine Grace a prisoner is able to turn his gaze back-
wards, he will see the fire casting the images on the
screen, the men on the parapet, and the opening of the
cave. With blurry eyes and much trouble and suffering,
he goes out of the cave and first looks at the stars and
the starry firmament at night. After his eyes get used to
daylight, he is able to see animals and the things of which
he had only seen the images on the cave wall. The former
cave prisoner, released from the dungeon, is at last able
to see the sun (representing the Ultimate Reality), which
is the cause of existence of things here on earth and
which gives the human eye the power to see and makes
things visible to us.[275]
   In a very beautiful simile that parallels Plato's allegory
of the cave, Rumi likens the existential condition of men
in this world to the predicament of the prophet Joseph,
who was thrown by his brothers into a well and was released through Divine Grace by travelers in a caravan
who were searching for water.

You are Joseph, full of beauty, this world is as the well,
and this rope is patience with the command of God.

79

O Joseph, the rope is come, put your two hands upon it.
Do not neglect the rope, for it has grown late.
Praise be to God, that this rope has been dangled,
and that grace and mercy have been blended together,
so that you may behold the world of the new spirit,
a world quite manifest though invisible to us now.
This world of non-existence has become like real existence,
while that world of real existence has become very hidden.
The dust is on the wind, it is playing,
it is making a false show and forming a veil.[276]

He whose spiritual senses have been unveiled sees
Divine Beauty and Perfections everywhere. All things become the vehicles manifesting God's signs. Wherever he
turns, he beholds traces of His Names and Attributes. He
who is not a lover, that is, he whose spiritual faculties
are dormant, sees things only in their phenomenal aspect.

The peerless God hath made all the six directions
a theatre for the display of His signs to the enlightened,
in order that, whatever animal or plant they look upon
they may feed on the meadows of Divine Beauty.
Hence He said unto the company of believers
"Wheresoever ye turn, His Face is there" (Quran 2:115).
If in thirst they drink some water from a cup
they behold God within the water.
He that is not a lover of God sees in the water his own image,
O man of insight.
But since the lover's image has disappeared in the Beloved,
whom now should he behold in the water? Tell us.[277]

One of the great tasks of prophets, sages, and saints
has been to open the spiritual eyesight of human beings
and to shed upon them a spiritual light whereby they are
able to see spiritual realities. They have been able to illuminate the souls of people and to deliver them from the
darkness of ignorance. They are the ones who have been
able to awaken humanity from the dogmatic slumber of
negligence and inadvertence. Those whose hearts and

spirits are not enlightened are spiritually asleep even though their eyes are open.

> Whosoever is awake is the more asleep;
> his wakefulness is worse than his sleep.
> When our soul is not awake to God,
> wakefulness is like closing our doors.[278]

In the Holy Quran this world is said to be the "world of play and pastime."[279] In reference to this verse Rumi says:

> All humanity are children except him that is intoxicated with God.
> None is grown-up except him that is freed from sensual desire.
> God said: "This world is a play and pastime" (cf. Quran 29:64),
> and ye are children and God speaks truth.
> If you have not given up play you are a child.
> Without purity of spirit how will you be fully intelligent?[280]

The above verses may be a reference to a tradition narrated from the Prophet, who said that people in this world are in a dream and when they die they awake. He is also reported to have said: "My eye sleeps but my heart never goes to sleep.

> Oh, how many there are whose eyes are awake
> and whose heart is asleep.
> What, in truth, should be seen
> by the eyes of creatures of water and clay?
> But he that keeps his heart awake
> though the eye of his head may sleep,
> his heart will open a hundred eyes.
> If you are not one of illumined heart, be awake.
> Be a seeker of the illumined heart and be always in strife.
> But if your heart hath been awakened,
> sleep sound;
> thy eye is not absent from the seven (heavens) and the six (directions).
> The Prophet said: "Mine eye slumbers,
> but when doth my heart slumber in drowsiness?"[281]

Humankind in the Thought of Rumi

The Human Reality

When considering the concept of humanity in Rumi, which being connected to the infinite Divine reality is profoundly multifaceted, we should bear in mind his precept:

> Even if we cannot weigh the imponderable water of the
>   Oxus,
> we can at least abate our thirst by drinking some of it.[282]

It is very difficult for the modern person to visualize the reality of himself and the cosmos surrounding him as Rumi conceived it, mainly because modern science has reduced the human being to his outmost form, to his flesh, skin, and sinews, as Mawlana would have it, and consequently has alienated the human being from his true nature. Modern philosophy has added a supererogatory note, making metaphysical questions about the reality of anything seem like a redundancy and a superfluity. It is opportune here to ask our great master the question "what is the human being?" and to wait for an answer. He will give us sure hints and allusions in his primordial *Mathnawi*, in his *Discourses* (*Fihi Ma Fihi*), and in his other writings.

If we posed the question about the reality of the human being to our great master, he would immediately inquire whether we were asking about the external human form or about his intrinsic and hidden nature. We too should therefore be able to make this distinction. It makes a great deal of difference which of the two is the object of our inquiry. He would say that outwardly and in his external form, the human being is in the world (*in-der–Welt–sein*) and hence is an insignificant offshoot of that great cosmic tree. In his appearance, the human being has a derivative existence. But this is not the case with the essential human reality, which is the originative cause of the universe, [283] for:

> Outwardly a gnat will cause his outward frame to whirl round (in agitation),
> but inwardly his nature encompasses the Seven Heavens.[284]

There has been much talk among the ancient sages about the relationship between the human being and the universe. How are we related to the universe right now? On sapiential and metaphysical grounds, it was taken for granted that the human being is a cosmos or a universe in his own right. But which is the greater universe, the interior world of the human being or the exterior world perceived by our senses? Again, our great master would respond by saying that in our outward form we are the microcosm or the lesser world, but in reality we are the macrocosm.

Let us consider a fruit-bearing tree. Externally, the branch is the origin of the fruit, but in reality the branch came into being for the sake of the fruit. If there had been no hope of the yield of fruit, the gardener would not have planted the tree to start with. Therefore, in reality, the tree was born of the fruit, even if in appearance the fruit was generated by the tree.[285] Muslim sages have traced this genealogical pedigree of things to a universal metaphysical principle to the effect that "what comes first in the intellect comes last in external reality."[286]

The Human Being, the Astrolabe of God

In his *Discourses*, Rumi makes an analogy of the reality of the human being with a sort of a Divine astrolabe. Medieval astronomers used an instrument called by this name to determine the position and the relative distances of stars. But to use the instrument requires the knowledge and skill of an accomplished astronomer—a greengrocer, for example, can derive no benefit from it. Just as the copper astrolabe is the mirror of the heavens, so the human being is the astrolabe of the Divinity. When a human being, through Divine Grace, comes to have knowledge of God and becomes familiar with Him, "through the astrolabe of his being, he beholds moment by moment and flash by flash the manifestations of God and His infinite Beauty, and that beauty is never absent from his mirror."[287]

This simile of the astrolabe is repeated in the *Mathnawi*[288] when Adam is declared to be the manifestation of the Attributes of the Divine Sublimity and the theophany of His Names. Prophets are said to be spiritual astronomers in possession of the spiritual mysteries, who by their keen spiritual insight can observe the stations of the spiritual world. Those deprived of this knowledge, short of this spiritual insight, fall upon their self-image, like the conceited lion, who, seeing his image in the well-bottom, plunged into self-destruction.

> The lion in the well, in his fury
> did not know himself at that moment from the enemy.
> He regarded his own reflection as his enemy:
> necessarily he drew a sword against himself.
> Oh, many an iniquity that you see in others
> is your own nature reflected in them, O reader!
> In them shone forth all that you are,
> in your hypocrisy and iniquity and insolence.[289]

The Human Being Made in the Image of God

In the Bible it is said that God made the human being in His own image, after His likeness (Genesis 1:26). In the Quran we read that God "taught Adam all the Names" (2:31). That is, He made the human being the locus of manifestation of all His Names and Attributes. All the attributes of perfection that we see anywhere in the world are but faint reflections of the Divine Attributes. The world in its totality manifests some of the Attributes of the Divine Perfections, but all the Attributes of God are manifested in the human being. Even angels do not partake of this totality and integrity. So we should see every perfection in human and non-human beings alike as projections, irradiations, and emanations of Divine Perfections.

The accomplished Sufi beholds the entire world as a mirror or as limpid water in which the Attributes of the Almighty are shining forth. The knowledge of the learned, the justice of the just, and the clemency of the clement are but the manifestations of the same Attributes of the Divinity. Kings are manifestations of His Kingship, the sages are manifestations of His Wisdom, and the beauteous are the mirrors of His Beauty; love for them is a projection of His Love. Just as the water of a stream changes ceaselessly, yet the image of the moon in the stream abides, so also generation after generation passes away, but those Divine Names are permanent and everlasting.

> Know that the world of created beings is like pure and
>   limpid water
> in which the attributes of the Almighty are shining.
> Their knowledge and their justice and their clemency
> are like a star of heaven reflected in running water.
> Kings are the loci of manifestation of God's kingship;
> the learned are the mirrors of God's wisdom.
> Generations have passed away, and this is a new genera-
>   tion:
> the moon is the same moon, the water is not the same
>   water.[290]

The Human Being as Substance and the World as an Accident

In a well-known poem in the *Mathnawi*, Rumi says:

> If you born of Adam, sit like him
> and behold all his progeny within yourself.
> What is in the jar that is not in the river?
> What is in the house that is not in the city?
> This world is the jar and the heart is like the river.
> This world is the chamber, and the heart is the wonderful
>   city.[291]

86

Jami, the great Persian Sufi poet of the ninth/fifteenth century elucidates this verse by explaining that Rumi's symbolic description of this world as a "jar" and a "house" and his allegorization of the heart of the perfect human being as a "river" and a "city" mean that whatever there is in the world also exists in the human being, whereas compared with the human being, there is something lacking in the world. This has two implications. First, the attributes of the perfect human being as the Divine image are universal, whereas the attributes in other creatures are particular; they are as if determinations and reflections of the perfect human being's reality. Second, the Divine Attributes are manifested in the human being *in toto*, whereas they exist in other beings partially and in a state of scatteredness and differentiation.[292]

Elsewhere in the *Mathnawi*, Rumi says:

How are you this form? You are that Unique One,
for you are fair and lovely
and intoxicated with yourself.
You are your own bird, your own prey and your own
    snare;
you are your own seat of honor, your own floor and your
    own roof.[293]

Time and again Rumi emphasizes that the human being is the true substance, and all the worlds are his accidents, and it makes little sense to seek the substance in the accidents.

The human being is the substance
and the celestial spheres are his accidents.
All things are a branch or the step of a ladder and he is
    the goal.
O thou to whom reason, foresight and intelligence are
    slaves:
how art thou selling thyself so cheaply?
Service to thee is imposed on all existence as a duty.
How should a substance beg for help from an accident?
Thou seekest knowledge from books? What a pity!
Thou seekest pleasure from sweetmeats? Alas!

Thou art the sea of knowledge hidden in a dewdrop.
Thou art the universe hidden in a body three cubits
    long.[294]

In the *Discourses*, Rumi elucidates this point with the parable of the bald man of Baalbek, who carries on his head a tray containing a pinch of every drug. The heaps from which the pinches were taken are infinite, but there is no room in his tray for more pinches.

> The human being is like the bald man of Baalbek, or a druggist's shop. He is loaded with pinches and pieces out of the treasuries of the attributes of God, all in boxes and trays, so that he may engage in this world in trade suitable to Him—a piece of hearing, a piece of speech, a piece of reason, a piece of generosity, a piece of knowledge.[295]

God-Centeredness

We use this term instead of others such as "theocentrism" or "theocracy," because the latter terms have developed ideological and political shades of meaning that are absent in Rumi, for whom the Divine Vision of things is part and parcel of the primordial human nature. To say that God is the center of everything is to say that He is the principle both transcendent of and immanent in everything. As the Quran teaches: "Wheresoever you turn, there is the face of God" (Quran 2:115).

Everything is the Face of God in the sense that it is His manifestation, and its very being, or "thereness" or *Dasein,* is the very presence of God in it. The true mystic sees the image of God in everything, or rather sees everything as the image of God.

> The peerless God hath made all the six directions
> a theatre for the display of His signs to the enlightened,
> in order that, whatever animal or plant they look upon
> they may feed on the meadows of Divine Beauty.
> Hence He said unto the company (of believers)
> "Wheresoever ye turn, His Face is there."
> If in thirst they drink some water from a cup
> they behold God within the water.

He that is not a lover of God sees in the water his own image,
O man of insight.[296]

But even if there is an inalienable relationship between God and every entity in the world, this relationship is even closer between the human being and God. It is one of mutual love existing between the lover and the beloved in which there is no separation between the two. It is a relationship where this duality has given way to and vanished in utter Union:

There is a union beyond condition or analogy
between the Lord of humanity and the Spirit of humanity.
But I said humanity (nas), not a monster (nasnas).
Humanity is naught but the spirit that knows the Divine
Spirit.
A human being is naught but humanity, but where is humanity?
You have never seen the head of man, but only the tail.[297]

The reality of a human being, according to Rumi, rests in his vision of reality. Take away this vision and what remains is his skin and sinews. But it is not the case that every vision is valid. The true vision is the vision of the Beloved.[298] By meeting God, the inner eye gains spiritual vision. How could God become the confidant of every fool?[299]

Life without repentance is the gradual eroding of the
spirit;
to be absent from God is instantaneous death.
Life and death are both sweet in the presence of God;
without God, the Water of Life is hellfire itself.[300]

The Human Being as a Friend of God

The concept of walayah plays a very prominent role in the writings of Rumi. This word and its cognate wali (one who possesses walayah) have been variously rendered into English as "proximity," "friendship," "sainthood," and "vicegerency." It is derived from the Arabic root w-l-

y, which signifies that two things are contiguous or consecutive, like two consecutive numbers between which no number intervenes. Therefore, this term means the proximity of the servant to God, or his friendship with God, which of course entails the sanctity of the Friend of God and his function of vicegerency of God among creatures. *Walay-ah*, according to the Sufis, is the inner core and kernel of religion. Considering that religion is the address of God to humanity, *walayah* is that aspect of religion that is oriented to God, uplifts the servant to the Divine Threshold, and finally absorbs him into the inner chamber of spiritual Union.

In the *Discourses*, Rumi postulates that a *wali* should not be counted among the "number" of ordinary people. To do so would be "a trial appointed by God." Rumi says:

> They say, "This man is one and they are a hundred," that is, they say the saint is one and humanity is many, a hundred and a thousand. This is a great trial. This view and this thought that makes a person see them as many and him as one is a great trial. *And their number we have appointed only as a trial* (Quran 74:31)...call them if you will sixty or a hundred or a thousand, and this man one, but on the contrary the truth is that they are nothing, whereas he is a thousand and a hundred thousand and thousands of thousands.[301]

In another parable, Rumi likens the spirit of saints to pure water, which is so limpid that it shows forth all that is beneath it, from pebbles to broken shards, and all that is above it, which is reflected in it. But in the breasts of the common and ordinary people, the same limpid water becomes muddy, dark, and sullied. "Then God most High sent forth prophets and saints like a great limpid water such as delivers out of darkness and accidental coloration every mean and dark water that enters into it."[302] The prophets and saints, therefore, remind him of his former state. They do not implant anything new in his substance.[303]

Saints are those who assist a person until his temperament returns to its right balance, and his religion and his heart are restored to their original harmony.[304]

> We are physicians, the disciples of God;
> the Red Sea beheld us *and was cleft* (Quran 26:63).
> Those natural physicians are different
> for they look into the heart by means of the pulse,
> We look well into the heart without intermediary,
> for through discrimination we see things from a higher
>   vantage point.
> Those others are physicians of food and fruit,
> by them the animal soul is made robust.
> We are physicians of deeds and words,
> the radiance of the light of Divine Majesty is our inspirer.
> We know that a deed like this will be beneficial to thee,
> while a deed like that will cut thee off from the Way,
> and that words like these will lead thee on (to Grace),
> while words like those will bring anguish to thee.
> To those physicians a sample of urine is evidence,
> whereas the evidence of ours is the revelation of the Al-
>   mighty.
> We do not desire a fee from anyone,
> our fee comes from a Holy Place.
> Hark, come hither for the incurable disease!
> We, one by one, are a medicine for the spiritually sick. [305]

When the Friends of God have the ultimate Union in view, to them death becomes sweet as sugar, and their sight is never dazzled by the fortunes of this world. The death of the body is not bitter to them, because they flee from the gloomy dungeons of the world to the verdant meadows of Paradise.[306] Companionship with saints makes one saintly, just as the laughing pomegranate makes the garden laugh. Association with the Friends of God turns one's heart into a precious gem, even if it is made of rock or marble. So one should implant the love of the Friends of God within one's spirit.[307] The Friends of God are the Israfils[308] of their time, who blow into the dead corpses the spirit of life.[309]

The possibility of friendship with God is no doubt one of the most important aspects of Rumi's thought, and we

RUMI: A PHILOSOPHICAL STUDY

will therefore return to it for more detailed consideration in a subsequent chapter.

The Human Being as Knower

It is the very essence of the human being to know, and to know is to be able to know Reality. For Mawlana, Reality is nothing other than *Haqq*, or God, and all of His manifestations. According to the well-known statement of Aristotle in the prologue to his *Metaphysics*, "The human being is that which he knows and no more."[310] The same idea is expressed by our master in the following verse:

> O my brother, you are the same as your thoughts, noth-
>   ing more.
> As for the rest, you are only bones and sinews.
> If your thought is a rose, you are a rose-garden;
> and if it is a thorn, you are a fuel for the bath-furnace.
> If you are rose-water you are sprinkled on head and
>   chest,
> and if you are like urine, you are cast out.[311]

All the infinite creatures were created as the result of one single thought, which, like a torrent, flowed over the vast expanse of the universe. In ordinary people's eyes that thought is slight, but like a voracious torrent it swallowed and swept away all the world. So if thought is the origin of every craft in the world, and if from thought houses, palaces, cities, mountains, and rivers derive their life, so why in our eyes does the body appear as great and worthy of respect as King Solomon, and thought appear unworthy and despicable as an ant?

> See the infinite creation, issued from a single thought,
> which has become like a torrent flowing over the earth.
> Small is that thought in the people's eyes,
> but like a flood it swallowed and swept away the whole
>   world.
> So when you see that upon a single thought
> every craft in the world is dependent;
> houses and palaces and cities,
> mountains and plains and rivers,

earth and ocean, as well as sun and sky,
are living from it as fish from the sea—
then why in your foolishness, O blind one,
does the body seem to you a Solomon, and thought only
    an ant?[312]

In a well-known verse, Mawlana furthermore beautifully declares that:

This world is one single thought
emanating from the universal intellect;
the intellect is like a king
and the ideas are his envoys. [313]

In order to understand what Mawlana means by
"thought" in the lines quoted above, we must remember
that for Muslim sages, knowledge is not confined to its
conceptual and ratiocinative aspects. There is a hierarchy of degrees of knowledge, among which the best, according to Mawlana, is the science of realization. In order
to explain what this science is we should bear in mind
the three stages of certainty discussed above: 1.
knowledge of certainty (*'ilm al-yaqin*); 2. vision of certainty (*'ayn al-yaqin*); and 3. realization of certainty (*haqq
al-yaqin*). Seyyed Hossein Nasr explains these stages
beautifully in the following terms:

In the Quran we read, "Moses said to his household: Verily,
beyond all doubt I have seen a fire. I will bring you tidings
of it or I will bring you a flaming brand that ye may warm
yourselves" (Quran 27:6). To bring tidings of the fire, to see
a fire brand, and to be warmed (which could also be translated as being burned) by the fire in this Quranic verse
symbolizes the three stages of attaining certainty of the
Truth, which is symbolized here as fire.[314]

Muslim sages and Sufis consider the science of realization as the most valid type of knowledge, and they call
it "the science of tasting" (*'ilm-i dhawqi*) or "the science of
unveiling" (*'ilm-i kashfi*). He who possesses this
knowledge is called a "realizer" (*muhaqqiq*). He who does

not possess the science of realization is a "blind imitator" (*muqallid*).

> Between the true knower and the blind imitators
> there are great differences;
> For the former is David, while the other is an echo.
> The source of the former's words is yearning ardor,
> whereas the imitator learns by rote...
> Even the imitator is not disappointed of the Divine recompense:
> the professional mourner gets his wages at the time of reckoning.
> Both infidel and true believer say "God,"
> but there is a good difference between the two.
> The beggar says "God" for the sake of bread;
> the devout man says "God" from his very soul.
> If the beggar knew what he was really saying,
> in his eyes neither more nor less would remain.
> For years that bread-seeker says "God,"
> like an ass, he carries the Quran for the sake of straw.[315]

An offshoot of this science of realization is the knowledge of the Self, of which the academicians of formal sciences are deprived.

> He knows a hundred thousand superfluous subjects
> connected with various sciences;
> but that unjust man does not know his own self.
> He knows the special properties of every substance,
> but in elucidating his own substance he is like an ass.
> Saying, "I know what is permissible and impermissible,"
> you know not whether you yourself are permissible (*yajuz*)
> or an old woman (*'ajuz*).
> You know this licit and that illicit matter,
> but are *you* licit or illicit? Consider well.
> Though you know the value of every commodity,
> if you do not know the value of yourself, it is folly.[316]

Those who possess the science of realization are truly "awakened" or "enlightened." They are the true human beings, and the rest of humankind are as children in comparison with them. They have truly attained the station of sobriety and the rest are in a state of spiritual dormancy.

> All humanity are children except him that is intoxicated
>   with God...
> The wars of humanity are like children's fights—
> all meaningless, pithless and contemptible.
> All their fights are fought with wooden swords
> and all their purposes end in futility.
> All of them riding on hobby-horses,
> say we are riding on Buraq and Duldul.[317]

The spiritually negligent and the unawakened people are like a hunter who instead of seeing the bird in the sky chases its shadow on the ground and speeds after it to the point of becoming exhausted. Not knowing that it is the reflection of the bird, he shoots arrows at the shadow until his quiver of life becomes empty. The awakened one on the contrary is the shadow of God on earth, who is dead to this world, but awake and living through God.[318]

> The shadow of God is the servant of God,
> who is dead to this world and living through God.
> Lay hold of his skirt most quickly without misgiving,
> that you may be saved in the end of the last days.
> *How He extended the shadow* (Quran 25:45) is the form of
>   the saints,
> which guides to the light of the Divine Sun.
> Do not go into the valley without this guide.
> Like Abraham say: *I do not love them that set* (Quran
>   6:76).
> Go from the shadow, gain a Sun.
> Pluck the skirt of the spiritual king, Shams-i Tabrizi.
> If you do not know the way to this bridal feast,
> ask of the Radiance of God, Husam-ad-Din.[319]

Life as Universal Joy

In the traditional worldview, life cannot be conceived without Divine Joy, even in the midst of horrible agitations. For Indian sages the ternary *sat* (being), *chit*

95

(knowledge), and *ananda* (bliss, spiritual joy) are the three inseparable facets of one and the same reality. Seyyed Hossein Nasr, in the prologue of his monumental *Knowledge and the Sacred*, while expounding the *sat-chit-ananda* doctrine has aptly remarked that the Arabic term *rahmah* (universal Divine Mercy), which according to the Quran "encompasses everything," embraces the two meanings of *sat* and *ananda* together.[320] In the traditional perspective no *sat* can be conceived without *ananda*, no being without Divine Bliss and without the universal Divine Mercy. The spiritual nexus between human beings and their Divine Source alone can bring about human bliss and felicity.

> If thou want the water of mercy, go,
> become humble and lowly
> and then drink the wine of mercy and become drunk.
> Mercy upon mercy rises up to the brim,
> do not limit thyself to a single mercy, O my son![321]

> I am the slave of him who will not sell his existence
> save to that bounteous and munificent Sovereign,
> so that when he weeps, the heavens begin to weep,
> and when he moans in supplication
> the celestial spheres cry out, "O Lord!"[322]

This universal spiritual joy is best manifested in the spiritual dance or *sama'*, which existed in certain Sufi orders but which Mawlana in particular made an ingredient of the spiritual economy of his order. According to Mawlana, this spiritual dance here below is but a faint imitation and reflection of the universal dance of the spheres.

> The shrill noise of the clarion and the clamor of the drum
> somewhat resemble that universal trumpet.
> Hence philosophers have said that we received these melodies
> from the revolution of the celestial spheres...
> The true believers say that the influences of paradise
> has made every unpleasant sound beautiful.
> We were all parts of Adam,

we all heard all these melodies in paradise.
Although the water and earth (of our bodies) have caused
    doubt to befall us,
something of those melodies comes back to our memory;
but since it is mingled with the earth of sorrow,
how should this treble and bass give us that same de-
    light?[323]

A Second Glance at What It Is to Be Human

One of the greatest mysteries of the human state is that we are able to question everything. To ask a question about something is an attempt to know the nature or the essence of that thing. Were this not the case, asking questions would amount to nothing; it would be utterly null and void. Asking questions about everything, on the other hand, presupposes that human beings have the capacity to know and to comprehend everything. It is this characteristic that distinguishes a human as a rational animal from all other beings. It is this quality, that is, the capacity to know everything, that amazed the ancient sages, who inquired into the problem of how it is possible for a being such as the human to search for the meaning and the reality of everything. The Greek philosopher Aristotle claimed that the human intellect is potentially everything. Moreover, he claimed that the human potential intellect becomes actualized to the extent that it acquires the actual knowledge of things. For Aristotle, just as the body is actualized by the assimilation of food, the human soul is actualized through the assimilation of knowledge. This permitted him to assert categorically: "A human is that which he knows and nothing more."[324]

n the same vein, Rumi believes that a human is what he thinks, or in other words, his being is the same as his thought. A human should never be identified with his bones or flesh or with his outward appearance.

> O my brother, you are the same as your thoughts, nothing more.
> As for the rest, you are only bones and sinews. [325]

The nature of the soul, according to Rumi, is consciousness, and consciousness by nature is spiritual; so one can say that the more aware a soul is, the more spiritual it is. Consciousness, moreover, has many levels, one level above another.

99

Since consciousness is the inmost nature and essence of
    the soul,
the more aware one is the more spiritual he is.
Awareness is the effect of the spirit:
anyone who has this in excess is a person of God.
Since there are consciousnesses beyond this bodily na-
    ture,
in that arena sensual souls are like inanimate matter.
The first soul is the theophany of the Divine Court;
the Soul of the soul is the theophany of God Himself. [326]

For Rumi, humans should never be identified with
their bodies. What constitutes the reality of humans is
their spiritual vision and their inner eye:

Thou art not this body; thou art that vision.
If thou hast beheld the spirit, thou art delivered from the
    body.
The human being is essentially vision;
The rest of him is mere flesh and skin:
whatever his eye has beheld, he is that thing.[327]

Rumi considers the human spirit to be the same as
knowledge and real self-awareness, which itself has
many degrees. The more the self-awareness of a creature,
the more intense and exalted is its being. The human being, for example, dominates and utilizes animals because
of his possession, and their lack, of knowledge and spiritual awareness. Angels are higher than ordinary humans, but prophets, sages, and saints are higher still
than the angels because the angels were commanded to
prostrate before Adam:

Spiritual life is naught but knowledge in times of trial,
the more knowledge one has, the more spiritual life one
    has.
Our spirit is more than the spirit of animals. Wherefore?
Insofar as it has more knowledge.
Hence, the spirit of the angels is more than our spirit,
for it transcends the common sense;
and the spirit of the masters of the heart
is more than that of angels.

100

Cease from bewilderment!
For that reason Adam is the object of their prostration;
his spirit is greater than their being.
Otherwise, it would not be fit to command
the superior to prostrate before the inferior.
When would it please the Justice and Grace of the Lord,
that the rose should prostrate before a thorn?[328]

Needless to say, one should not confuse Rumi's teaching about self-awareness or self-consciousness with so many of its modern equivalents, which are purely subjective and devoid of any spiritual and Divine Aspect. According to Rumi, our consciousness is a manifestation of the Divine Self-Consciousness, and in the final stages of the spiritual wayfaring of humans becomes identified with its Divine Source. The more advanced a human is in the spiritual path, the more he partakes of this Divine Consciousness.

In other contexts, when describing the spiritual stations of the Friends of God and the perfect saints, Mawlana says that they see, hear, and perceive through God.

God has said to the saint, "I am thy tongue and thy eye;
I am thy senses and I am thy good pleasure and thy
    wrath.
Go, for thou art 'By me he hears and by me he sees.'
Thou art the Divine consciousness itself:
How is it right to say, 'Thou art the possessor of Divine
    consciousness?'
Since thou hast become, through bewilderment,
'He that belongs to God,' I am thine, for 'God belongs to
    him.'"[329]

Knowledge of the Self

Perhaps there is no issue more consistently regarded as the most fundamental by the sages and the divines of all traditions than the knowledge of the self, for a deep knowledge of the self is the best, surest, and most direct way to know God. Indeed, the Prophet Muhammad is reported to have said: "He who knows his self, knows his Lord."

101

The knowledge of the self and the knowledge of God are so closely and intimately intertwined that the spiritual forgetfulness of the one entails oblivion toward the other, as also attested to by the following Quranic verse: "Be not as those who forgot God, and so He caused them to forget themselves," (59:18), which, contrapositively stated, can be used to deduce that the true knowledge of the self is the best way to attain the knowledge of God.

Rumi takes issue with those scholars and philosophers who inquire about everything in the heavens and the earth, from the minutest particles to the most stupendous galaxies, trying to untie every knot, but are totally oblivious to their own reality and their ultimate becoming. Suppose that they have left no knot unloosened, but have not realized their true nature and have no discrimination about their salvation or damnation, and cannot tell the causes of their felicity from the seeds of their adversity. Suppose, again, that someone knows the definition of everything; but if he does not know his own true definition, what then?

> Thou hast grown old in loosing knots:
> suppose a few more knots are loosed, what then?
> The knot that is fastened tight on our throat
> is that thou shouldst know whether thou art vile or fortunate.
> Solve this problem if thou art a human:
> spend thy breath on this if you have the Spirit of Adam.
> Suppose you know the definition of all substances and accidents:
> know the true definition of yourself, for this is indispensable.
> When thou knowest the definition of thyself, flee from this definition,
> that thou mayst attain to Him who has no definition, O sifter of dust!
> Thy life has gone to waste in logical predicates and subjects;
> thy life, devoid of insight, has been expended studying hearsay.
> Every proof without conclusion and effect is invalid:
> Consider the final conclusion of thyself![330]

Later, when we have drawn in clearer outline the ontological status of humans *vis-à-vis* God and other creatures, we will see why Rumi is so impatient with those who have cast into oblivion both their human and their Divine vocation.

> He knows a hundred thousand superfluous subjects
> connected with various sciences;
> but that unjust man does not know his own self.[331]

The reality of the human being, unlike his outward appearance, is the most hidden thing imaginable—even more hidden than fairies. This hiddenness is only apparent to people of intelligence. How more concealed is the reality of Adam, who was the Chosen of God (*Safi Allah*)!

> If, outwardly, the fairy is hidden, yet the human being
> is a hundred times more hidden than the fairies.
> Since in the view of the intelligent, the human being is
> hidden,
> how hidden must be Adam, the Chosen of God, in the unseen world.[332]

There are two ways of looking at a human: we can look at him and consider his external form—that which is revealed to us by our external senses; or we can penetrate to the core of his being and his inward essence with our Divine Intelligence. Considered outwardly, the human being is a very insignificant offshoot of the cosmic tree, but in reality he is the existential principle of the universe. Man is like a sun hidden behind a screen of dust, or like an ocean covered by straw.

> Therefore, the human being is in appearance the offshoot
> of the world,
> and intrinsically the world's root. Observe this!
> A gnat will set his outward frame whirling round;
> his inward nature encompasses the Seven Heavens.[333]

> Here is a sun hidden in a mote,
> a fierce lion in the fleece of a lamb.

103

Here is an ocean hidden beneath straw.
Beware, do not step on the straw by mistake.[334]

Rumi's simile reminds one of a similar one in Plotinus's *Enneads* where the ocean of the spirit is concealed by the froth and foam of the body, such that the deep water of the ocean cannot be seen.[335] Rumi staunchly supports the view that the human being is the real substance, and the universe with all its exorbitant magnitude is only an accident. The human being is the final cause and the ultimate purpose of creation, and the world as an offshoot depends on the root, which is the human being. This might seem to us moderns a poetic hyperbole, but we should not forget the fact that it is a view shared not only by many Muslim sages, but also by sages of other, especially eastern, traditions.

> The tiara of *We have honored* (the son of Adam) (Quran
>   17:70)
> is the crown upon thy head.
> The collar of *We have given you* (Quran 108:1) hangs
>   upon thy breast.
> The human being is the substance,
> and the celestial spheres are his accidents.[336]

Macrocosm and Microcosm

The human being, physically speaking, is approximately the middle point between the infinitely great and the infinitely small, between the almost indefinitely large cosmos and the infinitesimal particles studied by the physical sciences. He is in other words a mesocosm (a middle cosmos) situated between the microscopic and the macrocosmic. It is this ontological status that enables him to inquire about the minutest particles and the most gigantic galaxies. But human knowledge is not merely confined to material phenomena. Humans throughout history have considered the possibility of another or other worlds.

Contemplating the beauty, order, harmony, and innumerable perfections of the world, humans have borne witness to the existence of the Author of the universe, Who has bestowed existence, meaning, and perfection upon the entities in the world. So from one point of view, the human being is as if a tiny particle in the vast cosmos; but from another point of view, humans are able to comprehend (i.e. encompass and understand) the reality of things. This is a peculiar characteristic of humans, not shared by any other being. The vast cosmos with all its stupendous magnitude is never able to know or comprehend man. So the question naturally arises: what is greater in rank, value, and dignity: a human being or the cosmos? There have been many sages, especially in the oriental cultures, who believed in the essential priority of man over nature. If I am not mistaken, the Confucian view that the human being is the intermediary and the connecting link between Heaven and Earth is a good example of this perspective, especially if we bear in mind that by "Heaven" is never meant the physical sky.

The famous speculative Sufi metaphysician Ibn 'Arabi holds that the universe without the human being is like a lifeless body ready to receive the spirit, and that the human being is the very spirit of the cosmic body. In yet another simile, he envisions the cosmos without the human being as a mirror that has not been polished, and the human being is the very polishing of that mirror. By this he means that the human being is a being in whom the Divine Consciousness has been fully manifested.[337]

Let it be mentioned that by "human being" in this context Ibn 'Arabi means the Perfect Human Being (*al-insan al-kamil*), an idea that he has copiously elaborated on in his writings. Likewise, when a Buddhist believes that all things are manifestations of the Buddha-nature, are we not permitted to conclude that Buddha-nature (the Reality of Buddha) precedes and is prior to all things?

Rumi is decisively in favor of the view that the human being is the origin and the end-result of creation, in whom its final end is fulfilled. According to Rumi, in every human action and creation, and generally speaking in the act of any agent and the artifact produced by every artisan, the final product comes first in the mind of the agent, but is the last in the order of external existence.

The plan of a house, for example, is first conceived in the architect's mind; then he proceeds to procure the necessary preliminaries such as land, bricks, and doors; and the final product, the house, which is the end of the whole process, is the last to appear.

In Rumi's favorite example, the fruit is the final end of the gardener's labors. It is first in the gardener's mind but comes last after the planting, growth, and fruit-bearing of the tree.

> Therefore in form you are the microcosm,
> but in reality you are the macrocosm.
> Outwardly the branch is the origin of the fruit;
> inwardly the branch came into existence for the sake of
> the fruit.
> If there had not been desire and hope of the fruit,
> how should the gardener have planted the root of the
> tree?
> Therefore in reality the tree was born of the fruit,
> even if in appearance the fruit was generated by the tree.
> Hence Mustafa[338] said, "Adam and the other prophets
> follow behind me under my banner."
> For this reason, that all-knowledgeable one said allegori-
> cally,
> "Though we have come last we precede all.
> If in appearance I am born of Adam,
> in reality, I am the forefather of all forefathers." [339]

Rumi tells the story of a Sufi who in the Sufi fashion had his head on his knee for meditation in a garden. A busybody passer-by asked him why he had his head on his knee and recommended that he obey the command of God and lift up his head and enjoy the beauty of the garden, the aroma of sweet herbs, and the melodious song of the birds, and behold the traces of Divine Mercy. The Sufi answered:

> O man of vanity, His traces are within the heart.
> That which is outside is only the traces of the traces.
> The real gardens and verdure are in the very essence of
> the soul:
> the reflection thereof upon what is outside is as upon
> running water.

106

It is the image of the garden that is in the water,
which shimmers from the water's limpidity.
The real gardens and fruit are in the heart,
but the reflection of their beauty is upon this water and
    mud.[340]

The Second Birth

We are all familiar with the phenomenon of death. There
is scarcely a person who can escape or evade death. But
what we consider to be death is indeed birth into a new
life, which we call variously "the Hereafter" or "the life
after death." But there is another kind of birth in this
very life other than the physical birth, which is called the
spiritual birth or the second birth. It is in reference to
this birth that Jesus is related to have said that no one
shall enter the kingdom of God who is not born twice,
that is, having both a physical birth and a spiritual birth.
Just as physicians and midwives help women to give
birth to children, so prophets, Friends of God, spiritual
masters, and sages assist us in the birth of the spirit.

When a son of man is born twice,
he sets his foot upon the head of all causes.
The First Cause is not his religion;
the secondary cause does him no harm.
He flies like the sun in the spiritual horizon
with the bride of sincerity and with bodily form as a veil.
Nay, he is beyond horizons and the spheres
without locality like spirits and intelligences.[341]

Die Before You Die

A tradition related from the Holy Prophet affirms that one
should die before the natural death, which is no doubt a
reference to the second birth. This means that if a person
knows and believes in the first birth alone, he can never
experience the states of the spiritual birth. In order to be
born spiritually one should mortify the passions of the
concupiscent soul, which hinder and veil the effulgence
of the spiritual light. This kind of death, often referred to

as the voluntary death (*mawt-i iradi*), makes one witness in this very life the life of the spirit and its becoming as if after the natural death, causing one to be awakened to the spiritual realities.

> The mystery of "Die before death" is this:
> that the bounties come after dying.
> Except dying, no other skill
> avails with God, O artful schemer.
> One Divine favor is better
> than a hundred kinds of personal effort,
> such exertion is in danger
> from a hundred kinds of corruption,
> And that Divine favor depends on dying;
> the trustworthy authorities have put this doctrine to the
> test.
> Nay, not even this death is possible without the Divine fa-
> vor.
> Hark, hark! Do not tarry anywhere without the Divine fa-
> vor.[342]

To know better the significance of the spiritual rebirth, one should always bear in mind the fact that the spirit within us is a Divine Trust, deposited in us by God. It is His Spirit, that He has breathed into us: "I breathed into him of My own spirit," says the Quranic verse (15:29). The tenebrity of the body, brought about by its excessive worldly engagements, has tarnished the Divine aspect of the spirit. It is as if by spiritual rebirth one rejoins the spirit to its Divine Origin.

> Since by the grace of God, the Divine Spirit was breathed
> into me,
> I am the breath of God, kept apart from the windpipe of
> the body,
> so that the sound of His breathing should not fall in this
> direction,
> and that that spiritual pearl should escape the narrow
> bodily shell.
> Since God said: *Desire death, O ye that are sincere* (Quran
> 2:94, 62:6).
> I am sincere, I will sacrifice my soul for this purpose.[343]

The soul, freed from the turmoil of the body
is soaring on the wings of the heart, without bodily feet.
Like the prisoner in a dungeon who at night
falls asleep and dreams of a rose-garden,
And says, "O God, do not bring me back to my body,
so that in this garden I may walk with pomp and pride."
God says to him, "Thy prayer is granted:
go not back"—and God best knows the right course.
Consider how delightful is such a dream:
Without having seen death, he goes to paradise.[344]

Rumi calls the spiritual rebirth "the death by transmutation" (marg-i tabdili), in contrast to death by en-
tombment (marg-i dar gur). Abu Bakr, the first caliph, is
a clear instance of one who has undergone such a death,
regarding whom the Prophet said: "If anyone wants to see
a dead man walking, let him look at Abu Bakr."

O you who possess wisdom, if you want that reality unveiled,
choose death and tear off the veil.
Not such a death that you will enter the grave,
but a death of transformation so you will go into light...
Hence Mustafa said: O seeker of mysteries,
if you wish to see a dead man living,
walking on the earth like living men,
yet dead and his spirit gone to heaven...
behold Abu Bakr the devout, who through veracity
became the prince of the resurrected.[345]

Gnostics ('urafa') distinguish between three kinds of
death. The first kind is the instantaneous death of all
contingent beings, which at every moment go back to
their original non-being and are granted existence again
by the Author of all Being. The second is the natural
death experienced by all human beings, which is the separation of the soul from the body. The third is the cosmic
death associated with many cataclysmic events at the
end of the world.
Each kind of death is followed by a rebirth, called in
religious language a "resurrection." So when a human
being dies he will witness the existential states of the

109

Hereafter as a newborn child experiences the terrestrial mode of existence after being born into this world. In the spiritual rebirth, too, one will witness all the realities of the spiritual world. One will see with one's spiritual eye what others experience after death when all the veils are removed: "We have now removed from you your veil and so your sight today is piercing" (Quran 50:22). It is with reference to this Quranic verse that Imam 'Ali said: "If the veils were removed nothing would be added to my certainty."

Now for Mawlana, the exemplary paragon of this spiritual rebirth is the Prophet Muhammad. He had witnessed the reality of a hundred resurrections in this terrestrial life. His voluntary death or his spiritual birth was so perfect that he was able to communicate to us all the news about the other world. This can be seen as an allusion not only to the Quranic revelation, but also to the Nocturnal Ascent (mi'raj) of the Holy Prophet, when he even went beyond "the Lote-tree of the Boundary" and "he drew near and suspended hung, two bows'-length away, or nearer"(Quran 53:8–9).

> Muhammad, then, was a hundred spiritual resurrections here and now,
> for he was naughted in dying to temporal loosing and binding.
> Ahmad[346] is the twice-born in this world,
> he was manifestly a hundred resurrections.
> They asked him concerning the Resurrection saying:
> O (you who are) the Resurrection, how long is the way to the Resurrection?
> And often he would say with mute eloquence:
> Does anyone ask the Resurrection about the Resurrection?
> Hence, the Messenger of good tidings said, symbolically:
> "Die before you die" O nobles,
> even as I have died before death
> and brought from Yonder this fame and renown.
> Do you then become the Resurrection and thereby see the Resurrection.
> This is the condition for seeing anything.[347]

So Mawlana exhorts us all towards a spiritual renovation by being born into the life of the spirit:

> Oh happy is he who has died before death
> and has got the scent of the origin of this vineyard.[348]

Death as the Way to Perfection

For Mawlana, death at every level is a channel for attaining to a loftier and more sublime perfection. We see plainly that the elements die in the inorganic state and become endowed with growth. The plant again dies to the vegetative life and is born in animality. Death in animality causes it to be born in humanity. Once more one dies and leaves behind the human state to be reborn into an angelic life. Since "everything is perishing except His Face" (Quran 28:88), the angel must of necessity escape from the angelic world and shall become what one cannot even imagine. After all, according to the verse "Verily unto Him shall we all return" (Quran 2:156), everything will ultimately return to its Divine Source.

> I died to the inorganic state and became endowed with
>   growth,
> and then I died to vegetable growth and became an ani-
>   mal.
> I died from animality and became human.
> Why, then, should I fear? When have I become less by dy-
>   ing?
> At the next remove I shall die to human-ness
> that I may soar and lift up my head amongst the angels.
> And I must escape from even the angelic state,
> since *Everything is perishing except His Face.*
> Once more I shall be sacrificed and die to the angel;
> I shall become that which enters not into the imagination.
> Then I shall become non-existence.
> Non-existence tells me loud as an organ:
> *Verily, unto Him shall we all return.*[349]

The Soul and the Body

Rumi is well aware that in this life the soul or spirit cannot exist without the body. So he asserts, *prima facie*, that the soul and the body are intertwined and the one cannot exist here without the other.

> The spirit cannot function without the body;
> your body is frozen and cold without the spirit.
> Your body is visible, while your spirit is hidden from view.
> The business of the world is conducted by means of them
>   both.[350]

But though there is a union of the soul with the body in this terrestrial existence, the soul yearns for its original abode in the world of the spirit, and the body always gravitates to the world of the elements and prevents the soul from its flight towards the empyrean.

> The spirit, because of separation from the Divine Throne,
>   is in great want;
> the body from its passion for the thorn-shrub is like a
>   she-camel.
> The spirit unfolds it wings to fly upwards;
> the body has stuck its claws into the earth.[351]

The body and the soul are like two different species of birds. One is like a noble falcon and the other is as a crow. The human soul is imprisoned in the cage of the body. It should not become so accustomed to this cage as to forget its own liberation. Prophets, sages, and saints are the ones who have escaped safely from this prison, and they have shown us the way of escape.

> The bird that is a prisoner in a cage,
> if it is not seeking to escape, it is from ignorance.
> The spirits which have escaped from their cages
> are the prophets, those worthy guides.
> From without comes their voice of religion, crying:
> "This, this is the way of escape for thee.

By this we escaped from this narrow cage.
There is no means of escape from this cage but this
   way."352

Among human beings there are some who possess pristine and pure spirits, and there are others with vicious and tenebrous souls. Both of them are necessary in this world, in order to manifest the hidden mysteries of Divine Wisdom and Providence.

Amongst the created beings are pure spirits;
there are also spirits dark and muddy.
These shells are not of one degree:
in one of them is the pearl and in the other a counterfeit.
It is necessary to make manifest the difference between
   the good and the spoiled,
just as it is necessary to distinguish the wheat from the
   straw.
The creation of this world is for the sake of manifestation,
so that the treasure of Divine Wisdom may not remain
   hidden.
God said, "I was a hidden treasure." Listen!
Do not lose your substance: make it manifest!353

The Human Spirit and the Animal Spirit

By the animal spirit, Mawlana understands a spirit that has not been illuminated by the Divine Light and tends to remain in darkness. The sun has but one single light, but when it reaches the earth it becomes dispersed in different courtyards, which are separated from one another by partitions and walls. When you take away the partitions, the divided light once again becomes one single light. Such is the case of believers who partake of one single Divine Light, but because they are incarnated in various bodies seem to be different. So discord and disunion exist among animal souls; but human souls, thanks to their being illuminated by one single Divine Light, are united:

The animal spirit does not possess oneness:
seek not this oneness from this vital spirit.

113

If this person eats bread, that person is not filled,
and if this one bears a load, that one does not become
    laden.
Nay, but this one rejoices at the death of that one,
and dies of envy when he sees that one's prosperity.
The souls of wolves and dogs are separate, every one;
the souls of the lions of God are united.
I have spoken of their souls nominally in the plural,
for that single soul is a hundred in relation to the body.
Just as the single light of the sun in heaven,
is a hundred in relation to the courtyards of houses.
But when you remove the walls between them,
all the lights falling on them become one.
When the bodily houses have no foundation left,
the faithful remain *a single soul* (Quran 4:1, 31:28).[354]

The Sun of the spirits became separated
within the apertures of the bodies.
When you gaze on the Sun's disk, it is itself one,
but he that is veiled by the bodies is in some doubt.
Plurality is in the animal spirit;
the one single soul is the human soul.
Inasmuch as "God sprinkled His light upon mankind,"[355]
they are essentially one: His is never separated in real-
    ity.[356]

The Human Heart

By the human heart, we do not mean the physical heart, which is not a subject of study in the Divine Science, but is more aptly studied in physiology. By the human heart here is meant that spiritual organ in the human that is the center of his being, the focus of his consciousness and moral conscience, the locus of manifestation of all innate or adventitious ideas, all inspirations or revelations.

Modern philosophers are wont to regard the heart as the vehicle of the sentiments alone, which even though true in a sense, is nevertheless far from disclosing the heart's real nature. In the scriptures, especially the Quran, much emphasis is laid on the functioning of the heart as the highest vehicle of Divine Knowledge, as the following verses demonstrate:

Surely in that [the Quran] there is a reminder to him who has a heart, or will lend an ear and is a witness. (60:37)

They have hearts, but understand not with them... (7:179)

And we sent Jesus, son of Mary, and gave unto him the Gospel. And we set in the hearts of those who followed him love and mercy. (57:27)

In other verses, some hearts are said to be hardened, as stones:

Then your hearts became hardened thereafter and are like stones, or even harder. (3:74)

It was by the mercy of God that you were gentle to them; had you been harsh and hard of heart, they would have scattered from about you. (3:159)

The heart is moreover the locus of the Divine revelation to the Prophet, for "Truly this is the revelation of the Lord of all Being, brought down by the Faithful (Holy) Spirit, upon your heart" (Quran 26:194).

But what is most important for believers is that the heart is the locus of the invocation of the Divine Name and the vehicle of Divine Remembrance: for "Those who believe and their hearts are at rest in God's remembrance—indeed in God's remembrance are at rest the hearts of those who believe"(Quran 13:28).

Now, if God is one and infinite in the real sense of the term, this requires that the human heart, as the center of the human being, should be integrally one and at the same time infinite, so as to be able to encompass God. This fact has been alluded to by a sacred tradition attributed to the Holy Prophet, often referred to by Rumi and others: "My heavens and my earth cannot embrace Me, but the heart of my believing servant does embrace Me."

Mawlana, referring to the human heart, warns us that by the word "heart" he does not mean this cone-shaped visceral organ; the spiritual heart is above the Divine

Throne. The heart that is superior to the heavens and the earth is the heart of the prophets and the perfect saints, purified of every form of impurity and contamination. But our hearts are incarcerated in the prisons of our bodies.

> You say, "I too have a heart,"
> but the heart is above the Divine Throne, it is not below...
> The heart that is higher than the heavens,
> that is the heart of the saints or the prophets.
> That heart has become cleansed of earth and purified.
> It has come to full growth and has been made complete.
> It has taken leave of earth and has come to the Sea.
> It has escaped from the prison of earth and has become
>   the Sea,
> but our water has remained imprisoned in earth.
> O Sea of Mercy, draw us out of clay![357]

The relationship of the heart to the body is like that of a bird flying in the sky to its shadow on earth.

> A bird is flying in the atmosphere of the Unseen:
> its shadow falls on a piece of earth.
> The body is the shadow of the shadow of the shadow of
>   the heart:
> how is the body worthy of the lofty rank of the heart?[358]

The heart that is not illuminated by Divine Light is dark, narrow, and imprisoned as if in a tomb. As a result, one must direct the heart in such a way that it should be enlightened by the resplendence of the Divine Majesty.

> The house of that heart which remains unilluminated
> by the beams of the sun of the Divine Majesty
> is narrow and dark as the souls of deniers,
> destitute of the spiritual savor of the loving King.
> Neither the radiance of the Sun has shone into that heart,
> nor is there in it any spaciousness or opening of the door.
> The tomb is better for you than a heart like this.
> Come now, arise from this tomb which is thy heart.[359]

One often compares one's own heart to that of the great saints and, seeing them through the narrow mirror of one's heart, rejects them. This is, of course, a grievous

116

error. Again, one might judge them by their outward form, whereas the Prophet said: "God does not regard your outward forms, but regards your inmost hearts." Since the human heart is infinite, the seven heavens would be lost in one of its corners. Through the heart of the perfect man, God sends His Mercy in the six directions. It is through him that God accepts or rejects anyone among creatures, by virtue of his being God's mirror and the mediation between Him and the universe.

> Since thou hast deemed thy heart to be the Heart,
> thou hast abandoned the search after those who possess the Heart.
> The Heart into which if seven hundred like these Seven Heavens
> should enter, they would be lost and hidden from view.
> The owner of the Heart becomes a six-faced mirror:
> through him God looks upon all the six directions.
> Whosoever hath his dwelling-place in the world of six directions,
> God does not look upon him except through the mediation of the owner of the Heart.
> If God rejects anyone, He does it for his sake,
> and if He accepts one, he likewise is the authority.[360]

Rumi advises us to seek the possessor of the spiritual heart and to become of the same genus as the heart. He recommends that we liberate ourselves from the narrow dungeon of the body and take refuge in the vast vistas of the heart.

> Seek the owner of the heart if you are not soul-less;
> become of the same genus as the hearts
> if you are not an adversary of the Sultan.[361]

> You must set foot on the plain of the heart,
> because in the plain of the body
> there is no opening.
> The heart is the abode of security,
> O friends!
> It has fountains and rose-gardens within rose-gardens.[362]

117

Rumi and Divine Love

One of the most mysterious of all mysteries in human beings is the mystery of love. Love has many different aspects and can take on multifarious forms, such as love of money, love of position, love of wealth, love of one's country, love of children, love of one's spouse, love of truth and wisdom, and self-love. Without love of one kind or another, life would not be worth living and would be worse than the life of animals, plants, and minerals, which are not alien to love of a sort. Love, moreover, is love of something that one either lacks or desires and considers to be desirable in itself. Humans by nature desire that which seems to them to be good, that is, that which is perfect and beautiful. That is why all human beings love beauty and perfection of some kind and try to create beauty and perfection in whatever they do. They also appreciate the beauty of nature in its various forms, and since the beauty of nature has no end, the human soul ever enjoys more and greater manifestations of beauty. But for the ancients, beauty was not only physical beauty. More important than physical beauty was inner beauty, that is, the beauty of the soul, which consists of its various perfections and excellences, which we deem to be its virtues. A virtuous and perfect soul to them was more beautiful than a well-formed body. But higher still on the scale of beauty was the beauty of the intellect, which manifests itself in arts, sciences, various sorts of knowledge, and especially sapiential and Divine wisdom. A real sage, like Socrates, even if snub-nosed, was described by Alcibiades in Plato's *Symposium* as "one of those little sileni[363] that you see on the statuaries' stalls; you know the ones I mean—they're modeled with pipes or flutes in their hands, and when you open them down the middle there are little figures of the gods inside."[364]

But again, for ancient sages all kinds of beauty and love that we see in creation are manifestations and appearances of Beauty, and that is why they are sometimes beautiful and at other times not. Our world, after all, is the world of becoming and change, and this permits us

119

to say that nothing in this world is beautiful in itself. As a manifestation of Beauty, everything beautiful partakes of Beauty and shares in it, according to its capacity for Beauty as such. Beauty in itself, and also Love in itself, are Attributes of Being in Itself or the Absolute. This is again the case with all other perfect attributes, which first and foremost belong to the Being of the Real, and only contingently and secondarily to the created order.

According to Mawlana, this world of creation is like the limpid and clear water of a river in which the perfect Attributes of the Almighty God are manifested. All the perfections of creatures are reflections of Divine Names and Attributes. Their knowledge, justice, clemency, and the like are Divine theophanies, like the appearance of a star or the moon in running water. Kings are the locus of manifestation of God's Kingship; the learned divines are the mirrors of God's Wisdom. The moon is the same moon, but its image in a river is not the same; the water is constantly running and changing. Justice is the same justice, and knowledge remains unchanged. The Divine Attributes, or you could say with Plato the Divine Ideas, are permanent and everlasting; but generations after generations have passed away. So we should not seek the origin of these attributes of perfection in the running water, but rather we should raise our heads and seek them in the wide expanse of heaven. When we rub well our eyes we will see "that all of them are really He."

> Know that the world of created beings
> is like pure and limpid water
> in which the attributes of the Almighty are shining.
> Their knowledge and their justice and their clemency
> are like a star of heaven reflected in running water.
> Kings are the loci of manifestation of God's kingship;
> the learned are the mirrors of God's wisdom.
> Generations have passed away, and this is a new genera-
> tion:
> the moon is the same moon, the water is not the same
> water.
> The justice is the same justice, and learning is the same
> learning too;
> but those generations and peoples have been replaced.

Generations on generations have gone, O sire,
but these Ideas are permanent and everlasting.
The water in this channel has been changed many times:
the reflection of the moon and of the stars remains unal-
    tered.
Therefore its foundation is not in the running water;
nay, but in the regions of the breadth of Heaven.
These attributes are like Ideal Stars;
know that they are established in the sphere of the Ideas.
The beauteous are the mirror of His beauty;
love for them is the reflection of His being the object of de-
    sire.
This cheek and mole goes back to the source thereof.
How should a phantom continue in the water forever?
The whole sum of pictured forms
is a mere reflection in the water of the river.
When you rub your eyes you will see
that all of them are really He.[365]

The Meaning and Reality of Love

If we are looking for a definition for love, that is impossible, because love is not a concept to be conceived by the
mind; rather, it is a reality that must be realized in our
being. Any endeavor to attain to a definition is to be veiled
and debarred from its reality. One can, however, ap-
proach it through the illumination of Divine Knowledge.

O sincere one, a single atom
of the light of the mystic knowledge within
is better for you than a hundred definitions.
To confine one's attention to a definition
is a mark of being veiled
and of mere conjecture and opinion.
He whose scout is the eye of the heart,
his eye will behold with the clearest vision.
His soul is not content with continuous transmission.
Nay, his feeling of certainty comes from the inward eye.[366]

Love, moreover, is an infinite ocean whose depth cannot be fathomed and whose reality cannot be uttered in
narrow and limited human expressions. Love is an ocean
without an end whose drops cannot be numbered.

121

Love is not contained in speech and hearing:
Love is an ocean whereof the depth is invisible.
The drops of the sea cannot be numbered:
the seven seas are petty in comparison with that
    Ocean.[367]

Love is a stranger to the two worlds; it has seventy-two kinds of madness. Love is the most hidden of the hidden, and what is most apparent of its hidden nature is bewilderment. The Holy Prophet said: "My community will be divided after me into seventy-two denominations of which only one is on the right path." The group on the right path, according to Rumi, is those who follow the religion of love, which is alien to those other sects. Love is above all oppositions, such as servitude and lordship, infidelity and faith, and even being and non-being. It is nearer to the sea of non-being because in it all the distinctions that are in the proper domain of Being, and hence of the intellect, are shattered. Since humans are unable to express the mysteries of love, Mawlana hankers after an ideal situation in which love itself, which is the language of being, could speak in human terms and could divulge some of its secrets. But in our present predicament whatever we say about it, whatever we utter, we only add another veil to it and conceal it under our frigid words. Being imprisoned in the cage of phenomenal existence, Mawlana says that he has no choice but to breathe forth the hidden secrets of love into his reed-pipe.

Love hath estrangement with the two worlds;
in it are two-and-seventy madnesses.
It is exceedingly hidden and its bewilderment is manifest;
the Soul of the spiritual sultans are pining for it.
Its religion is other than that of the two-and-seventy
    sects;
beside it the throne of kings is but a splint-bandage.
At the time of *sama'*, Love's minstrel strikes up this
    strain:
"Servitude is chains and lordship headache!"
Then what is Love? The sea of Not-being;

122

there the foot of reason is shattered.
Servitude and sovereignty are known;
loverhood is concealed by these two veils.
Would that Being had a tongue
that it might remove the veils from existent beings!
O breath of existence, whatsoever words thou mayest ut-
     ter,
know that thereby thou hast bound another veil upon it.
That utterance and that state of existence
are the bane of perception:
to wash away blood with blood is absurd, absurd.
Since I am familiar with His frenzied ones, day and night
I am breathing forth the secrets of Love
in the cage of phenomenal existence.[368]

Love purges one of all covetousness and all defects. It
brings us good gain. It is the physician of all our ailments. It is the healer of all our spiritual maladies, like
Plato, and of our physical ills, like Galen. Through love
the earthly body has soared up to Heaven, so Mount Sinai became intoxicated and Moses fell into a swoon.

He whose garment is rent by a mighty love
is purged of covetousness and all defect.
Hail! O Love that bringest us good gain.
Thou that art the physician of all our ills,
the remedy of our pride and vainglory,
our Plato and our Galen.
Through Love the earthly body soared to the skies,
the mountain began to dance and became nimble.
Love inspired Mount Sinai,
O lover,
so that Sinai was made drunken
and Moses fell in a swoon.
Were I joined to the lip of one in accord with me,
I, too, like the reed could tell all that may be told.[369]

True love purges one's faith of all impurities, like a pure
     flame of fire.
It is far above belief and disbelief;
Because these are no more than husks
And the true love is the core and the kernel,

And there is no doubt that the husks should be consumed
in the oven of love.[370]

A lover is always in affliction; so you can always recognize a lover by the affliction of his heart. There is no
sickness to be compared with the sickness of a heart in
love. There are many kinds of ailment but the ailment of
love is different from all others. Love is the astrolabe of
God by which you can discover and decipher the Divine
Mysteries. Love is either earthly or heavenly, but no matter whether it is from this world or from the next, it will
ultimately lead us yonder, to the presence of the Beloved.
The reality of love is ineffable, because to express it you
must either do so by word of mouth or in written words,
but in either case you are doomed to failure. The commentary by the tongue, even if clearer than writing, will
mask the reality of love. The pen, again, is unable to bear
the onerous burden of love, and whenever its tries to give
an exposition of love, it splits upon itself. Intellect is also
unable to expound it because the more it endeavors to
explain its reality, the more it will be caught helplessly,
as in a mire. It is only love that can utter for us an exposition of love and loverhood.

Being in love is made manifest by soreness of heart;
there is no sickness like heart-sickness.
The lover's ailment is separated from all other ailments;
Love is the astrolabe of the mysteries of God.
Whether love be from this side or from that side,
in the end it leads us yonder.
Whatsoever I say in exposition and explanation of love,
when I come to love itself, I am ashamed of that explanation.
Although the commentary of the tongue makes all clear,
yet tongueless love is more clear.
Whilst the pen was making haste in writing
it split upon itself as soon as it came to Love.
In expounding Love, the intellect lay down like an ass in
   the mire;
it was love alone that uttered the explanation of love and
   loverhood.

124

The proof of the sun is the sun itself:
if you require the proof, do not avert your face from it.[371]

There are some who flee from love as soon as they experience a single humiliation; they feign love but are not real lovers. They know nothing of love except its name. Love has a hundred kinds of coquetry and pride, and is gained through many sorts of blandishment. It only seeks those who are sincere and faithful, and evades those who are disloyal comrades.

Thou art fleeing from love because of a single humiliation;
what dost thou know of Love except the name?
Love hath a hundred disdains and prides;
Love is gained by means of a hundred blandishments.
Since Love is loyal, it purchases him that is loyal;
it does not look at a disloyal comrade.[372]

God as Absolute Love

In philosophical literature God seldom appears as a Lover, not to mention as Absolute Love. But in religious literature, especially as interpreted by Sufis and Muslim sages, Love is one of the Attributes of God. In the Holy Quran, for example, we often encounter statements that God loves those who have this or that quality, or He loves those believers who do such and such an act. Love, on the other hand, is the motive impulse behind creation. Peripatetic philosophers such as Aristotle considered God to be the unmoved mover of the universe, required only to explain universal motion, or at best to be the cause needed to explain the actualization of the potentialities in the universe. He was never conceived of as having existentiated the universe for the sake of Love, nor was there a love relationship between God and human beings.

The theme of love has been the focus of much attention among Sufi saints and Muslim sages. A vast literature can be found in the various Islamic languages on this subject, of which one for example can mention *Treatise on Love* (*Risalah fi'l-'Ishq*) by Avicenna and the poetry of Ibn Farid and Ibn 'Arabi in Arabic, and the *The Narcissus of Lovers* (*'Abhar al-'Ashiqin*) of Ruzbihan Baqli Shirazi, *The Sparks of Love* (*Sawanih*) of Ahmad Ghazali, the *Treatise on Love* (*Risalah fi'l-'Ishq*) by Suhrawardi, *The Gleams of Love* (*Lama'at*) of Fakhr al-Din 'Iraqi, and *The Rays of the Gleams* (*Ashi''at al-Lama'at*) by Jami in Persian, in addition to many others. Besides the exquisite lyric poetry on Divine Love by the great poets of Persia, such as Rumi, Sa'di, and Hafiz, the motif of love has been beautifully depicted in such romances as *Layli and Majnun* (the paradigm of the human love), *Vis and Ramin*, *Khosrow and Shirin*, and many other works.

According to Rumi, love in the true sense of the word is one of the Attributes of God. Beauty in other things is borrowed and is at best a kind of gilded beauty.

> Love is one of the attributes of God,
> who is in need of nothing;
> Love for aught besides Him is unreal,
> because that which is besides Him
> is but a gilded beauty:
> its outside is shining light
> but it is like dark smoke within.[373]

In the Quran, God's love for humans is conjoined with humans' love for God, and it is declared: "He loves them and they love Him" (5:54). Love and Friendship are the Divine Attributes of God. Fear is not an Attribute of God, but it is an attribute of servants. Even if creatures, and above all humans, share in these Divine Attributes, what relation is there between the Attributes of the Eternal Being and the creature, who has come into being and is essentially non-existent?

> Since you have read in the Quran *They love Him*
> joined in a certain place with *He loves them*,
> know then that Love too is an attribute of God,
> O honored Sir.
> What relation exists between the attributes of God
> and those of a handful of earth?
> What relation exists between the attributes of him

126

who is originated in time
and those of the Holy One?[374]

When we love someone, we should seek the source of that love. It is not merely due to the body, because the love of the dead body is not lasting, whereas the love of the living is ever fresh. Mawlana wants us to understand that God is the author of life, beauty, and love in everything. So we should choose the Love of Him Who is the Source of every perfection and beauty and from whose Love all prophets have gained all their power and glory.

> Because love of the dead is not enduring,
> because the dead one is never coming back to us,
> but love of the living is every moment
> fresher than a bud in the spirit and in the sight.
> Choose the love of that Living One
> who is everlasting,
> who gives you to drink of the wine that increases life.
> Choose the love of Him from whose love
> all the prophets gained power and glory.
> Do not say: "We have no admission to that King";
> since dealings with the generous are not difficult.[375]

Mawlana time and again reiterates that love for the dead is not enduring and that one should guard one's love and constantly keep it fixed on the Living One Who is the source of one's spiritual life.

> Love for the dead is not lasting:
> keep your love fixed on the
> Living One who increases spiritual life.[376]

One of the virtues of love is that like a blazing fire it burns and consumes everything other than the beloved. It is as if it draws the sword of "There is no god" and destroys everything other than God, and all there remains is "except God." Hence only through love is the formula of unification (*tawhid*), "There is no god but God," realized. For the lovers only He becomes the object of joy and sorrow. He alone becomes the object of their reward and remuneration. If the lover has anything other than the beloved as the object of his love, it is idolatry; it is not love; it is simply idle passion.

> For His lovers He alone is their joy and sorrow,
> He alone is their wages and hire for service.
> If there be any spectacle except the Beloved
> it is not love, it is an idle passion.
> Love is that flame which when it blazes up
> consumes everything else but the Beloved.
> The lover drives home the sword of "No"
> in order to kill all other than God.
> Thereupon consider what remains after "No":
> there remains "except God,"
> all the rest is gone.
> Hail, O mighty love, destroyer of polytheism![377]

Phenomenal Love

By "phenomenal love" we mean the love of phenomena or mere forms without being bolstered by the Reality of Love. Mawlana wants to awaken us to the fact that we should not be content with the outward aspect of phenomena or with mere forms. True love should enable us to pierce the shell of phenomena and with our inner and spiritual eye witness the Reality that has appeared in those phenomena. When the Reality disappears, the phenomenon fades away. The most hideous error is to take the phenomenon for the Reality, and to confuse the Absolute with the relative that manifests it.

Rumi advises us to abandon the love of mere forms. The object of love is not the form, whether it be love of things in this world or in the next world. If we love our beloveds for their formal appearance, why do we abandon them when they are dead? If our love were for the mere form, the form is still there in the dead body. Both love and beauty are for the sake of the spirit, which has left the body. This means that both beauty and the corresponding love originally belong to the spirit, which is from the resplendence of the Divine Spirit, just like the shining of a sunbeam on a wall by which the wall receives a borrowed splendor. Likewise, the solar beauty of the

128

Divine Essence shines upon everything, and each thing accepts it according to its degree of preparedness. But little by little God takes away that beauty, and as a consequence the phenomenal beauty in that thing withers and fades away. Only the beauty of the heart and not that of the bones is the lasting beauty. So you must seek the heart and not set your heart on bones. When the lips of your heart drink the wine of love, the talisman of your shadowy and phenomenal existence will be shattered, and then you will see that the drink, the giver of the drink, and the drunken, all three, become one, and then you will taste the savor of unadulterated unification.

> That which is the object of love is not the form,
> whether it be love for this world or yonder world.
> That which you have come to love for its form,
> why have you abandoned it after the spirit has fled?
> Its form is still there; whence then this disgust?
> O lover, inquire who your beloved really is!
> ...The sunbeam shone upon the wall;
> the wall received a borrowed splendor.
> ...Beauty in humankind is like gilding;
> else how did your sweetheart become as ugly as an old
>   hag?
> She was like an angel, she became like a demon,
> for that loveliness in her was a borrowed thing.
> Little by little He takes away that beauty,
> little by little the sapling withers...
> Seek the heart, set not thy heart on bones;
> for that beauty of the heart is the lasting beauty:
> its lips give to drink of the water of life.
> Truly it is both the water, and the giver of drink, and the
>   drunken;
> all three become one when your talisman is shattered.[378]

Elsewhere, Mawlana points out that the merchant, the trader, and the carpenter in the final analysis work for love of someone living. So one also should exert oneself in the hope of a Living One Who does not become lifeless after a day or two. Our friendships with our nurse, the tutor, even with our father and mother, are not permanent. That friendship is a radiance of the Divine Friendship cast upon their wall. Their friendship in other words is a "borrowed" one.

> On whatsoever existent thing thy love is bestowed,
> that thing is gilded with Divine qualities.
> When the goldenness has gone to its original source
> and only the copper remains,
> thy nature is surfeited and proceeds to discard it.
> Withdraw thy foot from that which is gilded by His qualities;
> do not from ignorance call the base alloy beautiful...
> The light is going from the wall up to the sun:
> go to that Sun which ever moves in proportion.[379]

In the sixth book of the *Mathnawi*, Mawlana summarizes the whole argument about love:

> Love is one of the attributes of God who is in need of nothing;
> love for aught besides Him is unreal.
> Because that which is besides Him is but a gilded beauty:
> its outside is shining light, but it is like dark smoke within.
> When the light goes and the smoke becomes visible,
> at that moment the unreal love is frozen up.
> That beauty returns to its source;
> the body is left foul-smelling, shameful and ugly.
> The moonlight is returning to the moon;
> its reflection goes off the dark wall...
> When the gold flies from the surface of the base coin,
> that gold returns to its original mine and settles there.
> Then the shamefully exposed copper is left black like smoke
> and its lover is left looking blacker than it.
> But the love of them that have spiritual insight
> is fixed on the gold-mine;
> necessarily it grows greater every day.[380]

That is why Rumi always warns us to be on our guard lest we be deceived by love for illusory things.

130

Those loves which are for the sake of color
are not love:
in the end they are a disgrace.[381]

Most battles, wars, struggles, and skirmishes have
been due to envy and jealousy arising from false passions, gilded beauty, and fake loves.

How do the vulgar burn with envy
for the fleeting happiness of riches and the body?
Behold the kings, how they lead armies
and slay their own kinsmen because of envy.
The lovers of filthy dolls
have sought each other's blood and life.
Read *Vis and Ramin* and *Khosrow and Shirin*!
See what those fools did because of envy.
You will see that the lover perished and the beloved too:
they are naught and their passion is also naught.[382]

Cosmic Love

According to Rumi, love is the stimulus behind the motion of the spheres and even the cause for the existentiation of the universe. For many of us, the universe moves
automatically by virtue of some self-styled mechanical
forces and laws. This would be the case if we were to consider the universe quite superficially and from a purely
physical and material aspect. But if we consider being as
emanating "from that side," it is saturated with Power
and all other perfect Divine Qualities, such as Life,
Knowledge, Beauty, Wisdom, Love, and so on. God, as
the great Artisan of the Universe, loves His artifact, and
this Love permeates every particle of the universe.

For Rumi, the world floats like a fleck of foam on the
ocean of Love. Particles of the universe seek each other
like lovers. The whirling spheres revolve through the
agency of Love. Without Love, the world would be as frigid
as ice. It is the power of Love that uplifts inorganic matter
into plants, and from vegetative life evolves them into animal and then into spiritual life, as the Holy Spirit
breathes life into them as It did into the Virgin Mary. So

131

every mote in the cosmos is in love with that eternal Perfection, and hastens upward to assimilate to it.

> Love is an infinite ocean,
> on which the heavens are but a fleck of foam,
> distraught like Zulaykha in desire for a Joseph.
> Know that the wheeling heavens are turned by waves of
>   Love;
> were it not for Love the world would be frozen.
> How would an inorganic thing change into a plant?
> How would vegetative things sacrifice themselves
> to be endowed with Spirit?
> How would the Spirit sacrifice itself for the sake of that
>   Breath,
> by the waft whereof a Mary was made pregnant?
> ...Every mote is in love with that perfection
> and hastening upward like a sapling.[383]

For Mawlana, everything in the universe operates through the power of Love. Look how the grain grows from the earth and is baked into bread so that it becomes ready to be assimilated into our body, which in its turn has access to the Spirit. This assimilation process can only be rendered possible through the alchemical power of Love.

> If there had not been Love,
> how should there have been existence?
> How should bread have attached itself to you and become
>   you?
> The bread became you: through what?
> Through your love and appetite.
> Otherwise how should the bread have had any access to
>   the Spirit?
> Love makes the dead bread into Spirit;
> it makes the Spirit that was perishable everlasting.[384]

Love craves to drink and is also the seeker of those who are eager to drink. The lover and the beloved chase each other like day and night. Day is the lover of night and the more so night is in love with day. They are perpetually seeking and pursuing each other, moving at one another's heels.

To the lover one moment of separation is as a year;
to him a year's uninterrupted union is a fleeting fancy.
Love craves to drink and seeks him who craves to drink;
the lover and the beloved are at each other's heels like day
    and night.
Day is in love with night and has lost control of itself;
when you look, the night is even more in love with it.
Never for one instant do they cease from seeking;
never for one moment do they cease from pursuing each
    other.
This one has caught the foot of that one,
and that one the ear of this one;
this one is distraught with that one,
and that one is beside itself from this one...
In the lover's heart is naught but the beloved;
there is nothing to separate and divide them.[385]

When the cup-bearer of the primordial covenant
poured a draught upon this abject earth,
the earth seethed and we are of that seething.
O God, pour another draught, for we are without effort.[386]

Who Is a Lover?

Love is a sort of insanity, and in fact there is no one mad-
der than a lover. But it is no common kind of madness.
Medicine cannot help us to cure the melancholy of love.
If a physician were seized with the frenzy of love, he
would wash the pages of his book of medicine.

None is more mad than the lover.
Reason is blind and deaf to this melancholia,
because this is no common madness:
in this case medicine can give no right guidance.
If frenzy of this kind overtake a physician
he will wash the book of medicine with tears of blood.[387]

A lover who is grabbed in the grip of love has no
choice; like a cat in a bag, he is lifted high or flung low
by love. Or he is like one who is taken by a rapid torrent.
He has to submit himself to the ordinance of love.

133

In the hand of Love I am like a cat in a bag,
now lifted high and now flung low by Love.
He is whirling me round His head;
I have no rest either below or aloft.
The lovers have fallen in a fierce torrent;
they have set their hearts on the ordinance of Love.
They are like the millstone turning day and night
in continual revolution, moaning incessantly.
Its turning is evidence for those who seek the River,
lest anyone should say that the River is motionless.
If you see not the hidden River,
see the perpetual turning
of the celestial water-wheel.[388]

In the last two lines, Rumi indicates that the regular motion of the celestial spheres denotes the existence of the Divine Beloved, who actuates the movement of the spheres as the object of their love and desire.

Rumi tells a story of a Sufi who saw a food-bag hanging on a nail without any food in it. He began to whirl and rend his garments. When his whirling turned into an ecstasy, everyone who was a Sufi joined him. An idle busybody objected that the food-bag hung on the nail was without food. So what was the purpose of this tumult? To which the Sufi retorted:

The lover's food is love of the bread, without the bread;
no one that is sincere is in thrall to existence.
Lovers have naught to do with existence:
lovers have the interest without having the capital.
They have no wings and yet they fly round the world;
they have no hands and yet they carry off the ball from
    the polo-field.
The dervish who scented Reality used to weave baskets,
though his hand had been cut off.
Lovers have pitched their tents in non-existence:
they are of one color and one essence, like non-exist-
    ence.[389]

For the lovers the only lecturer is the Beauty of the Be-
    loved;
their only lecture, book and assigned chapter is His face.

134

Though they are outwardly silent, the shrill noise of their
    repetition
goes up to the Divine Throne.
Their only lesson is enthusiasm,
the whirling dance and quaking agitation.
They are not concerned with obligatory and optional
    courses,
or with discussions on the chain of infinite regress
and the vicious circle.
Their only chain is the musk-dropping curls of the Be-
    loved,
and their question about the "circle"
revolves around the circle of the Friend.[390]

The Friends of God

As discussed above, the term "Friends of God" (*awliya' Allah*) is mentioned many times in the Holy Quran. The word *awliya'* is the plural of *wali*, which is derived from the root *w-l-y*, meaning nearness or proximity between two things such that there is no intermediary between them. Hence, the Friends of God, according to this interpretation, are intimate with Him, such that there is no intervening medium between them.

However, another meaning of the same root is "protection and guardianship," so this means that the Friends of God have submitted themselves to the Divine Care, such that in all their states they are under His protection and guardianship, as in the case of minors and orphans in Islamic jurisprudence, who are entrusted to the care and protection of a legal custodian.

The word *tawalla*, taken from the same root, means "to take as a friend or as a protector or guardian." It also means "to get near to," and with the preposition *'an* ("from") it means "to get away from or to flee from something." In some verses of the Quran, the word *wali* and its cognates are often rendered as "friend," though they could be as easily rendered in English as "protector," and vice versa, as can be seen in the following verses:

> It is written down that whosoever takes him [Satan] for a friend [or "protector"], him he leads astray and he guides him to the chastisement of hellfire. (22:4)

> Have you not regarded those who have taken for friends [or "protectors"] against whom God is Wrathful. (58:14)

> Your friend [or "protector"] is only God, His Messenger and believers who perform the prayer and pay the alms while they bow down in prayer. (5:55)

> O believers do not take as your friends [or "protectors"] those among the People of the Book who take your religion as a mockery and as sport. (5:58)

> Or have they taken to themselves protectors [or "friends"] apart from Him? But God, He is the protector. (42:9)

> And it is He who sends down the rain after they have despaired and He unfolds His mercy; He is the protector, worthy of all praise. (42:28)

> You see many of them making unbelievers their friends [or "protectors"]. (5:80).

However, there are other verses where the word can only be rendered as "friend" and nothing else:

> That is Satan frightening his friends; therefore do not fear them, but fear Me if you are believers. (3:175)

> The good deed and the evil deed are not equal. Repel the evil deed with that which is better and then you will see that (your enemy) between whom and you there is enmity shall be as if your intimate friend. (41:34)

What is important for our purposes is that the term *awliya' Allah* mentioned in the Quran can only be rendered as "the Friends of God."

Sometimes the word *wali* in this sense is rendered by some translators, such as Nicholson and Arberry, as "saint," which may be accurate, especially in a Christian context; a "Friend of God" is no doubt a "saint," being endowed with Divine sanctity. But in the Islamic context, a *wali* is also a manifestation of Divine Knowledge, Divine Wisdom, and, in short, all Divine Qualities. A *wali* sees by God, hears by God, says what he says by God, and, in short, is the one who has annihilated his egoistic self in the Divine Self. He is nevertheless by definition a "saint" because the ever-presence of the Divine Self makes a thing sacred.

It is again interesting to note that in the Quran, *al-Wali* is a Divine Name, and as such, like all other Names and Attributes, must be manifested in the universe, and especially in human beings. God, in other words, has created humankind and sent prophets and revealed the scriptures in order to take some Friends to whom he might reveal His secrets. So, according to both the common view of the believers and that of Sufis in particular, if there comes a time when there are no Friends of God (*awliya'*) among humanity, that is an indication of the imminent end of that cycle of humanity. A tradition, in this context, is attributed to the Prophet Muhammad that says: "The Resurrection will not arise while there is on earth one single human who says 'Allah, Allah' (meaning a Friend of God)."

Walayah (Divine Friendship, Divine Proximity, or sainthood, you might say) is the very core of every Divine religion, without which religion loses its authenticity. According to some gnostics (*'urafa'*), including Ibn 'Arabi, a luminary in speculative Sufism and an elder contemporary of Rumi, the founders of the great world religions, namely the messengers (*rasul*, pl. *rusul*) have three different functions. First, as messengers they bring a new Divine message or a new Divine law. Second, they also function as prophets (*nabi*, pl. *anbiya'*),[391] that is, they give us valid knowledge about the realities of the invisible or spiritual world. Third, they have direct communion with the Divinity such that they receive directly and without an intermediary all the truths and realities from God Himself. With respect to the latter function, that is, their direct communion with the Divinity, they are also called *awliya'*, or Friends of God.

A messenger, according to Ibn 'Arabi, integrates in himself the three mentioned functions together. In other words, a messenger is at the same time a prophet and a saint. A prophet, on the other hand, embodies in himself two functions—prophet and saint—without being a messenger. Finally, a *wali* realizes in him the function of sainthood or *walayah*, without having the other two mentioned functions. A messenger, therefore, representing the three functions together, is higher in spiritual rank than a prophet or a saint. And for the same reason, a *wali* is lower in this regard than the other two, because he realizes in himself only one function.

But here Ibn 'Arabi also adds that in the messenger, considered as realizing in himself these three functions, the aspect of *walayah* is higher than his other two aspects, because it is through *walayah* alone that he has communion with the Divinity, without which the other two aspects would be impossible. For the same reason, though a prophet integrates in himself two functions, the aspect of *walayah* is superior to prophecy (*nubuwwah*) as such.

In a sacred tradition known as the tradition of the supererogatory acts (*hadith qurb al-nawafil*) narrated from the Holy Prophet, God says:

> He who makes enmity with a friend of Mine, he has indeed declared war on Me. My servant does not draw near to Me by anything more beloved to Me than what is made obligatory for him. My servant ceaselessly draws nigh unto Me by supererogatory acts until I love him. When I love him, I become his hearing wherewith he hears. I become his sight wherewith he sees. I become his hand wherewith he makes an assault. I become his foot whereby he walks. If he asks of Me something, I shall give it to him. If he takes refuge in Me, I will give him shelter. I never doubt anything I do save my vacillation about taking the soul of my believing servant who detests death. I abhor to do to him what he dislikes.

Referring to this famous hadith, which succinctly delineates for us the path of *walayah*, Rumi says:

> Hark! The saints are the Israfils of the time;
> from them the dead receive life (*hayat*) and modesty
>   (*haya'*).
> The dead souls in the grave of the body
> upon hearing their voice leap up in their shrouds.
> Awakening, they say, "This voice is different from all other
>   sounds,
> to give life is the work of the voice of God."
> O ye who are rotten with death under your skins,
> return from non-existence at the voice of the Friend.
> Absolutely, that voice is from the King,
> though it be from the larynx of God's servant.
> God has said to the saint, "I am thy tongue and thy eye;
> I am thy senses and I am thy good pleasure and thy
>   wrath."
> Go, for thou art 'By me he hears and by me he sees.'

140

Thou art the Divine consciousness itself:
how is it right to say, 'Thou art the possessor of Divine
   con-sciousness?'
Since thou hast become, through bewilderment,
'He that belongs to God,'
I am thine,
for 'God belongs to him.'"392

In the above verses there is allusion to the sacred tradition (*hadith qudsi*) "He who is for God, God is for him" (*man kana li-llahi kana Allahu lahu*), which Rumi interprets to mean that God sometimes speaks through him as "I" and sometimes as "thou," because the servant of God at this stage has annihilated his self in the Divine Self.

In another sacred tradition, God says: "My heavens and my earth cannot encompass Me, but the heart of My believing servant does encompass Me." On the basis of this tradition, Rumi argues that we should not seek God above or below or in any of the other directions of the spatio-temporal continuum. If He is ever to be sought and found anywhere, it is in the hearts of His Friends and saints.

The Prophet said that God has said:
"I am not contained in the jar of 'high' or 'low.'
Nor am I contained in the earth or the heaven of the
   Throne.
Know this for certain, O dear one.
But I am contained in the true believer's heart; how won-
   derful!
If you seek Me, seek Me in those hearts."393

The Friends of God are the shadows of God on earth. A Quranic verse asks: "Have you seen how your Lord has extended His shadow on earth? And if he had wanted He would have made it stand still" (25:45). Some commentators have taken this verse to be a reference to the manifestation of absolute being as the universal act of God. Rumi takes it to be a reference to the saints and the Friends of God. One should take hold of the skirt of a saint and benefit from his spiritual direction so as to be

141

saved from the tumult and confusion of the latter days of the present cycle of humanity. One should not go without a spiritual guide in this horrendous valley.

> The shadow of God is that servant of God
> who is dead to this world and living through God.
> Lay hold of his skirt most quickly without misgiving
> that you may be saved in the skirt of the last days.
> *How God extended the shadow* is the image of the saints,
> which guides to the light of the Divine Sun.
> Do not go in this valley without this guide.
> Say like Abraham, *I love not them that set*[394] (Quran 6:76).

We said earlier that in every age and epoch there must be Friends of God among whom only one possesses this spiritual rank of *walayah* in an absolute sense and whom Rumi calls "the standing and the living spiritual leader (*imam*)." He is both guided by God (*mahdi*) and the Guide (*hadi*). He has this function whether he is hidden from view or apparent. He is like the spiritual sun illuminating the world. The Divine Intellect guides him like the archangel Gabriel. But below him there is a hierarchy of saints. Just as physical light has many grades, from the resplendent source of light, the sun, to the reflected light of the moon, and the other stars, so too the light of Divine Friendship has many degrees and ranks, from the absolute light of the Imam to the lower ranks. The Light of God has 700 veils and many tiers. The lesser lights are like the lamps kindled by the Divine Light.

> Therefore in every epoch a saint arises;
> the probation lasts until the Resurrection.
> Whosoever has a good disposition is saved;
> whosoever is glass-hearted is broken.
> So the standing and living Imam is that saint (*wali*),
> whether he be the descendent of 'Umar or of 'Ali,
> he is the *Mahdi* (the Divinely guided) and the *Hadi* (the
>   Guide),
> O seeker of the Way.
> He is both hidden from you and seated before your face.
> He is the Light, and universal Reason is his Gabriel;
> the saint that is lesser than he is his lamp.

That saint who is lesser than this lamp is our lamp-niche;
Light has many gradations in degree.
Because the Light of God has seven hundred veils,
regard the veils of Light as so many tiers.
Behind each veil a class of saints has its abode.
These veils of theirs are rank upon rank,
up to the Imam.[395]

Those who are said to be alchemists try to change base metals into gold. But the true alchemists are the Friends of God, who by their spiritual illumination turn the darkness of the carnal passions into the gold of Divine Light. They lift the human soul from the abyss of selfish desire to the proximity of the Divine Union. They fathom the ocean of Divine Wisdom and bring forth precious pearls. By their spiritual alchemy they change every loss into gain.

It does not harm a man of the heart
if he drinks deadly poison for all to see...
He fetches pearls from the bottom of the sea,
from losses he brings gain to the surface.
If a perfect man take earth, it becomes gold;
if an imperfect one carries away gold, it becomes ashes.
Since that righteous man is the accepted of God,
his hand in all things is the hand of God.[396]

Friends of God, having attained proximity to God, Who is eternal bliss and joy, are full of delight and exultation. They are rid of all anguish and despair. One should plant their love in the midst of one's soul and should not submit one's heart to anyone except them. One should not allow the body to attract the heart towards earthly pleasures. One should seek the nourishment of the heart from the blessed Friends of God.

The sword of reality is in the armory of the saints;
to see them is for you the true alchemy.
All the wise have said the selfsame thing:
the wise man is *a Divine Mercy to all the worlds* (Quran
    21:107).
...The laughing pomegranate makes the garden laughing;
companionship with great men makes you great.

143

Though you be adamantine rock or marble,
you will become a jewel when you reach a man of heart.
Plant the love of the holy ones within your spirit.
Do not give your heart save to the love of the glad-
    hearted.
Go not to the neighborhood of despair.
There is hope.
Go not towards the darkness.
There are suns.
The heart will draw you to the neighborhood of the folk of
    the heart.
The body leads you into the prison of water and clay.
Here, give your heart food from a fellow-hearted one.
Go and seek blessedness from one who is blessed.[397]

Mawlana teaches that if someone wishes to sit with God, he should associate with His Friends. To break off from the presence of saints is to be lost in darkness. If Satan cuts someone off from the presence of the noble saints, he will find no one to help and protect him. This may be understood as a reference to the following verse in the Quran: "Whomsoever God guides, he is rightly guided and whomsoever He leads astray you will never find for him a *wali* [a Friend of God] to guide him" (18:17).

Whoever wishes to sit with God,
let him sit in the presence of the saints.
If you are broken off from the presence of the saints,
you are in perdition, because you are a part without the
    whole.
Whomsoever Satan cuts off from the noble saints,
he finds him without anyone to help him and he devours
    his head.
To go for one moment, a single span apart from that com-
    munity
is a result of Satan's guile.
Hearken and know it well.[398]

It is mentioned in the Quran that the messengers of God never deliver the Divine Message in exchange for worldly gain, reward, or remuneration. They do whatever they do not only for the sake of duty, but for the satisfaction and pleasure of God. Such is the case, according to

144

Rumi, with the Friends of God who have assumed the
nature of God, Who is absolutely Munificent and does
nothing in expectation of gain. This is not the case with
ordinary people, who do everything in the hope of some
compensation. Even their greeting each other is not without some expectation of gain, whether they know it or
not. The greeting (*salam*) of a saint is as if a greeting from
God Himself.

He who gives without expectation of any gains,
He is God, He is God, He is God,
or the friend of God who has assumed the nature of God
and has become luminous and has received the Absolute
   Radiance.
For He is rich, while all except him are poor.
How should a poor man say, "Take!" without compensation?
Till a child sees that an apple is there,
it will not hand over a rotten onion.
All these market-folk, for this reason
are seated on their benches: to sniff out compensation.
They proffer a hundred fine articles of merchandise
and within their hearts they are intent on compensation.
O man of religion, you will not hear a single *salam* (greet-
   ing)
which will not pluck your sleeve in the end...
except the *salam* of God, come and seek that *salam*,
from house to house, from place to place, and from the
   street to street.
From the mouth of the man who has a good scent for
   spiritual things
I heard both the message and the *salam* of God.
The saint's *salam* has become the *salam* of God
because he has set fire to the household of self.
He has died to self and become living through the Lord.
Hence, the mysteries of God are on his lips.[399]

Respect and Reverence for the Friends of God

The Friends of God have a heart that is intimate with the
Divine Mysteries. They want angelic hearers who are willing to listen to them. Being God-like, they have a kingly
glory and magnificence, and therefore they demand a

145

spiritual obeisance from human beings. One cannot gain any advantage from their Divine Message unless one pays the respect and reverence due to them. They have a Divine Trust deposited with them that they will not deliver to us unless we are humble and submissive to them.

> These mystery-telling Messengers of the hidden Mind
> require a hearer who has the nature of Israfil.
> They have a haughtiness and pride like that of kings;
> they require service from the people of the world.
> Until you perform the observances due to them,
> how will you gain profit from their message?
> How will they deliver that trust to you
> till you are bowed double before them?
> How is every kind of observance acceptable to them?
> Because they have come from the Sublime Palace.
> They are not beggars that they should be grateful to you,
> O impostor, for every service.[400]

In the presence of the people of the heart one should be duly reverential and courteous. The courtesy due to the people who cherish bodily pleasures is outward, because God has deprived them of things inward and hidden. But the courtesy and respect due to the Friends of God is inward, because their hearts are insightful of the most hidden thoughts. But we, on the contrary, pay respect to spiritually blind worldlings purely for worldly gain, and behave disrespectfully to the saints.

> Keep watch over your hearts, O fruitless ones,
> in the presence of the majesty of the men of heart.
> Before the man of body, respect is shown outwardly,
> for God has veiled the hidden mysteries from them.
> Before the men of heart, respect is shown inwardly,
> because their hearts have insight into the inmost secrets.
> Thou art contrariwise: for the sake of worldly position
> thou comest with reverence
> before the blind and sit in the vestibule,
> but before the Seers thou behavest disrespectfully.
> Hence, thou hast become fuel for the fire of lust.[401]

146

The Friends of God, the Knowers of Divine Mysteries

The Friends of God are also known by other names. Sometimes, as we saw, a Friend of God is called a saint. Most often he is called "one who knows by God" (*'arif bi'Llah*). At other times Friends of God are called "the poor with respect to God" (*al-faqir ila'Llah*). In English they are called "mystics," no doubt with reference to the fact that they are possessors of the Divine Mysteries. They are also known as Sufis, since, following the practice of the Prophet, they are usually dressed in woolen garments. But the plurality of names should not distract us from their being the total manifestation of the Divine Names and Attributes, which qualifies them to act as the vicegerents of God.

> Since in eternity it was the will and decree of God,
> the Forgiver, to reveal and manifest Himself
> —for nothing can be shown without an opposite;
> and that peerless King had no opposite—
> therefore, He made a vicegerent, one having a heart,
> that he might be a mirror for His sovereignty.[402]

Because they know everything by God, the Friends of God are aware of the Divine Mysteries unknown to others even while being embodied in human flesh.

> The guardians of the Sun of Reality are the saints;
> in human flesh they are aware of the Divine Mysteries.[403]

There are certain Friends of God who are known as "the spies of hearts" (*jawasis al-qulub*). They can, if they so desire, know what occurs in the hearts of others. The mysteries of all things are unveiled to them. Rumi explains and justifies this fact by pointing out that for those who are familiar with the secrets of the Divine Ipseity, it is not difficult to know the secrets of created beings. For him who can walk in the spheres, it is not difficult to walk on earth.

The chosen servants of God, the Knower of things unseen,
are in the spiritual world the spies of hearts.
They enter within the heart like a fancy;
the mystery of the real state is unveiled to them.
In the body of the sparrow what power and faculty is
      there
that is hidden from the intellect of the falcon?
He who has become aware of the secrets of *Hu* (He, God),
what to him is the secret of created things?
He who walks upon the spheres,
how is it difficult for him to walk upon the earth?[404]

In the sublunary world the members of the three kingdoms, that is, animals, plants, and minerals, do not
know of one another's inner states. Neither do most human beings, who are not aware of the pains and sufferings of each other. They are so much engaged with the
demands of the body and with sensual pleasures that
these suffocate the light of the spirit within them. It is
quite different with the Friends of God, who being disen-
gaged from bodily passions have become identified with
their spirit. They can permeate deeply into the spiritual
states and conditions of others, even those that are concealed from them.

Whatever kingdoms there are under the spheres,
whether mineral, animal or plant,
they are heedless, every one, of another's pain
except those persons that are discerning and perfect...
What the man of heart knows of your condition,
you do not know of your own condition.
O uncle!
Heedlessness was from the body;
when the body has become spirit,
it inevitably beholds the Mysteries.[405]

In the Holy Quran it is said that whatever exists, has
happened, or is going to happen is recorded in the
Guarded Tablet (*al-lawh al-mahfuz*). Now, the Friends of
God are able to behold this Tablet and read the Divine
Decree concerning everything as it is inscribed therein.

148

Ordinary people might think that this is a sort of astrology, geomancy, or wonder-working. However, the hearts of the Friends of God are the vehicles of Divine Inspiration and hence are immune from falling into error. "Beware of the spiritual insight of the believer, because he witnesses everything by the Light of God," said the Prophet. So, the Friends of God are secure from any kind of error and heedlessness.

> [Bayazid's][406] guide is the Guarded Tablet.
> From what is it guarded? It is guarded from error.
> It is not like astrology or geomancy, or dreams;
> it is the inspiration (*wahy*) of God and God knows best
>   what is right.
> The Sufis call it the inspiration of the heart
> in order to disguise it from the vulgar.
> Take it to be the inspiration of the heart,
> for it is where He is seen.
> How should there be error when the heart is aware of
>   Him?
> O true believer, thou hast become seeing by the light of
>   God.
> Thou hast become secure from error and inadvertence.[407]

The Friends of God, the gnostics or the "knowers by God," even though they know all the Divine Mysteries, which have been taught to them by God, are not permitted to divulge them. Their hearts are full of mysteries, but their lips are as if locked and sealed.

> That evil-doer went to a gnostic and said,
> "Remember me in a prayer."
> That liberated one knew his secret,
> but, like the forbearance of God, did not divulge it.
> On his lips is a lock, while his heart is full of mysteries;
> his lips are silent, though his heart is filled with songs.
> Gnostics, who have drunk the cup of God,
> have known the mysteries and kept them hidden.
> Whosoever has been taught the mysteries of the Real,
> his mouth is locked and his lips are sealed.[408]

Friends of God are not only the possessors of the Divine Mysteries. Being linked to the infinite Knowledge of

149

God, they also possess power from God, doing everything no doubt by Divine Concurrence, which means that they do not wield this power arbitrarily.

> The saints possess power from God:
> they turn back from its course the arrow that has been
>   shot.
> When he regrets he shuts the doors of effects from their
>   cause,
> but by the hand of God.
> By opening the door of Divine Grace,
> he makes unsaid what is said,
> so that neither skewer nor kabob
> is burnt thereby.[409]

The Friends of God, Like Water, Purify What Is Impure

Religion, having an absolutely Divine Source, is like rain water coming from heaven. It is very clear and pure, uncontaminated by any dirt or defilement. It washes away and clears any pollution, but by so doing it becomes dirty and sometimes ritually impure, such that the senses reject it and one detests drinking it. But God does not leave it in that state. He brings the water back to His sea of goodness and washes away all its impurities. He takes it back to heaven, purifies it of its filth, and sends it back again to earth to make clean and pure what is dirty and squalid. Saints and Friends of God are like that rain, sent from the spiritual Heaven to cleanse all the impurities of our souls. This parable may imply that any Divine Religion as revealed by God and preached by its messengers, prophets, great saints, or Friends of God is pure in origin, but when it passes through the bodies and souls of people, it gets sullied and soiled, as water that flows in dirty river-beds, whereas in the breasts and hearts of saints it rests ever pure and uncontaminated.

> The water rained from heaven
> that it might cleanse the impure of their defilement.
> When the water had done battle and had been made dirty,
> and had become such that the senses rejected it,
> God brought it back into the sea of Goodness

that the Origin of the water might generously wash it
   clean.
Next year it came sweeping proudly along,
"Hey, where have you been?"
"In the sea of the blessed.
I went from here impure;
I have come back pure.
I have received a robe of honor,
and have come back to the earth again.
Make haste! Come unto me, O polluted ones,
for my nature has partaken of the nature of God.
I will eagerly accept all your foulness;
like an angel I will bestow purity on the imp.
When I become defiled, I will return there;
I will go to the source of the source of purities.
There I will pull the filthy cloak off my head,
and He will give me a clean robe once more."
...Verily, what is meant by this water is the spirit of the
   saints,
which washes away all your dark stains.[410]

Medical Physicians and Spiritual Physicians

Ancients, unlike moderns, were as much concerned with
the treatment of the soul as they were with the care of
the body. As discussed above, the human being was considered to have two kinds of birth, physical and spiritual.
Just as medicine was the science dealing with the dis-
eases and the disorders of the body, so there was another
discipline that not only treated the disorders and maladies of the soul, but was more concerned with its whole-
ness and health. In one sense, one could say that most
ancient philosophy, as well as all religions, was deeply
engaged in this "spiritual medicine." Some of the great
physicians, such as al-Razi, were not only well-known
authors in medical science, but also wrote books and
treatises on "spiritual medicine." The one was concerned
with the body, the offspring of the first birth, and the second with the spirit, the outcome of the second. The whole
message of Rumi could in a sense be envisaged as a very
authentic spiritual medicine.

151

Just as one should have regard and reverence for the physicians of the body, even more so should one revere the physicians of the soul. The physicians of the body might be able to prevent physical blindness, but they cannot of necessity hold back the blindness of the soul. One should serve those healers of the spirit with one's whole heart.

> When you have regard for the hearts of the physicians,
> you will see yourselves and will become ashamed of yourselves.
> It is not in the power of created beings to remove this blindness,
> but the honoring of the physicians is from Divine guidance.
> Become devoted to these physicians with all your soul
> that you may be filled with musk and ambergris.[411]

The Spiritual Master

Treading the spiritual path (*tariqah*) without a spiritual master (called *shaykh* in Arabic and *pir* in Persian) is almost an impossibility. In a normal journey one starts from where one is and moves forward towards the destination. So the itinerant must have the destination clearly in his view; otherwise the journey would be more of a vagrancy. He must also know the stations of the way so as not to be lost irretrievably in the wilderness. Having some companions on the journey will relieve him from utter solitude and from the other dangers confronting him. But most important of all, this very hazardous journey is impossible without a guide who will lead him through very dangerous mountain passes, deep abysses, horrendous valleys, tortuous byways, and unknown bifurcations and crossroads.

But traveling a spiritual path no doubt is much more difficult. The starting-point of the spiritual wayfaring is one's own self. It takes place within one's self. The destination is the Divine Self. One should know well before the departure the destination and the stations of the way and the self-transformation that will take place at every

152

juncture. The spiritual way is very difficult to traverse without spiritual companions. But most important of all, it is not possible to tread the path without a spiritual master. It is a maxim, commonly repeated among the spiritual wayfarers and sometimes attributed to the Holy Prophet, that "He who has no spiritual master, his spiritual master is Satan" (*man la shaykha lahu fa shaykhuhu al-shaytan*).

According to Rumi, the spiritual path is the path of illumination, and the spiritual master is an enlightened person whose spiritual eyes have been unveiled such that he sees everything through the Divine Light. He is well aware of the way and can induce the same spiritual awareness in the disciple. The words of a spiritual master are luminous, and therefore one should endeavor to listen to and to understand his words so that his light permeates and accompanies one all the time. Knowledge is like rainwater descending from heaven. One should resemble the sky and the cloud and shed rain over all. The water-spout, no doubt, carries the rain from the roof, but the water of the spout is borrowed, whereas the water in the cloud and the sea is original. For Rumi, inspiration and revelation, being original, are symbolized by the clouds that bring rain and produce multicolored gardens, whereas thoughts and cogitations cut off from Divine revelations are like water running down the spouts, which even causes quarrels and skirmishes among neighbors.

> The illumined Shaykh makes the disciples cognizant of
>   the Way;
> moreover he causes the light of faith to accompany his
>   words.
> Strive to become intoxicated and illumined,
> in order that his light may be inseparable from you.
> When your knowledge is steeped in light,
> then *the contumacious folk* derive light from your
>   knowledge (Quran 19:97).
> Whatever you say, too, will be luminous,
> for the sky never rains aught but pure water.
> Become like the sky and become like the cloud and shed
>   rain.
> The spout rains too, but it is of no use:

the water in the spout is borrowed;
the water in the cloud and in the sea is primordial.
Your thought and cogitation resemble the spout;
inspiration and revelation are like the cloud and the sky.
The rain-water produces a many-colored garden;
the spout causes neighbors to quarrel.[412]

When one submits oneself to the injunctions of a spiritual master, one should not be peevish and faint-hearted. If one gets fretful and enraged by his injunctions or his reprimands, how can one benefit from his spiritual light? How can a mirror be polished without receiving blows from the polisher?

When thou hast chosen thy Pir, be not faint-hearted,
be not weak as water and crumbly as earth.
If thou art enraged by every blow
then how wilt thou become a clear mirror without being
polished?[413]

Here, Mawlana tells the story of a man from Qazwin who went to a barber to tattoo a lion on his shoulder-blade,[414] but as soon as the barber started to stick in the needle to tattoo the tail, the man felt extreme pain. He asked what limb the barber had begun with, and was answered: "with the tail." So the man said that a lion did not need a tail. But as soon as the barber started to tattoo another limb, the man yelled: "Which of his members is this?" and the answer came: "This is his ear, my good man." "Let him have no ears," the man said. "Please go on with another part." The barber started to prick his needle on a third spot. The man, feeling extreme pain, asked: "What is the member you are pricking in?" "This is the lion's belly," the barber rejoined. "Let the lion have no belly!" the man said. Whereupon the barber angrily flung the needle to the ground, and said:

Has this happened to anyone in the world?
Whoever saw a lion without tail, and head and belly?
God himself did not create a lion like this![415]

Then Rumi advises the disciple to endure the pain of spiritual training in order to escape from the poison of the miscreant self. It is not permissible to test and to make trial of the shaykh after the disciple has chosen him as a spiritual master, because one's ignorance and audacity will come to light. This would be like a mote trying to weigh a mountain: the scales of the balance would no doubt be shattered by the mountain. Such is the case if the disciple tries to weigh the shaykh with the judgments of his intellect.

> If a novice has made trial of a Shaykh,
> who is the spiritual leader and guide, he is an ass.
> If you make trial of him in the way of religion,
> *you* will be tried, O man without certainty.
> Your audacity and ignorance will become naked and exposed to view:
> how should he be made naked by that scrutiny?
> If the mote come and weigh the mountain,
> its scales will be shattered by the mountain, O youth.
> For he applies the scales of his own judgment
> and puts the man of God in the scales.
> But since the Shaykh cannot be contained by the scales of intellect,
> consequently he shatters the scales of intellect.[416]

As mentioned above, the spiritual master is called *pir* in Persian, a word that at the same time means "aged" or "with beard hoary with age." However, the spiritual master according to Rumi is not called *pir* because of his old age. On the contrary, he is young in fortune. He is made old by the Truth, not by time.

> The Pir is like summer and others are like autumn.
> Other people are like night and the Pir is the moon.
> I have bestowed on young Fortune the name Pir (old),
> because he is made old by Truth, not by Time.
> He is so old (*pir*) that he has no beginning.
> There is no rival for this unique pearl.[417]

The journey is hazardous and full of unspeakable perils, so one should choose a *pir* to show one the way and to make one secure from terrible dangers. One may have traveled on a road many times and yet on occasion be bewildered and dumb-founded; so one should not travel alone on a road that one has not seen even once. One should study the Quran to understand that a great many peoples in the past have gone the way of perdition because they disobeyed the prophets, who were the true guides of the way. One should, moreover, be on guard against the carnal passions of the concupiscent or the evil-bidding soul, symbolized in the following lines as an ass. The ass is ever desirous of grazing in a luxuriant pasture, so whenever it sees a meadow, it turns towards it. For this reason the ass is the enemy of the way, and one should beware lest its love for fodder and herbage should cause one to stray from the path.

> Choose a Pir, for without a Pir
> this Journey is exceedingly full of woe and affright and
>   danger.
> Without an escort you are bewildered,
> even on a road you have traveled many times before.
> Do not, then, travel alone on a Way you have not seen at
>   all.
> Do not turn your head away from the Guide.
> Learn from the Quran the perdition of the wayfarers,
> and what the evil-souled Iblis did unto them...
> He carried them for a journey of hundreds of thousands of
>   years
> From the highway and made them backsliders and devoid
>   of good works.
> Behold their bones and their hair.
> Take warning.
> And drive not your ass towards them.
> Seize the neck of your ass and lead him towards the Way,
> towards the good keepers and knowers of the Way.
> Beware! Do not let your ass go
> and do not remove your hand from him,
> because his love is for the place where green herbs are
>   plentiful.
> If you carelessly leave him free for one moment,
> he will go many leagues in the direction of herbage.

The ass is an enemy to the Way, he is madly in love with
    fodder.
Oh, many are the attendants on him that he has brought
    to ruin![418]

When one walks on the path with the shaykh it is as
if one is journeying in a safe and secure ship. Even if one
is sleeping in the ship, one is nonetheless going on the
way. This might be a reference to the saying of the Holy
Prophet that he is an ark in the flood of time and that his
Household and his Companions are like the ark of Noah;
whoever clings to them shall be saved, and whoever
abandons them is doomed to loss and perdition. A true
shaykh is also the spiritual heir and successor of the
Prophet. One should not break with him and rely on one's
own resources like self-conceited fellows. One should fly
with one's wings in the heaven of spirituality. One should
not consider the wrath and anger of the spiritual master
to be contrary to his mercy. As in the Divine Being, his
mercy precedes his wrath, or in other words, his wrath is
an offshoot of his mercy.

On this account the Prophet said,
"I am as the Ark in the Flood of Time.
I and my Companions are as the Ark of Noah:
whoso clings to us will gain spiritual openings."
When you are with the Shaykh, you are far removed from
    wickedness,
day and night you are a traveler and in a ship.
You are under the protection of a life-giving spirit,
you are asleep in the ship, yet you are going on the way.
Do not break with the prophet of your days;
do not rely on your own skill and desire.
Lion though you are, you are self-conceited, in error
and contemptible when you go on the way without a guide.
Beware! Do not fly except with the wings of the Shaykh,
that you may receive the aid of the armies of the Shaykh.
At one time the wave of his mercy is your wings,
at another moment, the fire of his wrath is your carrier.
Do not reckon his wrath to be contrary to his mercy.
Behold the oneness of both in the effect.[419]

The shaykh, who sees everything by and through the Divine Light, sees the beginning of everything that is prior to his existence, in the Divine Knowledge, and also the end of things after they have come into being. In other words, he has a view of the ultimate becoming of things (*akhir-bin*); he has shut for God's sake that eye that like animals sees the stable alone (*akhur-bin*).

> The Shaykh who has become seeing by the light of God,
> has become aware of the End and the Beginning.
> He has shut for God's sake the eye that sees the stable
>   (*chishm-i akhur-bin*);
> in the race of excellence, he has opened the eye that sees
>   the End
> (*chishm-i akhir-bin*).[420]

The spiritual master sees distinctly what will become of each person after many years. What ordinary people see in the mirror, the shaykh can ever behold in an unbaked mud-brick.

> The Pir is seeing distinctly, hair by hair,
> what will become of him after a hundred years?
> What does the common man see in the mirror
> that the Pir does not see in the crude mud-brick?[421]

The *pir* is the spiritual guide and director in the community. He opens the gate of the garden of Paradise. It is related that the Prophet said that a shaykh who is advanced in spiritual realization is like a prophet among his community.

> There was a Shaykh...like a prophet amongst religious
>   communities,
> an opener of the door of the garden of paradise.
> The Prophet said that a Shaykh who has advanced (to per-
>   fection)
> is like a prophet amidst his people.[422]

One should not give one's hand in allegiance except to the hand of the spiritual master. The novice's intellect, as a result of its association with the carnal soul, has become childish in disposition. Thus one must associate it with the perfect intelligence of the spiritual master so that the understanding may withdraw itself from that evil disposition.

> Do not surrender thy hand save to the hand of the Pir,
> for God hath become the aider of his hand.
> The Pir of your intellect has become childish
> from being a neighbor to the carnal soul, which is veiled.
> Associate the perfect intelligence of the Pir
> with your imperfect understanding
> in order that your understanding may return from that evil
> disposition. [423]

Placing one's hands in the hands of the spiritual master is a sign and symbol of swearing allegiance to him. It is a repetition of the oath of allegiance sworn by the Companions to the Prophet as each one laid his hands in the hands of the Prophet. As the Quran states: "Those who swear allegiance to thee, swear allegiance in truth to God; God's hand is over their hands" (48:10).

Again, ten choice Companions of the Prophet swore the oath of allegiance to him under a tree in a place called Hudaybiyyah: "God was well pleased with the believers when they were swearing allegiance to you under the tree, and He knew what was in their hearts, so He sent down the Divine Tranquility (*sakinah*) upon them and rewarded them with a nigh victory" (Quran 48:18). So according to the Quran, for someone to lay hands in the hands of the Prophet is to swear allegiance not only to the Prophet but in reality to God, and while doing so the hands of God are above his hands.

> When thou layest thy hand in his,
> then thou wilt escape from the hand of devourers,
> and thy hand will become one of the people of the Covenant
> *above whose hands is the hand of God* (Quran 48:10).
> When you have put your hand in the hand of the Pir,
> the Pir of wisdom who is knowing and eminent,
> who is the prophet of his own time, O disciple!
> so that the light of the Prophet is manifested by him:
> in this way you have been present at Hudaybiyyah

159

and have become associated with the Companions who
took the Covenant.
Therefore, you have become one of "the ten Companions
given glad tidings"
and have been made pure like sterling gold.[424]

A person often stumbles on the way, and might become completely blind and not be able to step forward in
the spiritual path, so he needs the help of an accomplished adept to take him safely to the destination. One
should expose oneself to the adept's Divine blessings, so
that through spiritual novitiate and apprenticeship, even
if one is a needle, one will become the sword of 'Ali (dhu'l-
fiqar).

> Unless thou desire this incessant stumbling on the way
> sharpen thy eye with the dust of the foot of a saint.
> Make the dust of his foot collyrium for thine eye
> that thou mayst strike off the head of the scoundrels.
> For through this pupilage and this poverty of spirit
> though you be a needle, you will become trenchant like
>   dhu'l-fiqar.
> Use the dust of the elect as collyrium;
> it will both burn the eye and do it good.
> The eye of the camel is so luminous
> because he eats thorns to increase the light of his eye.[425]

For Rumi, the story of Moses with the Green Prophet
Khidr is an illustrious instance of the relationship between a disciple and the spiritual master.[426] In his journey to the "meeting place of the two seas" (majma' al-
bahrayn), Moses met the Green Prophet. As the Quran
says: "Then they found one of Our servants unto whom
We had given mercy from Us, and We had taught him
knowledge from Us." Moses asked the Green Prophet if
he could follow him so that Khidr might teach him of the
mysteries he had been taught by God, whereupon the
Green Prophet answered: "Assuredly, you will not be able
to bear with me patiently. And how should you bear patiently what you have never encompassed in your
knowledge?" Moses promised: "Yet you shall find me, if

160

God will, patient, and I shall not rebel against you in anything." The Prophet Khidr stipulated: "Then if you follow me, question me not on anything until I myself introduce the mention of it to you."

So they departed until they embarked upon a ship and the Green Prophet started to make a hole in it. Moses objected that this would drown its passengers and that he had done a grievous thing. Khidr reminded him of his promise: "Did I not say that you could never bear with me patiently?" Moses apologized and begged him not to take him to task if he had forgotten the promise, but neither to constrain him to do something so difficult for him.

They departed until they met a youth, and the Green Prophet, without speaking a word, slew him. Moses immediately objected that he had slain an innocent soul, and it was surely not in retaliation for another slain soul. It would be a horrible sin in the Divine Law to murder an innocent soul. Khidr again reminded Moses of his impatience its passengers and that he had done a grievous thing. Khidr reminded him of his promise: "Did I not say that you could never bear with me patiently and of his violation of the promise he had made. Moses apologized again and promised that should he question him a third time, that would be the end of their companionship.

So they departed until they reached a city where they asked the inhabitants for some food, but they were refused and were not received hospitably. There they found a wall about to tumble down, so Khidr built it back up. Moses again objected, and said that if he had wished, he could have received a wage for his work. "This is a parting between me and you," said Khidr, and informed him of the interpretations of those things that Moses could not bear patiently.[427]

Now, for Rumi as for other Sufi masters, this story is the exemplary instance of the relationship between a master and a disciple. Moses, despite being a great messenger and prophet, lacked the purely esoteric knowledge concerning what is considered to be the most abstruse and most mysterious of matters, called by some "the mystery of the primordial Divine Decree" (sirr-i qadar). The Green Prophet did not begrudge him, but stipulated

161

that he should unconditionally accept what he was going
to do.

> As for the boy whose throat was cut by Khidr,
> the vulgar do not understand the mystery thereof.
> He that receives from God inspiration (*wahy*) and answer,
> whatsoever he may command is precisely what is right.
> If one who bestows life should slay, it is allowable;
> he is the vicegerent and his hand is the hand of God.
> Like Ishmael, lay your head before him;
> gladly and laughingly give up your soul before his dagger
> so that your soul may remain laughing unto eternity,
> like the pure soul of Ahmad with the One (*Ahad*).
> Lovers drain the cup of joy at the moment
> when the fair ones slay them with their own hand.[428]

The saint *par excellence* and the supreme spiritual
master in all Sufi orders is 'Ali, the cousin and son-in-
law of the Prophet, whom Mawlana has superbly eulo-
gized on several occasions in the *Mathnawi*. The spiritual
master of 'Ali, no doubt, is the Prophet himself, but the
following exhortation of the Prophet to 'Ali nevertheless
emphasizes the necessity of following a spiritual master.

> The Prophet said to 'Ali, "O 'Ali,
> thou art the lion of God, thou art a courageous knight,
> but do not even rely on thy lion-heartedness:
> come into the shade of the palm tree of hope.
> Come into the shade of the sage
> whom no conveyer can carry off from the Way.
> His shadow on earth is like mount Qaf.
> his spirit is like the Simurgh that soars exceedingly high.
> If I should tell of his qualities until the Resurrection
> do not expect any conclusion and end to them.
> The Divine Sun has veiled Himself in the human being;
> understand it, and God knows best what is right.[429]

Then Mawlana explains that there are different ways
for achieving Divine Proximity. One way, for example, is
the way of ritual acts. But even though this is a sure way
for deliverance, the best way is to take refuge in the
shadow of a sage, who is the one who helps us escape

from the most secret enemy within us. This is the best
act of devotion and the straightest path to salvation.

> O 'Ali, above all devotional acts in the Way
> choose the shadow of the servant of God.
> Everyone took refuge in some act of devotion
> and discovered for themselves some means of deliverance.
> Go thou, take refuge in the shadow of the Sage,
> that thou mayst escape from the Enemy who secretly op-
>   poses thee.
> Of all acts of devotion this is the best for thee:
> thereby thou wilt gain precedence over all those who have
>   precedence.
> When the Pir has accepted thee, take heed, surrender
>   thyself.
> Go, like Moses, under the authority of Khidr.
> Bear patiently, without hypocrisy, whatever is done by a
>   Khidr,
> so that Khidr would not say: "Be gone, this is our part-
>   ing."
> Though he stave in the boat, do not speak a word.
> Though he kill a child, do not tear thy hair.[430]

Finally, Mawlana recommends that we seek a *pir* and
make him our leader and guide in the spiritual way. By
pir, he again reiterates that he does not mean a person
who is aged, but one who is in right guidance. Those who
live in darkness are illuminated by the *pir*, provided that
they subject themselves to his authority. Some people
might suppose that subjecting oneself to the spiritual
master means to undergo unbearable and lengthy trouble. This is an erroneous opinion. It only means to surrender oneself unconditionally to the spiritual master.
Henceforth, one will not seek the way of the empyrean;
one will only seek the *pir*. Mawlana's thrice-repeated
phrase "I will seek the Pir" is a way of emphasizing that
his presence is a *sine qua non* of the Way.

> May none but the Pir be thy master and general,
> not that Pir, Father Time, but the Pir of right guidance.
> The devotee of darkness sees the light immediately
> as soon as he becomes subject to the authority of the Pir.
> What is required is self-surrender not long toil;

it is useless to rush about in error.
Henceforth, I will not seek the way to the Aether,[431]
I will seek the Pir, I will seek the Pir, the Pir, the Pir.[432]

Universal Reason, Intellect, and Knowledge in Rumi's Thought

Some philosophical terms are difficult to translate from one language into another without loss of meaning. A clear instance is the word *'aql*, which when rendered as "reason"—from the Latin root *ratio*, originally meaning "to calculate"—conveys only one aspect of the Arabic word. Perhaps a better alternative would be "intellect," from the Latin *intellectus*, which is derived from a root originally meaning "to harvest" or "to gather together." Thus, "reason" refers to the analytic and "intellect" refers to the synthetic, integrative, or unitive aspect of this faculty, and the word *'aql* embraces both of these two aspects.

The word *'aql*, moreover, like its Greek equivalent *nous*, had other connotations that are totally missing in these words as they are used today. For example, nowadays those who are rationalists regard *'aql* to be at best one faculty among other faculties of the soul. But for ancient philosophers, *'aql* or its equivalent, *nous*, was an immaterial *substance*, which for its existence did not depend on the existence of the body.

The Greek *nous*, like the Arabic and Persian *'aql*, as we shall also see in Rumi, has both a psychological and a cosmological function. In its psychological aspect, the rational soul, according to the Peripatetics, for example, has several levels.

The material intellect (*nous hylikos, intellectus materialis, 'aql-i hayulani*) is the intellect that has the potentiality to receive every intelligible form, without itself being actually any particular thing. It is considered to be like a blank tablet on which everything could be written.

A higher stage is the habitual intellect (*intellectus in habitu, 'aql-i bi'l-malakah*), which has acquired some self-evident or axiomatic truths.

The intellect that has actualized in itself most of the intelligibles is called the actual intellect (*intellectus in actu, 'aql-i bi'l-fi'l*).

In the highest stage, the human intellect, as acquired intellect (*intellectus acquisitus* or *intellectus adeptus, 'aql-*

165

i mustafad), does not receive the intelligibles from the sensibles by an act of abstraction, but receives them directly from the Divine Intellect, also called the Agent Intellect (*intellectus agens*, *'aql-i fa''al*), which itself is considered either to be the totality of the intelligibles in God as the Absolute self-thinking thought (*nous nouon*) or, according to the later Peripatetics, as the intellect of the lunar sphere.

In the Peripatetic view, the world consists of ten spheres, each governed by one planetary Soul and Intellect. The Tenth Intellect, identified with the archangel Gabriel, is the guardian of the sublunary world.

In Plato, however, the intellect is not confined to the ten celestial intellects associated with ten celestial spheres. For him the world is divided into the sensible or visible world (*kosmos aisthetikos, kosmos horatos*) on the one hand, and the intelligible or invisible world (*kosmos noetikos, kosmos ahoratos*) on the other. The intelligible world is the cause of the sensible world, and is far above it in rank, majesty, dignity, and luminosity. In Plato's view, since everything in our world descends from the One (God) through the intelligible world, everything has an intelligible or spiritual aspect. Contrary to the Peripatetic view according to which all things in the universe except a few are lifeless, in the Platonic universe all things coming from the spiritual or the intelligible world, which is identical with life itself, are intelligent and partake of Divine Life.

Rumi, on the other hand, makes a distinction between discursive reason (*'aql-i bahthi*) and a reason whose fountainhead is in the very core of the spirit. Discursive reason is what we use in our academic discourse as a means of obtaining knowledge by using hypotheses, concepts, definitions, judgments, syllogisms, proofs, and so on. The other type of reason is obtained without books and without using such axioms as the impossibility of the infinite regress and the vicious circle. The knowledge gained through this reason is Divine Inspiration, based on such spiritual practices as the purification of the soul, the mortification of the passionate and carnal self, and polishing the mirror of the heart such that it fully reflects the Divine Mysteries.

The same distinction in knowledge is to be found in Shihab al-Din Suhrawardi, the founder of the Ishraqi or the Illuminationist School of Philosophy. He maintains that there are two different kinds of knowledge: discursive knowledge, based on the sciences of logic and the art of demonstration; and knowledge by tasting, or sapiential knowledge ('ilm-i dhawqi), which is far superior in rank, depth, and dignity to knowledge by discursivity or the art of argumentation and demonstration. Suhrawardi calls the one who possesses sapiential knowledge a theosopher or Divine Sage (hakim muta'allih).

On the basis of this epistemic division, Suhrawardi classifies philosophers into two distinct categories: discursive philosophers, on the one hand, and sapiential philosophers on the other. Some philosophers such as Aristotle and the Peripatetics in general are adepts in discursive philosophy. Some thinkers, including all the Sufi masters, such as Junayd, Bastami, or Tustari, possess sapiential wisdom, but lack discursivity. Great philosophers like Plato, the Presocratics, and the ancient Persian sages, according to Suhrawardi, possess the two categories of discursive and sapiential wisdom together.[433]

It is interesting to note that ever since Imam Muhammad Ghazali launched his very severe and staunch attacks against philosophers in his various books such as The Incoherence of the Philosophers (Tahafut al-falasifah), The Deliverance from Error (al-Munqid min al-dalal), and Faysal al-tafriqah (Making a Distinction between Islam and Disbelief), attacking philosophers became a common theme, especially among Sufi poets such as Sana'i, 'Attar, Rumi, and others. However, these attacks also became a great incentive and stimulus for the burgeoning and efflorescence of sapiential philosophy, especially in Iran, the homeland of Ghazali. Great schools of philosophy came into being, such as the school of Illumination mentioned above, by correcting many of his grievous errors and benefiting from his many important metaphysical and epistemological insights.

The Greek word *nous*, which was rendered as *intellectus* in Latin or *'aql* in Arabic by the ancients, is today translated mostly by the word "spirit." The expression *kosmos noetikos* is rendered both as "the intelligible world" and "the spiritual world." Both renditions are correct because an immaterial and simple substance is both living, or better, is the source of life, and moreover is self-aware and has the power to know itself and other things.

In other words, *'aql* is a simple immaterial substance, and every immaterial substance possesses both knowledge and self-awareness. It is by virtue of these qualities that it is called *'aql* or "intellect." Moreover, it possesses life, without which knowledge would be impossible. By virtue of this life it is called *ruh*, or spirit. However, these are only two among a wide range of aspects with regard to each of which it has a different name. Thus, the selfsame entity can be spoken of using different names according to its various functions and aspects.

With regard to *'aql* in particular, there are some philosophers who lay greater stress on reason or intellect and others who emphasize knowledge, but it should be underscored here that knowledge and reason are coextensive and coterminous, so that the one implies the other. For example, some philosophers maintain that the first determination is the Divine Intellect, whereas others consider it to be Divine Knowledge. However, this is more a linguistic than a real difference.

According to Rumi, everything in the universe from the so-called minerals, to plants, animals, stars, and heavens, from the minutest particles to the greatest galaxies, is endowed with the Divine Intelligence, and everything works intelligently. This explains for us the prevalence of an astonishing order and unity in the universe. In the scriptures, this orderliness and beauty of the cosmos has been emphatically stated. Since many people are reluctant to understand this point, prophets tried to prove it by bringing knowledge into stone and rod.

> The Nile has learned from God to discriminate,
> for it opened for these Israelites and shut fast against those Egyptians.

His grace makes the Nile intelligent;
His wrath makes Cain foolish.
From kindness, He created intelligence in lifeless things;
by His wrath, He cut off intelligence from the intelligent
    one.
By His grace an intelligence appeared in lifeless matter,
and through His chastisement knowledge fled from the in-
    telligent.
There, by His Command, the rain-like intelligence poured
    down.
Here, intelligence saw God's anger and took flight.
Clouds and sun and moon and lofty stars
all come and go according to arrangement.
None comes but at its appointed hour
so that it neither lags behind its time nor arrives before.
Since thou didst not understand this from the prophets,
they brought knowledge into stone and rod,
that thou by analogy might undoubtedly deem
the other lifeless things to be like rod and stone.[434]

As Rumi puts it, the Universal Intellect is like a vast
ocean, and the forms of things are like bubbles on its
surface or like empty cups, which when filled sink into
the ocean. This reminds us of the above-cited simile of
the Universal Intellect in Plotinus where he likens the
Universal Intellect to an infinite ocean, which is covered
by the thick foam of phenomena such that it becomes
invisible to the eye.[435]

Think what worlds are in the hidden stores of the Intellect,
how wide is this ocean of the Intellect!
In this sweet ocean our forms are moving fast
like cups on the surface of water:
Until they become full, they float like bowls on top of the
sea,
but when the bowl is filled it sinks therein.
Intellect is hidden and a world of phenomena is visible;
our forms are spray from that hidden ocean.[436]

So the Universal Intellect is extremely hidden, but our
forms as phenomena are most apparent in this vast
ocean; but they are no more than spray in comparison
with that ocean.

In another poem, Mawlana considers the world to be a reflection or the manifested form of the Universal Intellect; it is like the father of every visible form. When a person does not reconcile himself with the Universal Intellect, he lives a canine life. We should therefore make our peace with this father so that the world becomes to us like a paradise. At every moment new forms of beauty shall appear. Heaven and Earth will be transfigured in our view. By the vision of beautiful forms, which are no doubt the appearances of the Universal Intellect, every kind of anguish will depart.

> The whole world is the form of the Universal Intellect,
> which is the father of whoever follows the Divine Word.
> When anyone shows excessive ingratitude to the Universal Intellect
> the form of the universe appears to him as a cur accordingly.
> Make peace with this father, abandon disobedience,
> that water and clay may appear to thee as a carpet of gold.
> Then the Resurrection will become thy present state;
> Heaven and earth will be transfigured before thee.
> Since I am ever at peace with this father,
> this world is like a paradise in my sight.
> At every moment appears a new form and a new beauty,
> so that from seeing new visions ennui dies away.
> I see the world to be full of bounty,
> the waters constantly gushing forth from the springs.
> The noise of their water is coming to mine ear;
> my inner consciousness and intelligence are becoming intoxicated.
> I see boughs dancing like penitents,
> the leaves clapping their hands like minstrels.
> The gleam of the mirror is flashing through the felt cloth;
> think how it will be if the mirror itself be displayed.
> I am not telling even one mystery out of thousands,
> because every ear is filled with doubt.
> To the imagination (*wahm*) what I say is glad tidings of the future,
> but the intellect says, "What glad tidings?" It is my cash in hand.[437]

In short, Mawlana maintains that our world is a world full of accidents.[438] Whence do these accidents arise? They arise from forms. Whence do the forms arise? They no doubt arise from thoughts. Is their origin our thoughts? No, how can our thoughts originate the forms of things in the external world? Rather, their origin should be sought in the Universal Intellect. The Universal intellect is like unto a king, and the forms of things are his envoys. In other words, the Universal Intellect is present in everything as the very form of that thing.

> Indeed, all created things are accidents
> so that in this sense it was revealed:
> *Did there not come...* (Quran 76:1)[439]
> Whence arise those accidents?
> From forms.
> And whence arise these forms?
> From thoughts.
> This world is one thought of the Universal Intellect.
> The Intellect is like a king and the forms are his envoys.[440]

Intelligence is the light and an intelligent person is one who has the lamp in his hand. He is like a leader who follows his own light. Because he has his own light, he has faith in himself. One should also follow the guidance of his light. One who is half-intelligent takes an intelligent person as his guide and lets him lead him the way as a blind man clutches a seeing man and lets him guide. But he who lacks intelligence and knows nothing of the way disdains to follow a guide.

> The intelligent person is he who has a lamp;
> he is the guide and leader of the caravan.
> That leader is one who follows his own light;
> that selfless traveler is the follower of himself.
> He is the one that puts faith in himself;
> and may you too put faith in the light on which his soul
>   has grazed.
> The other who is the half-intelligent
> deems an intelligent person to be his eye,
> and has clutched him as the blind man clutches the guide,

171

so that through him he has become seeing and active and
    illustrious.
As for the ass who had not a single barley-corn's weight of
    intelligence,
who possessed no intelligence himself and forsook the in-
    telligent guide,
who knows neither much nor little of the way
and yet disdains to go behind the guide,
he is journeying in a vast wilderness,
now limping in despair and now advancing at a run.
He hath neither a candle to make it his leader,
nor half a candle, that he should beg a light.[441]

Intelligence is like a wing by which a person soars up
to the heaven of truth. If someone lacks intelligence, he
should take a wise and intelligent person as his guide. If
he does not have spiritual insight, he must seek a master
who is endowed with such insight.

Intelligence is wings and feathers to a man.
When he lacks intelligence, he must rely on the intelli-
    gence of a guide.
Either be victorious or in search of a victor.
Either have insight or seek one endowed with insight.
Without the key, namely intelligence, this knocking at the
    door
is prompted by self-will, not by right motives.[442]

Intelligence is the embodiment of beauty. God has
given it a robe of honor and a thousand names, each
name betokening an aspect of its perfection. One of its
perfections is that being Divine in nature, it is self-sufficient and autonomous. Compared to its luminosity, the
daylight appears to be dark. If, on the contrary, the form
of foolishness were revealed, the darkness of night would
appear as daylight.

When the beauteous Intelligence unveiled its face from
    non-existence,
God gave it a robe of honor and a thousand names.
The least of those sweet-breathing names
is that it is not in need of anyone.
If the Intelligence display its face in visible form,

day will be dark beside its light.
And if the image of foolishness were to appear,
beside it the darkness of night would be radiant.[443]

There are different degrees of intelligence, and the differences between them are as great as the difference between the sunshine and a spark of light. In several places Mawlana attacks the view of the Mu'tazilites that all human beings share equally in intelligence and that superiority and diversity in intelligence are the result of learning and experience.

Know well that intelligences differ thus
in degree from the earth up to the sky.
There is an intelligence like the orb of the sun.
There is an intelligence inferior to Venus and the meteor.
There is an intelligence like a flickering lamp.
There is an intelligence like a star of fire,
because, when the cloud is removed from it,
it produces intellects that behold the Light of God.[444]

A single human comprises many degrees and levels of being and perception, differing from each other in the order of their priority and in the order of their emanation from their Divine Source. The more hidden and veiled they are from our physical sight, the higher they are in spiritual rank. The body, which is plainly seen by our eyes, is the lowest. The heavenly spheres are also visible to our sight so they are the husk, and the light of their spirit is the core and the kernel.

The spirit is concealed in the body; the body is as the sleeve, and the animal or vital spirit is as the arm that moves it. More concealed than the animal spirit is the intellect; it is easier to perceive the spirit than to apprehend the intellect. The spirit that is involved in the Divine Revelation is still more concealed than the intellect.

The heavenly sphere, then, is the husk,
and the light of the spirit is the kernel.
This sky is visible, that spirit is concealed;
do not stumble on this account.
The body is manifest, the (vital) spirit is concealed.

173

The body is as the sleeve, the spirit as the arm.
Again, the intellect is more concealed than the (vital)
    spirit;
perception apprehends the (vital) spirit sooner than the
    intellect.
If you see a movement, you know that he who moves is
    alive;
but you do not know that he is full of intellect
until regulated movements appear,
and he by means of knowledge
turns the motion of copper into gold.
From manual actions being conformable to intellect
you may perceive that there is intellect behind them.
The spirit that partakes of Revelation
is more concealed than the intellect,
because it is of the unseen; it belongs to yonder side.
The intellect of Ahmad was not hidden from any one,
but his spirit of revelation was not apprehended by every
    soul.[445]

It is related that the Holy Prophet said that God Most
High created the angels and deposited intellect in them,
and He created the beasts and set lust and vital passions
in them, but He created the sons of Adam and set in them
lust and intellect together. He whose intellect prevails
over his lust is higher than the angels, and he whose lust
prevails over his intellect is lower than the beasts.

It is related in the Hadith that the majestic God
created the creatures of the world in three kinds:
One class He made entirely reason and knowledge and
    munificence;
that is the angel: he knows nothing but prostration in
    worship.
In his original nature is no concupiscence and sensuality;
he is absolute light, living through love of God.
Another class is devoid of knowledge,
like the animal, being fat from fodder.
It sees nothing but the stable and its fodder;
it is heedless of misery and felicity.
The third class is Adam's progeny, the human being:
half of him is of the angel and half of him is ass.
The ass-half, indeed, inclines to that which is low;
the other half inclines to that which is intellectual.

Those two classes (angels and beasts) are at rest from war
    and combat,
while this person is in painful struggle with two adver-
    saries.[446]

As we saw, contrary to the Mu'tazilites, who said that
reason is equally distributed in all human beings, Mawlana staunchly holds the view that human beings are not
equal in their intelligence. They can ascend higher than
the angels and descend lower than the beasts. At the
higher, that is, the spiritual, level there is unity and harmony among believers, but at a lower, that is the animal
and bestial, level there is opposition and animosity.

The faithful are numerous, but the faith is one;
their bodies are numerous, but their soul is one.
Besides the understanding and the soul which is in the ox
    and ass,
man has another intelligence and soul.
Again, in the saint, who has that Divine Breath,
there is a soul other than the human soul and intelli-
    gence.
The animal spirit does not possess oneness:
seek not this oneness from this vital spirit...
The souls of wolves and dogs are separate, every one.
The souls of the lions of God are united.[447]

This explains, according to Rumi, the Quranic verse
"the faithful are brothers" (49:10) and the prophetic tradition that the Divine scholars are as one soul. It also
explains why disbelief in one prophet is disbelief in all
prophets. At the very least, it entitles us to say that if one
disbelieves in one prophet or perfect saint, his faith is not
perfect.

According to Rumi, there have been diverse modes
and stages in the nature of man from the beginning and
from which he has evolved, but which nonetheless still
exist in him right now. But these stages are vertical, rather than horizontal, and lead him back to the Divine
Source. The way up and the way down are the same. He
was mineral and turned into the organic and the vegetable state; from the vegetable he turned into the animal,

175

and from the animal he transformed into the human stage. There are again many stages in the human intelligence. The particular intelligence is derived from the universal intelligence. The human can advance, in this very life, from one stage of intelligence to another. He does not remember his former intelligences, but he can migrate to ever higher degrees of intelligence. How marvelous is the human situation! As one who falls asleep becomes oblivious of the past, or as one who is brought back to wakefulness mocks his pains and sufferings while asleep, so too this world, as a sleeper's dream, will fade away at the break of the dawn of death.

> First he came into the clime of inorganic things,
> and from the state of inorganic things he passed into the
>   vegetable state.
> For years he lived in the vegetable state,
> and did not remember the inorganic state because of op-
>   position.
> And when he passed from the vegetable into the animal
>   state,
> the vegetable state was not remembered by him at all...
> Again, the Creator, whom thou knowest,
> was leading him from the animal state towards humanity.
> Thus did he advance from clime to clime,
> till he has now become intelligent and wise and sturdy.
> He has no remembrance of his former intelligences;
> but from this intelligence also there is a migration to be
>   made by him,
> that he may escape from this intelligence full of greed and
>   self-seeking,
> and may behold a hundred thousand intelligences most
>   marvelous.
> Though he fell asleep and became oblivious of the past,
> how should they leave him in that self-forgetfulness?
> From that sleep they will bring him back again to wake-
>   fulness,
> that he may mock at his present state.
> ...Even so this world, which is the sleeper's dream:
> the sleeper fancies that it is really enduring,
> till all of a sudden there shall rise the dawn of death
> and he shall be delivered from the darkness of falsehood
>   and opinion.

Then laughter at those sorrows of his will take possession
    of him
when he sees his permanent abode and dwelling place.
Everything good or evil that thou seest in thy sleep
will be made manifest, one by one, on the Day of the Last
    Congregation.[448]

Reason and Faith

In Rumi's view there is no antagonism or clash between
faith and reason. Reason or intellect, rather than being
an adversary, is the guardian of faith. When the carnal
nature of man gets the upper hand and bids one to do
evil, the intellect is there to curb it and to put an iron
chain on the flesh. The intellect is like a just police-in-
spector in the city, striking terror into the hearts of
thieves, rogues, and scoundrels. It is like a tom-cat who
keeps all the mice in their holes. The intellect, in short,
is the guardian and the magistrate of the city of the heart.

> The reason that is allied to faith is like a just police-in-
>   spector:
> it is the guardian and the magistrate of the city of the
>   heart.
> It is mentally alert like a cat:
> the thief remains in the hole like a mouse.
> Wherever the mouse gets the upper hand,
> no cat is there, or there is just the image of the cat.
> What cat? The faith-regarding reason in the body
> is the lion which overthrows all lions.
> Its growl is the magistrate of the carnivorous animals;
> its roar prevents the herbivorous creatures.
> The city is full of thieves and robbers of clothes;
> you are free to choose whether there be a police-inspector
>   or not.[449]

Intellects and hearts have a celestial origin, but they
are blocked from the celestial light because of their im-
prisonment in the body. They are like the two angels,
Harut and Marut, in the Quran, who came to the earth
and were held captive in the pit of Babylon. They taught
people magic but admonished them not to use it in an

improper way. The good and the wicked learned magic from them, but the wicked abused it in their evil ways.[450]

> Without any doubt, intellects and hearts are celestial
> though they live debarred from the celestial light.
> Like Harut and Marut, those two pure ones
> have been confined here in a horrible pit.
> They are in the low and sensual world;
> they have been confined in this pit on account of sin.
> The good and the wicked learn magic
> and the opposite of magic from these twain involuntarily.
> But first they admonish him saying:
> "Beware! Do not learn and pick up magic from us!
> We teach this magic, O so-and-so,
> for the purpose of trial and probation."[451]

But Satan beguiles and deceives the foolish children. He buys their faith and reason in exchange for the kingdom of this world. This world is the world of ornamentation. Satan decks out the carcass of this world so finely by his delusive magic that he is able to exchange it for hundreds of rose gardens.

> From the foolish children the ghoul-like Satan
> is buying their reason and faith in exchange
> for the kingdom of this world.
> He decks out the carcass so finely that with it
> he buys from them two hundred rose-gardens.[452]

Different Levels and Kinds of Intellect in Rumi's Thought

At the beginning of this chapter we discussed the levels of the intellect according the Peripatetic philosophers. Rumi shows himself to be both a great sage and a great Sufi master through his own very subtle and clear-cut distinctions between the various kinds of intellect. We seldom find a philosopher who has delved so deeply into the various kinds of intellect and how they function, and especially their role in the attainment of truth and their function in the salvific economy. Now let us cast a cursory glance at his treatment of the various kinds of reason.

The first distinction to be mentioned is that between the acquired (*maksabi*) and the God-given (*wahbi, bakhshish-i yazdan*) intellect. The acquired intellect is the intelligence that we use in learning different sciences and disciplines. It is obtained through the good offices of a teacher, by reflection, through concepts, and by committing data learned to memory; we make definitions and hypotheses, and use the laws of logic and the science of demonstration. By applying this intelligence we try to gain superiority over others, but often our mind feels burdened with redundant things. The other intellect is the gift of God. Its fountainhead is in the very core of one's heart, whence Divine Knowledge gushes forth to one's tongue. Like water from a spring, it does not change its color, flavor, or scent, and never stinks. The acquired intelligence is like the water that runs from the streets into the house. It changes color, gets fetid, and stops when the water-way is blocked.

> The intellect is two intellects:
> the former is the acquired,
> which you learn like a boy at school,
> from book and teacher, and by reflection and memory,
> and from concepts and from excellent and virgin sciences.
> Thereby your intelligence becomes superior to others,
> but through preserving that knowledge you are heavily
>   burdened.
> You are a guarding tablet, ever-circling round in search;
> he is the Guarded Tablet who has passed beyond this.
> The other intellect is the gift of God;
> its fountainhead is in the midst of the soul.
> When the water of God-given knowledge gushes from the
>   breast
> it does not become fetid or old or yellow.
> And if its way of issue is stopped, what harm?
> For it gushes continually from the house of the heart.
> The acquired intellect is like the conduits
> that run into a house from the streets:[453]

if its waterway is blocked, it is without any supply.
Seek the fountain from within yourself![454]

Rumi does not totally deny the discursive method. His objection to the discursive philosophers is that they consider the discursive method to be the only valid, authentic, and reliable way for the attainment of the truth. But from the sapiential point of view, it has many shortcomings. The discursive method, if used properly, at most leads us to the knowledge, but not to the vision and the realization, of reality. That is why he calls it knowledge by imitation (*'ilm i-taqlidi*). Even if rational discourse is as precious as jewels, spiritual discourse is far above it in rank and dignity.

> Though rational discourse be precious as pearls and
>   coral,
> spiritual discourse is quite another thing;
> spiritual discourse is on another plane;
> spiritual wine has another consistency.[455]

Mawlana speaks of some discursive philosophers (which might be a reference to Avicenna and some other Peripatetics) who declare that it is impossible for human beings to know the quiddity of things as they are in themselves. According to Rumi, this is the philosophical stance of the vulgar and the common run of people. But to perfect human beings, the inmost secret of things is not hidden. How can it be concealed from them, while they are aware of the Divine Mysteries? Discursive reason, for example, says: "This is not reasonable! It is a vicious circle! It is a ditch! Do not fall into it." But the spiritual master would say that you merely deem to be absurd whatever is above your spiritual capacity. There are things, moreover, that at one time we consider to be impossible, but when we reach a more mature age, they not only become possible, but are actualized.

> To be unable to perceive the quiddity, O uncle,
> is the condition of common men:
> do not say it absolutely,
> inasmuch as quiddities and their inmost secret

180

are clearly visible to the eyes of the perfect.
Where in existence is anything more remote from under-
    standing
and spiritual perception
than the Mystery and Essence of God?
Since that does not remain hidden from His intimates,
what essence and attribute is there
that should remain concealed from them?
The discursive reason says this is far (from reasonable)
and deeply involved;
do not listen to an absurdity without some explanation.
The spiritual pole replies, "To you, O feeble one,
that which is above your state seems absurd."
Is it not the case that incidents that are now revealed to
    you
at first seemed impossible to you?[456]

It is worthwhile to elaborate a little on Rumi's concep-
tion of discursive and sapiential reason. He often uses
many other names for the discursive reason (*'aql-i
bahthi*), such as partial reason (*'aql-i juz'i*); particular reason (*'aql-i juzwi*); instrumental reason (*'aql-i kar-afza*);
acquired reason (*'aql-i muktasab*; *'aql i-tahsili*); academic
reason (*'aql-i maktabi*); worldly or mundane reason (*'aql-
i dunyawi*); and worldly cunning and astuteness (*daha,
ziraki*).[457]

Discursive reason is distinguished from the Universal
Intellect (*'aql-i kulli*) and the Total Intellect (*'aql-i kull*).[458]
One should bear in mind that discursive reason and universal intellect are not two totally different kinds of intelligence; rather, they refer to different levels and functions
of one and the same intelligence, which is either oriented
upwards towards Divine Unity, or downwards towards
worldly and mundane attachments. The first of these levels views everything from the Divine vantage point,
whereas the latter takes care of the body and seeks to
fulfill the insatiable desires of the ego and the carnal self,
which entraps it in the prison of lust, egoism, and sensuality.

According to Rumi, there is only one way to be released and liberated from this tenebrous dungeon of par-
tiality and boundedness, and that is by piercing the veils

of the particular reason and connecting it with the universal intellect, thus allowing the Divine Light to illuminate the dark cavern of discursivity. Mawlana is extremely harsh to those who obstruct the way of the universal intellect and incarcerate themselves in the confines of the partial, egoistic, and mundane reason.

The human intellect is by nature Divine and praiseworthy. It is particular reason (*'aql i-juzwi*) that has calumniated it and has given it a bad name. The particular reason is ever desirous of acquiring worldly gains, and this caprice and avarice eventually deprives man of his worldly desires.

> The particular reason has given
> the universal intellect a bad name.
> Worldly desire has deprived the worldly man of his desire.[459]

The particular reason is like a flash of lightning, which cannot guide us on the way, especially if we are journeying to a far-off city. The lightning is only a sign that the cloud is going to rain.

> The particular reason is like the lightning and the flash:
> how is it possible to go to the city of Waksh in a flash?
> The light of the lightning is not for guidance on the way.
> Nay, it is a command to the cloud to weep.[460]

In another beautiful allegory, Rumi compares the flight of the partial reason to the flight of vultures trying to reach the seventh heaven, and likens the soaring up of the universal intellect to the wings of Gabriel, which according to the Quran ascended as far as the reaches of the Lote-Tree.[461] Or rather, the universal intellect is like Abraham, and the partial reason is exemplified by Nimrod, the despot who was Abraham's staunch adversary. Abraham, the father and progenitor of Abrahamic religions, invited Nimrod, then the sovereign of Babylon, to accept faith in the primordial religion, but Nimrod refused to believe. He wanted to soar up physically to Heaven to see Abraham's God with his own eyes.

He ordered a magnificent throne to be made, decorated with light feathers that he fastened to hundreds of vultures he had trained for the purpose. On a specified day, after a jubilee, the flight to Heaven started, and the vultures flew to ever higher heights, but after no more than a few days, they became so exhausted that they were no longer able to draw the throne upwards, and after they traveled a great distance, the throne toppled and fell to the ground, and Nimrod lost his life.

According to Rumi, had Nimrod believed in Abraham and submitted himself to his spiritual direction, Abraham would have taken him to the Divine Throne with the wings of Gabriel without the need for carrion-eating vultures. He who relies on the partial or particular reason is like Nimrod, who tries to fly to the farthermost Heaven with the assistance of vultures. He who uses the universal intellect is like Abraham, who soars up on the wings of Gabriel.

> Was it not Abraham that caused the gross Nimrod
> to journey to heaven with the help of vultures?
> Impelled by self-will he went far upward;
> but no vulture can fly to heaven.
> Abraham said to him, "O traveler, I will be thy vulture.
> This will be more seemly for thee.
> When thou makest of me a ladder to go aloft
> thou wilst ascend to heaven without flying."
> As the heart, without provisions or riding camel,
> travels swiftly as lightning to West and East;
> as man's consciousness, wandering abroad whilst he is
>   asleep,
> travels during the night to remote cities;
> as the gnostic, sitting at ease,
> travels by a hidden track through a hundred worlds.
> If he has not been endowed with power to travel like this,
> from whom are these reports of that spiritual domain?
> Hundreds of thousands of Pirs are agreed upon
> these reports and veracious narratives.
> Amongst these dignitaries there is no single dispute,
> such as there is in knowledge based on opinions...
> Arise, thou who resembles Nimrod and seek wings from
>   the eminent;
> these vultures will not avail thee as a ladder.

The vulture is the particular reason, O petty one;
its wings are connected with eating carrion.
But the intellect of exalted saints (*abdal*) is like the wing
   of Gabriel;
it soars, mile by mile, up to the shade of the Lote-Tree.[462]

In another profound and highly symbolic metaphor, Rumi likens the human person to a kingdom ruled by a king and a vizier or minister, representing the spirit and the intellect respectively. Everything depends on who the king and the vizier ruling and governing the dominion are. In the Holy Quran, two kings and two ministers are mentioned who symbolize for Rumi the supreme spirit and the universal intellect on the one hand, and the animal spirit and particular or partial reason on the other.

The first is the prophet Solomon, concerning whom it is said that he was given a kingdom of which nobody after him would be worthy. His vizier, mentioned by commentators as being named Asaf, was the one who "had been given 'knowledge of the Book,'" by which he was able to bring Bilqis, the queen of Sheba, together with her throne to Solomon's court in the twinkling of an eye.[463]

Pharaoh, on the other hand, was assisted by a like-minded vizier named Haman, who corrupted Pharaoh's intellect to the extent that he claimed divinity for himself. So according to Rumi, the association of Solomon and Asaf, like the conjunction of the spirit and the universal intellect, is, to use a Quranic term, "light upon light" (24:35), whereas the association of the Pharaoh with Haman, representing the carnal, sensual, and evil-bidding soul with the partial reason, is "darkness upon darkness" (Quran 24:40). Finally, Mawlana exhorts us, as kings of our existential dominion, to take the universal intellect and not the partial reason as our chancellor.

Thy intellect is the vizier and is overcome by sensuality:
in the realm of your being it is a brigand on the Way to
   God...
Alas, for the king whose vizier is this carnal reason;
the abode of them both is vengeful Hell.
Happy is the king whose helper
in affairs is a vizier like Asaf.

184

When the just king is associated with him
it is called *light upon light*.
A king like Solomon and vizier like Asaf
are *light upon light* and ambergris upon ambergris.
When the king is Pharaoh and his vizier like Haman
ill-fortune is inevitable for both.
Then it is *darkness, one part over another*;
neither intellect nor fortune shall be their friend on the
    Day of Judgment.
I have not seen aught but misery in the vile.
If you have seen aught else,
convey to them my special salutations.
The king is as the spirit, and the vizier as the intellect;
the corrupt intellect brings the spirit to corruption.
Do not take the particular reason as your vizier.
Make the universal intellect your vizier, O King.[464]

Rumi has a lot to teach us in the above exhortation. In the realm of our existence as spirit, we are the vicegerents of the Divine Spirit, the sovereigns and the supreme rulers appointed by the Divinity. If we want to take a vizier to assist us in our terrestrial existence, it should be not the particular reason but the universal intellect.

Like Plato, Rumi believes that all the sciences, such as geometry, astronomy, medicine, and even discursive philosophy, when cut off and separated from the Divine and sapiential wisdom, are beneficial and salutary only in this world and have nothing to do with our post-terrestrial existence. They are, as he expressly states, "the science of building the worldly stable," which we share with other animals, albeit in a higher degree; we need them in order to preserve our animal existence during our sojourn here below. Those who are enchanted and fascinated by the charms of this world have given to those sciences the name of "mysteries," while being ignorant of "the knowledge of the Way to God."

The fine artifices of geometry or astronomy,
and the science of medicine and philosophy,
which are connected only with this world
and have no way up to the Seventh Heaven:
all this is the science of building the worldly stable,

185

which is the pillar of the existence of the ox and the
camel.
For the sake of preserving the animal for a few days
these confounded fools have given to those (arts and sciences)
the name of "mysteries."
The knowledge of the "Way to God"
and the knowledge of its stations,
only the owner of the heart knows
or his heart itself.[465]

According to Muslim philosophers such as Avicenna,
animals—in addition to the faculty of imagination (*kha-
yal*), which represents to them the particular forms of
things like the particular images in a mirror—have another faculty, found also in human beings, which apprehends particular (and not universal) meanings. This faculty, called *wahm* or the "estimative faculty," often leads
one to no more than a false opinion. For example, most
people walk easily on a short wall, half a yard wide. But
if the same wall happens to be too high, most people fall,
because of the operation of the estimative or the apprehensive faculty, which suggests to them falsely that one
falls at high altitudes. In contrast, a trained tight-rope
dancer would walk on the two with the same speed. Now,
according to Rumi the particular reason, unlike the universal intellect, is most often governed by the estimative
faculty and hence mostly by false opinion.

Apprehension (*wahm*) and opinion are the bane of the
particular reason
because its dwelling place is in darkness.
If there be a path half a yard wide on the ground
a man will walk safely without apprehension.
But if you walk on top of a high wall
you will stagger even if its width be two yards.
Nay, through apprehension and from trembling of heart
you will be on the point of falling.
Consider well and understand the fear that is due to apprehension.[466]

186

Now the important question is: how can we join the particular reason to the universal intellect? Rumi has several solutions for this problem, which at first glance seem to be different from one another but are in reality quite interrelated. According to Rumi, the particular reason is only the receiver of sciences and is not an intellect of production. If knowledge of the sciences were produced by the particular reason, then it should be able to derive them without the aid of a teacher or a master. The particular reason is capable of being taught, but only a man possessed of Divine Revelation or Divine Inspiration can give it the required instruction. Rumi, like many ancients, maintained that all trades, crafts, professions, and sciences were originally taught to man by Divine Inspiration. Some ancient philosophers, such as Plato, maintained that all arts, sciences, and crafts were taught to man by Hermes, a messenger who mediated between God and human beings. His peer in the Islamic world is the Prophet Idris, who, as his name indicates (the root *d-r-s* in Arabic means "to instruct"), was the teacher of all the arts and sciences to mankind. The prophet Enoch plays a similar role in the Judaic tradition. So one way to escape the dilemma is to rejoin all the arts and sciences to their Divine Origin as revealed to man by sages and prophets.

> This astronomy and medicine is Revelation (*wahy*) to the
> prophets;
> where is the way for intellect and sense towards the direc-
> tion-less?
> The particular reason is not the intellect of productivity
> (*'aql-i istikhraj*);
> it is only the receiver of science and is in need of teaching.
> This reason is capable of being taught and of understand-
> ing,
> but only the possessor of Revelation gives it instruction.
> Assuredly in their beginning all trades and crafts
> were from Revelation;
> but reason added something to them.
> Consider whether this reason of ours
> can learn any trade without a master.
> Although reason was hair-splitting in contrivance,

187

no trade was tamed without a master.
If knowledge of a trade were derived from this reason
any trade could be acquired without a master.[467]

Another way to rescue the partial and particular reason from the dungeon of its particularity is to connect it to the heart, which is the center of one's being and the mirror of the Divine Throne. Particular reason, imprisoned in its confined cell, claims for itself a fake autonomy while being severed from the universal intellect harbored in the human heart. It is not in fact autonomous; it is only a pupil of the heart and predisposed to learn from it. It is part of the heart, and so it must go back to its source and learn to serve it.

> God drove the devils from His place of watch,
> He drove the particular reason from its despotism,
> saying: "Do not domineer: you are not autonomous;
> nay, you are the pupil of the heart and predisposed to
>   learn from it.
> Go to the heart, go, for you are a part of the heart:
> take heed, for you are a slave of the just King."
> To be His slave is better than being a sovereign,
> for *I am better than him* is the word of Satan.[468] (Quran
>   7:12)

The last line is a reference to Satan, who was commanded by God to bow before Adam when Adam was created by God "in the best stature" (Quran 95:4). Satan refused to bow, arguing that he was "better than Adam." It was the autonomy of his reason that caused him to rebel against God. Obedience to God through the universal intellect is better than rebellion against Him through the autonomous functioning of the particular reason.

But the best solution, according to Mawlana, the way to liberate oneself from the boundedness and limitation of the particular reason, is through Divine Love. Using one's particular or partial intelligence to attain to the Ultimate Reality is like utilizing the art of swimming to cross a vast ocean. One will in all probability be drowned, and there is seldom the possibility of being saved. Swimming is no doubt good for traversing smaller rivers such as the Oxus, but not for crossing the deep and bottomless oceans. If one is eager to evade the calamity of being drowned, one should embark on an ocean-going vessel, which is the symbol of Divine Love. There is also reference to Noah, who asked his son to board the Ark to be saved from the Great Deluge, but his son retorted that he could save himself by swimming and taking shelter in the high mountains.

> He that is blessed and the confidant of mysteries
> knows that astuteness is of Iblis, while love is of Adam.
> Astuteness is like swimming in the seas:
> the swimmer is seldom saved, and is drowned in the end.
> Abandon swimming, let pride and enmity go;
> this is not an Oxus or a river, it is an ocean.
> And, moreover, the deep ocean without refuge
> sweeps away the seven seas like straw.
> Love is as a ship for the elite;
> seldom is there calamity, for the most part there is deliverance.
> Sell astuteness and buy bewilderment:
> astuteness is opinion, while bewilderment is vision.
> Sacrifice your intellect in the presence of Mustafa;
> say: "*Hasbiya'Llah*," for God suffices me.
> Do not draw back your head from the Ark
> like Kan'an, who was deluded by his cunning soul,
> saying: "I will go up to the top of the lofty mountain.
> Why must I be under an obligation to Noah?"[469]

According to Rumi, love is the ladder by which one can scale up to the universal intellect; so there is no disharmony between love and the intellect in its universal aspect. It is only the partial or particular reason that denies the reality of love, even though it pretends to be the confidant of love and as such the possessor of mysteries. The partial reason is conceited and inflated with the egoistic self. Unless it becomes self-less and devoid of self-existence, it is a plaything in the hands of Satan.

> Partial reason is a denier of love
> though it may pretend that it is a confidant of the mysteries.
> It is clever and knowing, but it is not naught;

189

so long as the angel has not been naughted, it is a Satan.
Partial reason is our friend in word and deed,
but when it comes to spiritual states, it is naught.[470]

According to Rumi, all our intellects have descended from the quarter of the Beloved, and those who are spiritually alert and intelligent are ever eager to send their intellects to that quarter. Only those who are spiritually indolent or lukewarm prefer to stay in this quarter without the vision of the Beloved. In that quarter there is no need for ratiocination, because everything is the presence and vision of the Beloved.

> Sacrifice reason in love for the Friend:
> anyhow all intellects are from that quarter where He is.
> The intelligent have sent their intellects yonder,
> only the fool has remained on this side where the Beloved
>   is not.
> If from bewilderment, negligence is abandoned on this
>   side (sar),
> every tip (sar) of your hair will become a new head (sar)
>   and intellect.
> On that side the brain is not suffered to think,
> for there the brain and intellect grow fields and or-
>   chards.[471]

Another way of connecting the partial reason to the universal intellect is through the demand of the partial reason to know the Divine Mysteries. If there is "demand upon demand," then that perpetual impulse for the Divine will necessitate the manifestation of those mysteries. Then the ocean of the universal reason will undulate, and its waves will reach the partial reason.

> Partial reason would not be telling of the mysteries
> of the Universal Intellect,
> if there were not demand after demand
> Since demand after demand is arriving,
> the waves of that sea reach this place.[472]

The particular reason, being engaged in the nether world of change, is not immune to the vicissitudes of time and changes of fortune, but the universal intellect, being secure from the hazards of time and space, is beyond troubles and tribulations.

Another key to open the treasury of the universal intellect is the bewilderment in God. The Prophet of Islam, the exemplary paragon of all prophets and sages, is reported to have said: "O My Lord, augment my bewilderment in Thee."

> The particular reason is sometimes dominant,
> sometimes overthrown.
> The universal intellect is secure from the vicissitudes of
>   Time.
> Sell reason and artfulness and buy bewilderment (in God).
> Betake thyself to lowliness (khwari), O Son, not to Bu-
>   khara.[473]

The partial reason is very strong in the head but very weak in the legs, which means that it knows many things conceptually but is very weak in spiritual wayfaring and journeying in the path towards God. It is sick of heart but wholesome in body, because it is immersed in sensuality and corporeal pleasures. According to Rumi, another way to awaken the spiritually feeble-minded and to melt their frozen intellects is the use of parables. A parable might illuminate their feeble intellect so that it can apprehend the truth.

> But the Sufis use comparison and illustration
> in order that a loving feeble-minded man may apprehend
>   the truth.
> It is not a simile but a parable
> to melt the frozen intellect.
> Reason is strong in the head but weak in the legs,
> because the heart is in ruins, while the body is sound.
> Their reason is deeply involved in the pleasures of this
>   world;
> never, never do they think of abandoning sensuality.[474]

Some Moral Virtues in the *Mathnawi*

In a sense it is true to say that the whole *Mathnawi* is a manual for the training of the soul and for cleansing it of all rust and impurities, which impede it from manifesting the Divine realities. It is very hard to elaborate on all the virtues mentioned in this great work and even more difficult to select a few from among them. Here we only mention some of the ethical maxims and virtues that are necessary for all humans to observe in daily life, and that moreover orient the soul in the right direction if it yearns to realize the spiritual stations in its journey towards God. But before proceeding to our discussion about these virtues, we should emphasize that Rumi, like all other Sufi masters and unlike almost all modern philosophers, is not interested in abstract, empty, and barren conceptual and merely theoretical discussions about moral virtues. He is rather more concerned with their realization in the human soul.

The Reward of Our Actions

No matter what we do, our actions are rewarded even in this life. This world like a mountain echoes our actions back towards us, as the shadow turns back to the wall that has cast it.

> Although the wall casts a long shadow
> yet at last the shadow turns back again towards it.
> This world is the mountain and our actions the shout;
> the echo of the shouts comes back to us.[475]

According to Mawlana, committing an evil act is like sowing a decayed seed: it will yield bad fruit. Thus one should not feel secure in doing evil acts.

> When you have done evil, be afraid, do not be secure,
> since the evil is a seed and God will cause it to grow.[476]

Referring to the story of Joseph in the Quran, whom his brothers had taken to the desert for a walk, returning

193

to declare he had been eaten by wolves and producing as an evidence a specious bloody garment, Rumi says:

> O you who have torn the coats of Joseph,
> know that it is your own fault if the wolf tear *you*.
> These continual pangs are the effect of your own action,
> this is the meaning of "The Pen has dried."[477]

The expression "the Pen has dried" is a reference to a prophetic tradition that states that in the Eternal Decree of God (*qada*) everything is finalized and unalterable as when the ink of the pen dries up after being written on the page. This has been taken by many to mean a kind of inscrutable determinism, where there remains no place for human choice and by which all human actions are pre-determined. But Mawlana, on the contrary, interprets the prophetic tradition to mean that whatever you do, the intrinsic effects of your acts will necessarily emerge. If you have done good acts, you will be rewarded accordingly, and if you have done evil acts, you will be punished accordingly. He underscores this point in several other places in the *Mathnawi*.

> How should the meaning of "The Pen has dried" be this:
> that acts of perfidy and acts of faithfulness are alike?
> Nay, perfidy in return for acts of perfidy: the Pen has
>   dried.
> And faithfulness in return for those acts of faithfulness:
>   the pen has dried.[478]

And again,

> Likewise, the true interpretation of "The Pen has dried" is
>   this:
> That this tradition is for the purpose of inciting us
> to the most important engagement.
> Therefore the Pen wrote that every action,
> has the effect and consequence appropriate to it.
> The Pen has dried that if you do wrong, you will suffer
>   wrong,
> and that if you act rightly the result will be your felicity.[479]

194

Mawlana tells the story of a callous person who planted a thorn bush in the middle of the road, and every time the wayfarers reproached him and told him to dig it up, he would refuse to do so. The people's clothes were torn by the thorns, and their feet were pitiably wounded. Even when the governor told him to dig it up, he would refuse and procrastinate. Every day that evil tree was growing younger while its digger was getting older; that thorn bush gained strength while its digger was aging and in decline. Now Mawlana, addressing us, says:

> (The thorn bush) is growing younger, you older;
> be quick and do not waste your time.
> Know that every single bad habit of yours is a thorn bush;
> many a time have you been wounded by your own evil
>   habits.
> You have no sense, you are very senseless.
> If to the wounding of other persons,
> which comes to pass from your evil nature,
> you are indifferent,
> yet are not indifferent to your own wounds:
> you are the torment of yourself and of every stranger.[480]

Always Tell the Truth

Being is founded on reality and truth. Whenever you say something that is the case in reality, it is true, and otherwise it is false. In other words, falsehood and its subjective referent, that is, a false judgment, do not point to or denote anything in reality. To tell a lie is to make a false judgment intentionally, and since it is intentional, it can be considered in a way to be a kind of sophistry, meant to deceive others. That is why telling the truth is the cause of the peace and tranquility of the mind, as telling lies is the agent of its disquiet and perturbation. The Prophet of Islam is reported to have said: "Always abandon what casts you into doubt for what does not cast you into doubt. For indeed truth is tranquility and falsehood is uncertainty."

> The heart is comforted by true words
> just as a thirsty man is comforted by water.[481]

195

Since the Shining Truth is the cause of tranquility,
the heart will not be calmed by lying words.[482]

The heart is not comforted by lying words;
water and oil kindle no light.
Only in truthful speech is there comfort for the heart
Truths are the bait that entraps the heart.[483]

One should again refrain from giving false promises,
owing to the fact that they cause disquiet, as true promises are a comfort to the heart.

There are true promises pleasing to the heart;
there are false promises fraught with disquietude.
The promise of the noble is sterling coin.
The promise of the unworthy becomes anguish of soul.[484]

When one tells a lie it is like a thorn or a thistle, which
pricks the mouth such that the mouth is continually disturbed until one spits it out.

Falsehood is like a piece of straw and the heart like a
       mouth;
a piece of straw never becomes hidden in the mouth.
So long as it is there he keeps moving his tongue,
in order that thereby he may eject it from his mouth.[485]

If a counterfeit coin gains currency it is due to the fact
that there are genuine coins. So also, if any falsehood has
ever gained any value, it is due to the intrinsic worth and
value of the truth.

How should there be imagination without reality?
How should any false coin pass without a genuine one?
How should a lie fetch a price without truth?
Every lie in both worlds has arisen from truth.[486]

One Should Guard One's Tongue

While living in this world, our soul is embodied, and each faculty of the soul functions through its proper bodily organ. So we might say that each organ or limb in the body has its peculiar excellences and deficiencies, its proper virtues and vices. Our tongue, for example, is the organ for speech. One of its virtues is silence, much emphasized in ancient literature, and its deficiency is inopportune and vainglorious talk.

A tradition attributed to the Holy Prophet or to Imam 'Ali states that "man is concealed under his tongue." We do not know what a person is as long as he has not opened his mouth to speak. We cannot say whether he is a sage or a fool. People are, so to speak, hidden under their tongues. Let them speak, and their real spiritual rank will become revealed to you. Mawlana likens the tongue to a curtain that covers the gate of the house, and speech to a wind that blows away the curtain. As long as one has not spoken, the interior of the courtyard, that is, the soul, is hidden from our view, and when the wind of speech blows, the interior becomes visible to us.

> Man is concealed under his tongue;
> this tongue is the curtain over the gate of the soul.
> When a gust of wind has rolled up the curtain,
> the secret of the interior of the house is disclosed to us. [487]

Patience and silence accompany each other, and they attract Divine Mercy, whereas vain talk and disputation cause feebleness of mind.

> Patience and silence attract the Divine Mercy,
> whereas to seek evidence is a sign of infirmity.
> Accept the Divine command *Be ye silent* (Quran 46:29),
> in order that the recompense of *Be ye silent*
> may come to your soul from the Beloved.
>
> Silence is the sea and speech is like the river;
> the sea is seeking thee, do not seek the river. [488]

Sometimes a single word is sufficient to destroy the whole world. There are persons who shut their eyes and by their vain words set the whole world ablaze. In a beautiful simile, Mawlana likens the tongue to a whetstone that produces by its words sparks of fire. It is surrounded on every side by a field of cotton. So one should beware lest the cotton is set on fire.

> This tongue is like stone and is also fire-like,
> and that which springs from the tongue is like fire.
> Do not vainly strike stone and iron against each other,
> —now for the sake of relating a story,
> now for the sake of boasting—
> because it is dark and on every side are fields of cotton.
> How should sparks be amongst cotton?
> Iniquitous are those persons who shut their eyes,
> and by such vain words set a whole world ablaze.
> A single word lays waste a whole world,
> and turns dead foxes into lions.[489]

Again, just as an arrow shot from the bow, once shot, shall never return to the bow, so too the words uttered by the tongue shall never return to the tongue. Hence, one should meditate well about the words one utters.

> Know that a word which has suddenly shot from the
>   tongue,
> is like an arrow shot from the bow.
> O son, that arrow does not turn back on its way;
> you must dam a torrent at the source.[490]

Moreover, one should keep account of one's speech. Words deposited in the breast are like income, and words uttered by the tongue are like expenditure. One should not expend too much of one's income and must beware lest the expenditure should exceed or exhaust the income. Words are husks, and meanings are their kernels; so gibberish is like a husk without a kernel.

> These words in the breast are an income of kernels;
> in silence, the spiritual kernel grows a hundredfold.

198

When the word comes onto the tongue, the kernel is ex-
    pended;
refrain from expending so the goodly kernel may remain
    with you.
The man who speaks little hath strong thoughts;
when the husk, namely speech, becomes excessive,
the kernel goes.[491]

Generosity and Magnanimity

Magnanimity means the greatness and nobility of the
soul, and, together with its twin virtue of generosity, is
the most characteristic trait of believers. The Holy
Prophet is related to have said: "Generosity is a tree
among the trees of Paradise." Generosity does not only
mean to give away one's possessions or property in the
way of God. More important is the abandonment of carnal pleasures and lustful concupiscence for the sake of
the Divine pleasure and satisfaction.

Shut the lips and open the palm filled with gold;
leave off being a miser with the body, exhibit munificence.
Munificence is the abandonment of lusts and pleasures;
no one who is sunken in lust rises up again.
This munificence is a branch of the cypress of paradise;
woe to him that lets such a branch go from his hand!
This abandonment of sensuality is the firmest handle;
this branch draws the spirit up to heaven.[492]

In Islam, moreover, one of the obligatory acts is the
payment of *zakat,* or the poor-tax, which consists of bestowing a portion of one's annual income on the poor and
needy as prescribed in the *Shari'ah,* or Divine Law. *Zakat,* etymologically, means "purification," which implies
that in addition to purifying the soul from all taints and
blemishes, one should likewise cleanse one's belongings
of all kinds of impurity.

Riches were never diminished by alms-giving;
in sooth, acts of charity are an excellent means
of attaching wealth to one's self.
In the poor-tax is the overflow and increase of one's gold;

in the ritual prayer is preservation from lewdness and in-
iquity.
The poor-tax is the keeper of your purse;
the ritual prayer is the shepherd who saves you from the
wolves.[493]

We must not imagine that by spending money in the
way of God we will lose it. In His Holy Book He has promised that He will replace it with that which is much better. It is Satan who instills dread in his friends when they
want to give away something in the way of God.

If because of your liberality
no wealth remains in your hand,
how should the bounty of God let you be downtrodden?
When any one sows, his barn becomes empty of seed,
but there is goodliness in his cornfield.[494]

Niggardliness is as bad as prodigality and extrava-
gance. But one should not squander one's wealth where
it would be a waste, that is, where it is not in accord with
the commands of God. Here, to be niggardly is much better than to be prodigal.

There is many an act of niggardliness that is better than
prodigality;
do not bestow what belongs to God except by the command of God,
that thou mayst gain infinite treasure in return,
and that thou mayst not be numbered among the infidels.[495]

Spiritual Self-Exertion

The human soul, which is of the Divine origin, has descended into this body and has become so habituated to
the body that it has forgotten its former spiritual abode.
Engagement in bodily pleasures has deprived it of its
soaring flight and bound it to the bodily prison. So this
heavenly bird must once more regain its spiritual wings
and liberate itself from the material prison so it can has-
ten aloft to its original habitation.

200

The bird that is a prisoner in a cage,
if it is not seeking to escape,
is it not from ignorance?
The Spirits which have escaped from the cages
are the prophets, those worthy guides.
From without comes their voice of religion,
crying: "This, this is the way of escape for thee.
By this we escaped from this narrow cage;
there is no means of escape from this cage but this
    way.[496]

In order to escape from the prison of the body and to attain to the Divine realm, what is required is the exertion of a spiritual concentration and devotion, mortification of the carnal soul, the realization of virtues, and the acquisition of Divine vision. In order to achieve this sublime peak, one needs spiritual self-exertion, a warfare with the carnal soul, coupled with prudence and patience.

Give thy life for this cup, O son;
how may victory be won without spiritual warfare and patience?
To show patience for the sake of this is no hardship.
Show patience, for patience is the key to joy.
From this ambush none escaped without some patience
    and prudence;
to prudence, indeed, patience is the foot and hand.[497]

The Divine Spirit in man is hidden among the faculties of the soul, such as the animal spirit, the imagination, and discursive reason, just as butter is hidden in buttermilk. The body, which is like the churn, and the buttermilk within it are visible, but the "lordly spirit" seems to be non-existent, because it is invisible.

Thy true substance is concealed in falsehood,
like the taste of butter in the taste of buttermilk...
Till God send a messenger, a chosen servant,
a shaker of the buttermilk in the churn.
that he may shake it with method and skill,
to the end that I may know that my true ego was hidden.[498]

201

The purport of this beautiful simile is that our Divine self, manifesting the Absolute Divine Self, is concealed and veiled amid multifarious lower faculties of the soul, which are nothing but its many refractions. The Spirit, which is the root and the principle, seems to be non-existent, whereas the body and the physical phenomena, which are no more than mere appearances, have the claim to real existence. In order to make our hidden Divine Self manifest, we must subject ourselves to the spiritual disciplines and mortifications of the soul prescribed by prophets and spiritual masters. This requires persistence, perseverance, spiritual effort, and self-exertion on the one hand, and "method and skill" on the other.

Spiritual Companionship

Perhaps very few things that we can find in this world and in our transient terrestrial existence are as precious and worthy as good friends. Ancient sages believed that a good friend is "one's other self," as if there were one spirit within two bodies. Accordingly, one can find a vast literature on the subject in nearly all cultures and civilizations.

For Rumi, a friend is "a mirror of the soul," according to the famous saying of the Holy Prophet: "The believer is a mirror unto the believer." One should therefore always keep the mirror away from dirt and defilement.

> Since the true believer is a mirror for the true believer
> his face is safe from defilement.[499]

You should keep this mirror entirely pure so that it may reflect your spiritual state and show you your true reality. In another parable, Mawlana likens a true friend to the eye by which one is able to see; one must not damage one's eyes with motes or sticks, so that friendship may always remain pure.

> The friend is thine eye, O huntsman;
> keep him unsoiled by sticks and straw.[500]

202

One must not cast dust on the eye with the tongue's broom. One ought not to breathe on the face of the mirror. For Mawlana, friendship is a universal principle. When the earth, for example, finds a friend, namely the springtide, it brings forth flowers. The tree, when united to a friend, that is, the sweet air of the spring, starts to blossom. But in autumn, when it meets a repugnant companion, "it withdraws its face and head under the coverlet."[501] One should always think of the neighbors before the house and of the companions before the journey.

> The friend is the support and refuge on the Way;
> when you consider well, the friend is the Way.[502]

It is evident that any true friend is of inestimable value, but for Rumi a true friend is first and foremost a spiritual friend.

> The mirror of iron is only for external forms;
> the mirror that shows the aspect of the heart is of great
>   price.
> The soul's mirror is naught but the face of the friend,
> the face of that friend who is of yonder land.[503]

So one should always take spiritual and Divine men as one's companions. Rumi often uses the expression "the folk of meaning" (*ahl-i ma'na*) for spiritual men, i.e., those whom God calls "the possessors of the kernel" (*ulu al-albab*) in the Holy Quran.

> Consort with the folk of meaning,
> that you may both win the gift and be generous.
> Beyond dispute, the spirit devoid of meaning in this body
> is even as a wooden sword in the sheath.[504]

Companionship with righteous people makes one righteous. In order to correct a set of scales, one usually uses another set of scales. So one ought to rectify one's soul through companionship with righteous people.

> Straighten your members with the help of the straight;
> turn not your head aside from that threshold,
> O you who would go straight.
> Balance makes balance correct;
> balance also makes balance defective.[505]

Friends are the cause for joy and exuberance as enemies are the cause of grief and adversity. So one must not vex friends by selfishness and egoism lest they become one's enemies.

> Whoever is sitting with friends is amidst a flower-garden,
> though he be in a bath-furnace.
> Whoever in the world sits with an enemy,
> he is in a bath-furnace though he be in a flower-garden.
> Vex not your friend with egoism,
> lest your friend become your adversary and enemy.[506]

One can tell the good friends from the bad ones in times of trials and tribulations, just as one can distinguish genuine and false gold in the blazing fire.

> A friend is like gold, tribulation is like fire;
> the pure gold is glad in the heart of fire.[507]

The Dangers of Bad Friends

A famous Persian poem, which has become a proverb in this language, says:

> It is always good to make friends with the wise,
> and a wise enemy is better than a foolish friend;
> for a wise enemy will raise you up,
> but a foolish friend will strike you down to earth.

A "fool," as defined by Rumi, is not one who has a low intelligence quotient or is not able to score high grades on examinations. A fool is one who robs one's religion and makes one stray from the straight path. As Jesus has said, the disease of folly is the sign of the wrath of God; so one should escape from the fool as Jesus did.

Jesus said: "The disease of folly is the wrath of God";
physical disease and blindness are not wrath,
they are a means of probation.
Probation is a disease that brings Divine mercy;
folly is a disease that brings Divine rejection...
Flee from the foolish, seeing that Jesus fled from them;
How much blood has been shed by companionship with
     fools!
The air steals away water little by little;
so, too, does the fool steal away religion from you.
The flight of Jesus was not caused by fear, he is safe from
     mischief;
it was for the purpose of teaching others.[508]

Rumi, again, narrates a tradition from the Prophet of
Islam who said: "A fool, whoever he is, is our enemy, and
whoever is intelligent is dear to our soul." Here, of course,
intelligence, we should be reminded, means the power of
discrimination between the truth and error, between the
Absolute and the relative, between the Real and the illusory, between the Creator and the creature. In other
words, as Rumi says above, it is "the way of true religion."

The Prophet said: "Whosoever is foolish,
he is our enemy and a ghoul who waylays the traveler.
Whosoever is intelligent, he is dear as our soul,
his breeze is our sweet basil...
If the fool put sweetmeat on my lip,
I am in a fever from tasting his sweetmeat."[509]

The fool's excuse is worse than his crime;
the excuse of the ignorant is the poison that kills wis-
     dom.[510]

To depict for us friendship with a fool, Rumi relates
the parable of a man who made friends with a bear. One
day the man fell asleep and the bear kept driving the flies
away from his face, but in spite of all his efforts they soon
came back again. Several times the bear drove back the
flies from the young man's face, but as soon as he did so
they would fly back. The bear became enraged by the
flies. He went off to the mountain and picked up a huge
stone, as big as a millstone. He fetched the stone and saw

the flies seated comfortably on the young man's face. To drive them away once and for all he took up the stone and struck it down upon the flies so that he would see them no more.

> The stone made powder of the sleeping man's face,
> and published to the whole world this adage:
> "The love of a fool is for sure the love of a bear:
> his hate is love and his love is hate."
> His promise is infirm and corrupt and feeble,
> his word stout and his performance weak.
> Do not believe him, even if he take an oath;
> the man whose speech is false will break his oath.[511]

So we see Mawlana often complaining bitterly of vicious friends who "are like an ugly nose on a beautiful face," and he advises us to seek and consort with good companions.

> Oh, alas, alas for the sorrow caused by an uncongenial
>   friend.
> O ye nobles, seek ye a good companion.[512]

Mawlana even invokes the Holy Name when swearing that an evil friend is worse than a bad snake:

> I swear by the truth of the Holy person of Allah, the Lord,
> that a malign snake is better than a malign friend.
> The malign snake takes the soul from the man it has bit-
>   ten;
> the malign friend leads him into the everlasting fire.[513]

So when love for a bad companion grows in us, we should be on our guard and try to uproot it, lest it should destroy our heart.

> The mosque is the heart to which the body bows down;
> wherever the mosque is, the bad companion is its de-
>   stroyer
> (like a tree that grows through the foundations of a build-
>   ing).
> When love for a bad companion has grown in you,
> beware, flee from him and do not converse.

206

Tear it up by the root, for if it shoots up its head,
it will demolish both you and your mosque.[514]

Do not listen to the friendliness of the fair-spoken ignorant man,
for it is like an old virulent poison.[515]

The Advisability of Taking and Giving Counsel

A human being is not the Universal Intellect, so as to
know everything, and the intellect is not equally distributed among humankind such that all humans actually
know the same things with equal profundity and preci-
sion. So human intellects gain enlightenment and
strength by consultation, a fact much stressed in the
Holy Quran and in the prophetic traditions, as indicated
by the following verses:

And ask the people of remembrance if you do not know.
(21:7)

And consult them in affairs. (3:159)

And their affair should be through consultation among
them. (42:38)

The Prophet of Islam also said that he whose counsel
is sought should be trusted (*al-mustasharu mu'taman*).
Again, he is reported to have said that intellects are like
lamps, meaning that their lights strengthen each other.

Counsel gives perception and understanding;
the mind is helped by other minds.
The Prophet said: O adviser, take counsel with the trustworthy,
for he whose counsel is sought is trusted.[516]

It is necessary to consult wise and knowledgeable
people in everything. Consultation in the right manner
prevents sorrow, regret, and repentance in the end. This
was the advice given by all the prophets to their commu-
nities.

It becomes necessary to take counsel concerning things to
    be done
so that there may not be repentance in the end.
The community said, "With whom shall we take counsel?"
The prophets answered: "With intellect, which is the
    Imam..."
Mind gains strength from another mind;
the sugar-cane is made perfect by the sugar-cane.[517]

One should take note of the Divine command to the
Prophet to consult with the community, because consultation makes error less frequent, and also because intellects, like luminous lamps, strengthen one another. However, there is a stronger reason for consultation, namely
that among the assembly of those who are consulted,
there may be one who is illuminated by the Light of
Heaven. The Wisdom of God has mingled everything here
below on earth with the lofty Heaven, but his jealousy
(*ghayrah*) has drawn a veil of concealment between the
two. The existence of that unveiled and illuminated one
in the assembly of consultants will no doubt shed a new
light on the problem at hand. That is why traveling has
been enjoined, because it helps one to try one's fortune
and seek among intellects such an illuminated intellect.
And again, this is the reason why monasticism is forbidden in Islam, because for the hermit in the mountains,
the opportunity of meeting such perfect intellects is lost.

Take counsel with the company of the righteous,
note the Divine command given to the Prophet, *Consult
    them* (3:159).

Their affair is consultation is for this purpose (Quran
    42:38)
for owing to consultation mistakes and errors occur less.
These human intellects are luminous like lamps;
twenty lamps are brighter than one.
There may happen to be amongst them a lamp
that has become aflame with the light of Heaven,
for the jealousy of God has produced a veil of conceal-
    ment,
and has mingled the low and the lofty together.
He hath said: "Travel." Always be seeking in the world,

208

and trying your fortune and destined lot.

In all assembly-places always be seeking amidst the intellects

such an intellect as is found in the Prophet.

For the only heritage from the Prophet is that intellect,

which perceives the unseen things

before and behind.

Amidst the inward eyes, too, always be seeking,

that eye which this epitome, the *Mathnawi*, cannot de-
scribe.

Hence the majestic Prophet has forbidden monkery,

and going to live as a hermit in the mountains,

in order that this kind of meeting should not be lost,

for to be looked on by them is fortune and an elixir of im-
mortality.[518]

True Meaning and Outward Form

The problem of appearance and reality is one of the most ancient problems in the history of human thought. There have been many approaches to the solution to this problem both in the East and the West, some of them converging to nearly the same result, even if diverging from one another in their expressions and terms.

There is no doubt that our external senses convey to us only the appearances of things and have no access to their reality. That is why the phenomenalists, that is, those philosophers who maintain that there is nothing beyond what the senses exhibit, make no distinction between appearance and reality; in other words, for them the appearance of things is the same as their reality. Early Greek philosophers from Parmenides down to Plato were concerned with the interrelationship between phenomenon (appearance) and noumenon (intellectually grasped reality). The well-known Atma-Maya doctrine in Hinduism might be considered a very subtle and profound answer to the same problem. There is also a vast literature in Islamic sapiential philosophy and again in speculative Sufism, especially in the works of the great Master Ibn 'Arabi, about this subject, which could be made the theme of an independent study. Rumi more often than not uses the terms "outward form" (*surat*) and "inner meaning" (*ma'na*) for appearance and reality, although, as will be explained, he sometimes employs other terms. It is interesting again to note that one of the Beautiful Names of God is "the Real" (*al-Haqq*), which is taken to mean that the Divinity is the Absolute Reality and the principle behind everything real. Again, the Holy Quran teaches that "He is the First, the Last, the Hidden and the Manifest" (57:3), which is again interpreted by Divine sages to mean precisely this.

For Rumi, moreover, "meaning" is not purely subjective, such that it has its existence solely in the human mind. It is objective in the sense that it has its proper sphere of being—what he calls "the world of meaning or reality" ('alam-i ma'na)—which, ontologically speaking, is beyond the phenomena of the present world.

For Mawlana, every outward form emanates from an inner reality, namely ma'na (meaning, intention). Our speech, for example, arises from our act of thinking, and thinking itself is a kind of spiritual motion or, in his own words, an "intellectual wave from the absolutely still and motionless ocean of Divine Knowledge and Wisdom." When the ocean of Divine Knowledge undulates, waves of thought, which are determinations of Divine Knowledge, emerge and are articulated in the form of speech and voice. As long as, so to speak, we "exhale" these words through the power of our breath, they exist; otherwise, just as waves return to the ocean, so too meanings, as soon as they are expressed, return to their Divine Origin. The outward forms of the words in like manner are continually created at each instant, and as soon as they are created they fall back to their origin, which is none other than the sea of thought. The ocean of Divine Knowledge itself is a determination of the Divine Essence, which is absolute simplicity and pure formlessness. So one can say that all the forms in Divine Knowledge, as to be explained below, have issued from a preternatural and primordial formlessness.

> Know that form (surat) springs from meaning (ma'na)
> as the lion from the jungle,
> or as a voice and speech from thought.
> This speech and voice arose from thought;
> thou knowest not where is the sea of thought,
> but since thou hast seen that the waves of speech are fair,
> thou knowest that their sea also is noble.
> When the waves of thought sped on from the sea of wisdom,
> wisdom made for them the form of speech and voice.
> The form was born of the Word and died again;
> the wave drew itself back into the sea.
> The form came forth from Formlessness
> and went back thither,
> for Verily unto Him are we returning (Quran 2:156).[519]

Mawlana puts forth the theory of instantaneous creation (*khalq-i jadid*). The existentiating act of God, called by some "the Breath of the Compassionate" (*nafas al-Rahman*), is renewed at every instant, such that the coming into being of each instant presupposes the non-existence of all other instants. Since these almost infinite instants follow one another, forming a temporal continuum, the act of existentiation and annihilation is so rapid that we never notice the death and rebirth of beings at each moment. This instantaneous death and rebirth is called the Lesser or Microcosmic Resurrection (*qiyamat-i sughra*), in contrast to the death and rebirth of man (Mesocosmic or Middle Resurrection, *qiyamat-i wusta*) and the cataclysmic death of the entire universe (Macrocosmic or Greater Resurrection, *qiyamat-i kubra*).

> Every instant, then, thou art dying and returning;
> Mustafa declared that this world is but a moment.
> Our thought is an arrow shot from Him (*Hu*) into the air (*hawa*).
> How should it stay in the air? It comes back to God.
> Every moment the world is renewed
> and we are unaware of its being renewed,
> whilst it appears the same.
> Life is ever arriving anew, like the stream,
> though in the body it has the semblance of continuity.[520]

Yes, everything seems to be the same in appearance because of the swiftness of this existential motion. Perhaps all of us have experienced something similar when we whirl around a firebrand very quickly and it appears as a continuous circle, and when we see that falling drops of rain seem to trace out a continuous line.

> From its swiftness it appears continuous,
> like the spark which thou whirlest rapidly with thy hand.
> If thou whirl a firebrand with dexterity,
> it appears to the sight as a very long fire.
> The swift motion produced by the action of God
> presents this length of duration, time,
> as arising from the rapidity of Divine action.[521]

213

When He recites spells over the non-existences,
which have no eye or ear, they begin to stir.
Because of His spells the non-existences at that very mo-
    ment,
are joyously dancing into existence.
When, again, He recited a spell over the existent,
at His word the existent marched back post-haste into
    non-existence.[522]

All, whether men or women, in the whole world,
are continually in the death-agony and are dying.[523]

The meaning or reality of things issues forth from the
invisible world, but the outward form is provided by this
world.

The wine belongs to the Unseen, the pot to this world;
the pot is apparent, the wine in it is very hidden,
very hidden from the eyes of the uninitiated,
but manifest and evident to the adept.[524]

Mawlana, addressing us, complains that what we
take to be the true meaning and reality is in fact the outward form, which is borrowed and subsidiary, and we
usually rejoice in things that are relative and secondary.
The true meaning, if we are ever able to grasp it, would
seize us, enrapture us, and make us die to ourselves. It
would not make us blind and deaf as lovers of outward
forms.

Your reality (ma'ni-yi tu) is the form and that which is bor-
    rowed;
you rejoice in what is relative and secondary like rhyme.
Reality is that which seizes you
and makes you independent of form.
Reality is not that which makes blind and deaf
and causes a man to be more in love with form.[525]

The meaning or reality of things is like the kernel, and
the outward form is as the husk. He who seeks the kernel
is not after the husk. For the saints and sages, what is
lawful is the kernel and not the husk.

214

If the outward form, moreover, has any value, it is due to the reality and the meaning behind it. Does the purse have any worth apart from the gold contained in it? Would the body have any worth without the radiance of the soul? Does not the soul itself borrow its intrinsic value from the spirit of all souls, namely God?

> He that seeks the kernel has a hundred loathings for the
>   husk;
> to the goodly, the kernel alone is lawful, lawful...
> The value of the purse is from the gold;
> without the gold, the purse is of no worth.
> Even as the worth of the body is derived from the soul,
> so the worth of the soul is derived from the radiance of
>   the Soul of the soul.[526]

The form again is nothing as compared with the meaning and reality of things. The reality of the sky, which keeps it upside down like an inverted bowl and makes it rotate like the wheel of a celestial water mill, is the Universal Intellect. The motion of the body is due to the spirit, which is veiled by the body as a shield. The motion of the wheel is caused by the water of the stream. The power of inhalation and exhalation is owing to the desire of the spirit. It is the spirit that causes the breath to articulate different words and makes the body engage in peace or strife. But what is the reality of all realities and cause of the meaningfulness of all meanings? It is God.

> What is form in comparison with meaning? Very feeble.
> It is the meaning of the sky that keeps it upside down.
> Judge by the analogy of the celestial wheel:
> from whom does its motion proceed? From directive Intel-
>   lect.
> The motion of this shield-like body,
> is derived from the veiled spirit, O Son.
> The motion of this wind is from its meaning,
> like the wheel that is captive to the water of the stream.
> The ebb and flow and incoming and outgoing of this
>   breath,

from whom does it proceed but from the spirit that is
  filled with desire?
Now the spirit makes the breath "J," now "H" and "D"
  [*jahd*, i.e. "strife"],
Now it makes it peace, now strife.
"The Meaning is Allah" said the Shaykh of the Religion,
the sea of spiritual meanings of the Lord of created beings.
All the tiers of earth and heaven
are but as straw in that flowing sea.[527]

Everything in the universe is the creation of a single
thought or idea in the Divine Mind. Again, everything
made or uttered by humans is the outcome of an idea in
their minds. So why is it that the thought or the idea that
can sweep away the whole world like a flood is so despicable in the view of the rabble? Everything in the universe,
from crafts, houses, palaces, cities, mountains, plains,
rivers, oceans, the sun, and the sky, as well as creatures,
is a creation of Divine Thought.[528]

Mawlana, speaking through the tongue of a frog, explains that congeniality among things is due to their
meaning and their intrinsic reality and not due to their
outward forms, and admonishes that one should not become a lover of forms and seek congeniality in mere appearances.

Intellect was saying to the frog: "It is certain that congeniality,
is by way of meaning and is not from water and clay.
Take heed, do not become a worshipper of form and do
  not say this.
Do not seek the secret of congeniality in the outward
  form."[529]

What is congenial or not can only be discriminated by
the intellect and not by the outward form. Jesus, for example, in outward form was a human, but was of the
same genus as the angels.

216

By intellect you can recognize what is of the same genus
and what is not;
you ought not to run at once to outward forms.
My being of the same genus as you is not in respect of
outward form;
Jesus in the form of man was homogeneous with the angels.[530]

One should knock at the door of reality, and it will be
opened. One should always, like a falcon, beat the wings
of thought. But because we are clay-eaters, our wings
have been stained with mud, and we are not able to soar
up to the domain of meaning.

When you knock at the door of meaning it will be opened
to you.
Beat the wings of thought, in order that you may be made
a king-falcon.
The wings of your thought have become mud-stained and
heavy,
because you are a clay-eater; clay has become to you like
bread.[531]

The World of Meaning

Rumi, like other sages, makes a distinction between the
world of phenomena and the world of reality or meaning.
In the language of the Holy Quran, these two are called
respectively the world of creation (*'alam al-khalq*) and the
world of command (*'alam al-amr*). Everything in the phenomenal world of creation issues forth from the world of
command. We read for example in the Book of Genesis
that God said: "Let there be light" (the world of command), "and there was light" (the world of creation) (Genesis 1:3). And in the Holy Quran, God declares: "And our
command to a thing when we will it (is such that) we say
to it be! And there it is" (2:117). The world of command is
also called the spiritual world (*'alam-i jan*) and sometimes
the intelligible world (*'alam-i 'aql*). As mentioned above,
Rumi sometimes calls it the world of meaning (*'alam-i
ma'na*).

217

The world of reality has many distinctive features. To begin with, the spiritual world, being beyond the spatio-temporal continuum, has no spatial directions such as north and south or above and below. The world of creation, being spatial, is endowed with direction and orientation. If the world of command has no direction, how much more true is this with respect to God the Commander.

> The world of creation is endued with diverse quarters and
>   directions,
> but know that the world of Divine command and Attrib-
>   utes is beyond direction.
> Know, O beloved, that the world of command is without
>   direction;
> of necessity the Commander is even more without the di-
>   rection.[532]

Another distinctive and characteristic feature of the spiritual world is that its beings are incapable of being divided, separated, and united. You can, for example, divide the body of a man into different limbs, but you cannot in the same way divide and apportion humanity between different men. Humanity is a unity and totality that is indivisible into parts. When, for example, you predicate humanity of John and say: "John is human," you have not cut humanity into multifarious parts and given one part to John. The whole of humanity is predicated of and attributed to John. That is why John, like any other human being, can become—and potentially is—a Perfect Man.

> Because in the spirit there is no separating and uniting,
> while our thought cannot think except of separating and
>   uniting.[533]

Separating (*fasl*) and uniting (*wasl*), in other words, are peculiar to material substances. Another peculiar feature of spiritual beings is that they are free from number, size, and quantity. An elephant is not more animal than a mosquito because of its incomparably larger size. Animality is equal in the two animals. Things of the spirit,

218

moreover, can only be known through the spirit and through spiritual vision, and not merely through sensation, conceptualization, and ratiocination.

> They that know the spirit are free from numbers:
> they are sunk in the Sea that is without quality and quantity.
> Become spirit and know spirit by means of spirit;
> become the friend of vision not the child of ratiocination.[534]

Mawlana, commenting on the verses of Hakim Sana'i according to which "in the realm of the soul there are skies lording over the sky of this world,"[535] says:

> The Unseen World has other clouds and water;
> it has another sky and sun
> that is not discerned save by the elect.
> The rest are *in doubt as to a new creation* (Quran
> 50:15).[536]

According to Mawlana, the spiritual world is pure intelligence, whereas forgetfulness is the prop and pillar of the present world. If intelligence were to prevail in this world, it would be destroyed. Only a trickle of intelligence permeates this world. If that trickle of intelligence were discontinued, selfish desires such as greed and self-conceit would prevail among mankind. And if the trickle of intelligence from the invisible world were to become greater, there would be left neither virtue nor vice in this world.

> Forgetfulness, O beloved, is the pillar of this world;
> intelligence is a bane to this world.
> Intelligence belongs to that other world,
> and when it prevails, this world is overthrown.
> Intelligence is the sun, and cupidity the ice.
> Intelligence is the water and this world the dirt.
> A little trickle of intelligence is coming from yonder world
> that cupidity and envy may not roar in this world.
> If the trickle from the Unseen should become greater
> in this world neither virtue nor vice will be left.[537]

219

The world of reality is an *outopia* ("the land of no-where"), radiant with the light of the Divine Glory, which, being eternal, possesses no past, future, or present. These expressions get their significance only in relation to us, as one individual becomes a father, son, or citizen with respect to different relations. Otherwise, the individual is one and the same person, just as a roof is in itself a single object, but becomes "above" or "below" with regard to two different viewers.

> A (land of) nowhere, in which there is the Light of God,
> where is its past, its present and its future?
> Its past or its future is only in relation to thee,
> both are one thing and thou thinkest they are two:
> one individual is to him father and to us son;
> the roof is below Zayd and above 'Amr.
> The relation of "below" and "above" arises from those two
>   persons;
> as regards itself, the roof is one thing only.[538]

The title of one section of Book Five of the *Mathnawi*, commenting on the Quranic verse "And lo, the afterlife is the real life, if they but knew" (29:64), reads:

> The gates and walls and area of that world and its water and pitcher and fruit and trees all are living and speaking and hearing. And likewise Mustafa, on whom be peace, has said that the present world is a carcass and those who seek it are curs. If the next world had no life, the next world too would be a carcass: A carcass is so called because of its being dead, not because of its evil smell and its foulness.[539]

Mawlana then declares,

> Since every atom of that world is living,
> able to understand discourse, and eloquent,
> [the prophets] have no rest in the dead world,
> for this worldly fodder is only fit for cattle.
> Whoever has the rose-garden to feast and dwell in,
> how should he drink wine in the bath-stove?
> The abode of the spirit is the Seventh Heaven (*'Illiyyin*);
> it is the worm that has its home in dung.[540]

220

There are no contraries in that world, and hence it is the abode of everlastingness. Tranquility and peace prevail there.

> That world is naught but everlasting and flourishing
> because it is not composed of contraries.
> This reciprocal destruction is inflicted by contrary on its
> contrary.
> When there is no contrary there is naught but ever-last-
> ingness.
> God, who hath no like, banished contraries from paradise,
> Saying, *Neither sun,* nor its contrary, *intense cold,* shall be
> there (Quran 76:13).
> Colorlessness is the origin of colors, peaces are the origins
> of wars.
> That world is the origin of this dolorous abode.
> Union is the origin of every parting and separation.[541]

The spirit in us is associated with knowledge and intellectuality. It has nothing to do with contingencies such as race and language.

> In thine essence thou art neither this nor that,
> O thou that art greater than imagination and more than
> more!
> The Spirit is associated with knowledge and intellect;
> what has the Spirit to do with Arabic and Turkish?[542]

The meaningless soul, which is a soul without reality, is like a wooden sword sheathed in a scabbard. While in the scabbard, it seems to be valuable, but when it is drawn, it cannot be taken into battle, but rather it is fit to be burnt.

> Beyond dispute in this body the spirit devoid of meaning
> is even as a wooden sword in a sheath.
> Whilst it remains in the sheath it is valuable,
> but when it has come forth it is an implement fit for burn-
> ing.[543]

Even if the word "spirit" (*ruh*) in Arabic is feminine, the spirit has nothing to do with masculinity and femininity. It is too exalted and sublime to be either one of

221

them. The spirit is not subject to wetness and dryness,
nor does it increase or diminish by food and drink.

> ...And the Arabs call the word for "spirit" feminine,
> but there is no harm to the Spirit from being feminine:
> The Spirit has no association with man and woman.
> It is higher than feminine and masculine;
> this is not that spirit which is composed of dryness and
>   moisture.[544]
> This is not that spirit which is increased by eating bread,
> or which is sometimes like this sometimes like that.[545]

God, the Reality of All Realities

One of the Holy Names of God is "the Real" (al-Haqq),
which means that the reality of everything real has its
source and origin in God. In other words, God is the
Meaning behind all meanings and the Ultimate Reality
from which every reality originates and to which it returns.

> "The Reality is Allah (al-ma'ni huwa'Llah)," said the
>   Shaykh of the Religion,
> who is the sea of the Spiritual realities of the Lord of the
>   Worlds.[546]

> O concealed One, who hast filled the world from East to
>   West
> and art exalted above the light of the Orient and Occident.
> Thou art an inmost Ground of consciousness revealing
>   our inmost thoughts,
> Thou art a bursting force that causes our rivers to burst
>   forth.
> O Thou whose Essence is hidden while Thy gifts are sen-
>   sible,
> Thou art as the water and we as the millstone.
> Thou art the wind and we as the dust;
> the wind is hidden while the dust blown by it is plainly
>   visible.
> Thou art the Spring, we are fair as the verdant orchard;
> the Spring is hidden while its bounty is manifest.
> Thou art as the Spirit, we are like hand and foot;
> the closing and opening of the hand is due to the spirit.

Thou art as intellect, we are like this tongue;
this tongue hath its expression from intellect.
Thou art like the joy and we are the laughter;
for we are the result of Thy blessed joy.
All our movement is really a continual profession of faith,
which bears witness to the Eternal Almighty One.[547]

A name or a word is not merely composed of letters. For example the word "rose" is not merely the juxtaposition of the letters *r-o-s-e*. No name is without a reality behind it. Each name is a particular manifestation of a Divine Name, and each Divine Name is identical with the Divine Ipseity. So when we have a name, we should seek its reality in the Name, which is to say the Comprehensive Divine Name, Allah. We should not contemplate the moon only in its reflections in the stream. We should lift our head and behold the beautiful moon in heaven. This reminds us of a story about the meeting of Rumi's master Shams with Awhad al-Din Kirmani in Baghdad. When Shams asked Awhad al-Din about the latter's spiritual state, he responded by saying that he was contemplating the moon in its reflections in the stream, meaning that he was contemplating the Divine Beauty in its manifestations in human beauties. Shams rejoined by saying to Awhad al-Din: "If you do not have a pimple on your neck, it would be better to raise your head and contemplate the beauty of the moon itself in the sky."[548]

Hast thou ever seen a subject that shows without an object that is shown?
Unless there is the road, there can never be the ghoul (which entices travelers to stray from the road).
Hast thou even seen a name without the reality,
or hast thou plucked a rose (*gul*) from the letters *g-u-l*?
Thou hast pronounced the name;
go, seek the thing named.
Know that the moon is on high,
not in the water of the stream.
If thou wouldst pass beyond name and letter,
make thyself wholly purged of self.[549]

223

It is not the case that everybody knows the reality of names. One should seek it from a true knower, that is, one who, like Adam, has been taught the reality of Names. What a name signifies to us is the outward appearance of things, but to God the name of every thing is its inmost reality.

> Hear the name of everything from the knower;
> hear the inmost meaning of the mystery of *He taught the Names* (Quran 2:31).
> With us, the name of every thing is its outward appearance,
> with the Creator, the name of every thing is its inward reality.[550]

We must make a distinction between a "name" and "the name of the name." When we give something a name, it is in reality "the name of the name" (*ism al-ism*). The "name" is "the thing itself"; its "real name" is its reality with God.

All names and attributes in the universe are manifestations of the Divine Names and Attributes, which are the grounds for the realities of everything in the universe. Most of these Attributes are mentioned in the Quran or in the prophetic traditions. Two of these Divine Names, for example, are "the Abaser" (*Khafid*) and "the Lifter" (*Rafi'*), which are manifested in the lowliness of the earth and the exaltedness of Heaven.

> This Divine Maker is He who abaseth and exalteth;
> without these two attributes no work is accomplished.
> Consider the lowness of the earth and the loftiness of the sky;
> without these two attributes its revolution is not possible.[551]

Look at the miracles of God, who through his Name "the Knower" (*al-'Alim*) has bestowed knowledge, understanding, and reason in the midst of blood and entrails; by his Name "the Seeing" (*al-Basir*) has given us the power of sight; and by His Name "the Speaker" (*al-Mutakallim*) has brought speech through a piece of flesh that is the tongue; or again, by His Name "the Hearing" (*al-Sami*) He has bestowed on us the faculty of audition through a cavity that we call our "ear."

> Save through Thy munificence it is impossible to convey,
> understanding and reason into the midst of blood and en-
> trails.
> This flowing light proceeds from two pieces of fat, the eye-
> balls;
> their waves of light reach up to the sky.
> The piece of flesh which is the tongue,
> from it the flood of wisdom is flowing, like a stream.
> Towards a cavity, whereof the name is "ears"
> up to the orchard of the soul,
> whereof the fruit is intellections.[552]

But the Giver of forms has no form. The forms come from formlessness and go back to it.

> The form came forth from Formlessness
> and went back thither,
> for *verily unto Him are we returning* (Quran 2:156).[553]

> Form is brought into existence by the Formless,
> just as smoke is produced by fire.[554]

> Since these forms are the slaves of the Formless,
> why, then, are they denying their Benefactor?
> These forms have their existence from the Formless;
> what means, then, their denial of Him who brought them
> into existence?
> ...Know that the form of the walls and roof of every dwell-
> ing-place
> is a reflection of the thought of the architect.
> Even though in the seat of his thought,
> there is no visible stone and wood and brick.
> Assuredly the Absolute Agent is formless;
> form is a tool in His hand.[555]

Man, the Epitome of Realities

According to an unstated and implicit doctrine of Aristotle, all human beings are hermeneuticians of a sort, because they always pass judgment on everything, and to make a judgment about something is to interpret it and then enunciate it in a judgment. What enables man, metaphysically speaking, to be the interpreter of all reality? Most modern philosophers are almost silent on this issue, and offer no acceptable thesis or even hypothesis to explain the fact. Ancient sages, however, were more concerned with this issue. Plato, by way of example, would say that the human soul is the epitome of all the Divine Ideas, which are the originating causes of everything. Aristotle would reply by saying that the human passive intellect is potentially everything, and hence has the capacity to know all things. And St. Augustine would have recourse to his theory of Divine illumination. To Mawlana, the human power to interpret everything is due to the fact that Adam and therefore also his progeny have been taught the reality of all the Names, so their souls potentially have the knowledge of everything. This is again the reason why man is a nomothetic being, that is, he is the giver of names to all things.

> The father of mankind who is the lord of *He taught the*
>   *Names* (Quran 2:31)
> hath hundreds of thousands of sciences in every vein.
> To his soul accrued knowledge of the name of every thing,
> even as that thing exists unto the end of the world.
> No title that he gave became changed,
> that one whom he called "brisk" did not become "lazy."[556]

> Inasmuch as the eye of Adam saw by means of the pure
>   Light,
> the soul and inmost sense of the names became evident
>   to him.
> Since the angels perceived in him the rays of God,
> they fell in worship and hastened to do homage.
> The Adam like this whose name I am celebrating,
> if I praise him till the Resurrection, I fall short.[557]

226

For Mawlana, as we said before, if we are the real progeny of Adam, we should, like him, see all the realities of the Names within ourselves. Our substance is Divine. The world is not the cause of our substance; rather it is merely our accident. This world is like the jar, and the human heart is like the river. What is in the jar that is not in the river? This world is the chamber and the heart is the wonderful city. The city can no doubt contain in itself myriad chambers.[558]

The Idolatrous Worship of Outward Forms

There are many people who love phenomenal forms to the point of worshiping them. This is a form of idolatry and is even worse, because an idolator worships an idol, imagining it to be the personification of a divinity, whereas these people idealize the outward form as the object of their adoration to the point of its divinization.

> Do not be intoxicated with these cups, which are phenomenal forms,
> lest thou become a carver of idols and an idolator.
> Abandon the cups, namely the phenomenal forms; do not tarry.
> There is wine in the cup, but it is not from the cup.
> Open thy mouth wide to the Giver of the wine.
> When the wine comes, the cup will not be lacking.[559]

The object of love is not the outward form. If it were merely the outward form, why would we abandon it after the spirit has departed from it? We should inquire who the true beloved is; we should seek out the Source, which with Its absolute Splendor shines perpetually within the forms.

> That which is the object of love is not the form,
> whether it be love for this world or yonder world.
> That which you have come to love for its form,
> why have you abandoned it after the spirit has fled?
> Its form is still there, whence then this disgust?
> O lover, inquire who your beloved really is.[560]

227

You are an idol-worshipper when you remain in forms.
Leave its form and look at the reality.[561]

But the worst idol is that of the egoistic self that is worshiped as the Absolute Self.

The idol of your self is the mother of all idols,
   because that idol is only a snake while this idol is a
      dragon.[562]

Rumi narrates a tradition from the Holy Prophet according to which when men die they feel sorrow and regret, not on account of death, but for having missed an opportunity in the former life. Why did they not make death the object of their attention, instead taking as their lifelong objects of desire those ephemeral phantoms that perished at the hour of death?

The grief of the dead is not on account of death,
it is because "we dwelt upon the phenomenal forms,
and this we did not perceive: that those are mere form
      and foam,
and that the foam is moved and fed by the Sea."
When the Sea has cast the foam-flakes on the shore,
go to the graveyard and behold those flakes of foam!
Then say to them, "Where is your movement and gyration
      now?
The Sea has cast you into crisis."
In order that they may say to you, not with their lips but
      implicitly,
"Ask this question of the Sea, not of us."[563]

If one passes beyond forms, one will feel the sense of Paradise in this very life. But before breaking the outward form of everything, one should break and destroy one's own form.

If ye pass beyond form, O friends,
it is paradise and rose-gardens within rose-gardens.
When thou hast broken and destroyed thine own form,
thou hast learned to break the form of everything.

After that, thou wilt break every form.
Like Haydar ('Ali), thou wilt uproot the gate of Khaybar.[564]

Attention to Form Is the Cause of Quarrels and Strife

Most of the wars and strife among humans are due to their extravagant attention to outward forms. If their attention were focused on the inner and hidden meanings, the differences would vanish, and the enemies would become friends through unanimity. Mawlana strikes here the parable of a master who gave a dirham to four servants to buy a fruit. One of them, a Persian, said: "I will spend this on *angur*." The second one, an Arab, said: "No, I want *'inab*, not *angur*." The third one, a Turk, said: "I do not want *'inab*, I want *uzum*." The fourth, a Greek, said: "Stop this talk. I want *istafil*." The four people did not know each other's language and were unaware of the hidden meanings of the names. They began to fight with one another, and in their folly smote each other with their fists. They were full of ignorance and empty of knowledge. If a polyglot scholar were there, he would tell them that they all wanted one and the same thing.

> If a master of esoteric knowledge had been there,
> a revered and many-languaged man, he would have pacified them.
> And then he would have said: "With this one dirham
> I will give all of you what ye wish.
> When without deceit ye surrender your hearts to me,
> this dirham will do all this for you...
> Your one dirham will gratify the wishes of all.
> Four enemies will become one through unanimity."[565]

> The difficulty over *angur* and *'inab* was not solved,
> by the contest between the Turk, the Greek, and the Arab.
> Until the Spiritual Solomon,
> skilled in tongues, shall intervene,
> this duality will not disappear.[566]

While writing these verses, Mawlana might have called to mind certain verses of the Quran that state that humankind was one single community, but there appeared many differences and dissentions among them, and they were divided into many hostile factions (2:213). One of the missions of all prophets, according to the Quran, has been to bring them back again to unity. Mawlana gives as an example the two hostile tribes of 'Aws and Khazraj in Medina, who had bloodthirsty feuds and battles with each other, but through the spiritual teachings of Islam became brothers through faith.

> The two tribes which were named 'Aws and Khazraj
> had a bloodthirsty spirit towards each other.
> Through the preaching of Mustafa their ancient feuds
> vanished in the light of Islam and of pureness of heart.
> First, those enemies became brethren
> like the units of a bunch of grapes in the garden.
> And then, at the admonition given in the words,
> *The true believers are brethren* (Quran 49:10),
> they dissolved and mingled and became one body.[567]

Spiritual Faculties of Perception

Besides the five physical senses, man has many other spiritual faculties, which are veiled and hidden for most people, but unveiled for gnostics and the folk of unveiling. Man is said to have seven levels of being, each one having its proper five senses, which become operative when the lower levels are transcended.

According to Mawlana, the physical senses, like bats, always run toward the sunset, whereas the spiritual senses always orient themselves towards the luminous sunrise. Man shares the physical senses with animals, but he possesses the spiritual senses in common with the cherubim and the angels.

> Besides these five physical senses there are five spiritual senses;
> those are like red gold while these senses are like copper.
> In the bazaar, where the buyers are expert,
> how should they buy the copper sense like the sense of gold?

The bodily sense is eating the food of darkness;
the spiritual sense is feeding from a Sun.[568]

The worldly sense is the ladder to this world;
the spiritual sense is the ladder to Heaven.
Seek ye the well-being of the former sense from the physician;
beg ye the well-being of the latter sense from the Beloved.
The health of the former arises from the flourishing of the
body;
the health of the latter arises from the ruin of the body.[569]

As waking and sleeping do not go together, so too are
the purely sensuous eye and the spiritual eye incompat-
ible. The sensuous eye is the enemy of religion and spirituality, because it sees the foam and not the deep sea. It
is deft in perceiving the phenomena and not the reality of
things.

Throw dust on your sense-perceiving eye;
the sensuous eye is the enemy of intellect and religion.
God has called the sensuous eye blind;
He has said that it is an idolator and our foe,
because it saw the foam and not the sea,
because it saw the present and not tomorrow.[570]

Jesus is reported to have said: "The kingdom of God
is within you." So one ought to seek the way of pleasure
from within oneself and not from the world outside. A
Sufi, for example, who takes delight in the remembrance
of God, takes joy in this remembrance and is enraptured
and delighted by invoking the Name of God in the corner
of a mosque. But those who take pleasure in things outside themselves, such as palaces and castles, are disappointed in the end because they have sought joy and
pleasure in things extrinsic to their nature.

Know that the way of pleasure is from within, not from
without;
know that it is folly to seek it in palaces and castles.
One man is enraptured and delighted in the nook of a
mosque,
while another is morose and disappointed in a garden.

231

The palace of the body is nothing:
ruin the body!
The treasure lies in the ruin, O my prince.
Don't you see that at the wine-feast
the drunkard becomes happy only when he becomes ruined?[571]

The vision of colors is impossible without an external light. But the perception of both color and light is impossible without the existence of an internal light. The outward light emanates from the sun, but the inward light is a manifestation of the beams of Divine Glory. To be more exact, the light that gives light to the eye, that is, the power to see, is the heart, and that which gives light to the heart is the Light of God. God is again the supreme cause of the external light. "God is the Light of the Heavens and the earth" (Quran 24:35).

There is no vision of color without the external light,
even so it is with the color of inward phantasy.
This outward light is from the sun and from *Suha*,[572]
while the inward light is from the reflection of the beams
of Divine Glory.
The light which gives light to the eye is in truth the light
of the heart;
the light of the eye is produced by the light of hearts.
Again, the light which gives light to the heart is the Light
of God,
which is pure and separate from the light of intellect and
sense.[573]

When a man is spiritually perfect, he is a unitarian, that is, he views everything from the vantage point of its primordial root and origin. But if a man is squint-eyed, he sees only the branch of phenomena and the outward appearances.

When the eye is quite perfect, it sees the root;
when a man is squint-eyed, it sees the branch.[574]

If the animal sense could see God, then oxen and asses would be perfect saints and sages. If, moreover,

232

there were no senses beyond the animal sense, how could God have said in the Holy Quran that He has honored man and has favored him over all his other creatures (17:70)?

> If the animal sense could see the King (God),
> then the ox and the ass would behold Allah.
> If besides the animal sense thou hadst not another sense,
> outside of the desire of the flesh,
> then how should the sons of Adam have been honored?
> How by means of the common sense should they become
>   privileged?[575]

Since foolish people only take appearances and the outward aspects of things into consideration, the subtle mysteries involved in things are hidden from them. They are prevented from attaining the mysteries, because when the reality presents itself to them its subtleties escape them.

> Since the foolish took only the external appearance into
>   consideration,
> and since the subtleties were very much hidden from
>   them,
> necessarily they were debarred from attaining to the real
>   object,
> for the subtlety escaped them on the occasion when it
>   presented itself.[576]

The external senses are barriers and veils to the internal senses. In order to make the latter operative one must make the external senses inactive, such that without sensation and without ratiocinative thought one may hear the call of God.

> Put cotton-wool in the ear of the low physical sense,
> take off the bandage of that sense from your eyes.
> The ear of the head is the cotton-wool of the inmost ear;
> until the former becomes deaf
> that inward ear remains deaf.
> Become without sense and without ear and without
>   thoughts
> that ye may hear the call of God, *Return* (Quran 89:28).[577]

233

The Parable of the Cow of Baghdad

Mawlana is very concerned that there are many people who see the world through the narrow spectacles of their wishes, whims, and desires. They have their premeditated biases and prejudices regarding every-thing.

> How many a one has gone as far as Syria and Iraq,
> and has seen nothing but unbelief and hypocrisy.
> And how many a one has gone as far as India and Herat,
> and seen nothing but selling and buying.
> And how many a one has gone as far as Turkistan and China,
> and seen nothing but deceit and hidden guile.
> Since he has no object of perception save color and perfume,
> let him seek through all the climes, he will see nothing spiritual.[578]

Baghdad, at the time of Rumi, even if devastated by the Mongols, had become once more a flourishing city, thanks mainly to the efforts of its very efficient Persian governors. The city was considered to be full of scholars, sages, and saints.

Let us suppose that a plump cow all of a sudden enters the city of Baghdad and passes through the city from one end to another. What does it see in the city? What pleasures, joys, and delights does it take from this cosmopolitan and majestic city? For sure, its pleasure would rest in the rinds of watermelon or in the straw and hay scattered on the way.

> If a cow come suddenly into Baghdad,
> and pass from this side to that farther side.
> Of all its pleasures and joys and delights,
> she will see nothing but the rind of a watermelon.
> If straw or hay has fallen on the road,
> it is suitable to her bovine or asinine disposition.[579]

In this symbolic parable, the voracious cow signifies the adherents of extreme sensuality.

To return to the question of how to allay the malady of prejudice and ignorance, Mawlana advises us not to look at everything from our own narrow and prejudiced point of view. Zayd, for example, is a single person. To one of us he may seem to have the scent of Paradise and to other to be disgusting and a total loss. If you are prejudiced against him, do not look at him with your own eye. Look at him with the eye of lovers. Rather, borrow an eye from God's lovers; since you and he and his face and your eye and sight are all from God, look at his face with His own eye.

> Zayd is one person, to that one he is as paradise,
> while to this other one he is wholly pain and loss.
> If you wish that to you he should be as sugar,
> then look on him with the eye of lovers.
> Do not look on that Beauteous One with your own eye:
> behold the Sought with the eye of seekers.
> Shut your own eye to that Sweet-eyed One:
> borrow an eye from His lover.
> Nay, borrow eye and sight from Him
> then look on His face with His eye.[580]

Rumi's Theory of Knowledge

There might be an objection to our application of the expression "theory of knowledge" to Rumi's thought, grounded first in the fact that this term is quite modern, and so to apply it to Rumi is, to say the least, an anachronism; and second, that Rumi is after all a "mystic," and mysticism, as understood in the West, being based on a sort of personal experience, is far from having a theory of knowledge.

To the first objection we might answer by saying that we should not be deluded by mere words and expressions, but should show more concern for their meanings and significations. A seeker of truth, in the traditional understanding of the term, takes as much interest in the reality of things as in what their names signify, simply because for a name to be a name and not merely a *flatus vocis*, it must point to some reality. Accordingly, even though the expression "theory of knowledge" and its equivalent "epistemology" are quite new, to confine such expressions to modern philosophy is to deprive non-modern schools of philosophy of their very substance, especially considering the fact that *sophia* itself was taken to be the highest type of knowledge. Besides, adepts of Sufism are called *'arif bi-Llah*, that is, those who have attained to the most veritable knowledge of things by and through God. Theories of knowledge, in the true sense of the word, are to be found in great thinkers such as Plato, Aristotle, Avicenna, Suhrawardi, Ibn 'Arabi, and Rumi, to mention only a few. Having carefully studied their epistemologies, one can identify innumerable aberrations in modern theories of knowledge.

As to the second objection, we should not forget that some terms that were very meaningful and significant in a metaphysical and sapiential context have totally lost their meaning and have been reduced to the very opposite of their original tenor. Such terms include "theosophy," "theosopher," "gnosis," "gnostic," "mystic," "mysticism," and "myth." "Theosophy," which in ancient Greek meant the Divine Wisdom of the highest kind, has recently come to mean the teachings of a deleterious movement founded in 1875 as the Theosophical Society; "gnosis," which means "knowledge" in Greek, has historically been associated with the deviant "Gnostic" movements in Christianity, and hence it is problematic to use the term to render 'irfan in Arabic, for which it is an exact equivalent.

The same could be said about "mystic," "mystery," and "myth," which are derived from the Greek infinitive *muein*, which means "to become silent" or "to close one's eyes and lips," which no doubt are associated with the practice of meditation and contemplation, demanding the blocking of all untoward emotions that might agitate the soul.

According to Sufi doctrine, at the highest stage of spiritual wayfaring, when one attains to the station of Union, one's attributes are annihilated in the Divine Attributes. As a result, all the phenomenal human attributes are returned to their primordial origin, namely the Divine Attributes, whereby the servant hears by God, speaks by God, and knows by and through God. This fact, which is corroborated by many Quranic verses, is the reason why the perfect Sufis are called "the knowers by God."

"Man by nature," says Aristotle, "desires to know."[581] Following from this it could be said that "a man is what he knows. " To know, in other words, is the essence of the soul, and there is no vice as sordid and ignominious as ignorance. Mawlana time and again reiterates the importance of knowledge for a human being, affirming that all the nobility of a human depends on his knowledge and on his spiritual vision.

> O my brother, you are the same as your thoughts, nothing more.
> As for the rest, you are only bones and sinews.
> If your thought is a rose, you are a rose-garden.
> And if it is a thorn, you are a fuel for the bath-furnace.

If you are rose-water you are sprinkled on head and
     chest,
and if you are like urine, you are cast out.[582]

Thou art not this body; thou art that vision.
If thou hast beheld the spirit, thou art delivered from the
     body.
The human being is essentially vision;
the rest of him is mere flesh and skin:
whatever his eye has beheld, he is that thing.[583]

Knowledge according to Mawlana is like the seal of
Solomon, which both safeguards and opens the treasures
of Divine Wisdom. "The whole world is form and
knowledge is the Spirit." This pithy statement enshrines
a jewel of profound wisdom. If we trace back the visible
forms of things to their origin, we will see that all things
in the material, angelic (intermediary or imaginal), and
archangelic (spiritual or intelligible) orders have their primordial origin in the Divine Knowledge. The whole world,
in other words, originates and has its archetypal paradigm in the Divine Knowledge, which can appropriately
be regarded as the spirit of the visible forms in the universe.

Knowledge is the seal of the kingdom of Solomon;
the whole world is form and knowledge is the spirit.[584]

Man is moreover distinguished from all other animals
by the theomorphic prerogative of knowledge, by which
he is able to know the nature of things and wield them to
his advantage. Other animals are deprived of this Divine
quality, and that is the reason why man is able to ma-
nipulate them to his own purposes.

Because of this virtue, the creatures of the seas
and those of mountains and plains are helpless before
     man.
Of him the leopard and lion are afraid like the mouse;
from him the crocodile of the great river is in pallor and
     agitation.[585]

239

Knowledge, according to Mawlana, is like an ocean without shore. The seeker of knowledge is like a swimmer who can never reach the shore, but at the same time never gets wearied of swimming. The more one drinks of this ocean, the more one gets thirsty. That is why in the Holy Quran, the Prophet is commanded to beseech God for an increase in knowledge: "And say, O My Lord, increase me in knowledge" (20:114). Had knowledge had a definite limit, the Holy Prophet would have reached it, and would not need any increase therein.

Mawlana tells the story of a learned man who once said that in India there is a tree with peculiar fruit. He who finds the tree and eats of its fruit will never grow old and will have an everlasting life. A king, having heard this tale, was fascinated and became the lover of this tree, yearning eagerly to eat its fruit. He sent an intelligent envoy to India in search of the tree. The envoy roamed from town to town and wandered from place to place, and left no island, mountain, or plain unvisited. But all his search was in vain. Everyone whom he asked about the tree mocked him and considered him to be insane.

> They extolled him sarcastically saying: "O great sir,
> in such and such a very tremendous and huge country,
> in such and such a forest there is a green tree,
> very tall and broad, and every branch of it is big."[586]

So the king's envoy heard different kinds of reports from everyone, causing him to travel there vainly for many years. He suffered much fatigue in that foreign land and became too exhausted to search for the tree any further. He decided to return to the king, his eyes full of tears. While traversing the way back home, being utterly hopeless, he betook himself to a spiritual master who asked him about the cause of his grief and despair.

> He answered: "The Emperor chose me out
> to seek a certain branching tree,
> for there is a tree unique in all quarters of the world,
> its fruit is of the substance of the Water of Life.
> I have sought it for years and seen no sign of it

except the gibes and ridicule of these merry men."
The Shaykh laughed and said to him: "O simpleton,
this is the tree of knowledge within the sage.
Very high and very marvelous and very far-spreading,
a Water of Life from the all-encompassing Sea of God.
Thou hast gone after the form; thou hast gone astray.
Thou canst not find it because thou hast abandoned the
    reality.
Sometimes it is named 'tree,' sometimes 'sun,'
sometimes it is named 'sea,' sometimes 'cloud.'
It is that one thing from which a hundred-thousand ef-
    fects arise;
its least effects are everlasting life.
Although in essence it is single, it hath a thousand ef-
    fects;
innumerable names befit that one thing."[587]

Two Types of Knowledge

In the traditional Islamic worldview, a rigid and clear-cut distinction is made between this-worldly and other-worldly knowledge. This-worldly knowledge is the kind of knowledge connected with our transient existence in the present life. The other kind of knowledge is related to the postmortem stage of our existence, which for a Muslim believer is much more noble, exalted, and lasting than the present life. The one is called *'ilm-i ma'ash* (knowledge related to our worldly means of subsistence) and the other is termed *'ilm-i ma'ad* (literally, knowledge of our ultimate return or becoming). Again, in a tradition attributed to the Prophet Muhammad, there are mentioned two kinds of knowledge, one related to bodies (*'ilm al-abdan*) and the other concerned with religions (*'ilm al-adyan*). Islam never ignores the terrestrial needs of man, but not at the expense of forgetting his spiritual requirements. It tries to strike a harmonious balance between them.

What is important for Rumi is that these are two totally different types of knowledge, which should not be confused with each other, nor should one be reduced to the other. As evidence he adduces a prophetic tradition stating: "There are two greedy ones who will never be sat-isfied: the seeker of the present world and the seeker of knowledge." Rumi argues that in order for there to be a true disjunction in this division, this "knowledge" must be different from "knowledge of the present world." If they were identical, there would be a meaningless repetition or an absurd tautology.

> Knowledge is an ocean without bound or shore;
> the seeker of knowledge is like a diver in those seas.
> Though his life be a thousand years
> never will he become weary of seeking.
> For the Messenger of God said in explanation thereof,
> "There are two greedy ones who are never satisfied:
> the seeker of the present world and its abundant opportu-
>   nities for acquisition,
> and the seeker of knowledge and the considerations
>   proper to it."
> Now when you fix your attention on the division you will
>   see
> that this knowledge must be other than the present
>   world, O father.
> What then is other than the present world? The next
>   world,
> the knowledge of which will seize you from here and be
>   your guide to God.[588]

Knowledge by and through God

Traditional theories of knowledge are in many respects different from their modern analogues, which reduce the source of human knowledge ultimately to human subjec-tivity. As existence is an emanation or a manifestation of the Absolute Being, so are knowledge and all other at-tributes of perfection the pale reflections of the Divine At-tributes, and they should in the last resort be brought back and merged with their Divine Origin. This is only possible when the spiritual traveler attains to the station of unification or non-duality, where he hears, speak, and knows "by God" or through God, which is called in Sufi parlance *al-'ilm al-ladunni*.

The sciences of the mystics bear them aloft;
the sciences of the sensual men are burdens to them.
When knowledge strikes on the heart, it becomes a com-
    panion;
when knowledge strikes upon the body, it becomes a bur-
    den.
God hath said, *like an ass laden with his books* (Quran
    62:5);
burdensome is the knowledge that is not from Him.
The knowledge that is not immediately from Him
does not endure, like the hairdresser's dye.
But when you carry this burden well,
the burden will be removed and you will be given joy.
Beware! Do not carry this burden for the sake of selfish
    desire
so that you may ride on the smooth-paced steed of
    knowledge
and that afterwards the burden may fall from your shoul-
    der.[589]

Mawlana utterly downgrades the validity of a purely
worldly knowledge and wisdom that is devoid and de-
nuded of Divine illumination. It is a cause for spiritual
misery; so one should banish such wisdom from oneself.
It is a wisdom born of human fancy, which lacks the benefit of Divine Grace. Unlike the wisdom of religion by
whose wings one is able to soar up to the Divine Threshold, purely worldly wisdom causes doubt and suspicion.
Mawlana, moreover, reprimands the clever and cunning
scholars of the latter days, who out of a supercilious self-
aggrandizement deprecate the wise sages of the past. All
they have learned is cunning and trickery, and they have
thrown away all the character traits of the ancient sages,
such as patience, altruism, self-sacrifice, and generosity.

If thou desire that misery should vanish from thee
endeavor to diminish wisdom from thyself:
the wisdom that is born of nature and phantasy,
the wisdom that lacks the overflowing grace of the Light of
    the Glorious.
The wisdom of this world brings increase of supposition
    and doubt;
the wisdom of religion soars above the sky.

243

The ingenious rascals of this latter time
have aggrandized themselves over the ancients.
The learners of cunning have consumed their hearts
and have learned feints and tricks.
They have thrown to the winds patience, altruism, self-
    sacrifice,
and generosity, which are the elixir of the spiritual
    profit.[590]

Purely worldly knowledge is for the sake of gaining wealth and reputation; it is a bait for hunting popularity and not for seeking enlightenment and gaining release from this world. Having no outlet to the world of light, the possessor of this knowledge is like a mouse who has no access to the light. When the mouse tries to go out of the entrance, it is immediately driven back by the light and starts to make more burrows in the ground.

Imitative and conventional knowledge is one of which the
    owner laments
because the hearer is averse to hearing it.
Since it is bait for popularity not for the sake of enlighten-
    ment
its seeker is as bad as that ignoble worldly knowledge.
For he is seeking knowledge for the vulgar and the elite,
not in order that he may win release from this world.
Like a mouse he has burrowed in every direction
since the light drove him back from the entrance.
Inasmuch as he had no way to the open country and the
    light
he continued to make such an exertion even in that dark-
    ness.
If God gives him wings, the wings of wisdom,
he will escape from mousiness and will fly like the birds.
But if he seeks not wings, he will remain underground
with no hope of traversing the path to the Pleiades.[591]

Earlier we saw that Rumi makes a distinction be-tween discursive and realized knowledge. Discursive knowledge, especially when it does not aim at the attain-ment of truth, is like a business transaction and the ex-change of material goods, where the shopkeeper is ex-

244

tremely delighted when he vends a commodity. The purchaser of realized knowledge, on the other hand, which is based on deep spiritual vision, is God.

> Discursive knowledge, which is soulless,
> is in love with the countenance of customers.
> Though it is robust at the time of disputation,
> it is dead and gone when it has no customer.
> My purchaser is God, He is drawing me aloft,
> for *God has purchased* (Quran 9:111).[592]

To attain realized knowledge one needs self-sacrifice, that is, one must annihilate the egoistic self. The reward would be the vision of the infinite Beauty and Glory of God. One should turn one's gaze upwards from a handful of contingent earthly hobbies toward that Eternal Beauty that is the source of every beauty and the alpha and omega of every reality. Wallowing in earthly trifles, like eating clay, makes one pale-faced; turning to the world of the spirit and the Divine Threshold, one becomes rosy-cheeked through Divine illumination.

> The blood-money of my self-sacrifice is the beauty of the
>   Glorious One.
> I enjoy my blood-money as a lawful earning.
> Abandon these insolvent customers;
> what purchase can be made by a handful of worthless
>   clay?
> Do not eat clay, do not buy clay, do not seek clay,
> because the eater of clay is always pale-faced.
> Eat your heart that you may be young always,
> that your visage may be rosy with Divine illumination.[593]

Knowledge Is Light

In the Holy Quran, God is called the "Light of the Heavens and the earth" (24:35), and each of the following, which in its own peculiar way manifests that Divine Light, is called "light": knowledge (*'ilm*), Divine guidance (*hidayah*), revelation (*wahy*), the prophets (*rasul, nabi*) and especially the Prophet Muhammad, and the Scriptures

245

(*kitab*, namely the Torah, the Gospels, and the Quran itself). That which strings all these mentioned lights together is knowledge, without which their luminous nature would turn into the tenebrosity of ignorance. Mawlana time and again stresses the illuminative aspect of
knowledge and its significance in spiritual illumination.

> The illumined Shaykh makes his disciples cognizant of
>   the way.
> Moreover he causes the light to accompany his words.
> Strive to become intoxicated and illumined
> in order that His light may be the rhyming letter of your
>   discourse...
> When your knowledge is steeped in the light
> then the contumacious folk derive light from your
>   knowledge.
> Whatsoever you say too, will be luminous,
> for the sky never rains aught but pure water.[594]

Even a philosopher as great as Avicenna cannot write
a commentary on that light. A theologian as celebrated
as Fakhr al-Din Razi (d. 1209) can never be a confident
of its profound mysteries.

> And he that hath vision of that light,
> how should the explanation of his state be the task of Avi-
>   cenna?[595]

> If reason could discern the true way in this question,
> Fakhr-i Razi would be an adept in religious mysteries.[596]

Now the question poses itself as to how it is possible
to gain illumination in this tenebrous world of appearances. Rumi's answer is somewhat similar to that offered
by Plato. In his famous simile of the cave, Plato declares
that in order to flee from the subterranean cavern (symbolizing this world) it is sufficient that one of the prisoners break his shackles and with painstaking labor turn
his gaze toward the mouth of the cavern to see a dim
light, and then, ascending the wall of the cave, escape
from it to see the effulgent Source of light in the infinite
heaven. Mawlana too recommends that in the course of

spiritual progress, it is enough that only one of our senses loosen its bonds and sneak away toward the realm of light, and then the secrets of the invisible world will become apparent to all the other senses. If one sheep of the flock jumps over the stream, then the rest follow suit.

> When one sense in the course of its progress has loosed
>   its bonds
> all the rest of the senses become transformed.
> When one sense has perceived things that are non-sensi-
>   ble,
> that which is invisible becomes apparent to all the senses.
> When one sheep of the flock has jumped over a stream
> then they all jump across on each other's heels.
> Drive the sheep, thy senses, to pasture;
> let them browse on *He who brought forth the pasture*
>   (Quran 87:4),
> that there they may browse on hyacinth and wild rose,
> that they may make their way to the verdant meadows of
>   realities,
> that every sense of thine may become a prophet to other
>   senses
> and lead all the senses into that Paradise.
> And those senses will tell their mystery to thy senses
> without tongue, without literal or metaphorical expres-
>   sion.[597]

If we are among the progeny of Adam, we should follow him constantly in order to share more and more in that Divine Light. We should persevere in seeking Divine forgiveness. We should quench the burning fire of lust with the flood of tears. We should make the belly empty of bread, so as to find in it precious spiritual jewels; we must wean our soul from the Devil's milk to make it the companion of the angels.

> If thou art from the progeny of Adam and from his loins,
> be constant in seeking forgiveness in his company.
> Prepare a dessert of heart-fire and eye-water;
> the garden is made blooming by cloud and sun.
> What dost thou know of the taste of the water of the eyes?
> Thou art a lover of bread, like blind beggars.

If thou make this wallet empty of bread
thou wilt make it full of glorious jewels.
Wean the babe, thy soul, from the Devil's milk
and after that make it consort with the angels.
Whilst thou art dark and vexed and gloomy
know that thou art sucking from the same breast as the
    accursed Devil.[598]

Mawlana, as all traditional Muslim divines, lays much stress on the fact that in order to have an illuminated soul, it is essential that we obtain our livelihood from purely lawful and pious means. To eat "a lawful morsel" that is also ritually pure is a *conditio sine qua non* for the purification of the soul. Wisdom and knowledge, as Mawlana asserts, are the fruit of eating this lawful morsel. From canonically unlawful earnings there arise envy, guile, animosity, ignorance, and heedlessness.

The mouthful that gave increase of light and perfection
is obtained from lawful earning.
The oil that our lamp draws up (*kishad*),
when it extinguishes (*kushad*) the lamp, call it water.
From the lawful morsel are born knowledge and wisdom;
from the lawful morsel come love and tenderness.
When from a morsel thou seest arise envy and guile
and ignorance and heedlessness, know that it is unlawful.
Hast thou ever sown wheat and it produced barley?
Hast thou seen a mare bring forth an ass's colt?
The morsel is the seed and thoughts are its fruit;
the morsel is the sea and thoughts are its pearls.
From the lawful morsel in the mouth is born the inclina-
    tion
to serve, and the resolve to go to yonder world.[599]

The Conditions of Knowledge

There are certain conditions to be fulfilled for acquiring a knowledge that is spiritually beneficial and rewarding. First, knowledge should be accompanied by righteous deeds and pious works.

Therefore the Prophet said, "For traversing the way
there is no comrade more faithful than works.

If they be good, they will be thy friends for ever,
and if they be evil, they will be snakes in thy tomb."[600]

Second, treading the true path of righteousness is very difficult without the guidance of a master.

How, O father, can one do this work and acquisition
in the way of righteousness without a master.
The meanest acquisition that goes on in the world,
is it ever without the guidance of a master?...
Seek help in acquiring craft, O possessor of intelligence
from a generous and righteous person versed in that
    craft.
Seek the pearl in the oyster-shell, my brother
and seek technical skill from a master craftsman.[601]

Third, any practice, action or work that is not preceded by proper knowledge is not fruitful and may even be extremely harmful.

Its beginning is knowledge, then follows action
that it may yield fruit after a time or after death.[602]

Fourth, humility is a virtue that should always accompany the lovers of knowledge; pride is inimical to the aspirants of truth. One should never show any disdain for masters and should always be ready to learn from them. If a master tanner, for example, wears a threadbare pinafore, or a skilled ironsmith puts on a patched frock while blowing the bellows, it does not diminish their ranks.

If ye see sincere advisers, deal fairly with them
and be eager to learn; do not show disdain.
If the man engaged in tanning wears a threadbare gar-
    ment
that does not diminish the master's mastery of his trade.
If the ironsmith wears a patched frock when blowing the
    bellows
his reputation is not impaired in the eye of people.
Therefore strip the raiment of pride from thy body;
in learning put on the garment of humility.[603]

249

Fifth, each kind of knowledge and each discipline has its own method of learning and its special way of acquisition. The way of acquiring theoretical disciplines is oral instruction, i.e. by means of the tongue and the ears. The way of gaining practical and technical knowledge is through exercise and practice, i.e. by manipulating the body and the limbs.

> If thou wouldst learn theoretical knowledge
> the way of acquiring it is oral.
> If thou wouldst learn a craft,
> the way of acquiring is by practice.[604]

But according to Mawlana the highest and noblest type of knowledge is that of spiritual poverty (*faqr*), and its acquisition depends on spiritual companionship (*suhbat*). Here tongues, hands, and other bodily organs in themselves are of no avail. Here one soul receives knowledge from another soul directly and without the intermediary of books, writing instruments, or bodily organs. Here, mere knowledge of mysteries is not the ultimate aim; what is required is the expansion and illumination of the heart that is so stressed in the Quran and that God, interrogatively addressing the Prophet, has declared the greatest blessing conferred upon him.

> If thou desire spiritual poverty, that depends on companionship;
> neither thy tongue nor thy hand avails.
> Soul receives from soul the knowledge thereof
> not by way of book nor from tongue.
> If those mysteries of spiritual poverty are in the traveler's heart
> knowledge of the mystery is not yet possessed by the traveler,
> until the expansion of his heart shall make it full of light:
> hence God has said: *Did not We expand [thy breast]?* (Quran 94:1).
> For We have given thee the expansion within thy breast,
> We have put the expansion into thy heart.[605]

When the spiritual breast is expanded and illuminated, knowledge of the Divine Mysteries gushes forth from the human heart with such effervescence that the human heart does not need to get this knowledge from outside; otherwise one becomes the target of the Divine reproach.

> Thou art still seeking it from the outside;
> thou art a source of milk, how art thou a milker of others?
> There is a boundless fountain of milk within thee:
> why art thou seeking milk from the pail?
> O lake, thou hast a channel to the Sea:
> be ashamed to seek water from the pool...
> Contemplate the expansion of the heart within thee
> lest there come the reproach *Do not ye see?* (Quran
>   51:21).[606]

The final words of these lines refer to the Quranic verses "And on the earth are signs for those who are certain, and within your own selves. Do you not see?" (51:20–21). This reminds us of the famous saying of Jesus: "The kingdom of God is within you" (Luke 17:21), and that we should not seek it outside ourselves.

The disposition of the teacher, moreover, impresses itself on the pupils, just as our spirit produces effects on the whole body or as our reason brings the entire body into discipline. The souls of pupils become imbued with whatever science the master possesses. The master is like a reservoir from which many pipes flow. The water within the pipes is sweet and pleasant to the taste or brackish and dirty, depending on the water in the reservoir. But on the day of death, the best provision for the road is the knowledge of spiritual poverty.

> For whatever science the master is renowned,
> the souls of his pupils become endued with the same.
> With the master-theologian, the quick and industrious
>   pupil
> reads the principles of the scholastic theology.
> With the master-jurist, the student of jurisprudence
> reads jurisprudence when the teacher expounds it, not
>   theology.

251

Then the master who is a grammarian:
the soul of his pupil becomes imbued with grammar.
Again the master who is absorbed in the Way,
because of him the soul of his pupil is absorbed in the
    King.
Of all these various kinds of knowledge, on the day of
    death
the best equipment and provision for the road
is the knowledge of spiritual poverty.[607]

As in many verses above, we see here too that Rumi lays stress on spiritual poverty (*faqr*). Another name for a Sufi is *faqir ila Allah*, or "poor in God," based on the fact that in the Holy Quran, God addresses all of humankind with the words "O men, you are poor in relation to God, and God is the All-Sufficient, intrinsically Worthy of Praise" (35:15). As Jesus said in the Sermon of the Mount: "Blessed are the poor in spirit, for whom is the kingdom of Heaven" (Matthew 5:3).

Rumi relates the story of a self-conceited grammarian who, boarding a boat, turned to the boatman and asked if he had studied grammar. On hearing the answer "No," the grammarian said to the boatman: "Half your life is wasted." After a while there came a tempest that cast the boat into a whirlpool, and now the boatman shouted to the grammarian: "Now, tell me! Do you know how to swim?" On hearing the answer "No," the boatman declared: "O grammarian, your whole life is wasted because the boat is sinking in the whirlpool." What is needed now is the science of *mahw* (self-effacement, self-annihilation), not grammar (*nahw*).

Know that here *mahw* (self-effacement) is needed, not
    nahw (grammar).
If you are *mahw* (dead to self) plunge into the sea without
    peril.
The water of the sea places the dead one on its head,
but if he be living, how shall he escape from the sea?
Inasmuch as you have died to the attributes of the flesh
the sea of Divine Mysteries will place you on the crown of
    its head.

If in the world thou art the most learned scholar of the
    time,
behold the passing-away of this world and this time.
We have stitched in the story of the grammarian
that we might teach you the grammar (*nahw*) of self-ef-
    facement (*mahw*).[608]

Degrees of Knowledge

Knowledge, like being, has different degrees, one above
the other. At the lowest level is plain opinion, which is a
belief susceptible to being true or false. Every opinion
thirsts for knowledge, and knowledge itself aspires to certainty, and every certainty is the seeker of vision and intuition. In the Holy Quran, as stated before, three degrees
of certainty, one above the other, are differentiated: 1.
knowledge of certainty (*'ilm al-yaqin*), as when one sees
smoke; 2. vision of certainty (*'ayn al-yaqin*), as when one
sees that fire burns; and 3. realization of certainty (*haqq
al-yaqin*), as when one puts one's hand in the blazing fire
and has direct experience of the fire. It could be safely
assumed that without the higher types of knowledge, the
lower ones would be impossible. If there were no
knowledge, there would be no opinion; if there were no
vision, there would be no knowledge; and without the ac-
tuality of realization, no vision or knowledge would be
possible. Hence the possessors of the highest type of
knowledge are called the realizers (*muhaqqiq*), and those
who have knowledge without having attained the level of
realization or spiritual vision are called imitators (*muqallid*).

O son, every opinion is thirsting for certainty
and emulously flapping its wings in its search.
When it attains to knowledge, then the wing becomes a foot
and its knowledge begins to aspire for certainty.
For as has been well tested,
knowledge is inferior to certainty but above opinion.
Know that knowledge is a seeker of certainty
and certainty is a seeker of vision and intuition.
Vision is immediately born of certainty,
just as fancy is born of opinion.

253

See in the chapter *Alhakum* the explanation of this,
namely, that *the knowledge of certainty* becomes *the vision
of certainty* (Quran 102:1–7).[609]

Every Being Has a Share in Knowledge

We saw previously that according to Rumi, all things, including the minutest particles, have life and see and hear
in their own way and are full of joy and happiness, but
since we perceive them by our external senses, they seem
to us to be inanimate and mute.[610] However, if we penetrate into the world of spirit and become familiar with
their spiritual aspect, we can hear the loud noise of the
particles whereby they glorify the Lord of the Universe,
and then we will not be carried away by false interpretations, which result from a lack of the Divine Light that
reveals to us the true nature of things.

Everything in the universe has a specific function to
fulfill, and the infinite multiplicity of things work together
in a harmonious order and in a well-integrated unity.
This beauty, due to the cosmic harmony, is not fortui-
tously brought about by the chance concurrence of phenomena, but betokens the absolute Wisdom of the Author of the universe.

According to Rumi, every particle of the universe, and
generally speaking every thing, is endowed with a Divine
consciousness by which it knows the Lord of the universe
on the one hand, and fulfills its proper function on the
other. The Holy Quran is explicit about the fact that God,
apart from creating every thing, has revealed to it its
proper function. It is said, for instance, that God determined the seven heavens in two days and revealed to
each heaven its proper task (Quran 41:12). He has revealed to the bee how to make beehives on mountains
and trees, and how to make honey by eating from every
manner of fruit, and how to follow the ways of the Lord
(16:68). It is again said that on the Last Day, the Earth
will relate what the Lord has revealed to her (99:5), so
according to the Quran, revelation takes on a universal
and ontological aspect. Even if in human language all Divine Activity is expressed in the past tense, which should

254

mean that it has taken place once in an unknown past, in reality it is renewed at every instant.

> That which God taught to the bees
> He did not teach to the lion and the wild ass.
> The bee makes houses of juicy sweetmeat;
> God opened to it the door of that knowledge.
> That which God taught to the silkworm,
> does any elephant know such an artifice?
> Adam, created of earth, learned knowledge from God;
> his knowledge shot beams up to the seventh Heaven.[611]

In Islamic law, dogs and hounds are considered to be ritually impure and are not to be touched by a wet hand, and their leftovers are canonically forbidden to be eaten or even touched. But if they are taught how to hunt and are trained in the proper way, they become ritually clean, and their prey is lawful to eat. This has been taken to signify how important training, teaching, and knowledge are in spiritual transformation, even in animals, for knowledge wipes out ignorance and replaces it with the light of discrimination. According to Mawlana, animals cannot only be knowers (*'alim*); they can even become knowers in God (*'arif*). A case in point is the dog accompanying the Seven Sleepers in the cave, who lived among a community of disbelievers and atheists.

> They were youths who believed in their Lord and we increased them in guidance. And we strengthened their hearts when they stood up and said, "Our Lord is the Lord of the heavens and earth; we will not call upon any god apart from Him, for then we had spoken outrage. These our people have taken to them other gods apart from Him. Ah, if only they would bring some clear authority regarding them." (Quran 18:13–20)

So in order not to be polluted and contaminated by disbelief and to keep intact the pristine purity of their faith, they betook themselves to a cave where God made them to go into a very deep sleep for many years until the light of faith shone forth, and God made them wake up from that deep slumber.

Now, the Seven Sleepers were accompanied by their dog, who outstretched its paws on the threshold of the cave and slept with them. According to Mawlana, upon this fortunate dog was conferred a Divine conscience whereby it could discriminate belief from disbelief. In other words, it was an *'arif*, or a knower by God; it too had been illuminated by the Divine Light.

> When the dog has learned knowledge, he has escaped
>   from error;
> he hunts lawful prey in the forests.
> When the dog has becomes knowing (*'alim*) he marches
>   briskly;
> when the dog has become a knower of God (*'arif*),
> he becomes a Companion of the Cave.
> The dog has come to know who is the Master of the hunt;
> O God, what is that knowing light?[612]

To give another example, the earth is able to discriminate between God's friends and foes. It was able to distinguish the Light of Moses and let him pass undisturbed. It could understand the false pretensions of God's enemies, and opened a wide chasm to swallow them.

> If the blind man knows it not, it is not from his having no
>   eye to see;
> nay, it is because he is drunken with ignorance.
> Truly, the blind man is not more eyeless than the earth,
> and this earth, by the grace of God, has become a seer of
>   God's enemies.
> It saw the light of Moses and showed kindness to him;
> but Korah it engulfed, for it knew Korah.
> It quaked for the destruction of every false pretender;
> it understood the words of God: *O earth, swallow* (Quran
>   11:44).[613]

Knowledge through the Purification of the Soul

In all religions, much emphasis is laid on the purification of the soul. The function of the Holy Prophet, as all other prophets and messengers of God, is said to have been to teach the believers the Book (al-Kitab, Scripture) and Wisdom (al-Hikmah), and to purify their souls (Quran 2:129, 3:164, 62:2). The salvation and deliverance of the human soul is again the main objective of all religions, and there are many conditions mentioned for the attainment of this sublime goal. But all those conditions are recapitulated in one, which is the purification of the soul. The Quran states: "By the heaven and That which built it; and by the earth and That which extended it! By the soul and That which made it in equilibrium; and inspired it with its vice and its virtue. Saved indeed is he who purifies it, and failed has he indeed who corrupts it" (91:5–10).

As our physical eyes, like the clearest and the purest mirrors, reflect in us the visible images of things, so too our heart, the seat of our inner and spiritual faculties, when polished of its impurities and contaminations, becomes enlightened by and mirrors the Divine realities.

> When the mirror of your heart becomes clear and pure
> you will behold images outside of the world of water and
> earth.
> You will behold both the image and the image-Maker,
> both the carpet of glory and the Carpet-Spreader.[614]

> The mirror of iron is only for showing the skin;
> the mirror showing the features of the spirit is of great
> price.
> The soul's mirror is naught but the face of the Beloved,
> the face of that beloved who is of yonder land.[615]

The mirror of the heart must be clear in order that it might reflect Divine realities.

> Dost thou know why the mirror of thy soul reflects noth-
> ing?
> Because the rust has not been cleared from its face.[616]

So in order to become a mirror for reflecting the Divine Attributes, one must purge oneself of the attributes of the self-assertive egoistic self. Like polished iron, one must lose the rusty color.

257

Like polished iron, lose the color of iron;
become in thy ascetic discipline like a mirror without
    rust.
Make thyself pure from the attributes of self
that thou mayst behold thine own pure untarnished es-
    sence,
and behold within thy heart all the sciences of the proph-
    ets,
without book, without preceptor and without master.[617]

Here Mawlana tells the story of the competition between the Greeks and the Chinese in the art of painting
as a parable symbolizing the significance of purification
of the heart. Both the Greeks and the Chinese claimed to
be the better artists, so the king tried to put them to the
test. He assigned for each of them one particular room.
The two rooms faced each other with a thick curtain separating them. The Chinese demanded of the king a hundred colors, so that the worthy monarch opened up his
treasury, and every morning the Chinese received of his
bounty their ration of paints from the treasury. But the
Greeks said: "No hues and colors are suitable for our
work. All we need is to get rid of the rust." So they shut
the door and set to work polishing.

When the Chinese had finished their work, they were
beating drums out of joy. The king entered and saw the
pictures there. They were so beautiful that they were
about to rob him of his wits. After that he came toward
the Greeks. They removed the intervening curtain, and
the reflection of the Chinese pictures and artifacts struck
upon those walls, which had been polished and purified
of every taint and stain. All that the king had seen in the
Chinese room seemed more beautiful here, so that his
eyes were almost snatched out of their sockets.

The Greeks, O father, are the Sufis,
free from repetition and books and erudition.
But they have burnished their breasts and made them
    pure
from greed and cupidity and avarice and hatred.
That purity of the mirror is, beyond doubt, the heart,
which can receive images without number,

258

like Moses, who holds in his bosom the formless infinite
   form
of the unseen reflected from the mirror of his heart.[618]

Harmful Knowledge

Knowledge can be extremely dangerous, especially when
it falls into the hands of those who are evil-natured and
use it for their evil ends. One reason that Holy War has
been made incumbent and obligatory on true believers is
so that they might remove the sword from the hands of
the madmen who are the enemies of humankind.

> To teach the evil-natured man knowledge and skill
> is to put a sword in the hand of a brigand.
> It is better to put a sword in the hand of an insane man
> than that knowledge should come into the possession of a
>   worthless person.
> Knowledge and wealth and office and rank and fortune
> are calamity in the hands of the evil-natured.
> Therefore the Holy War was made obligatory on the true
>   believers
> so that they might take the spear-point from the hand of
>   the madman.[619]

One of the highest kinds of knowledge possible for human beings is the perennial wisdom, which for Rumi is
the kernel of all religions and, as we saw, is obtainable
by Divine Grace and through spiritual realization. Dangerous again is the inculcation of such wisdom with mere
words without being backed and bolstered by the science
of realization.

> Know, O simple man, that the words of wisdom
> on the tongue of the unwise are as borrowed garments.[620]

Mawlana is an especially sharp critic of false claim-
ants to Sufi knowledge and wisdom, who use it as a snare
to deceive simple believers. They deftly use Sufi idioms
and expressions to dupe simpletons into their aberrant
ways.

These shameless persons have attached to their tongues
the speech of dervishes and the deep sayings of gnostics.[621]

They take great pains at learning the jargon of Sufis
in order to embellish their discourse and to give pomp
and gravity to their pulpits. They are like people who
learn to imitate the sound of birds while being ignorant
of its meaning. They will either remain with nothing more
than verbal expressions, or else the Divine Grace and
mercy may overtake them and guide them to the true
way.

> Many learned the language of dervishes
> and gave luster therewith to their pulpits and assemblies.
> Either nothing was bestowed upon them except those ex-
> pressions
> or at last the Divine mercy came and revealed the right
> way.[622]

Such impostors have no scent or trace of God in them
and yet claim to be greater in rank and dignity than
Adam and Seth. Even Satan has not shown them his image, and yet they pretend to be superior to the great
saints (*abdal*).

They pilfer the expressions of Sufis in order to make
an ostentatious display of their personality. They slander
the great Sufi saints such as Bayazid, while the vilest and
the most wicked of mankind, such as Yazid, would be
ashamed of them.

> He has no scent or trace of God
> but his pretension is greater than that of Seth and Adam.
> The Devil has not shown to him even his portrait
> yet he is saying, "We are of the Abdal and even superior to
> them."
> He has stolen many an expression used by dervishes
> in order that he may be thought to be a holy personage.
> In his talk he cavils at Bayazid
> although Yazid would be ashamed of his existence.[623]

So one should beware of these false masters who have the outward features of Adam, but in fact are the incarnations of the Devil. They are like fowlers who make a whistling sound to deceive the birds and to lure them into a trap. So also a wicked man borrows the language of Sufis to chant a spell over ignorant people.

> Since there is many a devil who hath the face of Adam,
> it is not well to give your hand to every hand;
> because the fowler produces a whistling sound
> in order to decoy the bird
> so that the bird may hear the note of its congener
> and come down from the air and find trap and knife-
>   point.
> The vile man will steal the language of dervishes
> that he may thereby chant a spell over one bitten by a
>   snake.
> The work of holy men is as light and heat
> the work of vile men is trickery and shamelessness.[624]

Moreover, there are many scholars and learned men who do not profit from their knowledge. For them knowledge is a kind of learning by rote and committing concepts to memory without a profound understanding.

> Oh, there is many a learned man that hath no profit of his
>   knowledge;
> that person is one who commits knowledge to memory,
>   not one who loves it.[625]

The worst age and epoch is one in which the pen is in the hands of the perfidious and fraudulent scholars. As a result, great saints such as Hallaj were crucified on the gallows. When fools take over the affairs of the dominion, they will inevitably kill the prophets. When the authority is in the hands of the dissolute and extravagant rulers, Dhu'l-Nun will inevitably be in prison.

> When authority is in the hands of profligates
> a Dhu'l-Nun is inevitably in prison...
> When the pen is in the hand of a traitor
> unquestionably Mansur (al-Hallaj) is on a gibbet

261

When this affair belongs to the foolish
The necessary consequence is that *they kill the prophets*
(Quran 3:112).[626]

Being and Non-Being

There has been a lot of discussion about being in the history of human thought, but because of the profundity of the problem, and also the difference in viewpoints, there is a wide variety of opinions about it. Some theologians, for example, consider it to be *flatus vocis*, like other universals merely a sound without any meaning. Others consider it the most general and universal concept, devoid of any content. Still others view it as the most concrete and real of all concepts and make a distinction between the concept and the reality of being. Again, others distinguish between Absolute Being and relative or determined existence. They even apply two different names to these two kinds of being. They call the Absolute, which is the reality beyond and behind everything, "Being," and apply "existence" to its manifestation outside the Divine Essence in the cosmic plane, going back to a medieval usage that applied the term *Esse* to the Divine Reality and *existere* to its determinations or manifestations in the world, similar to the distinction between *wujud* (Being) and *kawn* (existence) in Ibn 'Arabi. Mulla Sadra, following some commentators of Ibn 'Arabi, differentiated between two meanings of the Absolute. In one sense, Absolute Being is the opposite of determined being and is the universal being that permeates all determined beings. According to him, this is the creative act of God, which is manifest in all beings. However, "Absolute" in this sense cannot be applied to God. The other sense is the Absolute that is beyond both absoluteness in the latter sense and determination; though transcending both, it is capable of becoming both. "Absolute" in this second sense can be applied to God.

Some Muslim philosophers starting with Avicenna make a distinction between accumulative (*mujami'*) and non-accumulative (*ghayr mujami'*) non-being. Accumulative non-being is capable of receiving being. A contingent quiddity, for example, does not exist but is indifferent with respect to existence and non-existence, depending

263

on the presence or absence of the cause. But non-accumulative non-being is the contrary of being, and hence it is impossible for it to exist.

However, most important in this connection is what some philosophers call Beyond-Being, which is most probably the same as what in Chinese philosophy, in Buddhism, and in some speculative mystics such as Rumi, is called "Emptiness" or "Non-Being." Here some explanation is in order.

In *The Republic* of Plato, for example, the Idea of the Good is Beyond-Being (*epekeina tes ousias*). *Ousia* etymologically means "a being," "a being among beings," or "an entity," and is usually translated as "substance." As used in this context, "Beyond-Being" means that the Idea of the Good is beyond determination and is not a thing among things. It is "no-thing." In metaphysical parlance, and according to the Neoplatonic interpretation, it is the "thingifier of things" without itself being a thing. This means that Plato's Idea of the Good is beyond any entification.

Rumi is one of the first to apply the expression "Absolute Being" (*wujud-i mutlaq*) to God, but we should bear in mind the fact that here "Absolute Being" is not the same as the *fiat* or the creative act of God, namely His command "Be!" (*kun*) by which He brought everything into being. He is Absolute in the sense that He is beyond any determination, including that of absoluteness and determination, boundedness or unboundedness. See how Rumi, in the following verses, elucidates that the Absolute Being (God) by His creative act (universal being) confers existence on all things:

> Who are we, O thou Soul of our souls,
> that we should remain in being beside thee?
> We and our existences are really non-existences;
> Thou art the Absolute Being which manifests the perishable phenomena.
> We all are lions, but lions on a banner,
> because of the wind, they are rushing onward
> from moment to moment.[627]

264

In this parable, things are like images on a banner, and the universal creative act is symbolized by the wind, which, sent by God, moves all images into being, and because of the wind they rush into existence from moment to moment.

> Their onward rush is visible and the wind is unseen;
> may that which is unseen not fail from us.
> Our wind and our being are of Thy gift;
> our whole existence is from Thy bringing us into being.
> Thou didst show the delightfulness of Being unto non-being,
> after thou hadst caused non-being to fall in love with Thee.
> Take not away the delightfulness of Thy bounty;
> take not away thy dessert and wine and wine-cup.
> And if thou take it away, who is there that will make inquiry?
> How should the picture strive with the painter?
> Do not look on us, do not fix Thy gaze on us;
> look on Thine own kindness and generosity.
> We were not, and there was no demand on our part,
> yet Thy grace was harkening to our unspoken prayer.[628]

"We," that is, our realities in Your Knowledge, "were not," that is, did not have cosmic or extra-deic existence, and we never spoke out our demand to exist; but Your unbounded Grace was listening to our unspoken demand and called us into existence.

> Before the painter and the brush the picture is helpless
> and bound like a child in the womb.
> Before Omnipotence all the people of the Divine court of audience
> are as helpless as the embroiderer's fabric before the needle.[629]

According to Mawlana, our eyes came into being as if in a state of slumber, and consequently we see the reverse side of things. Non-existents appear to us as existents, and conversely real existents appear to us as non-existent. We see the foam, but the sea is concealed from our view. We see the dust, but are unaware and heedless

265

of the wind. We believe what we see by our senses and then try to make deductions and inductions. In sum, we misplace affirmations and negations.

> God hath caused the non-existent
> to appear existent and magnificent.
> He hath caused the existent to appear
> in the form of non-existence.
> He hath concealed the Sea
> and made the foam visible.
> He hath concealed the Wind
> and displayed to thee the dust.
> The dust is whirling in the air,
> high as a minaret.
> How should the dust rise aloft of itself?
> Thou seest the dust on high,
> O infirm of sight,
> but the wind not,
> except through knowledge by induction.
> Thou seest the foam moving
> in every direction.
> Without the Sea, the foam
> hath no power to turn.
> Thou seest the foam by sense-perception
> and the Sea by induction.
> Thought is hidden but speech manifest.
> We deemed negation to be affirmation;
> we had an eye that saw only the non-existent.[630]

> The eye of the Sea is one thing and the foam another;
> leave the foam and look with the eye of the Sea.
> Day and night there is movement
> of foam-flecks from the Sea;
> thou beholdest the foam,
> but not the Sea. Marvelous![631]

> That which seems to you to be really existent
> is mere husk,
> while that which seems to have perished,
> that in reality is the root.[632]

Most people are mistaken about non-existence, not realizing that it is the true refuge in which they can find

their salvation. How do we obtain knowledge? By renouncing knowledge. How do we find peace? By renouncing peace with our carnal self. How do we seek real existence? By forsaking illusory existence.

Hence all the world have taken the wrong way,
for they are afraid of non-existence,
though it is the refuge in which they find salvation.
Whence shall we seek knowledge?
From renouncing knowledge.
Whence shall we seek peace?
From renouncing peace.
Whence shall we seek existence?
From renouncing existence.
Whence shall we seek the apple?
From renouncing the hand.[633]

In the piercing and penetrating metaphysical eyes of
Mawlana, Non-Being is a veritable mirror, which reflects
in itself being. What does he mean by that? To answer
this question we must ask, what are the characteristics
of a mirror that permit it to reflect the images of things?
The answer is that the mirror is pure nothingness, that
is, it is pure receptivity, having no qualities that would
distort the image. It should for example have no color. If
it had a specific color, it would not show the true color of
things as they are. It should have a plane and level surface. A concave or convex mirror would distort the image.

The essences of things, likewise, as pure receptivities,
are non-existent in themselves, able to receive the light
of Being, each according to its capacity. Again, those who
are poor in spirit can receive the blessings of God and
attain to the Kingdom of Heaven. Those who are finan-
cially poor are the mirror for the generosity of the rich. A
physician administers medicine where there is disease.
An orthopedist exerts his medical art where there are
fractured bones. God again sets right the hearts of those
that have broken hearts.

What is the mirror of Being?
Non-being.
Bring non-being as your gift if you are not a fool;

Being can be seen only in non-being.
The rich bestow generosity on the poor;
the clear mirror of bread is truly the hungry man.
Tinder, likewise, is the mirror
of that from which fire is struck.
Non-being and defeat, wherever they arise,
are the mirror which displays the excellence of all
    crafts.[634]

Since such is the description of non-existence, we should try to seek and stand upon this sea. In another context, Mawlana strikes the parable of a workshop where the master craftsman is free to make any artifact. The foundation of his workshop is non-existence, because it is empty and void, but his beautiful and masterly products are found everywhere outside the workshop. Indeed, the workshop of God, Who is the master of all masters, is non-existence; that is why the whole world is filled with His artifacts. And that is also the reason why adept Sufis and dervishes have outstripped others, for they have preferred non-existence to existence.

Since you have heard the description
of the sea of non-existence,
continually endeavor to stand upon this sea.
Inasmuch as the foundation of the workshop
is that non-existence which is void
and traceless and empty,
all master-craftsmen seek non-existence
and an empty place to exhibit their skill.
Necessarily the Lord, the Master of all masters,
His workshop is non-existence and naught.
Wherever this non-existence is greater,
the more manifest in that quarter
is the work and workshop of God.
Since the highest stage is non-existence,
the dervishes have outstripped all others.[635]

In the second book of the *Mathnawi*, Mawlana gives the same parable of the craftsman and the workshop. In traditional cultures, craftsmen mostly worked inside the workshop and could not be seen. So in order to see the craftsman one had to go inside the workshop, which was found to be empty, although the whole town was replete with his masterful works of craftsmanship. According to Mawlana, a work is a veil over the craftsman because he is present in the work, but you cannot see him outside that work. In other words, the work cannot exhaust the almost infinite possibilities latent in his craftsmanship, and also because he is far beyond the art manifested in that particular artifact. He who is outside the workshop is unaware of the craftsman. In order to see him one has to go inside the workshop, which is empty, interpreted by Mawlana as symbolizing non-existence, because there the craftsman is seen unveiled, unconditioned, and undetermined by any of his works, and hence is able to bring into being any work that is seen outside the workshop.

> The Worker is hidden in the workshop;
> go you in the workshop, see Him plain.
> Inasmuch as the work has woven a veil over the Worker
> you cannot see Him outside of that work.
> Since the workshop is the dwelling place of the Worker,
> he that is outside is unaware of Him.
> Come, then, into the workshop,
> that is to say, non-existence,
> that you may see the work
> and the Worker together.
> As the workshop is the place of clear sight,
> outside of the workshop there is only blindfoldedness.[636]

Previously we mentioned that according to Rumi form is brought into existence by the formless, and that formlessness is the origin and cause of all forms.[637] We could say that formlessness is an equivalent of non-being and form is on a par with being. As all forms proceed from the formless, so too all beings proceed and emanate from non-being. In another parable Rumi employs the symbolism of color to explain the same point. He might have taken the similitude of being as color from a verse of the Quran in which God is symbolically declared to be the best dyer (2:138). In several verses of the *Mathnawi*, Mawlana takes the world to be the dyeing-vat of God. Colorlessness is the origin of color and becomes bounded

269

and captivated by color by its manifestation in the phenomenal worlds. The Dyer is no doubt beyond coloration, but when He dyes, namely when the ontological event of manifestation takes place, there appears a world of opposition where opposition among colors becomes evident, and "a Moses comes into conflict with another Moses." But when colors are taken back to their original colorlessness, all oppositions vanish, and Moses and Pharaoh are reconciled.

> Since colorlessness became the captive of color,
> a Moses came into conflict with a Moses.
> When you attain unto the colorlessness you originally
> possessed
> Moses and Pharaoh are at peace with each other.[638]

Mawlana compares four levels of reality: non-being, imagination, actual being, and the sensible world. The realm of non-being is much vaster than the world of being (that is, actual existence), and between the two lies the world of imagination, which is narrower and more restricted than the realm of non-being but much more unbounded than the sphere of actual existence. The narrowest of them all is the world of sensation. The world of Divine Unity lies beyond the worlds of sensation, being, and imagination, and he who desires it must move in that direction.

> O God, do Thou reveal to the soul that place
> where speech grows without letters,
> that the pure soul may make of its head a foot
> towards the far stretching expanse of non-existence,
> an expanse most ample and spacious
> from which imagination and being are fed.
> The realm of imagination is narrower than non-existence;
> on that account imagination is the cause of grief.
> Actual existence again was ever narrower than imagination,
> hence in it moons become like the crescent.
> Again, the existence of the world of sense and color
> is narrower than this, for it is a narrow prison.
> The cause of narrowness is composition and number,

the senses always move towards composition.
Know that the world of Unification lies beyond senses;
if you want Unity, march in that direction.[639]

Unity, Plurality, and Unification

In traditional metaphysics the interrelation between
unity and plurality is an issue of utmost importance, and
constitutes the focus for almost all other issues. Look for
example at Plato's *Parmenides* where the absolutely
unique one (*hen*) becomes "one and many," which in its
turn descends into "many and one," and finally ends in
the world of sensation, which is sheer multiplicity. To cite
another example, consider Lao Tzu's magnificent system
where the Tao that has no name (pure unity) becomes
named and then is differentiated into "the ten thousand
things." To give another example, let us take into consideration Ibn 'Arabi's worldview, in which *Ahad*, or the
Unique One beyond all Names, Attributes, and distinctions, becomes *Wahid*, which is the Divine Essence taken
with all the Names and Attributes, from which the longi-
tudinal and latitudinal worlds with their increasing orders of multiplicity emerge.

In the Islamic worldview, the problem of unity gains
an additional significance since the first article of faith as
formulated in the first testimony is *tawhid* or unification,
which simply means turning back all multiplicity to its
original unity. The detractors of Sufism, and especially of
Ibn 'Arabi and Rumi, accuse them of the belief in what
they call *wahdat al-wujud*, a term never to be found in
their writings and that according to the detractors' very
superficial understanding is taken to mean the unity or
the identity of being in God and creatures, which leads
to pure immanentism, incarnationism, and finally mate-
rialism. Rumi's understanding of *tawhid* is concurrent
and congruent with the deepest layers of the Quran and
the prophetic traditions, which are either totally neglected by the literalists or are interpreted by them in the
most vulgar and ready-at-hand way.

The problem is made still more complicated by some
Western scholars who characterize Rumi's thought by

271

such prosaic and ambiguous terms as "pantheism," "panentheism," or "monism," and so on and so forth. Rumi is no doubt one of the greatest, if not the greatest, Sufi and speculative metaphysicians, and one cannot unveil the hidden mysteries of his thought unless one becomes intimate with the inmost secrets of his being.

See how Mawlana describes for us his *magnum opus*, the *Mathnawi*, as the "shop of Unity" (*dukkan-i wahdat*).

> Our *Mathnawi* is the shop of Unity;
> anything that you see there except the One is only an idol.
> Know that to praise an idol for ensnaring the vulgar
> is like (the Prophet's reference to)
> "the most exalted Cranes."[640]

In order to expound and elucidate how the One is manifested in the many, Rumi strikes some parables such as the appearance of waves on the sea. Waves are nothing but inundations and determinations of the seawater, and as such have no independent existence. They appear on the sea surface and soon vanish. We should not be veiled by the waves and thwarted from beholding the sea. Notwithstanding the appearance and disappearance of the waves, the sea ever remains in its primordial unity.

> It is the Sea of Unity: it has no match nor mate;
> its pearls and fishes are not other than its waves.
> Oh absurd, absurd to make aught its partner,
> far be it from that Sea and its pure waves!
> In the Sea there is no partnership or perplexity;
> but what can I say to him that sees double?
> Nothing, nothing.
> Since we are the mates of those who see double, O idola
>   tor,
> it is necessary to speak in the fashion of him who attrib
>   utes a partner to God.
> That Unity is beyond description and condition;
> nothing comes into the arena of speech except duality.
> Either like the double-seeing man drink in this duality,
> or close your mouth and be completely silent.[641]

Those who see double are those who see the waves and the Sea as quite different from and independent of each other. In other words, in their specious piety they see creatures quite separate from the Creator and almost independent of Him. This double-seeing is a sort of idol-worship in the sense that for them this world in which they are inevitably engaged is present, and God, Who is the Reality of all realities, seems to be absent. Consequently, they see the Sea and its waves, namely God and the world, as two independent realities.

There are other parables in the *Mathnawi* concerning unity and multiplicity on the basis of the symbolism of light. In one parable, Mawlana reminds us that we can look at a single lamp from two different perspectives. If you look at a lamp outwardly, it is made of an earthenware vessel containing a wick over which is a glass that protects it from the wind. From this point of view, lamps are different from each other, and hence there is a manifoldness and multiplicity of lamps. But if you fix your gaze on the light emanating from different lamps, there is unity without plurality. So all differences of opinion arise from the point of view from which we consider things.

> This earthenware lamp and this wick are different,
> but its light is not different,
> it is from Yonder.
> If thou keep looking at the glass
> thou wilt be lost,
> because from the glass arise numbers and duality.
> But if thou keep thy gaze fixed upon light
> thou wilt be delivered
> from dualism and the numbers of the finite body.
> From the difference of viewpoint, O kernel of existence,
> there arises the difference
> between believer, Zoroastrian and Jew.[642]

In a second simile, he strikes the parable of the sun and the sunlight emanating from it, which is one by nature but becomes many in relation to the courtyards of houses, which are divided by fences and walls.

273

Just as the single light of the Sun in heaven
is a hundred in relation to the courtyards,
but when you remove the walls separating them,
all their lights once again become one.[643]

But here Mawlana reminds the reader of a very significant point regarding similes, parables, and metaphors. Since almost all scriptures and books of sapiential
wisdom frequently use parables, metaphors, and symbols, Mawlana's warning here is opportune and must be
taken seriously into consideration. A parable or a symbol
in this context should not be interpreted in a literal
sense, which would totally distort it and divest it of its
meaning. Suhrawardi, the founder of Ishraqi or Illuminationist philosophy, accused Aristotle of having misunderstood the Presocratic philosophers because he took their
allegories and symbolisms in a purely literal sense.[644]
With good insight one should consider the intended point
of similarity, and not the points of dissimilarity in the similitude. According to Mawlana, if you say, for instance,
that Zayd is like a lion, and if you take this simile in a
literal sense, you would say that it is false because a lion
has a mane, paws, and a tail, whereas Zayd lacks all of
these. But this was not the intended point of comparison.
What you really purported to say was that Zayd is like a
lion in courage. So in reading parables and similes in
such contexts, we should be careful not to miss the point.
Following the above parable, Mawlana says:

> Differences and difficulties arise from this saying
> because this is not a complete similitude,
> it is only a comparison.
> Endless are the differences between the corporeal figure of
>   a lion
> and the figure of a courageous son of man.
> But at the moment of making the comparison,
> consider O thou who hast good insight,
> their oneness in respect of hazarding their lives.
> For, after all, the courageous man did resemble the lion,
> though he is not like the lion in all points of the defini-
>   tion.

274

> This abode does not contain any form that is one (with
>   other forms)
> so that I might show forth to thee a complete similitude.
> Still, I will bring to hand an imperfect comparison
> that I may redeem thy mind from confusion.[645]

In another simile Mawlana compares the light of our
two eyes. In outer form the eyes are two, but it is impossible to distinguish between them when one only considers their light. If again we have ten or a hundred lights in
one place, it is impossible to discriminate between their
lights, and they seem to be one single light. If you have a
hundred apples and quinces, and you press them, they
do not remain many, and produce one consistent juice.
Unlike in material things, in things spiritual there is no
division and number.

> When you look at the form, your eye is two;
> look at its light, which grew from the eye.
> It is impossible to distinguish the light of the two eyes
> when a man has cast his gaze upon their light.
> If ten lamps are present in one place,
> each differs in form from another;
> to distinguish without any doubt the light of each
> when you turn your face towards their light,
> is impossible.
> If you count a hundred apples or a hundred quinces,
> they do not remain a hundred
> but become one when you crush them.[646]

While we were in the spiritual world, we were simple
and of one substance. We were all spirit, without physical
head and foot, luminous as the sun and knotless like
pure water. But when that Divine light descended into
the body, it became many in number like the shadows of
a battlement. In order to make differences vanish, one
should raze the battlements in order to restore them to
their primordial unity.

> Simple were we and all one substance;
> we were all without head and without foot yonder.
> We were one substance, like the Sun;

we were knotless and pure, like water.
When that goodly Light took form,
it became many in number like the shadows of a battle-
    ment.
Raze ye the battlement with the mangonel,
that difference may vanish from amidst this company (of
    shadows).[647]

For Rumi, reality or everything partaking of reality is
either the Divine Essence, the Divine Attributes, or the
manifestations, determinations, and traces of the Divine
Attributes. If God is the First, the Last, the Hidden, and
the Manifest, His all-encompassing infinitude leaves no
room for any other reality. People are usually veiled by
outward forms, but when the veils are removed, we see
God there behind the veils. In the words of the Quran,
"Like a mirage in a wilderness which the thirsty man
thinks to be water, but when he comes to it he finds it to
be nothing, and he finds God there" (24:39).

When, for example we hear something, the air trans-
mits the sound to the cavity of our ear, to the little bones
inside the ear that receive the words and sounds. We generally attribute speaking to the tongue, and hearing to
the action of the conveying of air onto the auditory bones,
but according to Mawlana, the tongue, the bones, and
the air are veils. God is the Hearer and Speaker behind
those veils. In other words, human sight and hearing are
related to God's Attributes of Sight and Hearing.

What is that air within that little bone,
that air which receives the words and sounds
uttered by the story-teller.
The bone and the air are only a veil,
in the two worlds there is none except God.
He is the Hearer, He is the Speaker, unveiled;
for the ears belong to the head,
O you who have merited Divine recompense.[648]

In the sixth book of the *Mathnawi*, Mawlana depicts
for us in the best manner how the world is filled with the
reflection of the Divine Attributes and how the attributes
of perfection that we see around us are manifestations of

the Divine Names. According to Mawlana, the world and the creatures in it are like pure and limpid water, which manifest the Attributes of the Almighty God. The knowledge, justice, and clemency observed in human beings, for example, are the appearances of the same Divine Attributes in men, just like the appearance of a star of heaven in a stream. Kings are the theater for the manifestation of God's Kingship; the learned divines are mirrors of God's Wisdom. Generations after generations have elapsed; the moon is the same moon, but the water and the images in it are not the same. Justice is the same justice, knowledge is the same knowledge, but generations and people have changed.

> These attributes are like Ideal stars;
> know that they are established
> in the sphere of the Ideas.
> The beauteous are the mirror of His Beauty;
> love for them is the reflection of His desirability.[649]

Mawlana concludes by saying that the world of phenomena is a mere reflection of the Divine Perfections. Like those who have fallen into a deep slumber, we only need to wake up, "rub our eyes," remove the veils, and "perceive that all of them are really He."

> The whole sum of pictured forms is a mere reflection
> in the water of the river,
> When you rub your eyes
> you will perceive that all of them are really He.[650]

In order to attain to the station of unification, one should first remove all the veils that are impediments on the way.

> The Divine Sun has veiled Himself in man;
> apprehend this mystery, and God knows best what is
>   right.[651]

> The bone and the air are only a veil;
> in the two worlds there is none except God.[652]

How is it possible to daub this Sun
with a handful of earth? Pray, tell me.
Though you pour earth and a hundred ashes over its
    light,
it will come up above them.
What is straw that it should cover
the face of the water?
What is clay that it should cover the sun?[653]

But we have spoken so far as if all the veils in the way of *tawhid* and unification were the external phenomena. That is no doubt true, but the greatest veil, which is the most difficult to remove, is one's ego. Though it has a Divine origin, it has immersed itself in mundane affairs, worldly gains, and carnal passions and desires, and forgotten its Divine Source, even claiming the prerogative of Divinity for itself. It is impossible to realize *tawhid* in oneself unless one annihilates one's self in the Divine Self.

What is the meaning of "to learn
the knowledge of God's unity?"
To consume yourself
in the Presence of the One.
If you wish to shine like day,
burn up your night-like self-existence.
Melt away your existence as copper in the elixir,
in the Being of Him
who fosters and sustains existence.
You have fastened both your hands
tight on "I" and "We."
All this spiritual ruin is caused by dualism.[654]

Self-Annihilation

The Prophet of Islam is reported to have said: "Your worst enemy is your carnal ego, which is between your two flanks." Nothing is a greater barrier in the way of Union than one's egoistic self, which declares its autonomy from the Divine Self to the point of even denying it. One of the formulations of the first testimony of faith in the Quran is "There is no god but I" (16:2, 20:14, 21:25), which,

278

metaphysically expressed, means that there is no absolute self but the Divine Self. To assert one's self in the face of the Divine Self is a sort of dualism and amounts to *shirk*, that is, to making a partner with God in His Divinity.

> The idol of your self is the mother of all idols,
> because that idol is a snake
> while this idol is a dragon.[655]

> This egoism is the ladder climbed by the creatures,
> they must fall from this ladder in the end.
> The higher one goes the more foolish he is
> for his bones will be worse broken.
> This is the corollary of the subject
> and its fundamental principle is this:
> that to exalt one's self
> is to claim copartnership with God.
> Unless thou hast died
> and become living through Him,
> thou art an enemy seeking
> to reign in copartnership with Him.[656]

Mawlana, speaking through the mouth of a falcon addressing an owl, remarks that since our genus is not the genus of the King, we should annihilate our self in the Divine Self. When this happens, He remains alone. The individual soul is burned up in the Divine Sun.

> Since my genus is not the genus of my King
> my ego has passed away
> for the sake of His Ego.
> Inasmuch as my ego passed away,
> He remained alone.
> I roll at the feet of His horse, like dust.
> The individual self became dust,
> and the only signs of it
> are the marks of His feet on its dust.
> Become dust at His feet
> for the sake of this mark,
> in order that you may become
> the crown on the head of the lofty.
> Oh, there is many a one whom the form waylaid:

279

he aimed at the form and in reality
struck at God.[657]

He who has lost his self in the Divine Self is the best
of beings. He has made his attributes vanish in the Divine Attributes, and by annihilating his ego he has gained
an everlasting selfhood. All spirits and bodies obey him.
One reaches this lofty and exalted station only through
the Divine Grace. This self-annihilation is not done by
compulsion, but by an act of free choice.

> God said: "This overpowered man
> is that non-existent one
> who is only relatively non-existent,
> have sure faith.
> Such a non-existent one
> who hath gone from himself
> is the best of beings
> and the great one among them.
> He hath passed away in relation to the Divine Attributes,
> but in passing away from selfhood
> he really hath the life everlasting.
> All spirits are under his governance,
> all bodies too are in his control.
> He that is overpowered in Our Grace
> is not compelled;
> nay, he is one who freely chooses
> devotion to Us.
> In sooth, the end of free-will
> is that his free-will should be lost here.
> The free agent would feel no savor
> if at last he did not become
> entirely free of egoism.[658]

Mawlana, alluding to the Quranic verse "Everything
is perishing except His Face" (28:88), remarks that this
verse implies the annihilation of the egoistic self, which
claims self-styled permanence. We should not seek to exist unless we are in His Face. When man has passed
away from his selfish ego, he has indeed passed from
"everything is perishing" to "except His Face."

Everything is perishing except His Face,
Unless thou art in His face, do not seek to exist.
When anyone has passed away from himself
in My Face,
everything is perishing is not applicable to him.
Because he is in *except*, he has transcended *not*,
Whosoever is in *except* has not perished.
Whosoever is uttering "I" and "we" at the door,
he is turned back from the door and is continuing in
    not.[659]

According to Mawlana, sometimes the Attributes of the Eternal God manifest themselves to the human being, and when this occurs, the mantle of the creaturely attributes is burnt up. As will be explained later, in Mawlana's view annihilation in God never means that the servant becomes God or God becomes the servant. As he remarks here, the man is the same man, but because of the manifestation of the Divine Attributes, the human attributes are merged and absorbed in their primordial Origin.

When the Attributes of the Eternal have shone forth,
then the mantle of temporality is burned.[660]

Thou art a lover of God
and God is such that when He comes,
there is not a single hair of thee
remaining.
At that look of His, a hundred like thee
vanish away,
Methinks, sire, thou art in love
with self-naughting.
Thou art a shadow and in love with the sun;
the sun comes, the shadow is naughted speedily.[661]

Annihilation of the self is a consequence of following in the footsteps of the Prophet and becoming his spiritual inheritor by performing both the obligatory and the supererogatory ritual acts and injunctions. In a sacred tradition known as the *hadith* of proximity by supererogatory acts (*qurb al-nawafil*), God says: "My servant ever draws nigh unto me until I love him, and when I love him

I become his hearing whereby he hears, I become his sight whereby he sees, I become his hand whereby he assails, and I become his foot whereby he walks." According to this tradition the servant remains the servant, but his attributes are transmuted. He becomes the theatre of manifestation of the Divine Attributes.

> Absolutely, that voice is from the King,
> though it be from the larynx of God's servant.
> God has said to the saint, "I am thy tongue and thy eye;
> I am thy senses and I am thy good pleasure and thy
>   wrath.
> ...Sometimes I say to thee, 'It is thou,'
> sometimes 'It is I';
> whatever I say, I am the Sun
> Illuminating all."[662]

The station of annihilation (*fana'*) is also called intoxication or spiritual inebriation (*sukr*), because as in drunkards the ego is lost; possessors of this station may make ecstatic utterances (*shatahiyyat*) that seem very paradoxical to laymen but are very significant for the adepts of Sufism, simply because according to them in such an exalted station the speaker is God Himself, the consciousness of the speaker having been absorbed in the Divine Consciousness. The most typical example in this connection is the *ana al-Haqq* ("I am the Truth") attributed to Hallaj, which ended in his crucifixion in Baghdad. Opinions about the statement of Hallaj vary, ranging from considering it utter disbelief (*kufr*) to the highest degree of glorification. Hafiz, the great Persian poet, alluding to Hallaj, says:

> That companion by whom the pinnacle
> of the gallows became exalted
> said that his crime was only
> that he divulged the Divine mysteries.[663]

The Sufi master Shaykh Mahmud Shabistari in his *Rose-Garden of the Divine Mysteries*, referring to God's addressing Moses through the burning bush, asks whether is it permissible that a fiery bush should say "I

282

am God" (or, "I am who I am") but it is not permissible that a felicitous man should say this.[664] In his *Diwan* of poetry, Hajj Mulla Hadi Sabzawari, the famous Persian sage-philosopher of the nineteenth century, has the following to say in this regard:

> There is no Moses now to hear the
> song of "I am God";
> otherwise there is no tree in which
> this whisper is not to be heard.[665]

Ibn 'Arabi believes that annihilation is not the supreme station for the spiritual wayfarer because the traveler is annihilated in Divinity, and Divinity essentially and primarily belongs to God, and can only belong to man secondarily and accidentally. A higher stage in spiritual realization is subsistence (*baqa'*) where the Sufi returns to the stage of servanthood (*'ubudiyyah*), a station intrinsically belonging to man. In a chapter on the ecstatic utterances in *The Meccan Revelations*, Ibn 'Arabi states that the ecstatic utterances, though made by great Sufis, indicate that the utterer has not yet reached the highest stage of perfection.[666]

Shams-i Tabrizi also believed that in the ecstatic utterances of Hallaj and Bayazid Bastami there are still some traces of the ego left. We saw earlier that in the first encounter of Mawlana and Shams, the latter asked him this question: "Who is greater in spiritual rank, Bayazid or the Prophet Muhammad? Why did Bayazid say, 'Glory be to Me, How majestic is my state?' and Prophet Muhammad said, 'O My Lord we did not worship Thee as we should have'?" Faced by this paradoxical koan, Rumi was awakened from his spiritual slumber.

However, since the detractors of Hallaj have been legion, Mawlana tries to defend him from many different angles.

To begin with, Mawlana compares Hallaj with Pharaoh. Both of them said: "I am God," but there is a great difference in the purport of the two statements. Mansur Hallaj claimed the Divinity for God and not for himself, and in order to realize *tawhid* he naughted his selfish ego

283

in the Divinity. But Pharaoh, on the other hand, denied
God and claimed the Divinity for himself.

> A Pharaoh said: "I am God," and was laid low,
> a Mansur said: "I am God" and was saved.
> The former "I" is followed by God's curse,
> and the latter "I" by God's mercy, O loving man.
> For that one (Pharaoh) was a black stone,
> and this one (Hallaj) a cornelian.
> That one was an enemy to the light,
> and this one passionately enamored of it.
> This "I," O presumptuous meddler,
> was "He" in the inmost consciousness;
> through oneness with the Light
> and not through the doctrine of incarnation.[667]

In this last line, Mawlana takes Hallaj's utterance, "I
am God," to mean "I am He," that is, I am not other than
the Divine Ipseity from which I have originated. There is
no duality between us that would lead to copartnership
in the Divinity. Furthermore, this union is that of light
with Light, and is not based on the doctrine of incarnationism, in which, like the immersion of wool in water,
God becomes one with the creature.

In the first testimony of faith, "There is no god except
God," there is both a negation and an affirmation. When
you have eliminated your existence, what remains? There
remains only "except God" (illa, magar). This means that
through self-annihilation one flees from everything other
than God and clings to "except God."

> When the Shaykh (Hallaj) said,
> "I am God" and carried it through,
> he throttled all the blind skeptics.
> When a man's "I" is naughted from existence,
> then what remains? Consider, O denier.
> If you have an eye, open it and look!
> After "no" what else remains?
> "Except."[668]

> To say that "I" out of the proper time
> is a curse;
> to say that "I" at the proper time

is a mercy.
The "I" of Mansur certainly became a mercy;
the "I" of Pharaoh became a curse, mark it well.[669]

Mawlana strikes some parables and similes in order
to clarify this complicated problem. Almost all these parables have one thing in common: that self-annihilation
as understood by the Sufis is a process of self-transformation whereby one's attributes and hence one's ego become Divine. If one does not follow an authentic spiritual
way, there is of course the possibility that one's ego will
become demonic.

In the first parable, Mawlana cites the example of lu-
natics, who were believed to be possessed by the genies.
When a genie gains possession of a man, the attributes
of humanity disappear from him. What the man says is
really said by the genie. If a genie has such an influence
over men, how much more could be the power of the Creator of the genie to reabsorb men in His Attributes.

When a genie prevails over a man,
the attributes of humanity disappear from the man;
whatsoever he says, that genie will have said it—
the one who belongs to this side will have spoken
from the one who belongs to yonder side.
Since a genie hath this influence and rule,
how much more powerful indeed
must be the Creator of the genie?[670]

In another simile, Mawlana gives the example of an
intoxicated man who has drunk down draughts of wine.
If such a pot-valiant fellow drinks the blood of a fierce
lion, you will say that the wine did it, and if he speaks
with perfect eloquence, you will say the wine has spoken
those words.

A wine hath this power to excite disturbance and commotion;
hath not the Light of God that virtue and potency
to make you entirely empty of self
so that you should be laid low
and He should make the Word lofty?

Though the Quran is dictated
from the lips of the Prophet,
if any one says God did not speak it,
he is an infidel.[671]

In the fifth book of the *Mathnawi*, Mawlana strikes the parable of a lover and his beloved. The beloved asks the lover: "Do you love yourself or me more?" He replies:

> I am dead to myself and living by thee. I have become non-existent to myself and my own attributes and existent through thee. I have forgotten my own knowledge. I have lost all thought of my own power and have become powerful through thy power. If I love myself, I must have loved thee and if I love thee, I must have loved myself.[672]

In other words, according to Mawlana, the lover is totally absorbed and annihilated in the Attributes of the Beloved, and through this annihilation he is purged of his self-conceited ego.

According to the ancients, some minerals could be transformed into nobler ones as the result of the action of the celestial spheres or heavenly bodies. A stone, for example, could be turned into a ruby by the steady and blazing radiance of the sun. This forms the foundation for another parable regarding the transformation of attributes.

> As the stone that is entirely turned
> into pure ruby,
> it is filled with the qualities of the sun.
> That stony nature does not remain in it,
> back and front, it is filled with sunniness.
> Afterwards, if it love itself,
> that self-love is love of the sun, O youth!
> And if it love the sun with all its soul,
> it is undoubtedly love of itself.
> Whether the pure ruby loves itself
> or whether it loves the sun,
> there is really no difference
> in these two loves:
> both sides are naught
> but the radiance of the sunrise.[673]

In the second book of the *Mathnawi*, Rumi gives many other similes. But the reader should again be reminded that he should not take these parables in a quite literal sense. Rather, he should be mindful of the hidden allusions in the similes.

When, for example, lifeless bread is eaten and is associated with life, it becomes living and is turned into the substance of life. When dark firewood becomes the companion of fire, its darkness departs and is turned into light. Even a dead ass when thrown into a salt-mine abandons its asininity. God as the supreme dyer has dyed everything in His dyeing vat. If a Sufi fell into the dyeing-vat and you told him to arise, he would say in rapture: "I am the vat. Do not blame me!"

To give another simile, if you put dark iron in hot fire, little by little it loses its darkness and takes on the qualities of the fire; it starts to boast of its fieriness, and without a fleshy tongue it would tell you: "I am fire, I am fire."

> The color of the iron is naughted
> in the color of the fire,
> the iron boasts of its fieriness
> though it is silent.
> When it has become like gold of the mine in redness,
> then without tongue its boast is "I am the fire."
> It has become glorified by the color and nature of the fire,
> it says, "I am the fire, I am the fire.
> I am the fire; if thou have doubt and suspicion,
> Make trial, put thy hand upon me.
> I am the fire, if it seem dubious to thee
> lay thy face upon my face
> for one moment."[674]

But nonetheless Mawlana, like Shams, maintains that the state of Divinity belongs to God alone, and having his encounter with Shams in mind, he says that it is always better in the Muhammadan Way to return to what is essential to man, namely humanity, or in other words to spiritual poverty (*faqr*) and servanthood (*bandigi*) rather than Lordship (*rububiyyah, khudawandi*). Like the Prophet, one should live in the community as one among many. In other words, one should advance from the station of annihilation to that of subsistence (*baqa'*) and live as a servant who sees everything in the mirror of God.

The matter is most beautifully explained in the story of a bird and a fowler who had wrapped himself up in grass and drawn over his head a handful of roses and red anemones like a cap in order that the birds might think he was a clump grass.

> A bird went into a meadow:
> there was a trap set for fowling.
> Some grain had been placed on the ground
> and the fowler was ensconced there in ambush.
> He had wrapped himself in leaves and grass,
> that the wretched prey might slip off from the path.
> A little bird approached him in ignorance,
> then it hopped round and ran up to the man.
> (The clever bird immediately guessed that he was a man)
> and said to him, "Who are you, clad in green,
> in the desert amidst all these wild animals?"
> He replied, "I am an ascetic severed from mankind,
> I have become content to live here with some grass.
> I adopted asceticism and piety as my religion and practice,
> because I saw before me the appointed end of my life.
> My neighbor's death had given me warning
> and upset my worldly business and shop.
> Since I shall be left alone at the last
> it behooves me not to become friendly
> with every man and woman.
> I shall turn my face to the grave at the last;
> it is better that I should make friends with the One.[675]

There goes on a very long controversy between the fowler and the bird. The fowler defends his original stance, that is, the superiority of a life of monasticism, and the bird upholds life in a community as enjoined by the Prophet Muhammad. In his long argument the fowler says:

> Have you not the verse
> *The present life is only a play?* (Quran 47:36)
> You have squandered your goods

and have become afraid.
Look for your clothes ere night comes on,
do not waste the day in idle talk.
I have chosen a place of seclusion in the desert,
I have perceived that mankind are stealers of clothes.
Half of life is lost in desire for a charming friend,
the other half of life in anxieties caused by foes.[676]

The bird starts a debate with the fowler concerning monasticism and reminds the fowler that the Prophet has forbidden his community to practice monasticism, and is reported to have said: "There is no monasticism in Islam."

The bird said to him: "O Khwaja,
don't stay in monastic seclusion;
Monasticism is not good in the religion of Ahmad.
The Prophet has forbidden monasticism;
how have you embraced a heresy, O trifler?
The conditions of Islam are the Friday worship and the
    public prayers,
to enjoin good and forbid evil,
to bear patiently affliction caused by the ill-natured,
and to confer benefit on God's creatures
bounteously as the clouds.
O father, the best of the people is he who benefits the peo-
    ple;
If you are not a stone, why are you consorting with the
    clod?
Live amongst the community that is the object of Divine
    Mercy;
do not forsake the religion of Ahmad, be ruled by his
    practice...
Since the Messenger of Allah was the Prophet of the
    sword,
the people of his community are heroes and champions.
In our religion the right thing is war and glory;
in the religion of Jesus, the right thing is cave and moun-
    tain."[677]

There is a long debate between the two interlocutors on this theme. Finally, Mawlana wants to bring the story to an end, or as he says, make it "short and nimble."

The fowler spoke on one side
and the bird spoke on the other.
Their debate on this subject was prolonged
by the vehemence with which they argued.
Make the *Mathnawi* nimble and pleasing to the heart,
abridge and shorten their controversy.[678]

In short, the bird asked him: "Whose is this wheat?"
and he replied that it was the deposit of an orphan who
had no guardian. It had been entrusted to him because
people considered him to be trustworthy. So the bird,
driven by necessity and in a sore plight, with the permission of the fowler, while giving the guarantee for payment, ate something of the wheat. The poor bird had no
sooner eaten than it was caught in the trap because of
the artifice, cunning, and hypocrisy of the ascetic.

The bird said: "This is a fit punishment
for one who listens
to the beguiling talk of ascetics."
"Nay," said the ascetic: "It is a fit punishment
for the greedy wretch who incontinently devours
the property of orphans."[679]

The bird being entrapped began to lament so much
that the trap and the fowler trembled at the grief displayed by the bird. But the bird little by little came to
realize that to be caught in the trap was the cause of its
good fortune and felicity, and the best choice was the way
of submission and contentment.

Afterwards, the bird began to lament in such wise
that the trap and the fowler trembled at the grief,
crying: "My back is broken by conflicting motives in my
    heart.
Come, O Beloved, rub Thy hand on my head.
Under Thy hand my head hath a great relief from pain,
Thy hand is a miracle in bestowing favor.
Do not take away Thy shadow from my head,
I am restless, restless, restless.
All sorts of sleep have quitted mine eye,
in my passion for thee, O Thou who art envied
by the cypress and the jasmine.

290

Though I am not worthy of Thy favor,
what matter if for a moment,
Thou ask after an unworthy one
in a great anguish?
What right to Thy favor,
forsooth, had Not-being,
to which Thy grace opened such doors?
...O Thou by whom my shop and dwelling is ruined,
how shall not I wail when Thou rackest my heart?
How shall I flee from Thee since without Thee none liveth,
and without Thy lordship no slave hath existence?
Take my life, O Source of my life,
for without Thee
I have become weary of my life."[680]

Mawlana as usual ends the story with the adventure of love. Love never falls prey to anyone. It can never be ensnared by cunning and subterfuge. It is better to be caught in the trap of love. Love silently whispers into our ears: "To be the prey is better than to be the hunter." It is better to remain a mote than to claim to be the sun, to be a moth rather than a candle, to remain a servant of God rather than to claim Lordship.

That which is worth pursuing is Love alone,
but how should He be contained
in anyone's trap?
Yet perchance thou mayst come
and be made His prey,
thou mayst discard the trap
and go into His trap.
Love is saying very softly into my ears,
"To be the prey is better than to be the hunter."
Make thyself My fool and be a dupe;
Renounce the high estate of the sun,
become a mote!
Become a dweller at My door and be homeless;
do not pretend to be a candle, be a moth,
that thou mayst taste the savor of life,
and contemplate the sovereignty
hidden in servitude.[681]

As Plato's prisoner of the cave, having beheld and contemplated the glory of the sun, upon returning to the cave sees everything as the reverse of what he used to see in the cave, so too the servant who claimed Divinity in the state of annihilation, being restored to his normal state of humanity, observes that everything in this world is topsy-turvy, and its real nature is not apparent.

> In this world you see the shoes upside down;
> the title of "Kings" is conferred on bondsmen.
> Many a one who deserves to mount the scaffold
> with a halter on his throat,
> a crowd gathers round him
> crying, "Behold an emperor!"
> They are like the tombs of infidels,
> outwardly the robes of paradise;
> while within them is the Wrath of God,
> Almighty and Glorious.
> The worldling has been plastered like the tombs,
> the veil of self-conceit has been drawn over him.[682]

> It is certain that every seeker of princedom
> is thrown into captivity before he gains it.
> Know that what is depicted on this mundane frontispiece
> is preposterous;
> every slave to the world is named "lord of the world."
> O wrong-thinking perversely-acting body,
> thou that hast enthralled
> a hundred-thousand freemen,
> abandon this guileful plotting for a time,
> live free a few moments ere thou die.[683]

Eternal Decree (*Qada*) and Apportionment (*Qadar*)

There are two words much used in Islamic literature that have also found their way into the common and day-to-day language of Muslims. The first word, *qada*, is derived from a root that means to make a decisive judgment. Let us imagine a judge who has perfect knowledge about a certain legal case and also about all the laws and principles of jurisprudence; in other words, he is a perfect judge with perfect knowledge of his vocation. This means that all his judgments are decisive, because they are not made according to his arbitrary will, but are rather based on his truly flawless and impeccable knowledge. So the root *qada* in Arabic (from which the active participle *qadi*, meaning "judge," is derived) means to make a decisive judgment in accordance with certain and indubitable knowledge. Now, the two words *qada* and *qadar* are specifically applied to God with regard to His Acts. *Qada* in this context means the decisive judgment or the "eternal Decree" of God concerning all things as required by their realities in the Divine Knowledge. In the Quran we find the word in its different grammatical moods and cases, for example *wa qada rabbuka* ("your Lord has eternally decreed..." (17:23)). We use here the word "eternally" because Divine Knowledge is eternal and beyond contingencies such as time and space.

Qadar, which here we have translated as "apportionment," means the determination of a thing that existed eternally in the Divine Knowledge in a specific space and time when it comes into being in the sensible world. In other words, something that has been decreed eternally comes into being in due time and place according to its specific measures.

Now, things are determined as things in accordance with their realities as objects (*ma'lum*) in the Divine Knowledge (*'ilm*). The Divine Essence, being absolutely simple, is beyond any determination. The first determination occurs when the Divine Names and Attributes, which are the entifications of the Essence, together with

293

all their concomitant determinations (i.e. the realities of all possible things), are manifested in the Divine Knowledge. In this so-called cognitive determination (*ta'ayyun-i 'ilmi*) or epistemic self-manifestation (*tajjali-yi 'ilmi*) things have eternal self-subsistence (*thubut*) on the ontological level of Absolute Hiddenness (*ghayb-i mutlaq*).

These self-subsistent realities in the Divine Knowledge demand of God that He give them existence outside the Divine Essence. As stated by the Quranic verse "And He giveth you all that you ask of Him" (14:34), God does not begrudge them existence in the external world. In Sufi terminology, this is called the second de-termination (*ta'ayyun-i thani*). It is also called "the Breath of the Compassionate" (*nafas al-Rahman*) in analogy with human breath, which by being articulated creates letters and words. In the language of the Quran, it is called *qadar*, which means "measure": "Surely we have created everything in due measure" (54:49); "And there is not a thing but its treasuries are with us, and We send it not down but in a known measure (*bi-qadarin ma'lum*)" (15:21).

In Arabic it is said *qadara'l-shay'*, that is, "he made a thing by measure" or "he proportioned it according to a measure." This world of ours, moreover, is called *'alam al-taqdir*, "the world of measure," because nothing comes into being except at an apportioned time and in a specific space measured according to its own proper and peculiar specifications, just as things existing in the Divine Knowledge exist on the level of the eternal Decree (*qada*). One night in the latter nights of Ramadan, the month of fasting, is called *laylat al-qadr*, because it is believed that the Holy Quran was revealed on this night and that it is the night wherein the means of subsistence are appor-tioned.[684]

Before proceeding to a discussion about these two sig-nificant terms in the *Mathnawi*, it is necessary to under-score certain points: first, that belief in the eternal De-cree) of God does not mean a sort of determinism and fatalism as is usually understood or as is interpreted by some who do not know enough about Sufi metaphysics, as we shall discuss in a section on determinism and free choice; second, that according to some, for example Ibn 'Arabi, the *a priori* knowledge of the eternal Decree of God is extremely rare and hence is the most perfect kind of knowledge, as evidenced by the Holy Quran in the story of Moses and the Green Prophet; third, that just as the number two cannot complain and say: "Why am I the number two and not the number three or another number?" because each number is unique and a number in its own right and a real possibility in the order of numbers, so too every being is a real possibility in the almost infinite order of entities being both unique and irreplaceable; and fourth, that Divine Knowledge is not arbitrary, that is, subject to capricious volition, but is congruous with the reality of the object known (*ma'lum*) as existing in the Divine Knowledge. That is why according to the Quran, "God has the all-conclusive proof over every thing (*fa li'Llah al-hujjah al-balighah*)" (6:159) because this knowledge is not arbitrary and is in accord with the nature of the thing known.

The hand of the eternal Decree (*qada*) according to Mawlana is very strong, so one should not grapple with it, because otherwise one will be defeated. It is irresistible, so the best thing is to surrender to it.

> Do not grapple with the eternal Decree),
> O fierce and furious one,
> lest the eternal Decree also
> pick a quarrel with thee.
> One must be dead
> in the presence of the Decree of God
> so that no blow may come
> from *the Lord of the daybreak* (Quran 113:1).[685]

When we proceed to do something or take a task at hand, its faults and defects are concealed from our view. We have given ourselves up to the task because the Creator has veiled its faultiness from our vision. If it had become visible to us, we would have surely shunned it and distanced ourselves from it. If repentance, which is the outcome of the work, had shown itself in the beginning, we would never have ventured to do it.

Therefore God at first veiled that from souls
in order that we might perform that action
in accordance with the Divine Decree.
When the Divine Decree brought its ordainment into view
the eye was opened so that regret arrived.
This regret is another manifestation of the Divine Decree.
Abandon this regret, worship God.[686]

When the Divine Decree comes to pass, the whole world becomes straitened and cramped so that there is no escape. By the Divine Decree the sweet becomes bitter and brings anguish to the mouth.

The Holy Prophet said, "When the Decree comes,
the widest expanse becomes narrow;
when the Decree comes the eyes are veiled."[687]

When the Divine Decree comes
wisdom goes to sleep,
the moon becomes black,
the sun is stopped from shining.
How is this disposal of things by the Divine Decree singu-
lar?
Know that it is by the Divine Decree
that the denier disbelieves in the Divine Decree.[688]

Every disease has its proper cure; a fur, for example, is a cure for the pain of cold; but if God wills, cold will penetrate a hundred furs and one will feel tremors even if one wraps oneself up in manifold furs.

When the Decree comes, the physician is made foolish,
and the medicine loses its beneficial effect.[689]

However, according to Mawlana, the perception of the perfect gnostic (*'arif*) is never veiled by secondary causes; it can penetrate to the root and origin of things. But when a man is squint-eyed, metaphysically speaking, he is only able to see the branches.[690]

When something is decreed, it is inescapable; there can be no scheming and no stratagems to prevent it. One cannot tell friends from foes. What is one to do in such circumstances? The best choice, according to Rumi, is supplication, humble prayer, glorification of God, and the performance of ritual acts.

> When the Divine Decree comes to pass
> you see naught but the outward;
> you do not distinguish enemies from friends.
> Since such is the case
> begin humble supplication,
> set about lamenting, glorifying God and fasting.
> Lament continually,
> crying, "O Thou who well knowest the hidden things,
> do not crush us beneath the stone of evil contrivance."[691]

Another way of putting this is that one should take flight from the Divine Decree (*qada*) to the Divine Destiny (*qadar*). Once a great saint was standing by a wall. The wall suddenly started to fall down, and the saint immediately fled from it lest he should be hurt by the falling rubble. His disciples, objecting, asked: "Why are you escaping the Divine Decree?" He promptly answered: "I am fleeing from the Divine Decree to the Divine Destiny."[692]

> When the Decree puts forth its head from Heaven
> all the intelligent become blind and deaf;
> fishes are cast out of the sea,
> the snare catches miserably the flying bird...
> All are lost except that one
> who has taken refuge with the Decree...[693]

In the above verses, Heaven is a reference to the sphere of Divine Decree (*qada*), and earth naturally indicates the realm of the spatial and temporal measure (*qadar*), as also indicated by the following verses:

> Whatsoever may come from Heaven to the earth,
> the earth has no refuge or device or hiding-place...
> O thou who art a part of this earth,
> do not lift up thy head in rebellion.
> When thou seest the decree of God,
> do not withdraw disobediently.[694]

297

Contentment with the Divine Decree is one of the highest stations in the spiritual path, and some of the sages and saints are so absorbed in and content with the Divine Decree that they never ask or beg anything of God lest they should transgress their submission to it.

> I know another class of saints
> whose mouths are closed to supplication
> because of the contentment
> that is subservient to those noble ones.
> It has become unlawful for them
> to seek to avert destiny.
> In submitting to destiny
> they experience a peculiar delight.
> It would be an act of infidelity
> for them to crave release.[695]

In short, one should say that absolutely nothing happens in this universe except in accordance with the Divine Decree. We can also safely say that all the laws governing the universe are nothing but instruments for executing and effectuating the Divine Commands. So the best thing to do is first to take cognizance of this fact and then to submit oneself humbly to the ordainment of Heaven.

> Hear this much: since all action in the universe
> only comes to pass by the command of the Maker,
> when the Decree of God becomes the pleasure of His servant
> the servant becomes a willing slave to His Decree.
> Wheresoever the Eternal Command takes its course,
> living and dying are one to him.
> He lives for God's sake, not for riches;
> he dies for God's sake, not from fear and pain.
> His faith is for the sake of doing His will,
> not for the sake of paradise and its trees and streams.
> His abandonment of infidelity
> is also for God's sake,
> not for fear lest he go into the Fire.

298

The servant of God whose disposition and character is
like this:
does not the world move according to His command and
behest?[696]

Determinism and Free Choice

Are human beings determined and doomed to a predestined fate, or are they on the contrary free to choose their
courses of action? To be free means to be able either to
do or not to do something. Those who believe in determinism or fatalism (*jabr*) maintain that since everything
in the universe including the chain of causality is determined, there is no room for free choice (*ikhtiyar*), and
even what we consider to be our free choice is not free
from the concatenated chain of causality, and hence is
determined. The proponents of free choice (or *liberum ar-
bitrium*) maintain that man is not doomed to one course
of action, and he can, in other words, choose among different alternatives. When you say: "I will do such and
such an act," or: "I will not do it," this means that your
will is free to choose either of the two alternatives. Let us
start our discussion about determinism and free choice
by relating a story from the fifth book of the *Mathnawi*,
in which Mawlana absolutely rejects any kind of determinism and confirms man's power of free choice, showing that determinism in human acts is not acceptable in
any religion.

A certain man in the manner of thieves climbed up
the walls of an orchard and started to scatter the fruits.
Suddenly the owner of the orchard arrived and asked
him: "What are you doing?" The man replied: "Why do
you vulgarly blame a servant of God if he eats from God's
orchard the dates that God has bestowed upon him as a
gift? Why are you stingy at the table of the All-Rich Lord?"
Upon hearing this the owner of the orchard fetched a rope
to give an answer to that fine fellow. He at once bound
him tightly to the tree and thrashed him on the back and
legs with a cudgel. The thief cried that he was innocent
and begged him to have mercy and to have reverence for
God and stop hitting him with the cudgel.

299

He answered, "With God's cudgel this servant of His
is soundly beating the back of another servant.
It is God's cudgel and the back and sides belong to Him;
I am only the slave and instrument of His command."
The thief said, "O cunning knave,
I make a recantation of necessitarianism (*jabr*):
there is will, there is free will, there is free will."[697]

There are various theories advanced by determinists
and advocates of free choice. The absolute determinists
(also called necessitarians) hold that all our actions, including even their content and their intention, are determined, and so there is no room left for free choice. The
metaphysical libertarians, on the contrary, believe that
we are free to choose both the course and the content of
our actions. One can perhaps adduce the Mu'tazilites as
an example of this position. They believe in the so-called
theory of "the creation of acts" (*khalq al-a'mal*) by which
they mean that humans create both the course and the
content of their actions.

Their antagonists, the Ash'arites, on the other hand,
believe in the so-called theory of acquisition (*kasb*). According to this theory, when we intend to do something,
it is God who creates the course of action related to that
intention, and we only acquire it.

The Shi'ite theologians, however, hold that "there is
neither absolute determinism nor absolute free choice,
but the real solution rests in the middle way between the
two" (*la jabr wa la tafwid bal al-amr bayn al-amrayn*).
They might mean perhaps that man's freedom of choice
is not absolute like God's, but he is not at the same time
determined like pebbles and stones. It is in this vein that
Hajj Mulla Hadi Sabzawari, the nineteenth-century Persian philosopher, in his *Sharh-i Manzumah*, enunciates
his belief in this regard: "The act is God's act, but it is
our act" (*al-fi'l fi'l Allah wa huwa fi'luna*).[698]
Analogously, Mawlana has said:

Consider both our action and the action of God,
regard our action as existent; this is evident.
If the action of created beings be not in the midst
then say not to any one, "Why have you acted thus?"

300

The creative act of God brings our action into existence,
our actions are the effects of the creative act of God.[699]

Rumi does not expect us to accept the freedom of human choice (*ikhtiyar*) on kind faith. He wants to bolster it
with the following reasons or arguments:
First, it is self-evident in our moral awareness:

Beyond doubt we possess a certain power of choice;
you cannot deny the plain evidence of the inward
    sense.[700]

There is a power of choice in injustice and wrongdoing;
this is what I meant by this Devil and carnal soul.[701]

There is an invisible power of choice within us;
when it sees two objects of desire it waxes strong.[702]

Second, hesitation between two alternatives is another proof demonstrating free choice. Sometimes it so
happens that we are bewildered and caught between several alternatives, and we hesitate as to which of them to
choose. This itself proves that we are free in our choice.

When you say, "Tomorrow should I do this or should I do
    that?"
it is a proof of free will, O idol.[703]

When we are left vacillating between two actions,
how can this vacillation be without free will?
How should he whose hands and feet are chained
say, "Shall I do this or shall I do that?"
Can there ever be in my head such a dilemma as this:
"Shall I walk on the sea or shall I fly aloft?"
But there is this vacillation,
"Shall I go to Mosul for trade or shall I go to Babylon for
    magic?"
Vacillation, then, must have with it a power to act;
otherwise, it would be a mere mockery.[704]

Third, the difference between the tremor of the hands
caused by palsy and the motion in the hands of a writer
proves the difference between necessity and free choice.

O heart, bring a parable illustrating a difference
whereby thou mayst know compulsion from free will.
Take the example of a hand trembling from palsy,
and a hand that you cause to shake.
Know that both movements are created by God,
but it is impossible to compare the latter with the former.
You are sorry for having caused his hand to shake;
why does the man with palsy not feel regret?[705]

Fourth, commands, prohibitions, promises, threats, rewards, and punishments all presuppose freedom of choice.

Command and prohibition, anger, conferment of honor
and rebuke,
concern him who possesses the power of choice, O pure-
bosomed one.[706]

One never says "Come" to a stone;
how should any one request a brick to keep faith?[707]

The entire Quran consists of commands, prohibitions,
and threats;
whoever saw commands given to a marble rock?
Does any wise man, does any reasonable man do this?
Does he show anger and enmity to bricks and stones?[708]

Fifth, regret and remorse for doing evil deeds is another proof for freedom of choice in humans.

'Tis the Justice of the Dispenser,
'tis an act of just dispensation:
the wonder is this, that in Divine dispensation
there is neither compulsion nor injustice.
Were there compulsion (*jabr*), how would there be repentance?
Were there injustice, how would there be protection?[709]

And the penitence which you have felt for an evil deed
you have been led to through your power of choice
(*ikhtiyar*).[710]

Sixth, blushing, shame, and bashfulness are all indications of the existence of free choice.

Our lamentation is evidence of compulsion,
our sense of guilt is evidence of free will.
If there were not free will, what is this shame?
And what is this sorrow and guilty confusion and abash-
    ment?[711]

Seventh, we often change our plans, and this is further evidence for the existence of free will.

Why is there chiding between masters and pupils?
Why is the mind changing from plans already formed?[712]

Eighth, anger, wrath, and vengefulness all attest to
the reality of free choice.

The anger within you is a clear demonstration of a power
    of choice,
so that you must not excuse yourself after the fashion of
    the necessitarians.[713]

Even animals such as camels and dogs are aware of
human free will, and when humans take a course of action, they react. So how is it that some humans deny
their own freedom of choice?

If a camel-driver goes on striking a camel,
the camel will attack the striker.
The camel's anger is not directed against his stick,
therefore the camel has some notion of the power of
    choice in man.
Similarly, a dog: if you throw a stone at him
he will rush at you and will be contorted with fury...
Since the animal intelligence is conscious of the power of
    choice in man,
do not thou, O human intelligence hold this necessitarian
    doctrine.
Be ashamed![714]

Even if man is free, his freedom is of no account as
compared to the infinite freedom of God. So man is im-
potent in the face of the infinite power and the free choice
of God. It would be a great metaphysical error to take the

303

essentially bounded and limited freedom of man to be absolute.

> What in sooth is man's sovereignty and power of choice
> beside the light of the Everlasting Abode?
> His speaking organ is a piece of flesh,
> the seat of his vision is a piece of fat,
> the seat of his hearing consists of two pieces of bone,
> the seat of his intellectual perception is two drops of
>   blood, namely the heart.
> Thou art a little worm and art stuffed with filth,
> yet thou hast made a great display of pomp in the
>   world.[715]

In the end Mawlana beseeches God to deliver him from the two horns (*di-lemma*) of free choice, and guide him to that straight path which is free of any duality and bifurcation, which leads him right away to His Presence.

> O Thou who art the Help of those who seek help,
> help me to escape from this pillory of wicked acts of free
>   will...
> The one-way pull on the straight path
> is better than the two ways of perplexity,
> O Gracious One.
> Although Thou art the entire Goal of these two ways,
> yet indeed this duality is agonizing to the spirit.[716]

Transcending the duality involved in the bifurcation of human choice is only possible by an act of Divine Grace, which uplifts the servant to the station of unification, and the annihilation of his egoistic self in the Divine Self. So according to Mawlana, book-learning or discursive reasoning cannot solve the dilemma of determinism and free choice. This two-horned puzzle can only be solved and dissolved by Divine love.

> O dear soul! Love alone cuts disputation short,
> for it alone comes to the rescue
> when you cry for help against arguments.
> Eloquence is dumbfounded by love;
> it dare not engage in altercation,

for the lover fears that if he answer back
a pearl may fall out of his mouth.[717]

Rumi's Use of Tales, Parables, and Similes

The *Mathnawi* is replete with parables, allegories, and tales of various sorts, and it is necessary to say a few words about their significance in Sufi literature in general and in the *Mathnawi* in particular. In ancient scriptures, literature, and even philosophy, especially in the orient, one can find many fables, myths, allegories, and similes that are now little understood and even misinterpreted. For the ancients, an allegory or a myth could be the best way of expressing a universal truth as directly and plainly as possible; to use three words from a single Greek root (*muein*, to be silent), mystics would speak mysteries in the form of myths.

According to the Persian sage Suhrawardi, the founder of Illuminationist philosophy, the fact that the myths, allegories, and similes employed by the ancient sages have a symbolic significance indicates that they enunciate a universal truth, which is by nature metahistorical and can never be erroneous. To explain this point he distinguished between discursive knowledge (*'ilm-i bahthi*) on the one hand and sapiential wisdom (*hikmat-i dhawqi*) on the other. Discursive knowledge, which includes the various sciences, utilizes facts, whereas sapiential wisdom instead of facts deals with symbols. Indeed, sapiential wisdom may even take discursive facts as symbols, or use symbols that have no factual basis or are even factually untrue, but are allegorically and symbolically significant and hence eternally true. One is mistaken, according to Suhrawardi, if one takes an allegory, a symbol, or a myth (in the original sense of the word) literally, as a fact, as was done by discursive philosophers such as Aristotle (with regard to the ancients), and, we could argue, following Suhrawardi, as is done by many modern interpreters. A true allegory, according to Suhrawardi, can never be wrong. However, there is the possibility that it can be misunderstood if not viewed from a sapiential point of view.

307

The Holy Quran, like other scriptures, makes use of parables, allegories, and incidents in the lives of many prophets as symbols. In one context, it says that God is not ashamed of striking the parable of a gnat as an example (2:26). In another context, it gives us a general rule for understanding their significance, asserting: "We strike these parables for the people, but they are not fully understood except by those rooted in knowledge" (29:43).

It is for these reasons that fables and allegories are found with such regularity in Islamic and Persian literature. Apart from the Quran and the Bible, from which many parables permeated Islamic literature, parables were also borrowed from other cultures. To note just a few examples, in the field of statecraft, the "Mirrors for Princes" tradition was borrowed from the Sassanid writings of pre-Islamic Persia, and animal fables giving ethical teachings were taken from Sanskrit sources. *Kalilah and Dimnah*, for example, is the Arabic translation by the Persian Ibn al-Muqaffa' (d.759) from a Pahlavi (Middle Persian) translation of an original Sanskrit text known as *Panchatantra*, or the fables of Bidpai.

In addition to these, some of the stories of Rumi are taken from the life of the Holy Prophet, his companions, and early Sufis. Early Sufis, who were also competent scholars of prophetic traditions, mentioned the acts and sayings of the Holy Prophet, his companions, and the early generations of scholars in their ascetic manuals. These were later developed by such authors as Abu Talib al-Makki in his *Qut al-Qulub* (*The Nourishment of Hearts*), al-Kalabadhi in *al-Ta'arruf* (*A Survey of Sufism*), al-Sarraj in his *al-Luma'* (*The Sparks*), al-Qushayri in his *al-Risalah* (*The Epistle*), Hujwiri in *Kashf al-Mahjub* (*Unveiling of the Veiled*), and Khwajah Abdullah Ansari and Abu Sa'id Abu'l-Khayr in their various epistles in Persian, finally leading to the monumental works of Muhammad al-Ghazali, and his less well-known, but probably more influential, brother Ahmad.[718]

No less important in this regard were the works of philosophers such as Avicenna and Suhrawardi. Avicenna, in the second phase of his philosophical develop-

308

ment, turned from the Peripatetic to what he called "Oriental Philosophy," as evidenced in the introduction of his magnum opus, *Kitab al-Shifa*, and also in the introduction to the *Oriental Philosophy* itself. Most of his so-called oriental writings, such as *Salaman wa Absal* (now lost), *Hayy ibn Yaqzan* (*The Living, Son of the Awake*), and the *Risalat al-Tayr* (*The Treaties of the Bird*) are allegorical romances imitated by many later authors.

Perhaps more important in this connection is Suhrawardi, some of whose writings, especially those in Persian, are written in allegorical and symbolic language, and who has established, as mentioned, a philosophical foundation for the use and employment of symbolic allegories in sapiential theosophy.

But among the more immediate predecessors of Rumi who had greater influence on him in terms of Sufi doctrine and especially in the use of allegory, one can mention especially Sana'i. Sana'i's *Hadiqat al-Haqiqah* (*The Garden of Truth*) was considered by Rumi to be of high value. There are at least nine references to the *Hadiqah* in the *Mathnawi*.

Another Sufi author, who perhaps influenced Rumi to a far greater extent, was Farid al-Din 'Attar, whom as mentioned Rumi had possibly met en route to Anatolia as a boy, and by whom Rumi may have been given a copy of his *Asrar Nameh* (*The Book of Mysteries*). There is no doubt that 'Attar is a master of allegorical poetry. His *Mantiq al-Tayr* (*The Conference of the Birds*), a poetic elaboration and articulation of Ahmad Ghazali's *Risalat al-Tayr*, perhaps based on the treatise of the same name by Avicenna, is a story of a community of birds, led by the hoopoe, who set out to seek their king, the Simurgh. They have to traverse seven dangerous valleys (representing the seven main Sufi stations), and all but thirty perish on the way. After passing the seven valleys and attaining the station of Union, they realize that as thirty birds (*si-murgh*) they themselves are nothing but the King, Simurgh. 'Attar has moreover authored other works of allegorical poetry such as the *Ilahi Nameh* (*The Divine Book*) and the *Musibat Nameh* (*The Book of Suffering*). What is common among most of this genre of poetry is that a great many of the characters, speaking in human or in animal language, are varieties of birds or land and sea animals.

Rumi, great poet and mystic that he is, is far from being an imitator. Although he might have borrowed the material of some of his parables from other sources, he has taken them to such meaningful heights and given them such a new mold that they appear to us in a totally new light and seldom as an imitation. It is sufficient here to give a few examples of his parables.

The Story of the Greengrocer and the Parrot

There was a greengrocer who had a parrot, a green parrot with a sweet voice. It used to sit on a bench and look after the shop. It would address human beings and talk to them, attracting many customers to the shop. Once, while springing from the bench and taking flight, it spilled the bottles of rose-oil. The master, coming from his house and seating himself on the bench, found it covered in oil and his clothes ruined. Getting angry, he struck the parrot on the head, and the blow caused the poor parrot to turn completely bald.

For days the parrot did not speak. The merchant, regretting what he had done, drew deep sighs and tore his beard, saying:

> "Alas, the sun of my prosperity has gone under the
>   clouds.
> Would that my hand had been broken at that moment.
> How did I strike such a blow
> on the head of that sweet-tongued one?"[719]

He gave presents to every passing dervish in the hope that by his bestowal of charity, his misfortune would be brought to an end, and his bird would regain its speech. Three days and three nights passed. He was sitting on his bench, full of sorrow and in utter despair. He showed the bird all sorts of marvelous things, hoping to make it speak again. Meanwhile, a bare-headed dervish clad in sack-cloth passed by, with his head as hairless as the

310

outside of a bowl. Immediately, the parrot began to talk. It screeched at the dervish and said: "Hey, fellow! How did you get mixed up with the bald? Did you perhaps also spill oil from a bottle?" All the people present laughed at the inference the parrot had made, for it considered the wearer of the frock, the dervish, to be like itself.

The moral of the story is that we should not judge the actions of holy men by our own standards.

> On this account the whole world is gone astray:
> scarcely anyone is cognizant of God's *Abdal*.[720]
> They set themselves up equal with the prophets;
> they suppose the friends of God like themselves.
> "Behold!" they said, "We are men, they are men;
> both we and they are in bondage to sleep and food."
> In their blindness, they did not perceive
> that there is an infinite difference between them.
> Both species of insect ate and drank from the same place:
> but from the hornet came a sting and from the bee,
> honey.
> Both species of deer ate grass and drank water:
> from this one came dung, and from that one pure musk.
> Both reeds drank from the same water:
> but this one is empty and that one full of sugar...
> This one eats, and filth is discharged from him
> That one eats and becomes entirely the light of God;
> This one eats and of him is born nothing but avarice and
> envy;
> That one eats and of him is born nothing but love of
> God.[721]

The Parable of the Elephant in a Dark Room

Some Hindus had brought an elephant for exhibition and placed it in a dark house. Many people were going into that darkness to see the elephant. Since it was impossible to see the animal in the darkness, each person had to feel what it was with the palm of his hand.

> The hand of one fell on the trunk:
> "It is a creature like a drain-pipe," he said.
> The hand of another touched its ear,
> to him it appeared to be like a fan.

311

Another rubbed against its leg:
"I found the elephant's shape like a pillar."
Another laid his hand on its back:
"Truly, this elephant was like a throne."
...If there had been a candle in each one's hand,
the difference would have gone out of their words.
The eye of sense-perception is only like the palm of the
    hand;
the palm hath not power to reach the whole of the ele-
    phant.
The eye of the Sea of Reality is one thing
and the eye of the foam of phenomena another;
leave the foam and look with the eye of the Sea.[722]

By this parable, Rumi wants us to understand that we should always see the truth and the reality of things in their totality, which is only possible by a profound intellectual and spiritual vision, symbolically expressed as the light of a candle. Those who use only sense perception and, symbolically speaking, only use "the palm of their hands" can obtain no more than phenomenal knowledge. Such is the case with those who use the partial reason to grope the reality of things. They can only attain to partial and fragmented knowledge of reality.

This fragmented and partial view of reality causes dissension and sectarianism in religions because of the fact that the dissenters are not able to view religion in its primordial totality.

The Story of Moses and the Shepherd

One of the most famous parables of Rumi describes Moses' meeting with a shepherd. One day Moses saw a shepherd on the road who was saying: "O God, who choosest whomsoever Thou wilt, where art Thou that I may sweep Thy little room? May all my goats be Thy sacrifice, O Thou in remembrance of Whom are all my cries of 'Hay-Hay' and 'Hay-Hah.'"

The shepherd was talking nonsense in this fashion when Moses asked him: "To whom are you addressing these words?"

"To Him Who created us," the shepherd answered. "By Whom this earth and this sky were brought into sight."

"You have become impudent," Moses said.

> You have ceased to be a Muslim, you have become an unbeliever. What is this babble, this blasphemy, this gibberish! Stuff some cotton into your mouth; the whole world is stinking with the stench of your blasphemy; your blasphemy has turned the silk robe of religion to rags. Shoes and socks are fitting for you; how are they fit for the Divine Sun? If you do not stop your mouth from uttering such words a fire will come and burn up all the world.

"Moses, you have stitched up my mouth and burned my soul with repentance," the shepherd said. Heaving a sigh, he rent his garment and hastily turned toward the desert and departed. Following this:

> A revelation came to Moses from God:
> "Thou hast parted My servant from Me!
> Didst thou come (as a prophet) to unite
> or didst thou come to sever?
> So far as thou canst, do not set foot in separation:
> of all things the most hateful to Me is divorce.
> I have bestowed on every one a special way of acting:
> I have given to every one a peculiar form of expression.
> In regard to him it is praise,
> and in regard to thee it is blame:
> in regard to him honey,
> and in regard to thee poison.
> I am independent of all purity and impurity,
> of all slothfulness and alacrity (in worshipping Me).
> I did not ordain worship that I might make any profit;
> nay, but that I might do a kindness to (My) servants.
> Among the Hindus the idiom of India is praiseworthy;
> among the Sindians the idiom of Sind is praiseworthy.
> I am not sanctified by their glorification of Me;
> 'tis they that become sanctified and pearl-scattering.
> I look not at the tongue and the speech;
> I look at the inward and the state.
> I gaze into the heart to see whether it be lowly,
> though the words uttered be not lowly,
> Because the heart is the substance, speech only the accident;

313

so the accident is subservient, the substance is the real
 object.
How much more of these phrases and conceptions and
 metaphors?
I want burning, burning: become friendly with that burning!
Light up a fire of love in thy soul,
burn thought and expression entirely away!
O Moses, they that know the conventions are of one sort,
they whose souls and spirits burn are of another sort."
To lovers there is a burning at every moment:
tax and tithe are not imposed on a ruined village.
If the lover speak faultily, do not call him faulty;
and if he be bathed in blood, do not wash those who are
 martyrs.
For martyrs, blood is better than water:
this fault is better than a hundred right actions.
Within the Ka'ba the rule of the qibla does not exist:
what matter if the diver has no snow-shoes?
Do not seek guidance from the drunken:
why dost thou order those whose garments are rent in
 pieces to mend them?
The religion of Love is apart from all religions:
for lovers, the (only) religion and creed is God.[723]

After that, God hid in the inmost heart of Moses
mysteries which cannot be spoken.
Words were poured upon his heart:
vision and speech were mingled together.
How oft did he become beside himself and how oft return
 to himself!
How oft did he fly from eternity to everlastingness!
If I should unfold his tale after this, 'tis foolishness in me,
because the explanation of this is beyond our understanding;
And if I should speak thereof, 'twould root up men's
 minds;
and if I should write thereof, 'twould shatter many pens.
When Moses heard these reproaches from God,
he ran into the desert in quest of the shepherd.
He pushed on over the footprints of the bewildered man,
he scattered dust from the skirt of the desert...
At last Moses overtook and beheld him;
the giver of glad news said, "Permission has come from
 God.

Do not seek any rules or method of worship;
say whatsoever your distressful heart desires.
Your blasphemy is religion, and your religion is the light
of the spirit:
you are saved, and through you a whole world is in salvation.
O you who are made secure by *God doeth whatso He wil-
leth* (cf. Quran 22:18),
go, loose your tongue without regard for what you say."
He said, "O Moses, I have passed beyond that:
I am now bathed in my heart's blood.
I have passed beyond the Lote-tree of the farthest bourn,
I have gone a hundred thousand years' journey on the
other side.
Thou didst ply the lash, and my horse shied, made a
bound,
and passed beyond the sky.
May the Divine Nature be intimate with my human nature;
blessings be on thy hand and on thine arm!
Now my state is beyond telling:
this which I am telling is not my real state."[724]

The Stations of the Way

Sufism as we said is a spiritual journey where the point of departure is the wayfarer's self and of which the goal and destination is the Union of this self with the Divine Self. This spiritual journey, like terrestrial journeys, is marked by many stations, which the wayfarer must realize in himself. Unlike outward journeys, the spiritual journey takes place within the soul of the wayfarer and is actualized within his or her very own self. For this reason, the wayfarer does not leave behind the stations reached, but rather they remain ever with him after he has realized them.

Each Divine religion is a totality symbolized by a circle comprising a center, which even if invisible constitutes the reality of the circle. In addition to the center, a circle, moreover, is made up of a circumference and the radii that connect each point of the circumference to the center. The circumference, allegorically speaking, represents the outward or the exoteric aspect of the religion in view, called in Islam the *Shari'ah* or the Divine Law. The radii symbolize the *tariqah* (the Way) or esoteric aspect of the religion, which the spiritual wayfarer must tread to attain to the center, which represents the *Haqiqah* or Absolute Reality. For each point in the circumference, representing a particular believer, there is only one radius directed to the center. The radii, although outwardly different from each other, are essentially the same in that all define the same circle and ultimately lead to one and the same center.

By employing several similar analogies, Mawlana endeavors to elucidate the relationship between the *Shari'ah* (Divine Law), the *tariqah* (The Path, the Way), and the *Haqiqah* (the Absolute Reality). In one simile in the fifth book of the *Mathnawi*, the *Shari'ah* or the religious law is said to be like a candle. Unless one gains possession of a candle, one cannot find the way, and there can be no wayfaring. When one has found a candle and has come to the way, one's wayfaring is called the

317

path (*tariqah*). When one has reached the destination or the journey's end, that is Truth (*Haqiqah*).

In another simile, which uses the science of alchemy, Mawlana says that the Law is like learning the theory of alchemy from a teacher or from a book, the path is like making use of chemicals and rubbing the copper on the philosopher's stone, and the Truth is like the transmutation of the copper into gold.

> Those who know alchemy rejoice in their knowledge of it saying: "we know the theory of this science"; and those who practice it rejoice in their practice of it saying, "We perform such works"; and those who have experienced the reality, rejoice in the reality, "We have become gold" and are delivered from the theory and practice of alchemy; we are God's freedmen.[725]

Or again, the law could be compared to the science of medicine, the path to regulating one's diet according to the laws of that science and taking medicine in due proportion, and the Truth to gaining everlasting health and becoming independent of both.

When a person dies, the law and the path are cut off from him, and there remains only the Truth. In short the Law is knowledge, the path action, and the Truth attainment to God.

Certain points must be mentioned with regard to the spiritual stations (*maqamat*). There is a difference of opinion among the gnostics about the number and the order of the stations. However, all of them are agreed upon the major ones, all of which are mentioned in the Quran. Moreover, even though these stations are known and sought after by Muslims, their realization is not obligatory upon all of them. In other words, they belong to the order of the supererogatory, which being Divine injunctions were practiced by the Prophet and hence become obligatory only for those who want to follow in the footsteps of the Holy Prophet, who was the embodiment of the whole Quran. In addition, each station is essentially connected with one Divine Name. For example the following stations are connected with the mentioned Divine Names on the one hand, and constitute noble character traits and virtues on the other: repentance corresponds to the Divine Name *al-Tawwab*, "the Giver of Repentance"; faith to *al-Mu'min*, "the Believer/the Giver of Security"; generosity to *al-Karim*, "the Generous"; justice to *al-'Adl*, "the Just"; forgiveness to *al-Ghaffar* and *al-Ghafur*, "the All-Forgiving"; patience to *al-Sabur*, "the Patient"; gratitude to *al-Shakur*, "the Grateful"; forbearance to *al-Halim*, "the Forebearing"; wisdom to *al-Hakim*, "the Wise"; love to *al-Wadud*, "the Loving"; knowledge to *al-'Alim*, "the Omniscient"; and so on.[726] Such being the case, the wayfarer realizes in himself one Divine Name at each station, and by treading the path to the final destination, the wayfarer becomes the manifestation of all the Divine Names and Attributes and attains to a stage where he sees, hears, speaks, and knows by and through God, while remaining at the same time a servant of God. This is the highest stage of Divine proximity and sanctity. Here let us mention briefly some of those stations as they are presented in the *Mathnawi*.

Spiritual Wayfaring (*sayr wa suluk*)

There is a prophetic tradition in which the Holy Prophet is reported to have said: "Love of one's fatherland is a sign of faith." But Mawlana warns us that we should not take this in its purely literal sense. Our "fatherland" (*watan*) is not here; it is on the other side of the shore.

> Pass on from the expression
> "Love of the fatherland";
> do not stop,
> for thy real "fatherland" is Yonder.
> My dear one, it is not on this side.
> If thou desire thy fatherland
> cross to the other side of the stream.
> Do not misread this authentic tradition.[727]

In the spiritual journey, one is unconscious of the way and is "lost in God." One does not walk with bodily feet on the earth, for the lover of God walks on his heart. Being intoxicated with the Beloved, the traveler does not know whether the Way is long or short, for these are attributes of earthly journeys. To give us an inkling of what a spiritual journey is like, Mawlana reminds us that we were first semen in the womb, and then became embryos, and after birth grew up to rationality, unconditioned by time and space.

> Do not regard these feet that walk on the earth,
> for assuredly the lover walks on his heart.
> The heart that is intoxicated with the Sweetheart,
> what should it know of road and stage,
> of short and long?
> That "long" and "short" are attributes of the body;
> the faring of spirits is another faring.
> You have journeyed from the seed to rationality;
> it was not by a step or a league
> or moving from place to place.
> The journey of the spirit is not conditioned by distance
>   and time;
> our body learned from the Spirit how to journey.
> Now it has relinquished the corporeal journeying
> it moves unconditioned
> masked in conditioned-ness.[728]

> This longness and shortness appertains to the body;
> where God is, what is "long" and "short"?
> When God has transmuted the body
> He makes its faring without league or mile.[729]

We are used to traveling on land, but seem to be strangers to the sea voyage necessary to seek the Water of Life. Journeying on earth, we make use of our imagination and understanding, but swimming in the torrential waves of the sea requires self-effacement and intoxication. We are all accustomed to sensual drunkenness but alien to spiritual inebriation:

> Since thy life has passed in travelling on land,
> now mountain, now river, now desert,
> whence wilt thou gain the Water of Life?
> Where wilt thou cleave the waves of the Sea?

320

The waves of the earth
are our imagination, and understanding, and thought;
the waves of Sea
are self-effacement, and intoxication, and death.
Whilst thou art in this intoxication
thou art far from that intoxication.
Whilst thou art drunken with this,
thou art blind to that cup.[730]

Treading the path requires self-discipline and mortification of the carnal passions. It is not really mortification of the soul, but is its revivification and the attainment of an eternal life.

The death of the body in self-discipline is life,
the sufferings of this body are everlastingness to the
    spirit.[731]

These austerities of the dervishes,
what are they for?
Because that tribulation on the body
is the everlasting life of spirits.[732]

The Valley of the Search (*talab*)

If one does not seek something, one will never find it. So seeking the way and exerting oneself in the spiritual journey are necessary conditions for the wayfarer. No matter what state we are in, we should always keep searching. Only one with dry lips will reach the springhead. Has anyone learned a handicraft or acquired wealth without a quest?

In whatsoever state thou be
keep searching;
O thou with dry lip, always be seeking the water.
For that dry lip of thine gives evidence
that at last it will reach the springhead.
Dryness of lip is a message from the water
that this anxious search
will certainly bring thee to the water.
For this seeking is a blessed motion;

321

this search is the killer of obstacles
on the Way to God.[733]

If an ant has sought the rank of Solomon;
do not look contemptuously on its quest.
Everything that thou hast of wealth and handicraft,
was it not at first a quest and a thought?[734]

One gains one's daily bread by doing work and labor,
just as one gains one's livelihood by practicing a profession. So one should always gain one's apportioned nourishment through appropriate means, just as one should
enter one's house through the door without climbing the
walls.

The way of getting daily bread
is work, labor and fatigue.
God hath given every one
a handicraft and means of livelihood.
"Seek ye your daily portions
in the means thereof;
enter your dwellings by their doors."[735]

The outcome of the spiritual quest is best illustrated
in the following verses, which incidentally remind us of
similar verses in the Gospels.

The shadow of God
is over the head of His servant;
he who seeks at last shall be a finder.
The Prophet said that when you knock at a door
at last there will come forth a head from that door.
When you wait on the way of a certain person,
at last you will see the face of that person.
When, every day, you keep digging the earth from a pit,
at last you will arrive at the pure water.
Even if you may not believe it,
know that one day you will reap whatever you are sow-
    ing.[736]

322

Abandonment (*tark*)

By "abandonment" is meant giving up what is other than God, or that which is an impediment on the way to attaining Him. In order to "flee to God" (Quran 51:50), one first has to abandon the world insofar as it is considered as a reality totally separated and cut off from God. Furthermore, one must also abandon the egoistic self, which, having forgotten its Divine Origin, is idolized and worshiped instead of God. We should always bear in mind the fact that when Mawlana exhorts us to abandon the world, he is referring to the world insofar as it is sought after as a self-sufficient reality, independent of God:

> Plots for gaining this world are worthless;
> plots for renouncing this world are authenticated.
> The right plot is that the prisoner digs a hole in his
>   prison;
> if he blocks up the hole that is a foolish plot.
> This world is a prison and we are the prisoners;
> dig a hole in the prison and let yourself out.
> What is this world?
> To be forgetful of God;
> it is not merchandise and silver and weighing scales and
>   women.
> As regards the wealth that you carry for religion's sake;
> "How good is righteous wealth," as the Prophet recited.
> Water in the boat is the ruin of the boat;
> water underneath the boat is its support.[737]

As we can see clearly from the above verses, the world that is denounced is not constituted of such things as trinkets, wealth, gold, silver, luxuries, and women. Rather it is the forgetfulness of God. It is a world that is totally autonomous and self-enclosed. It is like a prison cut off from God. To make a hole in this prison means to deliver oneself by linking oneself to the Hereafter, and specifically to one's Divine Origin. Moreover, wealth spent in the way of God is like water underneath a ship in an ocean on which it sails with safety. But wealth expended for purely mundane purposes is like water inside a ship, which causes it to capsize. So, everything depends on

how and for what ends we use it. It was only for this reason and with this end in view that the Holy Prophet called
the world "carrion." Very few people can escape from the
charms and fascinations of the world. Those who can
evade its illusory splendor are "men of God," that is,
sages and saints.

> Since the Prophet's eye was fixed on the end;
> looking by that eye he called the world "carrion."[738]

> All humanity are children
> except him that is intoxicated with God;
> none is grown-up
> except him that is freed from sensual desire.
> God said: "This world is a play and pass-time" (cf. Quran
>   29:64)
> and ye are children, and God speaks truth.
> If you have not given up play,
> you are a child;
> without purity of spirit
> how will you be fully intelligent?[739]

Much more difficult than renouncing the world is renouncing the desires of the carnal soul; as the Holy
Prophet said, one's worst enemy is between one's two
flanks. The ego is the mother of all idols; it is worse than
even a dragon. The idol of the self is like a flint that produces innumerable sparks. The material idol is like a
spark that can be extinguished by water. It is easy to
break the stone idol but very difficult to subdue the demonic self. If one desires to know the true nature of the
egoistic self, one should read in the Quran about the
seven gates of Hell.[740]

> The idol of your self is the mother of all idols;
> because that idol is a snake
> while this idol is a dragon.
> The carnal self is as iron and stone
> while that idol is the sparks;
> Those sparks can be extinguished by water,
> but how should the stone and iron be allayed by water?
> How should a man, having these twain, be secure?
> The idol is the black water in the jug;

the self is the spring of the black water.
A single piece of stone will break a hundred pitchers;
but the spring is jetting forth water incessantly.
It is easy to break an idol,
very easy;
to regard the self as easy to subdue
is folly, folly.
O son, if you seek to know the reality of the self
read the story of Hell with its seven gates.[741]

It is extremely painful to subdue the passions of the miscreant self, so one ought to be patient in bearing the pain. The stars, the sun, the moon, and the spheres bow in submission to the one who has mortified his self.

O brother, endure the pain of the lancet;
that you may escape from the sting
of your miscreant self,
for spheres and sun and moon bow in worship
to the people who are delivered
from self-existence.
Anyone in whose body the miscreant self has died,
sun and cloud obey his command.[742]

The carnal self and the Devil were once one person, but manifested themselves in two different forms. Likewise, the intellect and the angels are of the same spiritual substance, but became two because of the wise purposes of the Divine dispensation. People should be on their guard because they have a home-grown adversary within themselves.

The fleshy soul and the Devil
both have been one body
manifesting themselves in two forms,
like the angel and the Intellect
which were really one
but became two forms for the sake of His wise purposes.
You have such an enemy as this
in your inmost being;
he is an obstacle to the intellect
and the adversary of the spirit and of religion.
At one moment he dashes forward

325

like the Libyan lizard;
then in a flight he darts away into a hole.[743]

In the Holy Quran, God has called the Devil *khannas*, a furtive sneaker, because like a hedgehog he hides his head, sticking it out when he finds the opportunity to catch his prey. The carnal soul likewise waylays us from within when it gets the opportunity.

> For God hath called the Devil *khannas*
> because he resembles the head
> of the little hedgehog.
> The head of the hedgehog is continually being hidden
> because of its fear of the cruel hunter
> until when it has found an opportunity
> it sticks out its head;
> by such stratagem the snake becomes its prey.
> If the fleshy soul had not waylaid you from within;
> how would the brigands have any power to lay a hand
>   upon you?[744]

Nothing can help us in subduing the carnal soul better than a spiritual master. So one should take hold of the hem of his robes and grasp it tightly. When you place your hand in the hand of the spiritual master, that is a sure sign of the Divine Grace.

> Nothing will slay the fleshy soul
> except the shadow of the Pir;
> grasp tightly the skirt
> of the slayer of the flesh.
> When you grasp it tightly,
> that is the aid of God;
> whatever strength comes to you
> is due to His attraction.[745]

Repentance (*tawbah*)

Tawbah is to ask the forgiveness of God when one has sinned or committed a grievous error. It is said that the repentance of the common people (*'awamm*) is from sin, the repentance of the spiritual elites (*khawass*) is from

326

negligence (*ghaflah*), and the repentance of the accomplished and realized gnostics is from everything other than God.[746] The Holy Prophet of Islam is reported to have said: "God accepts the repentance of His servant until he emits the death rattle." This means that the door of repentance is open to the end of one's life, or in Mawlana's terminology until the sun rises from the west. This is a reference to a Prophetic tradition according to which at the end of the time the sun will rise from the west.

Hark, do not act so henceforth,
but take precaution;
for through God's bounty
the door of repentance is open.
From the quarter of the West
a door of repentance
is open to mankind till the Resurrection.
Till the sun lifts up its head
from the West
that door is open:
do not avert thy face from it.
By the mercy of God
Paradise hath eight doors;
one of those eight is the door of repentance, O son.
All the others are sometimes open,
sometimes shut;
and never is the door of repentance but open.
Come, seize the opportunity,
the door is open;
carry thy baggage thither at once
in spite of the envious Devil.[747]

We must learn repentance from our progenitor Adam, who having sinned asked forgiveness for his sin from God, and humbly addressing God said: "Lord, we have wronged ourselves, and if Thou dost not forgive us and have mercy upon us we shall surely be among the lost" (Quran 7:23).

Learn from thy Father, for in sin
Adam came down willingly
to abase himself.
When he beheld that Knower of secrets

327

he stood up on his two feet to ask forgiveness.
He seated himself on the ashes of contrition;
he did not jump from one branch of idle pleading to an-
    other.
He said only, "O Lord we have done wrong,"
when he saw the angelic lifeguards
in front and behind.[748]

Thou, too, O lover,
since thy crime has become manifest;
abandon specious pretexts
and be broken-hearted.
Those who are the elect children of Adam;
sigh forth *verily we have done wrong* (cf. Quran 7:23).
Submit thy petition, do not argue
like the accursed hard-faced Iblis.[749]

Mawlana goes on to argue that sin in man is not innate; otherwise repentance and forgiveness would be impossible. Since it is a borrowed disposition, the confession of sin and repentance is possible. In Satan alone is
sin original, and for this reason he never has the desire
to repent.

The evil disposition was not innate in thy essence,
for from original evil comes naught but denial.
That is a borrowed evil
because he makes confession and seeks to repent,
like Adam whose lapse was temporary,
he inevitably showed penitence at once.
Since the sin of Iblis was original,
for him there was no way
to precious penitence.[750]

Iblis did not repent, but rather asked God to give him
a respite until the Day of Resurrection to waylay and
snare the children of Adam (Quran 7:14). Would that he
had repented like Adam.

The cawing and noisy cry
of the black crow
is ever asking for long life in this world.
Like Iblis it besought the Holy and incomparable God

for the life of the body till the Day of Resurrection.
Iblis said, "Grant me a respite
till the day of retribution."
Would that he had said:
"We repent, O our Lord."[751]

Even if the scroll of one's deeds is blackened by sins, it is never too late to repent. The past is gone and is not real. What is real is the present moment, which is the right moment for repentance. God has promised that all your past evil deeds will be made good, and the living water of repentance will make the tree of your life verdant again.

If you have blackened the scroll of your life,
repent of the deeds you did formerly.
Though your life has passed,
this moment is its root;
water it with repentance if it lacks moisture.
Give the Living Water to the root of your life
in order that the tree of your life may become verdant.
By this Water all past sins are made good;
bygone poisons are made sweet as sugar.[752]

One should not break one's repentance, for the violation of a covenant with God and a vow of repentance becomes a cause of calamity and affliction. In the case of "the followers of the Sabbath," such violation was the cause of their metamorphosis.[753] But in the case of the community of Muhammad, such metamorphosis is not in the body, but rather in the heart.

To violate a pact and break vows of repentance
becomes the cause of accursedness in the end.
The violation of vows of repentance by "the followers of the
    Sabbath"
became the cause of their metamorphosis, destruction
    and abomination.
Therefore God turned those people into apes,
since they rebelliously broke their covenant with God.
In this community there has never been metamorphosis
    of the body;

329

but there is metamorphosis of the spirit,
O man endowed with perception.[754]

Patience (*sabr*)

Another station on the way of the realization of unification is patience, which is much praised and recommended in the Holy Quran, as the following verses attest:

> Surely, the patient will be paid their reward in abundance
> without reckoning. (39:13)

> So be thou patient as the Messengers possessed of con-
> stancy were also patient. (46:35)

> Yet none shall receive it except those who are patient and
> none shall receive it save one of mighty fortune. (41:35)

> By the afternoon (*'asr*), surely man is in the way of loss,
> save those who believe and do righteous deeds and counsel
> each other unto the Truth and counsel each other to be
> patient. (103:1–3)

Mawlana, referring to Luqman, the proverbial sage
mentioned in the Quran, says that once he went to see
the prophet-king David, as according to tradition the two
of them were contemporaries. He observed that the king
was making rings of iron. He had not seen the armorer's
handicraft before and was therefore seized with astonish-
ment, and curiosity incited him to ask David about what
he was making with those interfolded rings.

> Again he said to himself, "Patience is better;
> patience is the quickest guide to the object of one's quest."
> When you ask no question
> the sooner its secret will be disclosed to you;
> the bird of patience flies faster than all others.
> And if you ask, the more slowly will your object be gained;
> what is easy will be made difficult
> by your impatience.[755]

330

So Luqman kept silent. He did not say a word until
the work was finished through David's craftsmanship.
David finished fashioning a coat of mail and put it on in
the presence of the patient and wise Luqman, and explained to him that it was an excellent garment that one
wears on the battlefields and in wars to ward off the
blows of the enemy. Then Mawlana concludes the story
by alluding to the last of the Quranic verses mentioned
above.

> Luqman said, "Patience too is of good effect;
> for it is the protection and defense
> against pain everywhere."
> God hath joined patience (*sabr*) with Truth (*haqq*);
> O reader, recite attentively
> the End of the chapter "The Afternoon."
> God created hundreds of thousands of elixirs,
> but man hath not seen an elixir like patience.[756]

The most patient among mankind are the messengers
of God, for they suffered much at the hands of their enemies, detractors, and denigrators. But through suffering
such afflictions they gained all this glory and intimacy
with God. If you see someone wearing a beautiful garment, be sure that he has obtained it through hard work
and patience. If you see a soul full of anguish, know that
he was an associate of impostors who knew no patience
and loyal friendship.

> The patience shown by all the prophets to the unbelievers
> made them the elect of God
> and the lords of the planetary conjunction.
> When you see anyone wearing goodly raiment
> know that he has gained it by patience and work.
> If you have seen anyone naked and destitute,
> that is a testimony of his lack of patience.
> Anyone who feels lonely and whose soul is anguished
> must have associated with an imposter.
> If he had shown patience and loyal friendship
> he would not have suffered this affliction
> from his separation.[757]

We, like Joseph, have been cast into the well of the present world. God has sent us a rope to save us from this fearful dungeon, and this is the rope of patience. We must seize this rope firmly and ascend by it to the world of spirit.

> You are Joseph, full of beauty
> and this world is as the well,
> and this rope is patience,
> with the command of God.
> O Joseph, the rope is come.
> Put your two hands upon it;
> do not neglect the rope,
> it has grown late.
> Praise be to God, that this rope has been dangled,
> and that grace and mercy have been blended together,
> so that you may behold the new world of the spirit;
> a world very manifest, though invisible.[758]

One of the companions of the Holy Prophet came to him and complained that he was being swindled in every business and transaction that he made. The Holy Prophet advised him that in every transaction he should stipulate three days for deliberation, and then uttered this famous statement: "Deliberation (ta'anni) is from the All-Merciful and haste comes from the Devil." According to Mawlana even animals deliberate before doing something. A dog, for example, before eating a morsel will sniff at it. We should not be less than animals in our deeds and actions. The dog smells with its nose, but we should deliberate with wisdom and our purified intellect.

> A certain companion said to the Prophet,
> "I am always being swindled in commerce.
> The deceit of everyone who sells or buys
> is like magic and leads me off the track."
> The Prophet said, "When thou art afraid
> of being duped in a commercial transaction
> stipulate for thyself three days
> for the option to deliberate.
> For deliberation is assuredly from the All-Merciful;
> thy haste is from the accursed Devil.
> when you throw a morsel of bread to a dog

he first smells, then he eats, O diligent one.
He smells with the nose,
we with wisdom;
we, again, smell it by our discerning intellect.
This earth and the spheres were brought into existence
by God, with deliberation, in six days."[759]

Thankfulness (*shukr*)

One of the greatest stations in the spiritual path is thankfulness (*shukr*). God has given us innumerable bounties for which we should be grateful to Him. As the Quran states:

> It is God who brought you forth from your mothers' wombs, and He appointed for you hearing and sight and the hearts, that perchance you might be thankful. (16:78)

> But there are few people among humankind who are really thankful to God. Truly God is bounteous to people, but most of the people are not thankful. (2:243)

Thankfulness to God causes an increase in His boons and blessings, and ungratefulness causes His chastisement. "If you are thankful, surely I will increase you but if you are thankless My chastisement is surely terrible" (Quran 14:7).

The results of our thankfulness or ungratefulness all return to us and not to God, Who, being self-sufficient and possessing infinite perfections, is not in need of our gratefulness. "Give thanks to God; whosoever gives thanks gives thanks only for his own good, and whosoever is ungrateful, surely God is All-Sufficient, All-Praiseworthy" (Quran 31:12).

The Holy Prophet is reported to have said: "He who is not thankful to the creatures is not thankful to the Creator." In other words, all Attributes of Divine Perfection are manifested in His creatures, and a diligent and discerning believer should recognize them and pay to them what is their due. Gratitude to a benefactor is gratitude to God, because if he has displayed munificence, it is a manifestation of the Divine Bounty and Grace. It is quite

333

improper to thank God and show ungratefulness to a benefactor. Again, love of God should be accompanied by the love of one's parents, because they are the most perfect earthly manifestations of the Divine Love. In other words, one who does not love one's parents does not love God in the true sense of the word. That is why in certain verses of the Quran, the command to worship God is immediately followed by the command to love one's parents.[760] Similarly, God has commanded us to send our blessings and benedictions upon the Prophet Muhammad whenever his name is mentioned because he was the vehicle and the locus of manifestation of all Divine perfections, both to the Islamic community and to the world at large.

> Gratitude to the benefactor is certainly gratitude to God;
> since the Divine favor caused him to show beneficence.
> To be ungrateful to him is to be ungrateful to God;
> beyond doubt his right to gratitude is attached to God.
> Always give thanks to God for His bounties,
> and always give thanks to and praise the Khwaja (the
>   benefactor) too.
> Though a mother's mercy is from God,
> yet it is a sacred duty and a worthy task to serve her.
> For this reason God hath said, *Do ye bless the Prophet*
>   (Quran 33:56);
> for Muhammad was the locus of the Divine Perfections.[761]

Ungrateful people should pay more heed to the lifestyle of birds and animals and learn something from their joyfulness, contentment, and gratefulness. The Holy Prophet is reported to have said: "Be ye like birds who go out empty-bellied in the morning and come back filled in the evening." It is only human beings who in virtue of their illusory whims and vain desires are full of anguish and anxiety.

> In this world thousands of animals
> are living happily without anxiety.
> The dove on the tree is uttering thanks to God,
> though her food for the night is not yet ready.
> The nightingale is singing glory to God

saying: "I rely on Thee for my nourishment,
O Thou the Answerer of prayers."
The falcon has made the king's hand his joy;
and has given up hope of all carrion.
Similarly, take any animal
from the gnat to the elephant:
They all have become God's Household;
how great is God's Household.
All these griefs within our breasts arise
from the vapor and dust of our existence.[762]

Giving thanks for a bounty is more pleasant than the bounty itself. The bounty is like the shell, and giving thanks is like the kernel, because thanksgiving brings us to the Beloved, while the plentifulness of bounties might cause negligence and forgetfulness.

Thanksgiving for the bounty
Is sweeter than the bounty itself;
how should he that is addicted to thanksgiving
go towards the bounty?
Thanksgiving is the soul of the bounty
and the bounty is as the husk,
because thanksgiving brings you
to the abode of the Beloved.
Bounty produces heedlessness
and thanksgiving alertness;
hunt after bounty with the snare
of thanksgiving to the King.
The bounty of thanksgiving
will make you contented and princely,
so that you will bestow
a hundred bounties on the poor.[763]

For these reasons, it is necessary to be thankful to our Benefactor; otherwise the door of everlasting chastisement will be opened. "The All-Thankful" (al-Shakur) is one of the Names of God; see how for a single thanksgiving He opens the doors of so many benefits.

In view of reason it is necessary
to give thanks to the Benefactor;
otherwise the door of everlasting wrath

335

will be opened.
Behold the loving kindness of God;
would anyone but God
be content with a single thanksgiving
for such benefits?[764]

The Quran asks us: "Hast thou not seen those who exchanged the bounty of God with unthankfulness and caused their people to dwell in the abode of ruin?" (14:28). Again, as the Holy Quran states, if one tries to count the blessings of God, they are infinite and cannot be numbered (14:34). In the words of Mawlana:

If the tip of every hair of me
should gain a tongue,
yet the thanks due to Thee
can never be expressed.[765]

Contentment (*rida*)

Those who attain the station of contentment are well pleased with God, as He is well pleased with them (Quran 5:119). They seek always God's good pleasure (Quran 2:207) and consider it to be the greatest of all blessings (Quran 9:72),

According to Mawlana, those who have realized in themselves this station have their mouths closed to any supplication, because to make a supplication for them is an objection to the Divine Decree, which they consider an act of infidelity.

Now listen to a story of those travelers on the Way
who have no objection in the world.
Those of the saints who make supplication
are in sooth different;
sometimes they sew and sometimes they rend.
I know another class of saints
whose mouths are closed to supplication.
Because of the contentment
which is subservient to those noble ones
it has become unlawful for them to seek to avert destiny.
In submitting to Destiny

they experience a peculiar delight;
it would be infidelity for them to crave release.
God hath revealed to their hearts
such a good opinion
that they do not put on the blue garb
on account of any sorrow.[766]

Mawlana, making use of his usual narrative style, illustrates the significance of contentment in the spiritual
Way by relating a dialogue between Buhlul, the famous
sage-lunatic (*'aqil-i majnun*) of Islam, and a certain dervish. Buhlul asked him how he fared, and the dervish
answered:

He said, "How should that one be
according to whose desire
the work of the world goes on,
according to whose desire
the torrents and rivers flow,
and the stars move in such wise as He wills,
and Life and Death are his officers,
going to and fro according to His desire?...
The travelers on the Way
go according to His pleasure;
they that have lost the Way
are in His snare.
No tooth flashes with laughter in the world;
without the approval and command
of that imperial Decree."[767]

Buhlul gives his assent to what the dervish has said
and declares that the veracity of his statement is evident
not only in his words, but also in his spiritual radiance
and his glorious aspect. But Buhlul asks him to expound
it more clearly, in such a way that both the wise and the
vulgar may benefit from it.

The dervish said, "This at least is evident to the vulgar:
that the world is subject to the Command of God.
No leaf drops from a tree without predestination
and the ordainment of that Ruler of Fortune.
No morsel goes from the mouth towards the gullet,
until God says to that morsel, 'Enter.'

337

The inclination and desire which is man's nose-rein,
moves subject to the Command of that Self-sufficient
     One.
In all the earths and heavens not an atom
moves a wing, not a straw turns
save by His eternal and effectual command.
To expound this is impossible
and presumption is not good.
Hear this much, since all action in the universe
only comes to pass by the Command of the Maker.
When the Divine Decree becomes the pleasure of His serv-
     ant
the servant becomes a willing slave to His Decree.
Not for dissimulation and not for reward and punishment;
nay, his nature has become goodly and gracious.
Wheresoever the Eternal Command takes its course,
living and dying are one to him.
He lives for God's sake, not for riches;
he dies for God's sake, nor for fear of going to the Fire.
The servant of God
whose disposition and character is like this,
does not the world move
according to his command and behest?"[768]

Trust in God (*tawakkul*)

Tawakkul is one of the great stations on the Way and it
means to put one's trust in God and in Him alone. One
of the beautiful Names of God is "the Trustee" (*al-Wakil*);
that is why the Holy Quran commands believers to take
Him as their trustee and repeatedly calls upon them to
have trust in Him.

> Lord of the East and the West, there is no god but He; so
> take him for a trustee. (73:9)

> Put thy trust in God and God suffices as a Trustee. (33:3)

Tawakkul in the true sense of the word requires that
believers should consider God to be All-Sufficient, and in
the last resort they should depend only on God, as shown
by the following Quranic verses:

Say: God is sufficient for me, there is no god but He. In Him I have put my trust. (9:129)

My succor is only with God. In Him I have put my trust, and to Him I turn penitent. (11:85)

And whosoever puts his trust in God, He shall suffice him. (65:3)

God loves those believers who put their trust in Him. (3:159)

According to Mawlana, no work is better than trust in God. To depend on one's power alone without having trust in God can cause one to flee from one affliction to another and from bad to worse. If the servant devises something, his device may become a trap in which he is ensnared. He might lock the door to ward off the enemy while the enemy is already within the house. Since there is a defect in our eyesight, it is better to let it join to the sight of the Friend.

There is no work better than trust in God;
what, indeed, is dearer than resignation?
Often do they flee from affliction to affliction;
often do they recoil from the snake to the dragon.
Man devised, and his device was a snare;
that which he thought to be life
was the drainer of his blood.
He locked the door while the foe was in the house;
the plot of Pharaoh was a story of this sort.
That vengeful man slew hundreds of thousands of babes,
while the one he was searching after was in his own
      house.
Since in our eyesight there is much defect,
go, let your own sight pass away in the sight of the
      Friend.
His sight for ours—what a goodly recompense!
In His sight you will find the whole object of your desire.[769]

We should know that God alone is the source of our sustenance and we should seek it from Him alone and

339

not from this or that person. We should seek intoxication from Him and not from wine or from hemp leaves. All wealth comes from Him and not from treasures. As the Holy Quran has commanded, we should in the last resort seek aid from Him and not from our kinsmen. In the end we shall lose all these things and we shall be left in the presence of God, so it is advisable to leave all the rest and return to Him alone.

> So that you may know that He
> is the Source of the source of all sustenance,
> and that the seeker of sustenance
> may seek only Him,
> seek sustenance from Him,
> do not seek it from Zayd and 'Amr.
> Seek intoxication from Him,
> do not seek it from beng and wine.
> Desire wealth from Him,
> not from Treasure and possession.
> Desire aid from Him,
> not from paternal and maternal uncles.
> At the last you will be left
> without all these things;
> hark, unto whom
> will you call at that moment?
> Call unto Him now, and leave all the rest
> that you may inherit the kingdom of the world.[770]

Mawlana tells the story of an ascetic who had heard the saying of the Holy Prophet that one's daily bread comes from God, and he wanted to put it to the test. That man went into the desert and lay down near a mountain, saying: "I will see whether my daily bread will come to me." It happened that a caravan lost its way and marched towards the mountain. The travelers saw someone lying there, and in their surprise asked each other how that man was lying there far from the road, destitute in the wilderness. Some thought him to be dead, and if he was alive he must have no fear of wolves and wild animals. They came and touched him, but the venerable man neither stirred nor said anything because he was making his experiment. Then they said: "This poor man has had a

340

stroke of apoplexy caused by hunger." So they fetched bread and food and were competing to pour it into his mouth and down into his throat, but the man purposely clenched his teeth in order to see the truth of that promise. They felt pity for the man and his starving and perishing with hunger. So they brought a knife and hastily made a rift in his closed teeth. They poured soup in his mouth and forced into it fragments of bread. [771]

> He said to himself, "O my heart,
> even though thou art keeping silence;
> thou knowest the secret, and art showing disdain."
> His heart replied, "I know the secret,
> and am purposely behaving thus;
> God is the Provider for my soul and body." [772]

Some might think that to put trust in God means that one should abandon all work and human endeavor. This is not true at all. A Bedouin came to the Holy Prophet and said that he had put his trust in God and left his camel in the desert, but his camel had gotten lost. The Prophet replied: "First bind the feet of your camel, and then trust in God." The Holy Prophet is again reported to have said: "The earnest worker is the beloved of God," which means that one should never be forgetful of the ways and means.

> The Prophet said with a loud voice,
> "While trusting in God, bind the knee of thy camel."
> Hearken to the signification of "The earnest worker is
>   God's beloved";
> through trusting in God, do not become neglectful of the
>   means. [773]

> If you trust in God, put trust in Him in your work;
> first earn the means, then rely upon the Almighty. [774]

Forbearance (*hilm*)

One of the Beautiful Names of God is "the All-Forbearing" (*al-Halim*). Only one of the signs of His Forbearance is that He sees all the sins, evils, and misdeeds of human beings and tolerates them with patience. All the creatures in the natural order partake in this exalted Divine Attribute. Look at the forbearance of Mother Earth, how she tolerates all the grievous excesses and extravagances of her children, especially in our age.

According to Mawlana, the sword of forbearance is sharper than the sword made of iron and leads more easily to victory.

> The sword of forbearance is sharper than the sword of
>   iron;
> nay it is more productive of victory than a hundred ar-
>   mies.[775]

The above verse comes in reference to Imam 'Ali, the model *par excellence* of all Sufi saints. Once he overcame a fierce enemy in a battle and was about to kill him, but at that very moment the adversary spat on his face. 'Ali immediately released him. The antagonist asked why 'Ali had released him when he had the power to kill him. 'Ali responded: "When you spat on my face, my fleshly self was aroused and then I could no longer act with sincerity towards God. Half my action would be for God and half of it for my idle passion. In God's affair partnership is not permitted." The antagonist of 'Ali said:

> "I was sowing the seed of wrong;
> I fancied thee otherwise than thou art.
> Thou hast always been the Balance of the Unique One;
> nay thou hast been the tongue of every balance.
> I am the slave of that eye-seeking Lamp
> from which thy lamp received splendor.
> I am the slave of the billow of that Sea of Light
> which brings a pearl like this into view.
> Offer me the profession of the Faith,
> for I regard thee as the exalted one of the time."
> Nearly fifty persons of his kindred and tribe
> turned their faces towards the religion.
> By the sword of forbearance 'Ali redeemed
> so many throats of such a multitude from the sword.[776]

It was due to their unshakable forbearance that all the great messengers were able to deliver the message of God and to establish the Divine religion in their community.

> This company of the elect have a hundred thousand for-
> bearances;
> every one of which is immovable as a hundred mountains.
> Their forbearance makes a fool of the wary
> and causes the keen-witted man with a hundred eyes
> to lose his way.
> Their forbearance, like fine choice wine,
> mounts by nice (*naghz*) degrees up to the brain (*ma-
> ghz*).[777]

But the best examples of human forbearance are only faint shadows of the Divine Forbearance. The Divine Decree has spread for us the carpet of indulgence and has allowed us to speak in boldness and without fear like an only child with his father, without his taking offence.

> Within My forbearance the forbearance of a hundred fa-
> thers
> and a hundred mothers at every moment are born and
> vanish.
> Their forbearance is but the foam of the sea of My forbear-
> ance;
> the foam comes and goes but the sea is always there.
> What indeed shall I say?
> Compared with that pearl this oyster-shell is naught
> but the foam of the foam of the foam of the foam.[778]

But one should not abuse the Divine Clemency and Forbearance too much. One should not exceed the bounds of modesty, for otherwise He will expose the sinner:

> Although God's forbearance bestows kindnesses;
> yet when the sinner has gone beyond bounds, He exposes
> him.[779]

There is a Persian proverb that says: "Even if the lid of the cooking-pot is open, but where is the modesty of the cat?" That is, the cat should be modest enough not to trespass its bounds. Although we know that God has His gaze fixed on everything we do and in virtue of His infinite forbearance pretends to be ignorant of our evil acts, this is an occasion for us to be modest and to know a little more about ourselves. We should not trample the bounds of modesty and decency.

> Though His forbearance has feigned to be ignorant
> one must come to know one's self a little.
> If tonight the mouth of the cooking-pot is open,
> yet the cat must have a little modesty.[780]

According to Mawlana, all messengers of God were the perfect paragons of forbearance. He gives the example of the Prophet Moses, who before being chosen as a prophet herded a flock of sheep. One day a sheep fled from the herd. Moses went the whole day searching for it but all in vain. He ran so much in the desert that his feet began to blister, having cast off his shoes in order to run faster. He continued to search for it until nightfall, and on the way he had lost sight of the flock. The lost sheep grew exhausted by fatigue and Moses was finally able to overtake it. He gently stroked its back and head to remove the dust and caressed it like a loving mother.

> Not even half a mite of irritation and anger,
> nothing but love and pity and tears!
> He said to the sheep, "I grant you had no pity on me.
> But why did your nature show cruelty to itself?"
> At that moment God said to the angels:
> "So-and-so is suitable for prophethood."[781]

Sincerity (*ikhlas*)

To be sincere in one's actions and intentions is the core of religious devotion and piety. According to the Holy Quran one should make religion itself pure and sincere for God, as is seen in the following verses:

344

So worship God making thy religion His sincerely. Indeed, only sincere religion belongs to God. (39:2–3)

Say, I have been commanded to worship God, making my religion His sincerely. (39:14)

Set your face in every place of worship and call on Him, making your religion sincerely His. (7:29)

Furthermore, Satan cannot seduce and pervert those who have been made sincere by God: "Said he [Satan]: By Thy glory I shall pervert them all together, excepting those of Thy servants among them that are made sincere." (38:83)

According to Mawlana, if you test the words and deeds of the insincere, they are stinking like a rotten onion. They are pithless and without marrow, while in the case of sincere people, each of their efforts is more excellent than the last. The reprobates of religion have no device but deceit and cunning.

If you scrutinize the labor
of them that are insincere
it is stinking layer upon layer
like an onion.
Every one of their efforts
more pithless than the other;
in the case of the sincere
each effort is more excellent than the last...
The black-faced hypocrites of religion
have indeed no equipment
but cunning and deceit and contentiousness.[782]

The insincere man worships God against his will, while the sincere one worships Him willingly. The one is like a child who loves the nurse only for her milk, while the other has a purely disinterested love for this pious maid. The child does not know anything about her beauty and has no desire in his heart except milk, while the other is a true lover of the damsel.

345

The command, *Come against your will* is for the blind fol-
 lower;
Come willingly is for him who is molded of sincerity (cf.
 Quran 41:11).
The former loves God for the sake of some cause;
While the other hath indeed a pure disinterested love.
The former loves the Nurse but for the sake of the milk;
while the other has given his heart for the pious maid.
The child hath no knowledge of her beauty,
he hath no desire of her in his heart except for milk;
while the other is, truly, the lover of the nurse;
he is disinterested, single-minded in love.
Hence he that loves God because of hope and fear
reads studiously the book of blind imitation.
While he that loves God for God's sake—Where is he?
For he is far from all self-interests and maladies.[783]

Hypocrisy is the worst enemy of sincerity. Mawlana
tells the story of a jurisprudent who in order to show himself "big and grand in the assembly" collected old rags of
various colors and wound them in his turban, and em-
bellished the exterior of his turban with pieces of gaudy
and charming colors. So the exterior of the turban was
beautiful as Paradise, but it was shameful within like the
soul of a hypocrite, for its interior was filled with shreds
of cotton and old rags clipped from old garments. A
clothes-robber, being enchanted by the outward beauty
of the turban, waylaid him in the dark to practice his
craft. He snatched the turban and started to run away.
The scholar, now bare-headed, shouted at him and said:
"O son, first undo the turban and then take it away."

Even as you are flying with four wings,
undo the gift which you are taking away.
Undo it and rub it with your hand,
then take it if you like, I sanction that.
When he who was fleeing undid it,
a hundred thousand rags dropped on the road.
Of that big improper turban of his
there remained in his hand only a yard of old cloth.
He dashed the rag on the ground saying, "O worthless
 man,
by this fraud you have put me out of business."[784]

346

Remembrance of God (*dhikr*)

The remembrance of God is the most sacred act in any religion because more than any other ritual act it embodies the presence of God. The most important ritual act in Islam is the canonical daily prayers (*salat*), concerning which God says: "...and perform the prayer; prayer forbids obscene deeds and evil, but the remembrance of God is greater" (Quran 29:45). In other verses, the Holy Prophet is commanded to remember God as often as possible (3:41); it is said of the hypocrites that they do not remember God except a little (Quran 4:142); and again, the Prophet is commanded to remember God when he becomes forgetful (Quran 18:24). Moreover, God says: "Remember Me and I shall remember you" (Quran 2:152), which according to the Sufi interpretation means that in the act of invoking the Divine Name there is "a unification between the invoker and the Invoked." Moreover, if someone forgets God, this means that God has already forgotten him. "They [the hypocrites] have forgotten God and God has forgotten them" (Quran 9:67). Likewise, in the following verse the forgetfulness of God has been associated with the forgetfulness of one's own self: "Be not as those who forgot God so that He caused them to forget themselves" (59:19). This verse, when construed contrapositively, signifies that he who knows truly his own self, knows God.

According to Mawlana, the Name of God is pure, and when you invoke it with devotion, it will clean you of every impurity and all defilement. When the Holy Name of God is invoked, there remains neither impurity nor sorrow, because one is joined to an inexhaustible source that is absolute purity, endless joy, and eternal bliss.

> Remembrance of God is pure;
> when purity has come
> defilement packs up and leaves.
> Contraries flee from contraries;
> night flees when light shines forth.
> When the pure Name comes into the mouth,
> neither impurity remains nor sorrow.[785]

347

Sometimes, because of routine everydayness, one's thought becomes as if frozen and congealed. In such cases Mawlana advises us to resort to the invocation of the Divine Name, because like the brilliant sun in the noontide, it melts away the ice of our frigid and congealed thought.

> We have said so much, think of the remainder;
> if thought be frozen, practice invocation of the Name.
> Invocation brings thought into movement;
> make invocation the sun for this congealed thought.[786]

When one invokes the Holy Name, one should do it with full devotion and love. This is lacking in the vulgar when they remember the Divine Name.

> The vulgar are always pronouncing the Holy Name;
> but it does not do this work
> since they are not endowed with love.[787]

By repeating the Divine Name, one exterminates the false cry of the ghouls and closes one's eyes to this world, which as with the vulture is used only for eating carrion. One gains spiritual insight and a sense of discrimination, by which one can distinguish between Truth and error, the Absolute and the relative, between the Real and the illusory.

> Prevent these voices from entering your heart
> so that Divine mysteries may be revealed to you.
> Repeat the Name of God, drown the cry of the ghouls;
> close your narcissus-eye to this vulture.
> Know the difference between the false dawn
> and the true;
> distinguish the color of the wine
> from the color of the cup.
> That perchance, from the eyes that see the seven colors
> patience and perseverance may generate an eye
> whereby you may behold colors other than these colors,
> and may behold pearls instead of stones.
> What pearl?
> Nay you will become an ocean;
> you will become a sun traversing the sky.[788]

348

In the Holy Quran it is said of the hypocrites that they do not remember God except a little (4:142). Having perhaps this Quranic verse in view, Mawlana comments that one should not rub musk on the body, but should rub the musk of the Holy Name within one's heart. The hypocrite on the contrary rubs musk on his body while his spirit is at the bottom of the bath-furnace. He has only the Divine Name on the tip of his tongue, whereas his heart stinks with disbelief. So his glorification of the Divine Name reminds one of the existence of roses and lilies on a dunghill.

> Do not put musk on your body,
> rub it on your heart;
> What is musk? The Holy Name of the Glorious God.
> The hypocrite puts musk on his body;
> and puts his spirit at the bottom of the ash-pit.
> On his tongue the Name of God,
> and his soul stinks from his infidel thought.
> With him the remembrance of God is the herbage of the
>   ash-pit;
> it is roses and lilies upon a dunghill.[789]

As we mentioned earlier, there is a vast amount of literature in Islamic culture about love, to an extent that is almost unique in world literature. Such love stories as Joseph and Zulaykha, Layla and Majnun, Khusraw and Shirin, Shirin and Farhad, Vis and Ramin, and many others, which are found in many different versions in multifarious languages, are not to be taken as mere stories for entertainment. According to Mawlana, they all have one thing essential in common, and it is that for all the lovers in these stories, their loved ones are the earthly reflections of that Absolute Beauty, which is most perfectly manifested in their own beloved. Mawlana gives a totally different interpretation to what we find in literary textbooks of the story of the famous pagan Arab king-poet Imra'u al-Qays, who is blamed for having abdicated his royal throne. According to Mawlana, he was a paragon of love. As the title to one section of the *Mathnawi* puts it:

Since all the women desired him with heart and soul, one may well wonder what was the object of his love songs and lamentations. Surely he knew that all these beauteous forms are copies of a unique picture which have been drawn by the Artist on frames of earth. At last there came to this Imra'u al-Qays such a spiritual experience that in the middle of the night he fled from his kingdom and children and concealed himself in the garb of a dervish and wandered from that clime to another clime in search of him who transcends all climes.[790]

In the following story about the love of Zulaykha, Mawlana well illustrates the Sufi precept that the invoker (*dhakir*) of the Divine Name, through the constant act of invocation (*dhikr*), becomes one with the invoked (*madhkur*). He compares allegorically the constant absorption of the Friends of God in their act of remembrance with the extent of Zulaykha's infatuation with Joseph, which caused her to conceal his name under all names. She applied to Joseph the name of everything. Their inner meaning was only known and revealed to her confidants.

> Zulaykha had applied to Joseph the name of everything
> from rue-seed to aloes-wood.
> She concealed his name in all names
> and made the inner meaning thereof known to her confidants.
> When she said, "The wax is softened by the fire,"
> this meant, "My beloved is very fond of me."
> And if she said, "Look the moon is risen,"
> or if she said, "The willow-bough is green..."[791]

That is to say, when she said: "Look, the moon is risen," she meant that the beauty of Joseph's countenance had appeared to her, and by saying: "The willow-bough is green," she was referring to the spiritual joy and delight associated with remembering the name of Joseph.

> Or if she said, "The leaves are quivering mightily,"
> or if she said, "The rue-seed is burning merrily..."[792]

350

If she said: "The leaves are quivering mightily," she meant that lovers were dancing cheerfully because of enchantment with his exquisite and majestic beauty. If she said: "The rue-seed is burning merrily," she was understood to mean that Joseph's beauty blinded the eyes of the envious and the jealous, as the rue-seed is burned to avert the evil eye.

> Or if she said, "The rose has told her secret to the nightingale,"
> or if she said, "The king has disclosed his passion for Shahnaz..."[793]

If Zulaykha said: "The rose has told her secret to the nightingale," she meant that Joseph had divulged all the secret mysteries of love to her. If she said: "The king has disclosed his passion for Shahnaz," she meant that God, by creating Joseph, had manifested all the mysteries of His beauty.

> Or if she said, "How auspicious is Fortune,"
> or if she said, "Give the furniture a good dusting..."[794]

If she said: "How auspicious is fortune," she wanted to signify how blessed was her fortune in virtue of her love for Joseph, and that "her furniture needed a good dusting," that is, her soul was in distress from being separated from her beloved and was in need of spiritual recreation and expansion.

> Or if she said, "The water-carrier has brought the water,"
> or if she said: "The sun is risen..."[795]

...she wanted to convey that the beauty of Joseph had allayed the passion of her heart, and that the bright sun of his beauty had illuminated her aggrieved heart.

> Or if she said, "Last night they cooked a potful of food,"
> or, "The vegetables are cooked to perfection."[796]

351

...she meant that her rawness and inexperience in love had given way to ripeness and perfection, and that her lustful and illusory love had been transmuted into a veritably real and Divine love.

> If she said, "The loaves have no salt,"
> or if she said, "The heavenly sphere
> is going round in the contrary direction..."[797]

...she meant that without the love of Joseph, life would not be gracious and worth living, and that the present circumstances were not yet favorable for her union with Joseph.

> If she said, "My head aches,"
> or if she said, "My headache is better."[798]

...she meant that she was quite aggrieved in virtue of her separation from Joseph, and that her pain and suffering from that separation had diminished.

> If she praised, it was his caresses that she meant;
> and if she blamed, it was separation from him.
> If she piled up a hundred thousand names,
> her meaning and intention was always Joseph.
> Were she hungry, as soon as she spoke his name
> she would be filled and intoxicated by his cup.
> Her thirst would be quenched by his name;
> the name of Joseph would be a sweet drink to her soul.
> And if she were in pain, by that exalted name
> her pain would immediately be turned into profit.
> In cold weather it was a fur to her.
> This, this the beloved's name can do
> in love.[799]

As mentioned earlier, the vulgar always pronounce the Holy Name, but since it is not imbued with true love, it does not do that work and does not have the same effect. In short what Jesus wrought by pronouncing the Divine Name was manifested to Zulaykha through the name of Joseph. But the upshot of the whole story, nay, the whole of the *Mathnawi* is recapitulated in the following verse:

> When the spirit has been united with God
> to speak of the one
> is to speak of the other.[800]

This can only be achieved in the station of unification, where any sign of duality is removed, and He alone remains as the unity of invoker, the invocation and the invoked.

Bibliography

Aflaki, Shams al-Din Ahmad. *Manaqib al-'Arifin*, ed. Tahsin Yaziji. Ankara, 1961.

Ibn 'Arabi, Muhyi al-Din. *Fusus al-Hikam*, ed. A. A. Affifi. Cairo, 1946.

Ibn 'Arabi, Muhyi al-Din. *al-Futuhat al-Makkiyyah*, ed. M. A. al-Mar'ashi. Dar Ihya' al-Turath al-'Arabi, Beirut, [n.d.].

Arberry, A. J. *The Discourses of Rumi*. John Murray. London, 1961.

Arberry, A. J. *More Tales from the Masnavi*. George Allen & Unwin. London, 1963.

Arberry, A. J. *Tales from the Masnavi*. George Allen & Unwin. London, 1961.

de Bruijn, J.T.P. *Of Piety and Poetry*. Brill. Leiden, 1983.

Chittick, William. *Me and Rumi: The Autobiography of Shams-i Tabrizi*. Fons Vitae. Louisville, 2004.

Chittick, William. *The Sufi Doctrine of Rumi: An Introduction*. Ariyamehr University Press. Tehran, 1974.

Chittick, William. *The Sufi Path of Knowledge*. SUNY Press. Albany, 1989.

Furuzanfar, Badi' al-Zaman. *Ma'akhidh-i Qasas wa Tamthilat-i Mathnawi*. Intisharat-i Danishgah Tehran. Tehran, 1347 [1968].

Furuzanfar, Badi' al-Zaman. *Risalah dar Tahqiq-i Ahwal wa Zindigani-yi Mawlana Jalal al-Din Muhammad Mashhur bih Mawlawi*. Zawwar. Tehran, 1333 [1954].

Furuzanfar, Badi' al-Zaman. *Sharh-i Mathnawi-yi Sharif*, 3 Vols. Intisharat-i Danishgah Tehran. Tehran, 1348 [1969].

Gulpinarli, 'Abd al-Baqi. *Mawlana Jalal al-Din*, Persian trans. by Tawfiq Subhani. Mu'assaseh-yi Mutala'at wa Tahqiqat-i Farhangi. Tehran, 1370 [1991].

Gulpinarli, 'Abd al-Baqi. *Mawlawiyyah ba'd az Mawlana*, Persian trans. by Tawfiq Subhani. Mu'assaseh-ye Kayhan. Tehran, 1366 [1987].

Hafiz. *Diwan*, Qazwini edition. Zawwar Publications. Tehran, [n.d.].

Huma'i, Jalal. *Mawlawi Nameh: Mawlawi Chi Miguyad*. Zawwar Publications. Tehran, 1393 [2014].

Jami, 'Abd al-Rahman. *Naqd al-Nusus fi Sharh Naqsh al-Fusus*, ed. William Chittick. Intisharat-i Anjuman-i Shahanshahi-yi Falsafah-yi Iran. Tehran, 1977.

Kirk, Raven, and Schofield. *The Presocratic Philosophers: A Critical History with a Selection of Texts*. Cambridge University Press. Cambridge, 1984.

Lewis, Franklin. *Rumi: Past and Present, East and West: The Life, Teaching and Poetry of Jalal al-Din Rumi*. Oneworld. Oxford, 2000.

Mudarris-Radawi. *Diwan-i Sana'i*. Sana'i Publications. Tehran, 1354 [1975].

Muwahhid, Muhammad 'Ali. *Bagh-i Sabz*, Karnameh Publications. Tehran, 1387.

Nasr, Seyyed Hossein. *The Garden of Truth*. HarperOne. San Francisco, 2007.

Nasr, Seyyed Hossein. *Jalal al-Din Rumi: Supreme Persian Poet and Sage*. Shura-yi 'Ali-yi Farhang wa Hunar. Tehran, 1974.

Nasr, Seyyed Hossein. *Knowledge and the Sacred*. SUNY Press. Albany, 1989.

Nasr, Seyyed Hossein et. al. (eds.), *The Study Quran*, editor in-Chief Seyyed Hossein Nasr. HarperOne. San Francisco, 2015.

Nicholson, Reynold A. *The Mathnawi of Jalaluddin Rumi* (English Translation), 6 Vols. Gibb Memorial Trust. London, 2013.

Oral, Osman. *I Believe in the Divine Destiny and Decree*. Tughra Books. Izmir, 2013.

Plotinus, *The Enneads of Plotinus*, trans. Stephen MacKenna. Faber and Faber. London, 1969.

Rumi, Mawlana Jalal al-Din. *Fihi ma Fihi*, ed. Furuzanfar. Amir Kabir Publications. Tehran, 1369 Solar [1990].

Rumi, Mawlana Jalal al-Din. *Kulliyat-i Shams (Diwan-i Kabir)* (ed. Furuzanfar), 10 Vols. Tehran University Press. Tehran, 1336–1346 [1957–1967].

Rumi, Mawlana Jalal al-Din. *Majalis-i Sab'ah*, ed. Taw-fiq Subhani. Intisharat-i Kayhan. Tehran, 1365 [1986].

Rumi, Mawlana Jalal al-Din. *Maktubat-i Mawlana Jalal al-Din Rumi*, ed. Tawfiq Subhani. Markaz-i Nashriyyat-i Danishgahi. [n.p.], 1381.

Rumi, Mawlana Jalal al-Din. *Mathnawi-yi Ma'nawi*, ed. Nicholson. Intisharat-i Amir Kabir. Tehran, 1339 [1960].

al-Sarraj, Abu Nasr. *Kitab al- Luma'*, ed. R. Nicholson. Brill. Leiden, 1914.

Shabistari, Mahmud. *Gulshan-i Raz*, ed. J. Nurbakhsh. Khanaqah-i Ni'matullahi Publications. Tehran, 1355 [1976].

Shahidi, Sayyid Ja'far. *Sharh-i Mathnawi*. Intisharat-i 'Ilmi-Farhangi. Tehran, 1383 [2004].

Shamisa, Sirus. *Guzideh-yi Ghazaliyyat-i Mawlawi*. Dadar. Tehran, 1379 [2000].

Shams-i Tabrizi. *Maqalat-i Shams-i Tabrizi*, edited by Muhammad 'Ali Muwahhid. Intisharat-i Khwarazmi. Tehran, 1369 [1990].

Shari'at, Muhammad Jawad. *Kashf al-Abyat-i Math-nawi*. Intisharat-i Kamal. Isfahan, 1363 [1984].

Sipahsalar, Faridun ibn Ahmad. *Zindigi-Nameh-yi Maw-lana Jalal al-Din-i Mawlawi*, ed. Sa'id Nafisi. Iqbal. Tehran, [n.d.].

Suhrawardi, Shihab al-Din Yahya. *Oeuvres philosophiques et mystiques,* Tome II. Academie Iranienne de philosophie. Tehran, 1977.

Sultan Walad. *Allah Nameh*, ed. Muhammad Ali Muwahhid and Alirida Haydari. Khwarazmi Publications. Tehran, 1389 [2010].

Sultan Walad. *Rubab Nameh*, ed. Ali Sultani-Gard-Faramarzi. McGill University Publications (Tehran Branch). Tehran, 1980.

Sultan Walad. *Walad Nameh*, ed. Jalal Huma'i. Kitabfurushi-yi Iqbal. Tehran, 1316 [1937].

Tilmidh Husayn. *Mir'at al-Mathnawi*. Silsilah-yi Nashriyat-i Ma (reprint edition). [n.p.], 1352.

Zamani, Karim. *Sharh-i Jami'-i Mathnawi-yi Ma'nawi.* Intisharat-i Mu'assaseh-yi Ittila'at. Tehran, 1372 [1993].

Zarrinkub, 'Abd al-Husayn. *Sirr-i Nay*, 2 Vols. Intisharat-i 'Ilmi. Tehran, 1369 [1990].

Endnotes

[1] Another version of this verse has as its second hemistich, "I burned, I burned, I burned."

[2] Quran, 102:5.

[3] Quran, 102:7.

[4] Quran, 56:95 and 69:51.

[5] *Mathnawi*, 2:860–61m.

[6] *Mathnawi*, 2:493–95.

[7] *Mathnawi*, 2:3265–66m.

[8] Because of his residence in Konya—formerly belonging to the Byzantine Empire, called by Muslims *al-Rum*.

[9] Badi' al-Zaman Furuzanfar, *Risalah dar Tahqiq-i Ahwal wa Zindigani-yi Mawlana Jalal al-Din Muhammad Mashhur bih Mawlawi* [henceforth *Zindigani-yi Mawlana Jalal al-Din*], Zawwar, Tehran, 1333 [1954], pp. 3–5.

[10] Ibid., p. 6; 'Abd al-Baqi Gulpinarli, *Mawlana Jalal al-Din*, Persian trans. by Tawfiq Subhani. Mu'assaseh-yi Mutala'at wa Tahqiqat-i Farhangi, Tehran, 1370 [1991], pp. 76–78.

[11] Furuzanfar, *Zindigani-yi Mawlana Jalal al-Din*, p. 6.

[12] Ibid., p. 9.

[13] Ibid.; Gulpinarli, *Mawlana Jalal al-Din*, p. 89.

[14] See Furuzanfar, *Zindigani-yi Mawlana Jalal al-Din*, p. 8.

[15] According to Sultan Walad, his grandfather, Baha' Walad, was being antagonized by the inhabitants of Balkh when, addressed by God perhaps in a dream, he was commanded to leave Balkh so that God might chastise its people. Accordingly, he departed for a pilgrimage to Mecca, in obedience to the command of God. He was on the way to Mecca when the news reached him of the Mongol invasion. Gulpinarli, *Mawlana Jalal al-Din*, p. 88.

[16] Franklin Lewis has cast doubt on this meeting, pointing out that it is neither mentioned by Rumi nor by his earliest biographers, but only enters the biographical tradition much later. See Franklin Lewis, *Rumi: Past and Present, East and West: The Life, Teaching and Poetry of Jalal al-Din Rumi*, Oneworld, Oxford, 2000, pp. 64–65. Readers seeking further information on the historical sources on the life of Rumi, his family, and the Mawlawiyya order are advised to consult this valuable work.

[17] Furuzanfar, *Zindigani-yi Mawlana Jalal al-Din*, p. 17.

359

[18] Sultan Walad passes over the period between Baha' Walad's return from the Hajj and his taking up residence in Konya without giving details. He only mentions that he went to Anatolia so that the people there might benefit from him, and among all its provinces chose Konya for his residence. See Sultan Walad, *Walad Nameh*, ed., Jalal Huma'i. Kitabfurushi-yi Iqbal, Tehran, 1316 [1937], p.191.

[19] Faridun ibn Ahmad Sipahsalar, *Zindigi-Nameh-yi Mawlana Jalal al-Din-i Mawlawi*, ed. Sa'id Nafisi, Iqbal, Tehran, [n. d.], p. 14.

[20] Shams al-Din Ahmad Aflaki, *Manaqib al-'Arifin*, ed. Tahsin Yaziji, Ankara, 1961, Vol. 1, p. 24.

[21] Furuzanfar, quoting Jami, mentions Baha' Walad's meeting with the great Sufi master Shihab al-Din Suhrawardi in Baghdad. Furuzanfar, *Zindigani-yi Mawlana Jalal al-Din*, p. 18.

[22] See Sipahsalar, *Zindigi-Nameh-yi Mawlana Jalal al-Din-i Mawlawi*, p. 14; Gulpinarli, *Mawlana Jalal al-Din*, pp. 87–88.

[23] Ibid., pp. 24–25.

[24] Furuzanfar, *Zindigani-yi Mawlana Jalal al-Din*, pp. 24–5; Aflaki, *Manaqib al-'Arifin*, Vol. 1, p. 26.

[25] Furuzanfar, *Zindigani-yi Mawlana Jalal al-Din*, p. 23.

[26] Gulpinarli, *Mawlana Jalal al-Din*, p. 90.

[27] Sultan Walad, *Walad Nameh*, p. 193; Gulpinarli, *Mawlana Jalal al-Din*, p. 90.

[28] Furuzanfar, *Zindigani-yi Mawlana Jalal al-Din*, p. 31.

[29] Ibid., Gulpinarli, *Mawlana Jalal al-Din*, p. 90.

[30] Sultan Walad, *Walad Nameh*, p. 193; Furuzanfar, *Zindigani-yi Mawlana Jalal al-Din*, p. 34.

[31] Furuzanfar mentions the *Manaqib* of Aflaki in particular. See *Zindigani-yi Mawlana Jalal al-Din*, p. 35.

[32] Ibid.

[33] Furuzanfar, *Zindigani-yi Mawlana Jalal al-Din*, p. 37; see also Sultan Walad, *Walad Nameh*, pp. 193–94.

[34] Sultan Walad, *Walad Nameh*, p. 196.

[35] Gulpinarli, *Mawlana Jalal al-Din*, p. 94.

[36] Furuzanfar, *Zindigani-yi Mawlana Jalal al-Din*, p. 39.

[37] Ibid., p. 44.

[38] Ibid.

[39] Sultan Walad, *Walad Nameh*, p. 169.

[40] Furuzanfar, *Zindigani-yi Mawlana Jalal al-Din*, p. 44; Gulpinarli discusses several of the reasons for preferring this date in *Mawlana Jalal al-Din*, pp. 97–98.

[41] Furuzanfar, *Zindigani-yi Mawlana Jalal al-Din*, p. 45.

42 Ibid., p. 46 (Quoting *Tadhkireh-yi Dawlat-Shah*).

43 Sultan Walad, *Walad Nameh*, p. 197; quoted in Furuzanfar, *Zindigani-yi Mawlana Jalal al-Din*, p. 47.

44 Ibid., p. 47.

45 Ibid.

46 Ibid.

47 Jalal Huma'i, *Mawlawi Nameh: Mawlawi Chi Miguyad*, Zawwar Publications, Tehran, 1393 [2014], p. 23.

48 Sipahsalar, *Zindigi-Nameh-yi Mawlana Jalal al-Din-i Mawlawi*, pp. 122–23.

49 Furuzanfar, *Zindigani-yi Mawlana Jalal al-Din*, p. 50.

50 Ibid.

51 Furuzanfar rejects this view. See *Zindigani-yi Mawlana Jalal al-Din*, p. 51.

52 Ibid.

53 Gulpinarli, *Mawlana Jalal al-Din*, pp. 102–3.

54 Furuzanfar, *Zindigani-yi Mawlana Jalal al-Din*, p. 56.

55 Ibid.

56 Ibid., pp. 62–63.

57 Sultan Walad, *Walad Nameh*, p. 198.

58 Furuzanfar, *Zindigani-yi Mawlana Jalal al-Din*, p. 67.

59 Ibid.

60 Ibid.

61 Ibid., p. 70.

62 Ibid., pp. 69–70.

63 Gulpinarli, *Mawlana Jalal al-Din*, pp. 147–48.

64 Ibid., pp. 148–49.

65 Furuzanfar, *Zindigani-yi Mawlana Jalal al-Din*, p. 70.

66 Ibid., p. 73. See also Sultan Walad, *Walad Nameh*, p. 49.

67 Ibid., p. 50.

68 This version, from Furuzanfar (*Zindigani-yi Mawlana Jalal al-Din*, p. 73) differs in its second hemistich from that given by Nicholson, which he translates "like beggars, snatched away the viands." *Mathnawi*, 1:84, where it is Jesus's request for sustenance from God that is being discussed.

69 Sections of which have been translated into English by William Chittick as *Me and Rumi: The Autobiography of Shams-i Tabrizi*, Fons Vitae, Louisville, 2004.

70 Furuzanfar, *Zindigani-yi Mawlana Jalal al-Din*, p. 74. See also Sultan Walad, *Walad Nameh*, p. 43.

71 Ibid., pp. 74–5.

72 Ibid., pp. 75–6.

73 Lewis, *Rumi: Past and Present, East and West*, p. 184.

[74] Gulpinarli, *Mawlana Jalal al-Din*, p. 150.

[75] Furuzanfar, *Zindigani-yi Mawlana Jalal al-Din*, p. 76; Sultan Walad, *Walad Nameh*, p. 52.

[76] Furuzanfar, *Zindigani-yi Mawlana Jalal al-Din*, pp. 76–77.

[77] Ibid., p. 77.

[78] Ibid.

[79] He explains the silence of Sultan Walad on the issue and Shams's prediction about his imminent absence by the fact that Sultan Walad was quite aware of the incident but concealed it from his father to the end of his life. Gulpinarli, *Mawlana Jalal al-Din*, pp. 151–52.

[80] Lewis, *Rumi: Past and Present, East and West*, pp. 185–93.

[81] Furuzanfar, *Zindigani-yi Mawlana Jalal al-Din*, p. 79; Gulpinarli, *Mawlana Jalal al-Din*, p. 159.

[82] Sana'i Ghaznawi, Abu'l-Majd Majdud ibn Adam (d. 1131), the author of *Hadiqat al-Haqiqah*. See Mudarris-Radawi, *Diwan-i Sana'i*, Sana'i Publications, Tehran, 1354 [1975], and J.T.P. de Bruijn, *Of Piety and Poetry*, Brill, Leiden, 1983.

[83] See Ibid., p. 166, and Furuzanfar, *Zindigani-yi Mawlana Jalal al-Din*, p. 79n.

[84] Ibid., p. 80. See also Gulpinarli, *Mawlana Jalal al-Din*, p. 160.

[85] Furuzanfar, *Zindigani-yi Mawlana Jalal al-Din*, p. 79; Gulpinarli, *Mawlana Jalal al-Din*, pp. 80–81.

[86] Ibid., p. 84.

[87] Ibid.

[88] Ibid.

[89] Ibid.

[90] Ibid., p. 85; Sultan Walad, *Walad Nameh*, pp. 57–58.

[91] Furuzanfar, *Zindigani-yi Mawlana Jalal al-Din*, p. 85; Sultan Walad, *Walad Nameh*, p. 58.

[92] Furuzanfar, *Zindigani-yi Mawlana Jalal al-Din*, p. 85.

[93] Ibid., p. 87.

[94] Furuzanfar, *Zindigani-yi Mawlana Jalal al-Din*, p. 88.

[95] Ibid., p. 86n; Sultan Walad, *Walad Nameh*, pp. 60–61.

[96] See *Mathnawi*, 2:1350.

[97] *Mathnawi*, 2:2163–66m.

[98] Sirus Shamisa, *Guzideh-yi Ghazaliyyat-i Mawlawi*, Dadar, Tehran, 1379 [2000], p. 15.

[99] Ibid.

[100] Ibid., p. 16n. *Mathnawi*, 5:2339m.

[101] Shamisa, *Guzideh-yi Ghazaliyyat-i Mawlawi*, p. 16.

[102] *Mathnawi*, 2:1112–14m.

103 *Mathnawi*, 1:119–24m

104 Furuzanfar, *Zindigani-yi Mawlana Jalal al-Din*, p. 92; Shamisa, *Guzideh-yi Ghazaliyyat-i Mawlawi*, p. 17.

105 Aflaki, quoted in Furuzanfar, *Zindigani-yi Mawlana Jalal al-Din*, p. 93.

106 Ibid., p. 95; Sultan Walad, *Walad Nameh*, p. 64.

107 Furuzanfar, *Zindigani-yi Mawlana Jalal al-Din*, pp. 95–96; Sultan Walad, *Walad Nameh*, p. 71.

108 Furuzanfar, *Zindigani-yi Mawlana Jalal al-Din*, p. 96; Sultan Walad, *Walad Nameh*, p. 71.

109 Furuzanfar, *Zindigani-yi Mawlana Jalal al-Din*, p. 97; Sultan Walad, *Walad Nameh*, pp. 74–75.

110 Furuzanfar, *Zindigani-yi Mawlana Jalal al-Din*, p. 98.

111 *Mathnawi*, 2:1320–1324.

112 *Mathnawi*, 2:159–60.

113 Furuzanfar, *Zindigani-yi Mawlana Jalal al-Din*, p. 100.

114 Lines by Sultan Walad from *Walad Nameh*, quoted in ibid., p. 100n.

115 Ibid., p. 101.

116 Sultan Walad, *Walad Nameh*, p. 113.

117 *Mathnawi*, 1: Preface.

118 Furuzanfar, *Zindigani-yi Mawlana Jalal al-Din*, pp. 103–4.

119 Ibid., p. 104.

120 Ibid.

121 Ibid., pp. 104–5.

122 Ibid., pp. 107–8.

123 Ibid., pp. 108–9.

124 *Mathnawi*, 2:1–7m.

125 Pronounced "*Zia al-Haqq*" in Persian.

126 *Mathnawi*, 4:1–6m.

127 *Mathnawi*, 1–3.

128 *Mathnawi*, 3:6.

129 Furuzanfar, *Zindigani-yi Mawlana Jalal al-Din*, p. 110.

130 Ibid., pp. 110–1.

131 Ibid., p. 111; *Mathnawi*, 6:4619m.

132 Furuzanfar, *Zindigani-yi Mawlana Jalal al-Din*, p. 111.

133 Ibid., p. 113n.

134 Ibid., p. 110. See also Sultan Walad, *Walad Nameh*, p. 121.

135 Gulpinarli, *Mawlana Jalal al-Din*, p. 236. According to Aflaki (*Manaqib*, Vol. 1, p. 353), Qunawi performed the funeral prayer after recovering from his faint. While unconscious, he is reported to have seen the Prophet Mohammad followed by hosts of angels praying the funeral prayer for Mawlana.

[136] Furuzanfar, *Zindigani-yi Mawlana Jalal al-Din*, p. 113n.

[137] Ibid., p. 114n.

[138] Ibid., p. 115; Gulpinarli, *Mawlana Jalal al-Din*, p. 239.

[139] Sultan Walad, *Walad Nameh*, Editor's Introduction, pp. 62–63.

[140] See Ibid., p. 62. For an extensive discussion of the Mevlevi Order and the descendants of Mawlana, see 'Abd al-Baqi Golpinarli, *Mawlawiyyah ba'd az Mawlana*, Persian trans. by Tawfiq Subhani, Mu'assaseh-ye Kayhan, Tehran, 1366 [1987].

[141] Furuzanfar, *Zindigani-yi Mawlana Jalal al-Din*, p. 158.

[142] Gulpinarli, *Mawlana Jalal al-Din*, p. 222.

[143] Classical Persian poetry is usually divided into three distinct styles: Khurasani, Iraqi, and Hindi.

[144] Mawlana Jalal al-Din Rumi, *Kulliyat-i Shams (Diwan-i Kabir)*, Tehran University Press, Tehran, 10 Vols, 1336–46 [1957–67].

[145] Mawlana Jalal al-Din Rumi, *Fihi Ma Fihi*, edited by Furuzanfar, Amir Kabir Publications, Tehran, 1369 Solar [1990], Editor's Introduction.

[146] See Furuzanfar, *Zindigani-yi Mawlana Jalal al-Din*, p. 167.

[147] Intisharat-i Kayhan, Tehran, 1365 [1986].

[148] Ibid., p. 168.

[149] Ibid., p. 169.

[150] Chittick, *Me and Rumi*, p. xi.

[151] Shams-i Tabrizi, *Maqalat-i Shams-i Tabrizi*, edited by Muhammad 'Ali Muwahhid, Intisharat-i Khwarazmi, Tehran, 1369 [1990], p. 77; *Me and Rumi*, p. 4.

[152] *Maqalat*, p. 340; *Me and Rumi*, p. 9.

[153] *Me and Rumi*, p. 74.

[154] *Maqalat*, p. 681; *Me and Rumi*, p. 192.

[155] *Maqalat*, p. 767; *Me and Rumi*, p. 192.

[156] *Maqalat*, p. 225; *Me and Rumi*, p. 192.

[157] *Maqalat*, p. 186; *Me and Rumi*, p. 193.

[158] *Maqalat*, p. 744; *Me and Rumi*, p. 16.

[159] *Maqalat*, pp. 759–60; *Me and Rumi*, p. 179.

[160] See M. Muwahhid, *Bagh-i Sabz*, Karnameh Publications, Tehran, 1387, p. 63.

[161] *Maqalat*, p. 734.

[162] *Maqalat*, p. 763; *Me and Rumi*, p. 179.

[163] *Maqalat*, p. 290; *Me and Rumi*, p. 184.

[164] *Maqalat*, p. 690; *Me and Rumi*, p. 184.

[165] *Maqalat*, pp. 618–19; *Me and Rumi*, p. 185.

[166] *Maqalat*, p. 142; *Me and Rumi*, p. 187.

167 *Maqalat*, p. 622; *Me and Rumi*, p. 187.

168 *Maqalat*, pp. 78–79; *Me and Rumi*, p. 117.

169 *Maqalat*, p. 730; *Me and Rumi*, p. 209.

170 *Maqalat*, p. 761; *Me and Rumi*, p. 56.

171 *Maqalat*, p. 643; *Me and Rumi*, p. 87.

172 *Maqalat*, p. 741; *Me and Rumi*, p. 82.

173 *Maqalat*, p. 657; *Me and Rumi*, pp. 82–83.

174 *Maqalat*, p. 690; *Me and Rumi*, p. 84.

175 *Maqalat*, p. 106, *Me and Rumi*, p. 190.

176 *Maqalat*, pp. 210–11; *Me and Rumi*, p. 87.

177 *Maqalat*, p. 280; *Me and Rumi*, p. 88.

178 *Maqalat*, p. 262; *Me and Rumi*, p. 93.

179 *Maqalat*, pp. 649 and 761; *Me and Rumi*, pp. 57 and 64.

180 *Maqalat*, pp. 239–240; *Me and Rumi*, p. 31. The question of whether the "Shaykh Muhammad" that Shams speaks of is indeed Ibn 'Arabi is a point of contention among scholars. Muhammad 'Ali Muwahhid firmly believes that "Shaykh Muhammad" is Ibn 'Arabi, and Franklin Lewis would like to believe the same (see Lewis, *Rumi: Past and Present, East and West*, p. 149). William Chittick, however, believes that there is insufficient evidence to draw a conclusion (see *Me and Rumi*, xviii–xix) However, given the large amount of circumstantial evidence, including the type of utterances regarding "the Necessary Being" and the status of Ibn 'Arabi in Damascus of the time, it is highly likely that these two figures are one and the same.

181 *Maqalat*, pp. 239–240; *Me and Rumi*, p. 31.

182 *Maqalat*, p. 94; *Me and Rumi*, p. 31.

183 *Maqalat*, p. 777; *Me and Rumi*, p. 33.

184 *Maqalat*, p. 697; *Me and Rumi*, p. 28.

185 *Maqalat*, p. 304; *Me and Rumi*, pp. 33–34.

186 *Me and Rumi*, p. 147.

187 *Maqalat*, pp. 321–23; *Me and Rumi*, pp. 147–48.

188 *Maqalat*, p. 249; *Me and Rumi*, p. 41.

189 *Maqalat*, p. 111; *Me and Rumi*, p. 25.

190 *Maqalat*, p. 193; *Me and Rumi*, p. 27.

191 *Maqalat*, p. 339; *Me and Rumi*, p. 27.

192 *Maqalat*, p. 192; *Me and Rumi*, p. 26.

193 *Maqalat*, p. 231; *Me and Rumi*, p. 64.

194 *Maqalat*, p. 716; *Me and Rumi*, p. 68.

195 *Maqalat*, p. 86; *Me and Rumi*, pp. 66–67.

196 *Maqalat*, p. 716; *Me and Rumi*, p. 103.

197 *Maqalat*, p. 145; *Me and Rumi*, p. 120.

[198] *Maqalat*, p. 718; *Me and Rumi*, p. 137.
[199] *Maqalat*, p. 212; *Me and Rumi*, p. 136.
[200] *Maqalat*, p. 203; *Me and Rumi*, p. 137.
[201] *Maqalat*, p. 203; *Me and Rumi*, p. 137.
[202] *Maqalat*, pp. 296–97; *Me and Rumi*, pp. 64–65.
[203] *Maqalat*, p. 275; *Me and Rumi*, p. 28.
[204] *Maqalat*, p. 345; *Me and Rumi*, p. 86.
[205] *Maqalat*, p. 23; *Me and Rumi*, p. 635.
[206] *Maqalat*, p. 18; *Me and Rumi*, p. 25.
[207] *Maqalat*, p. 678.
[208] *Maqalat*, p. 128; *Me and Rumi*, pp. 48–49.
[209] *Maqalat*, p. 288; *Me and Rumi*, p. 66.
[210] *Maqalat*, pp. 249–50; *Me and Rumi*, pp. 93–94.
[211] *Maqalat*, pp. 739–40; *Me and Rumi*, p. 63.
[212] *Maqalat*, p. 649; *Me and Rumi*, p. 64.
[213] *Maqalat*, pp. 192–93; *Me and Rumi*, p. 27.
[214] *Maqalat*, p. 75; *Me and Rumi*, p. 69.
[215] *Maqalat*, p. 62; *Me and Rumi*, p. 88.
[216] *Maqalat*, p. 231; *Me and Rumi*, p. 97.
[217] *Maqalat*, p. 160; *Me and Rumi*, p. 106.
[218] *Maqalat*, p. 146; *Me and Rumi*, p. 119.
[219] *Maqalat*, p. 212–13; *Me and Rumi*, p. 136.
[220] *Maqalat*, p. 84; *Me and Rumi*, p. 64.
[221] *Maqalat*, p. 691; *Me and Rumi*, p. 71.
[222] *Maqalat*, p. 209; *Me and Rumi*, p. 71.
[223] *Maqalat*, p. 303; *Me and Rumi*, p. 71.
[224] *Maqalat*, p. 645; *Me and Rumi*, p. 79.
[225] *Maqalat*, p. 643; *Me and Rumi*, p. 87.
[226] *Maqalat*, p. 657; *Me and Rumi*, p. 158. *Taha*, with which Sura 20 of the Quran begins, and which is alluded to in this passage, is considered to be a name of the Prophet.
[227] *Maqalat*, pp. 196–97; *Me and Rumi*, p. 70.
[228] *Maqalat*, p. 134; *Me and Rumi*, p. 198.
[229] *Maqalat*, pp. 299–300; *Me and Rumi*, p. 85.
[230] *Maqalat*, p. 657; *Me and Rumi*, p. 134.
[231] *Maqalat*, pp. 316–17; *Me and Rumi*, pp. 103–4.
[232] *Maqalat*, pp. 236–37; *Me and Rumi*, p. 97.
[233] *Maqalat*, p. 97; *Me and Rumi*, p. 102.
[234] Sultan Walad, *Walad Nameh*, p. 268.
[235] *Maqalat*, p. 294; *Me and Rumi*, p. 34.
[236] *Maqalat*, p. 127; *Me and Rumi*, pp. 180–81.
[237] *Maqalat*, p. 115.

238 Rumi, *Fihi ma Fihi*, p. 88.

239 *Maqalat*, p. 148.

240 *Maqalat*, p. 202; *Me and Rumi*, p. 45.

241 *Maqalat*, p. 227; *Me and Rumi*, p. 46.

242 *Maqalat*, p. 75; *Me and Rumi*, p. 46.

243 *Maqalat*, p. 178; *Me and Rumi*, pp. 50–51.

244 *Maqalat*, pp. 78–79; *Me and Rumi*, p. 127.

245 *Maqalat*, p. 718; *Me and Rumi*, p. 137.

246 Cf. Quran, 30:50.

247 *Maqalat*, p. 624; *Me and Rumi*, p. 137.

248 See Seyyed Hossein Nasr et.al. (eds.), *The Study Quran*, HarperOne, 2015, p. 452.

249 *Maqalat*, pp. 174–75; *Me and Rumi*, p. 171.

250 *Maqalat*, p. 627; *Me and Rumi*, p. 198.

251 *Maqalat*, 184; *Me and Rumi*, p. 152.

252 *Maqalat*, p. 698; *Me and Rumi*, pp. 152–53.

253 This section is found in *Maqalat*, pp. 634–35. Compare Chittick's translation in *Me and Rumi*, pp. 155–56.

254 *Me and Rumi*, p. 134.

255 *Maqalat*, p. 728; *Me and Rumi*, p. 135.

256 *Maqalat*, pp. 280–81. Compare Chittick's translation in *Me and Rumi*, p. 71.

257 Huma'i, *Mawlawi Nameh*, p. 45. Mawlana attributes this position to the theologians he is criticizing, with the words: "This is the interpretation of the Mu'tazilites and of those who do not possess the light of immediate (mystical) intuition." See *Mathnawi*, 3:1025–27.

258 *Mathnawi*, 3:1496–1500m.

259 *Mathnawi*, 3:1508–9m.

260 *Phaedrus*, 253a–256d.

261 *Mathnawi*, 2:1759m.

262 See Kirk, Raven, and Schofield, *The Presocratic Philosophers: A Critical History with a Selection of Texts*, Cambridge University Press, Cambridge, 1984, Chapter 6, pp. 181–212.

263 *Mathnawi*, 3:4725–7.

264 *Mathnawi*, 3:1019–24. The first line translated is missing in Nicholson but is mentioned in other editions.

265 *Mathnawi*, 2:691–5.

266 *Mathnawi*, 5:780–3m.

267 *Mathnawi*, 4:3499–3501.

268 *Mathnawi*, 3:2219–20m.

269 *Mathnawi*, 6:2344.

270 *Mathnawi*, 1:3279.

271 *Mathnawi*, 1:3280.

[272] *Mathnawi*, 4:409–10m.

[273] *Mathnawi*, 1:1459–62m.

[274] *Mathnawi*, 2:1942–49m.

[275] Plato, *The Republic*, 514a–521b.

[276] *Mathnawi*, 2:1277–81m.

[277] *Mathnawi*, 6:3640–44m.

[278] *Mathnawi*, 1:409–10.

[279] See Quran, 6:32, 49:64, 47:36, 57:20.

[280] *Mathnawi*, 1:3430–32m.

[281] *Mathnawi*, 3:1222–26.

[282] *Mathnawi*, 6:66. Author's translation.

[283] See *Mathnawi*, 4:3766.

[284] *Mathnawi*, 4:3767.

[285] *Mathnawi*, 4:521–24.

[286] *Awwal al-fikr akhir al-'amal.*

[287] A. J. Arberry, *The Discourses of Rumi*, John Murray, London, 1961, p. 22.

[288] *Mathnawi*, 4:313–45.

[289] *Mathnawi*, 1:1317–20.

[290] *Mathnawi*, 6:3172–75m.

[291] *Mathnawi*, 4:809–11.

[292] The reality of the perfect man, called the "Muhammadan Reality" in Sufism, is the isthmus or the intermediary between God and all creation. As an intermediary it represents the perfect Attributes of God and moreover comprehends in itself the reality of all things. In other words, the Muhammadan Reality as the first determination comprises in itself all other determinations and the realities of all things. See 'Abd al-Rahman Jami, *Naqd al-Nusus fi Sharh Naqsh al-Fusus*, ed. William Chittick, Intisharat-i Anjuman-i Shahanshahi-yi Falsafah-yi Iran, Tehran, 1977, p. 92.

[293] *Mathnawi*, 4:806–8.

[294] *Mathnawi*, 5:3575–79m.

[295] *The Discourses of Rumi*, p. 73.

[296] *Mathnawi*, 6:3640–43.

[297] *Mathnawi*, 4:760–62.

[298] *Mathnawi*, 1:1406–7.

[299] *Mathnawi*, 2:2309.

[300] *Mathnawi*, 5:770–71m.

[301] *The Discourses of Rumi*, pp. 19–20.

[302] *The Discourses of Rumi*, p. 45.

[303] Ibid.

[304] *The Discourses of Rumi*, p. 61.

305 *Mathnawi*, 3:2700–9m.

306 *Mathnawi*, 6:1713.

307 *Mathnawi*, 1:721–24.

308 Israfil is the archangel of the resurrection, who by blowing on his horn raises the dead to life on the Day of Judgment.

309 *Mathnawi*, 1:1030.

310 Aristotle, *Metaphysics*, 980a.

311 *Mathnawi*, 2:277–79m.

312 *Mathnawi*, 2:1032–36m.

313 *Mathnawi*, 2:978m.

314 Nasr, *The Garden of Truth*, HarperCollins, New York, 2008, p. 30.

315 *Mathnawi*, 2:494–500m.

316 *Mathnawi*, 3:2648–52m.

317 *Mathnawi*, 1:3430–36m. Buraq is the horse-like creature with a human face that the Prophet rode on his nocturnal journey and celestial ascent (*isra'*, *mi'raj*), and Duldul is the horse given to 'Ali by the Prophet.

318 *Mathnawi*, 1:416–23.

319 *Mathnawi*, 1:24–29.

320 Seyyed Hossein Nasr, *Knowledge and the Sacred*, SUNY Press, Albany, 1989, p. 6.

321 *Mathnawi*, 2:1940–1941m.

322 *Mathnawi*, 5:490–91m.

323 *Mathnawi*, 4:732–38m.

324 Aristotle, *Metaphysics*, 980a.

325 *Mathnawi*, 2:277m.

326 *Mathnawi*, 6:149–52m.

327 *Mathnawi*, 6:811–12m.

328 *Mathnawi*, 2:3326–3332m.

329 *Mathnawi*, 1:1937–9m. These lines refer to two Prophetic traditions: the first (discussed below) is the "hadith of supererogatory works" in which God says of the servant whom He loves: "I become the hearing by which he hears, the sight by which he sees, the hand by which he grasps, and the foot by which he walks..."; the second states: "He who belongs to God, God belongs to him."

330 *Mathnawi*, 5:561–67m.

331 *Mathnawi*, 3:2648.

332 *Mathnawi*, 3:425–57m.

333 *Mathnawi*, 4:3766–67m.

334 *Mathnawi*, 1:2502–3m.

335 See Paul Henry's Introduction to *The Enneads of Plotinus*, trans. Stephen MacKenna, Faber and Faber, London, 1969, p. xxxi.

336 *Mathnawi*, 5:3574–5m.

337 Ibn 'Arabi, *Fusus al-Hikam*, ed. A. A. Affifi, Cairo, 1946, Chapter One (*Fass Adami*).

338 i.e. the Prophet Muhammad.

339 *Mathnawi*, 4:521–27m.

340 *Mathnawi*, 4:1363–66m.

341 *Mathnawi*, 3:3576–79m.

342 *Mathnawi*, 6:3837–41m.

343 *Mathnawi*, 3:3935–37m.

344 *Mathnawi*, 5:1721–25m.

345 *Mathnawi*, 6:738–39m.

346 Ahmad is the celestial name of the Prophet Muhammad.

347 *Mathnawi*, 6:750–56m.

348 *Mathnawi*, 4:1373m.

349 *Mathnawi*, 3:3901–6m.

350 *Mathnawi*, 5:3423–24.

351 *Mathnawi*, 4:1545–47m.

352 *Mathnawi*, 1:1541–44m.

353 *Mathnawi*, 4:3025–29m.

354 *Mathnawi*, 4:411–18m.

355 This is a reference to the tradition of the Prophet: "Verily God created the creatures in darkness, then He sprinkled upon them of His light."

356 *Mathnawi* 2:186–89m.

357 *Mathnawi*, 3:2245–51m.

358 *Mathnawi*, 6:3306–7.

359 *Mathnawi*, 2:3129–32m.

360 *Mathnawi*, 5:871–76.

361 *Mathnawi*, 5:902.

362 *Mathnawi*, 3:514–15.

363 "Silenus was a minor woodland deity of ancient Greek mythology having usually human form but with a horse's ears and tail, and occasionally with the legs of a horse or a goat and being one of the companions of Dionysus." *Webster's Third New International Dictionary*, "Silenus."

364 Plato, *Symposium*, 215b.

365 *Mathnawi*, 6:3172–83m.

366 *Mathnawi*, 6:4403–6m.

367 *Mathnawi*, 5:2731–32.

368 *Mathnawi*, 3:4719–28m.

369 *Mathnawi*, 1:22–27m.
370 *Mathnawi*, 4:3279–83.
371 *Mathnawi*, 1:109–16m.
372 *Mathnawi*, 5:1163–65.
373 *Mathnawi*, 6:971–72m.
374 *Mathnawi*, 5:2186–88.
375 *Mathnawi*, 1:217–21m.
376 *Mathnawi*, 5:3272.
377 *Mathnawi*, 5:586–90m.
378 *Mathnawi*, 2:703–17.
379 *Mathnawi*, 3:554–59m.
380 *Mathnawi*, 6:971–79m.
381 *Mathnawi*, 1:205.
382 *Mathnawi*, 5:1201–5.
383 *Mathnawi*, 5:3853–58.
384 *Mathnawi*, 5:2012–14.
385 *Mathnawi*, 6:2674–80.
386 *Mathnawi*, 5:390–91m.
387 *Mathnawi*, 6:1979–81m.
388 *Mathnawi*, 6:908–13m.
389 *Mathnawi*, 3:3020–24.
390 *Mathnawi*, 3:3847–50m.
391 *Nab,* comes from the word *naba',* meaning "news," just as "prophet" in English is from the Greek *pro-phenai,* "to foretell."
392 *Mathnawi*, 1:1930–9m.
393 *Mathnawi*, 1:2653–55m.
394 *Mathnawi*, 1:423–26m.
395 *Mathnawi*, 2:815–22m.
396 *Mathnawi*, 1:1603–10m.
397 *Mathnawi*, 1:716–26m.
398 *Mathnawi*, 2:2163–67.
399 *Mathnawi*, 3:3352–64m.
400 *Mathnawi*, 3:3605–10m.
401 *Mathnawi*, 2:3218–22m.
402 *Mathnawi*, 6:2151–53m.
403 *Mathnawi*, 3:3333m.
404 *Mathnawi*, 2:1478–82m.
405 *Mathnawi*, 3:3562–66m.
406 The story in which these lines occur tells of Bayazid Bastami's prognostication of the coming of the great saint, Bu'l-Hasan Kharaqani, who would be born in Kharaqan near Bastam. Rumi asks how Bayazid knew of Kharaqani's birth centuries before it happened, and answers that Bayazid could read it in the Guarded Tablet.

[407] *Mathnawi*, 4:1851–55m.

[408] *Mathnawi*, 5:2238–40m.

[409] *Mathnawi*, 1:1669–71m. The phrase "neither skewer nor kabob is burnt" (*na sikh besuzad na kabab*) has now become an idiom meaning "to solve a situation with no harm done to either side by taking a middle way."

[410] *Mathnawi*, 5:199–221m.

[411] *Mathnawi*, 3:2730–32m.

[412] *Mathnawi*, 5:2484–93m.

[413] *Mathnawi*, 1:2979–80.

[414] *Mathnawi*, 1:2981–3012.

[415] *Mathnawi*, 1:3000–3001.

[416] *Mathnawi*, 4:374–79m.

[417] *Mathnawi*, 1:2939–41m.

[418] *Mathnawi*, 1:2943–54m.

[419] *Mathnawi*, 4:538–56m.

[420] *Mathnawi*, 2:1567–68m.

[421] *Mathnawi*, 6:2025–26m.

[422] *Mathnawi*, 3:1772–74m.

[423] *Mathnawi*, 5:736–38m.

[424] *Mathnawi*, 5:739–44m.

[425] *Mathnawi*, 4:3372–76m.

[426] The story is found in Quran 18:60–82.

[427] The Green Prophet explained: "Now I will tell thee the interpretation of that thou couldst not bear patiently. As for the ship, it belonged to certain poor men, who toiled upon the sea; and I desired to damage it, for behind them there was a king who was seizing every ship by brutal force. As for the lad, his parents were believers; and we were afraid he would impose on them insolence and unbelief; so we desired that the Lord should give to them in exchange one better than he in purity, and nearer in tenderness. As for the wall, it belonged to two orphaned lads in the city, and under it was a treasure belonging to them. Their father was a righteous man; and thy Lord desired that they should come of age and then bring forth their treasure as a mercy from thy Lord. I did it not of my bidding. This is the interpretation of that thou couldst not bear patiently." Quran 18:78–82, trans. Arberry.

[428] *Mathnawi*, 1:224-229m.

[429] *Mathnawi*, 1:2959-64m.

[430] *Mathnawi*, 1:2965-2971m.

[431] The element of which all the celestial spheres are composed, which is different from the four elements of the sub-lunar sphere.

[432] *Mathnawi*, 6:4121–24m.

[433] See the introduction to Suhrawardi's *Hikmat al-Ishraq*, Shihab al-Din Yahya Suhrawardi, *Oeuvres philosophiques et mystiques*, Tome II, Academie Iranienne de philosophie, Tehran, 1977, p. 11.

[434] *Mathnawi*, 4:2818–26m.

[435] *The Enneads of Plotinus*, trans. Stephen MacKenna, p. xxxi.

[436] *Mathnawi*, 1:1109–12m.

[437] *Mathnawi*, 4:3259–70m.

[438] Not traffic accidents, though there are many of those, but rather accidents in the Aristotelian sense, as opposed to substance.

[439] "Has there come on a while of time when he was a thing unremembered. We created man of a sperm drop, a mingling, trying him; and We made him hearing, seeing. Surely We guided him upon the way whether he be thankful or unthankful." Quran 76:1–3, trans. Arberry.

[440] *Mathnawi*, 2: 976–78m.

[441] *Mathnawi*, 4:2188–96m.

[442] *Mathnawi*, 6:4075–77m.

[443] *Mathnawi*, 4:2179–89m.

[444] *Mathnawi*, 5:459–69.

[445] *Mathnawi*, 2:3252–59m.

[446] *Mathnawi*, 4:1497–1504m.

[447] *Mathnawi*, 4:408–14m.

[448] *Mathnawi*, 4:3637–57m.

[449] *Mathnawi*, 4:1986–91m.

[450] See Quran 2:102.

[451] *Mathnawi*, 5:619–24m.

[452] *Mathnawi*, 6:993–94.

[453] In many traditional Persian cities, most houses had pools in their courtyards, which were supplied with water through channels cut next to the roads throughout the city.

[454] *Mathnawi*, 4:1960–68m.

[455] *Mathnawi*, 1:1501–2m.

[456] *Mathnawi*, 3:3650–56m.

[457] Imam 'Ali was asked whether his adversary, Mu'awiyah, had 'aql, and he replied that he did not have 'aql in the true sense, but had daha, which could be translated as "cunning" or "astuteness," or which in a modern context could be called "Machiavellian reason."

[458] The terms Universal Intellect ('aql-i kulli) and the Total Intellect ('aql-i kull) are both applied to the Cosmic Intelligence and the highest level of intellect within human beings. When

the former meaning is intended, they should be capitalized, and when the latter is indicated, they may be uncapitalized.

[459] *Mathnawi*, 5:463m.
[460] *Mathnawi*, 4:3319–20m.
[461] See Quran 53:14.
[462] *Mathnawi*, 6:4126–39m.
[463] See Quran 27:40.
[464] *Mathnawi*, 4:1246–58m.
[465] *Mathnawi*, 4:1516–20m.
[466] *Mathnawi*, 3:1558–61m.
[467] *Mathnawi*, 4:1294–1300m.
[468] *Mathnawi*, 4:3339–42m.
[469] *Mathnawi*, 4:1402–10m.
[470] *Mathnawi*, 1:1982–84m.
[471] *Mathnawi*, 4:1424–28m.
[472] *Mathnawi*, 1:2214–15m.
[473] *Mathnawi*, 3:1145–46m.
[474] *Mathnawi*, 6:117–20m.
[475] *Mathnawi*, 1:214–15.
[476] *Mathnawi*, 4:165.
[477] *Mathnawi*, 5:3180–2.
[478] *Mathnawi*, 5:3152–53.
[479] *Mathnawi*, 5:3131–33m.
[480] *Mathnawi*, 2:1239–43.
[481] *Mathnawi*, 6:4276.
[482] *Mathnawi*, 6:2576.
[483] *Mathnawi*, 2:2735.
[484] *Mathnawi*, 1:180–81m.
[485] *Mathnawi*, 6:2577–78.
[486] *Mathnawi*, 6:2219–20.
[487] *Mathnawi*, 2:845–46.
[488] *Mathnawi*, 4:2062.
[489] *Mathnawi*, 1:1593–97m.
[490] *Mathnawi*, 1:1658–59m.
[491] *Mathnawi*, 5:1175–77.
[492] *Mathnawi*, 2:1271–74.
[493] *Mathnawi*, 6:3573–75.
[494] *Mathnawi*, 2238–39.
[495] *Mathnawi*, 1:2226–27m.
[496] *Mathnawi*, 1:1541–44m.
[497] *Mathnawi*, 3:211–13.
[498] *Mathnawi*, 4:3030–34.
[499] *Mathnawi*, 2:30.

500 *Mathnawi*, 2:28.
501 See *Mathnawi*, 2:28–35.
502 *Mathnawi*, 6:1591.
503 *Mathnawi*, 2:95–96m.
504 *Mathnawi*, 1:711–712m.
505 *Mathnawi*, 2:121–22.
506 *Mathnawi*, 4:1976–78.
507 *Mathnawi*, 2:1461.
508 *Mathnawi*, 3:2592–98.
509 *Mathnawi*, 4:1947–51.
510 *Mathnawi*, 1:1160m.
511 *Mathnawi*, 2:2129–32.
512 *Mathnawi*, 6:2950m.
513 *Mathnawi*, 5:2634–35.
514 *Mathnawi*, 4:1383–85m.
515 *Mathnawi*, 6:1431.
516 *Mathnawi*, 1:1043–44.
517 *Mathnawi*, 2:2268–69, 77.
518 *Mathnawi*, 6:2611–21m.
519 *Mathnawi*, 1:1136–41m.
520 *Mathnawi*, 1:1142–45.
521 *Mathnawi*, 1:1146–48m.
522 *Mathnawi*, 1:1448–50m.
523 *Mathnawi*, 6:761.
524 *Mathnawi*, 5:3305–6.
525 *Mathnawi*, 2:719–21.
526 *Mathnawi*, 3:2529, 2534–35m.
527 *Mathnawi*, 1:3330–39m.
528 *Mathnawi*, 2:1032–40.
529 *Mathnawi*, 6:2952–53m.
530 *Mathnawi*, 6:2971–72m.
531 *Mathnawi*, 1:2870–1m.
532 *Mathnawi*, 4: 3692–93.
533 *Mathnawi*, 4: 3696.
534 *Mathnawi*, 3: 3191–92.
535 This verse is only paraphrased in prose in the title to this section of the *Mathnawi*, so it is not possible to trace its origin.
536 *Mathnawi*, 1:2035–36.
537 *Mathnawi*, 1:2066–70.
538 *Mathnawi*, 3:1151–54m.
539 *Mathnawi*, 5:3590.
540 *Mathnawi*, 5:3591–94m.
541 *Mathnawi*, 6:56–60.

542 *Mathnawi*, 2:55–56.

543 *Mathnawi*, 1:712–13.

544 i.e. the animal or vital spirit.

545 *Mathnawi*, 1:1974–77.

546 *Mathnawi*, 1:3338.

547 *Mathnawi*, 5:3308–16m.

548 Furuzanfar, *Zindigani-yi Mawlana Jalal al-Din*, p. 53.

549 *Mathnawi*, 1:3455–58.

550 *Mathnawi*, 1:1238–40m.

551 *Mathnawi*, 6:1847–48m.

552 *Mathnawi*, 2:2450–53.

553 *Mathnawi*, 1:1141.

554 *Mathnawi*, 6:3712.

555 *Mathnawi*, 6:3737–42.

556 *Mathnawi*, 1:1234–36.

557 *Mathnawi*, 1:1246–48m.

558 *Mathnawi*, 4:809–811.

559 *Mathnawi*, 6:3707–9.

560 *Mathnawi*, 2:703–5.

561 *Mathnawi*, 1:2893.

562 *Mathnawi*, 1:772.

563 *Mathnawi*, 6:1454–58.

564 *Mathnawi*, 3:578–80.

565 *Mathnawi*, 2:3687–90m.

566 *Mathnawi*, 2:3741–42.

567 *Mathnawi*, 2:3713–16.

568 *Mathnawi*, 2:49–51m.

569 *Mathnawi*, 1: 303–5m.

570 *Mathnawi*, 2:1607–9.

571 *Mathnawi*, 6:3420–23m.

572 "An obscure star in the Lesser Bear," F. J. Steingass, *A Comprehensive Persian-English Dictionary*.

573 *Mathnawi*, 1:1124–27.

574 *Mathnawi*, 5:1709.

575 *Mathnawi*, 2:65–67.

576 *Mathnawi*, 5:1331–32.

577 *Mathnawi*, 1:566–68m.

578 *Mathnawi*, 4:2373–76.

579 *Mathnawi*, 4:2377–79.

580 *Mathnawi*, 4:73–77m.

581 Aristotle, *Metaphysics*, 980a.

582 *Mathnawi*, 2:277–79m.

583 *Mathnawi*, 6:811–12m.

584 *Mathnawi*, 1:1030.
585 *Mathnawi*, 1: 1031–32m.
586 *Mathnawi*, 2:3651–52.
587 *Mathnawi*, 2: 3665–73m.
588 *Mathnawi*, 6:3880–85m.
589 *Mathnawi*, 1:3446–52m.
590 *Mathnawi*, 2:3201–6m.
591 *Mathnawi*, 2:2429–34m.
592 *Mathnawi*, 2:2435–38.
593 *Mathnawi*, 2:2439–42m.
594 *Mathnawi*, 5:2484–89m.
595 *Mathnawi*, 4: 506.
596 *Mathnawi*, 5: 4144m.
597 *Mathnawi*, 2: 3240–46m.
598 *Mathnawi*, 1:1636–41m.
599 *Mathnawi*, 1:1642–48m.
600 *Mathnawi*, 5:1053–54m.
601 *Mathnawi*, 5:1055–59m.
602 *Mathnawi*, 5:1057.
603 *Mathnawi*, 5:1060–63m.
604 *Mathnawi*, 5:1063.
605 *Mathnawi*, 5:1064–69m.
606 *Mathnawi*, 5:1070–74m.
607 *Mathnawi*, 1:2829–34m.
608 *Mathnawi*, 1:2841–46m.
609 *Mathnawi*, 3: 4118–23m.
610 *Mathnawi*, 1:1019
611 *Mathnawi*, 1:1009–12m.
612 *Mathnawi*, 2:2363–65m.
613 *Mathnawi*, 2:2366–71m. The Quranic verse quoted here refers to God's command to the earth to swallow the water that had been sent down in the flood of Noah, bringing it to an end.
614 *Mathnawi*, 2:72–73m.
615 *Mathnawi*, 2:95–96m.
616 *Mathnawi*, 1:34.
617 *Mathnawi*, 1: 3459–62m.
618 *Mathnawi*, 1:3483–86m.
619 *Mathnawi*, 4: 1436–39m.
620 *Mathnawi*, 2:670.
621 *Mathnawi*, 4:1703.
622 *Mathnawi*, 5:1443–44.
623 *Mathnawi*, 1:2272–75.
624 *Mathnawi*, 1:316–320m.

625 *Mathnawi*, 3:3038.

626 *Mathnawi*, 2:1393–99.

627 *Mathnawi*, 1:601–3m.

628 *Mathnawi*, 1:604–10m.

629 *Mathnawi*, 1:611–12.

630 *Mathnawi*, 5:1026–32m.

631 *Mathnawi*, 3:1270–71.

632 *Mathnawi*, 4:3047.

633 *Mathnawi*, 6:822–24.

634 *Mathnawi*, 1:3201–4m.

635 *Mathnawi* 6:1466–71m.

636 *Mathnawi*, 2:759–63m.

637 *Mathnawi*, 6:3712; 1:1141.

638 *Mathnawi*, 1:2467–68.

639 *Mathnawi*, 1:3093–99m.

640 Namely, idols worshiped by the pagan Arabs. *Mathnawi*, 6:1528–29m.

641 *Mathnawi*, 6:2030–5m.

642 *Mathnawi*, 3:1255–58m.

643 *Mathnawi*, 4:416–17m.

644 See Shihab al-Din Yahya Suhrawardi, *Oeuvres philosophiques et mystiques,* Tome II, p. 10.

645 *Mathnawi*, 4:419–24.

646 *Mathnawi*, 1:676–80m.

647 *Mathnawi*, 1:686–89.

648 *Mathnawi*, 6:1022–24.

649 *Mathnawi*, 6:3180–1m.

650 *Mathnawi*, 6:3183m.

651 *Mathnawi*, 1:2964.

652 *Mathnawi*, 6:1023.

653 *Mathnawi*, 4:825–27.

654 *Mathnawi*, 1:3009–12.

655 *Mathnawi*, 1:772.

656 *Mathnawi*, 4:2763–66m.

657 *Mathnawi*, 2:1173–38m.

658 *Mathnawi*, 4:397–403m.

659 *Mathnawi*, 1:3052–55m.

660 *Mathnawi*, 3:1391.

661 *Mathnawi*, 3:4621–23.

662 Mathnawi, 1:1936–40m.

663 Hafiz, *Diwan*, Qazwini edition, Zawwar Publications, Tehran, [n.d.], p. 97.

664 Mahmud Shabistari, *Gulshan-i Raz*, ed. J. Nurbakhsh, Khanaqah-i Ni'matullahi Publications, Tehran, 1355 [1976], p. 30.

665 Huma'i, *Mawlawi Nameh*, p. 232.

666 See Ibn 'Arabi, *al-Futuhat al-Makkiyyah*, ed. M. A. al-Mar'ashi, Dar Ihya' al-Turath al-'Arabi, Beirut, [n.d.], Chapter 221, Vol. 3:164.

667 *Mathnawi*, 5:2035–38.

668 *Mathnawi*, 6:2095–97m.

669 *Mathnawi*, 2:2522–23m.

670 *Mathnawi*, 4:2112–15.

671 *Mathnawi*, 4:2120–22.

672 *Mathnawi*, 5:2020–35.

673 *Mathnawi*, 5:2025–30.

674 *Mathnawi*, 2:1348–52m.

675 *Mathnawi*, 6:435–44.

676 *Mathnawi*, 6:457–60.

677 *Mathnawi*, 6:478–83, 493–94m.

678 *Mathnawi*, 6:524–25.

679 *Mathnawi*, 6:557–58.

680 *Mathnawi*, 6:559–72.

681 *Mathnawi*, 5:409–14.

682 *Mathnawi*, 5:415–18.

683 *Mathnawi*, 6:4441–44.

684 See Lane, *Arabic-English Lexicon*, "qadr."

685 *Mathnawi*, 1:910–11m.

686 *Mathnawi*, 4:1337–39m.

687 *Mathnawi*, 3:381.

688 *Mathnawi*, 1:1232–33m.

689 *Mathnawi*, 5:1707.

690 *Mathnawi*, 5:1707-9.

691 *Mathnawi*, 1:1194–96m.

692 For a report in which 'Umar ibn al-Khattab turns back from entering Damascus after hearing of a plague in the city, explaining to Abu Ubayda ibn Jarrah that he was "fleeing from what Allah has prescribed, only towards that which Allah has ordained," see Osman Oral, *I Believe in the Divine Destiny and Decree*, Tughra Books, Izmir, 2013, [n.p.].

693 *Mathnawi*, 3:469–72.

694 *Mathnawi*, 3:449–53.

695 *Mathnawi*, 3:1880–3m.

696 *Mathnawi*, 3:1905–15m.

697 *Mathnawi*, 5:3084–86.

698 Huma'i, *Mawlawi Nameh*, p. 81.

[699] *Mathnawi*, 1:1480–2m.
[700] *Mathnawi*, 5:2967.
[701] *Mathnawi*, 5:2974.
[702] *Mathnawi*, 5:3005.
[703] *Mathnawi*, 5:3024m.
[704] *Mathnawi*, 6:408–12m.
[705] *Mathnawi*, 1: 1496–99m.
[706] *Mathnawi*, 5:2973.
[707] *Mathnawi*, 5:2968m.
[708] *Mathnawi*, 5:3026–27m.
[709] *Mathnawi*, 4:1644–45.
[710] *Mathnawi*, 5:3025.
[711] *Mathnawi*, 1:618–19m.
[712] *Mathnawi*, 1:620.
[713] *Mathnawi*, 5:3049.
[714] *Mathnawi*, 5:3050–54.
[715] *Mathnawi*, 5:1852–55m.
[716] *Mathnawi*, 6:200–5.
[717] *Mathnawi*, 5:3240–42.
[718] According to Aflaki, Rumi traced back his spiritual lineage through his father to Ahmad al-Ghazali. See Furuzanfar, *Zindigani-yi Mawlana Jalal al-Din*, p. 8.
[719] *Mathnawi*, 1:254–55m.
[720] The unseen saints and sages.
[721] *Mathnawi*, 1:264–72m.
[722] *Mathnawi*, 3:1262–70m.
[723] *Mathnawi*, 2:1750–70m.
[724] *Mathnawi*, 2:1772–91m.
[725] See Rumi's introduction to Book 5 of the *Mathnawi*, trans. Nicholson, Vol. 3, p. 3.
[726] See William Chittick, *The Sufi Path of Knowledge*, SUNY Press, New York, 1989, p. 22.
[727] *Mathnawi*, 4:2211–12m.
[728] *Mathnawi*, 3:1976–81m.
[729] *Mathnawi*, 4:533–534m.
[730] *Mathnawi*, 1:573–76m.
[731] *Mathnawi*, 3:3365.
[732] *Mathnawi*, 3:3349m.
[733] *Mathnawi*, 3:1439–42.
[734] *Mathnawi*, 3:1448–49.
[735] *Mathnawi*, 3:1465–66m.
[736] *Mathnawi*, 3:4781–85m.
[737] *Mathnawi*, 1:980–85m.

[738] *Mathnawi*, 6:3475m.

[739] *Mathnawi*, 1:3430–32m.

[740] See for example Quran 15:44.

[741] *Mathnawi*, 1:772–79m.

[742] *Mathnawi*, 1: 3002–4.

[743] *Mathnawi*, 3:4053–56m.

[744] *Mathnawi*, 3:4060–63m.

[745] *Mathnawi*, 2:2527–28m.

[746] See Abu Nasr al-Sarraj, *Kitab al- Luma'*, ed. R. Nicholson, Brill, Leiden, 1914, p. 44.

[747] *Mathnawi*, 4:2503–8.

[748] *Mathnawi*, 4:324–27m.

[749] *Mathnawi*, 4:346–48m.

[750] *Mathnawi*, 4:3412–15m.

[751] *Mathnawi*, 5:767–79m.

[752] *Mathnawi*, 5:2221–24m.

[753] See Quran 2:65.

[754] *Mathnawi*, 5:2591–94m.

[755] *Mathnawi*, 3:1846–48m.

[756] *Mathnawi*, 3:1852–54.

[757] *Mathnawi*, 6:1410–14m.

[758] *Mathnawi*, 2:1276–79m.

[759] *Mathnawi*, 3:3494–3500m.

[760] See Quran 2:83, 4:36, 6:151, 17:23.

[761] *Mathnawi*, 6:3254–58m.

[762] *Mathnawi*, 1:2291–96m.

[763] *Mathnawi*, 3:2895–98.

[764] *Mathnawi*, 3:2671–72m.

[765] *Mathnawi*, 5:2315m.

[766] *Mathnawi*, 3:1878–83m

[767] *Mathnawi*, 3:1885–90m.

[768] *Mathnawi*, 3:1898–1915m.

[769] *Mathnawi*, 1:916–22.

[770] *Mathnawi*, 5:1495–99m.

[771] *Mathnawi*, 5:2401–17.

[772] *Mathnawi*, 5:2416–17.

[773] *Mathnawi*, 1:913–14m.

[774] *Mathnawi*, 1:947m.

[775] *Mathnawi*, 1:3989m.

[776] *Mathnawi*, 1:3981–88m.

[777] *Mathnawi*, 4:2092–94.

[778] *Mathnawi*, 1:2675–77m.

[779] *Mathnawi*, 3:2487m.

[780] *Mathnawi*, 4:2088–89m.

[781] *Mathnawi*, 6:3285–87.

[782] *Mathnawi*, 2:2900–2901, 2905m.

[783] *Mathnawi*, 3:4590–96m.

[784] *Mathnawi*, 4:1587–91m.

[785] *Mathnawi*, 3:186–88m.

[786] *Mathnawi*, 6:1475–76m.

[787] *Mathnawi*, 6:4038m.

[788] *Mathnawi*, 2:753–58m.

[789] *Mathnawi*, 2:267–70m.

[790] The story begins at *Mathnawi*, 6:3986.

[791] *Mathnawi*, 6:4021–24.

[792] *Mathnawi*, 6:4025.

[793] *Mathnawi*, 6:4026.

[794] *Mathnawi*, 6:4027.

[795] *Mathnawi*, 6:4028.

[796] *Mathnawi*, 6:4029.

[797] *Mathnawi*, 6:4030.

[798] *Mathnawi*, 6:4031.

[799] *Mathnawi*, 6:4032–37m.

[800] *Mathnawi*, 6:4040m.

Quranic References

Index

A

'Ala' al-Din (son of Rumi), 10, 11, 21, 38
abandonment (*tark*), 323, 324
Abdal, 184, 160, 311
Abhari, Athir al-Din, 2
Abraham, 3, 59, 95, 142, 182, 183
Abu Bakr, 16, 63, 109
Abu'l-Khayr, Abu Sa'id, 308
accidents, *see* substance and accidents
acquisition, theory of (*kasb*), 242, 300
Adam, 3, 59, 85, 86, 96, 100–104, 106, 174, 188, 189, 224, 226, 227, 233, 247, 255, 260, 261, 327, 328
Aflaki, 10–12, 16, 22, 23
alchemy, 45, 75, 132, 143, 318
Aleppo, 3, 13, 55
'Ali ibn Abi Talib, 15, 110, 142, 160, 162, 163, 197, 229, 342
allegory, 43, 88, 90, 106, 150, 182, 191, 202, 205, 229, 234, 258, 265, 268, 269, 272–275, 285–288, 302, 307–312, 317, 318, 350

allegory of the cave, 79, 246, 292
Anatolia, 2, 3, 11, 12, 26, 38, 47, 309
annihilation, 33, 51, 61, 76, 138, 141, 213, 238, 245, 252, 278, 280–286, 288, 292, 304
Ansari, Khwajah Abdullah, 308
appearance, phenomenon, 211, 212, 213, 217, 224, 228, 232, 233, 246, 277
apportionment. *See* Divine Destiny (*qadar*)
Aristotle, xi, 92, 99, 125, 167, 226, 237, 238, 274, 307
ascetic, 14, 15, 35, 41, 258, 288, 290, 308, 340
Ash'arites, 9, 57, 300
Asiya, 59
Athens, 3
'Attar, Farid al-Din, 10, 36, 42, 167, 309
Attributes of God. *See* Divine Attributes
Avicenna, xi, 3, 52, 54, 57, 64, 72, 125, 180, 186, 237, 246, 263, 308, 309
awliya', *see wali*, *awliya'*; Friends of God

385

B

Baghdad, 223, 234, 282
Baghdadi, Majd al-Din, 9
Baha' al-Din Walad (Baha' Walad), 9, 10, 11, 12
Balkh, 8, 10, 11, 378
Bayazid Bastami, 3, 16, 17, 49, 50, 56, 59, 149, 167, 260, 283
beauty, xiii, 19, 26, 29, 32, 47, 53, 78, 80, 85, 86, 88, 104, 106, 119, 121, 126, 128, 129, 130, 131, 170, 172, 223, 245, 254, 277, 349
Being, Absolute, 52, 72, 95, 109, 115, 120, 122, 123, 126, 141, 263, 264
being, concept of, 60, 71–73, 122, 131, 263
beloved, 39, 45, 48, 60, 61, 65, 66, 80, 89, 124, 127, 128, 129, 131, 132, 133, 190, 227, 286, 320, 335, 349
bewilderment, 101, 122, 141, 156, 189, 190, 191
Beyond-Being, 264
body-soul relationship, see soul-body relationship
Buddha-nature, 105

C

caravanserai, 16, 46
certainty, degrees of, 7, 8, 93, 110, 121, 253
character, 10, 15, 40, 44, 243, 299, 319, 338
Chelebi, Husam al-Din, 34, 35, 36, 37, 38, 41, 42, 95
childhood, 2, 7, 11, 46, 67, 77, 81, 94, 110
Christians, 40, 58, 60, 138
command, 18, 23, 25, 55, 66, 169, 197, 200, 208, 217, 218, 299, 300, 302, 332, 338
companionship, 14, 19, 33, 39, 47, 49, 63, 91, 143, 152, 153, 202–205, 206, 250
consciousness, 75, 99, 100, 101, 105, 114, 141, 170, 183, 222, 254, 282, 284
contemplation, 15, 29, 238
contentment (*rida*), 290, 298, 334, 336, 337
cosmos, 1, 7, 74, 83, 84, 104, 105, 132, 168, 170
counsel, consultation, 207, 208
craft, 92, 105, 187, 216, 249, 250, 268, 321, 322

389

92, 96, 99, 100, 104,
114, 120, 121, 138,
149, 153, 158, 166,
168, 169, 174, 179,
221, 224, 238, 239,
245, 246, 248, 253,
255, 267, 295, 319

N

nabi, 58, 139, 245 (*see also* prophet)

Names of God, *see* Divine Names

negligence, 47, 75, 80, 95, 190, 327, 335

Night of Power (*laylat al-qadri*), 61, 294

Nishapur, 10, 56

Noah, 3, 59, 157, 189

Nocturnal Ascent (*mi'raj*), 59, 110

non-being, 109, 122, 126, 134, 140, 172, 263–270, 280, 286, 291

ocean, 37, 39, 40, 44, 46, 63, 88, 93, 103, 104, 116, 121, 122, 131, 132, 143, 150, 153, 154, 160, 169, 188, 189, 190, 197, 212, 216, 219, 222, 228, 231, 239, 240, 241, 242, 248, 251, 252, 265, 266, 268, 272, 273, 297, 301, 312, 320, 323, 343, 348

opinion, 70, 78, 121, 176, 183, 186, 253, 273

outward form (*surat*), 50, 84, 117, 211, 212, 214–217, 225, 227–229, 233, 239, 241, 269, 276

P

Paradise, 54, 91, 97, 109

particulars, 186

Parwaneh, Mu'in al-Din, 41

path, xiii, 27, 41, 50, 58, 62, 101, 152, 153, 156, 157, 160, 191, 318, 321, 333, 337, (*see also tariqah*)

patience (*sabr*), 5, 30, 48, 75, 79, 160, 161, 163, 197, 201, 243, 244, 289, 319, 330, 331, 332, 342, 348

peace, 170, 195, 215, 216, 221, 267

perception, faculties of, 296, 304

perception, levels of, 77, 78, 80

Pharaoh, 59, 184, 185, 270, 283, 284, 285, 339

phenomenon, *see* appearance

philosophers, xi, 1, 9, 13, 45, 53–55, 59, 64, 77, 96, 102, 114, 125, 167, 178, 193, 226, 264

philosophy, xi, 1–4, 13, 54, 57, 71, 72, 83, 151, 167, 185, 237, 264, 307

physicians of the soul, 91, 123, 152, 267

pir, 7, 12, 13, 26–28, 107, 152–163, 172, 178, 180, 183, 193, 202, 240, 249, 251, 326

Plato, xi, 3, 54, 70, 79, 119, 120, 123, 166, 167, 185, 187, 211, 226, 237, 246, 264, 271, 292

Plotinus, xi, 104, 169

poverty, 17, 33, 145, 147, 160, 250–252, 267, 268, 287

praise, 12, 21, 33, 69, 70, 73–75, 313

prayer, 31, 40, 43, 74, 75, 76, 109, 137, 149, 200, 265, 289, 297, 347

predestination, 55, 299, 337

prejudice, 235

prohibitions, 55, 66, 302

proof, *see* demonstration (proof)

prophets, 1, 14, 53, 54, 57–60, 65, 80, 85, 90, 100, 106, 107, 112, 116, 127, 138–140, 150, 156, 158, 168, 169, 175, 187, 201, 202, 207, 220, 230, 245, 308, 331, 344

purification, 2, 33, 58, 116, 150, 166, 193, 199, 248, 256, 257, 258, 286, 347

purity, 44, 202, 230, 232, 255, 313, 324, 347

Q

Qunawi, Sadr al-Din, 2, 39, 40

Quran, 7, 13, 31, 43, 59, 66, 67, 69, 74, 81, 94, 114, 115, 125, 126, 137, 156, 246, 271, 286, 294, 302, 308, 318

Qushayri, 59, 308

R

Razi, Fakhr al-Din, 9, 56, 57, 151, 246

Razi, Najm al-Din, 2

realization, 2, 7, 8, 15, 93, 94, 158, 180, 193, 245, 253, 259, 330

realization of certainty (*haqq al-yaqin*), 253

realizer (*muhaqqiq*), 8, 93, 253

reason, 20, 54, 56, 78, 123, 133, 142, 165, 168, 174, 175, 177, 178, 187, 190, 225

reason, academic (*'aql-i maktabi*), 181

reason, instrumental (*'aql-i kar-afza*), 181

reason, partial (*'aql-i juz'i*), 181–184, 188, 189, 190, 191, 312

rebirth, 107–111, 151, 213